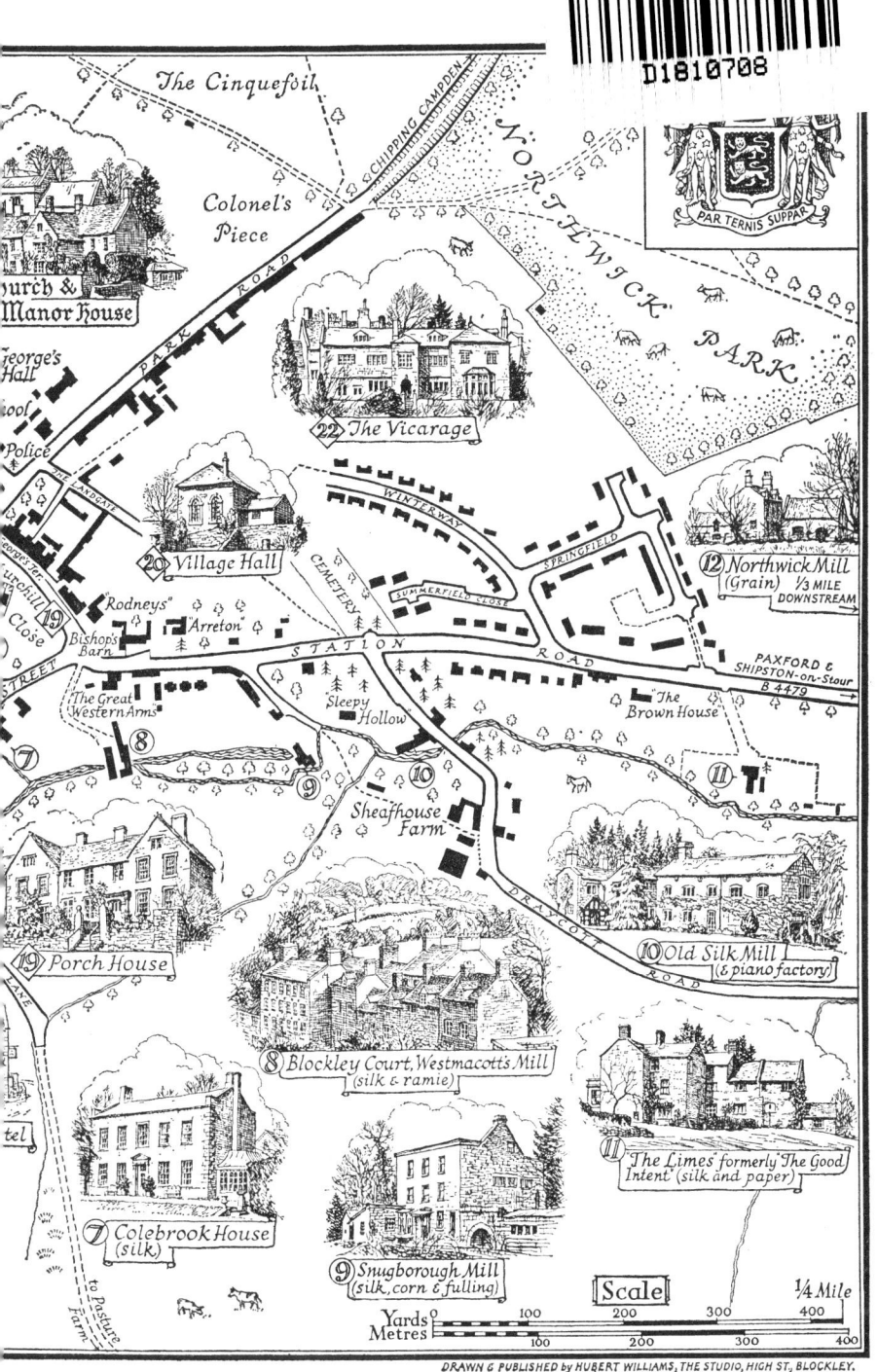

The Cinquefoil

Colonel's Piece

CHIPPING CAMPDEN

NORTHWICK PARK

PAR TERNIS SUPPAR

Church & Manor House

George's Hall

School

Police

PARK ROAD

22 The Vicarage

WINTERWAY

STRINGFIELD

12 Northwick Mill (Grain) ⅓ MILE DOWNSTREAM

20 Village Hall

SUMMERFIELD CLOSE

CEMETERY

"Rodneys"

"Arreton"

19 Bishop's Barn

STREET

Close

STATION ROAD

PAXFORD & SHIPSTON-on-Stour B 4479

"The Great Western Arms"

Sleepy Hollow

"The Brown House

7

8

9

10

11

Sheafhouse Farm

DRAYCOTT ROAD

19 Porch House

10 Old Silk Mill (& piano factory)

8 Blockley Court, Westmacott's Mill (silk & ramie)

11 "The Limes" formerly "The Good Intent" (silk and paper)

7 Colebrook House (silk)

9 Snugborough Mill (silk, corn & fulling)

to Pasture Farm

Scale ¼ Mile

Yards 0   100   200   300   400
Metres   100   200   300   400

DRAWN & PUBLISHED by HUBERT WILLIAMS, THE STUDIO, HIGH ST, BLOCKLEY.

To Sir George & Lady Baker –
with very best wishes Christmas 1974
& many many thanks for great help over the Congress
I felt knowing this area you would enjoy
this history by a BNC delightful old friend
Harry Ic[...] – (a great supporter here to all good
endeavours – Very good wishes for 1975
Please both come + visit again when near –

Blockley Through Twelve Centuries

[signature]

BLOCKLEY
Through Twelve Centuries

Annals of a Cotswold Parish

H. E. M. ICELY
M.A. (Oxon.)

Kineton: The Roundwood Press: 1974

Published for the Blockley Antiquarian Society by
The Roundwood Press (Publishers) Limited, Kineton,
in the County of Warwick

Set in 'Monotype' Times, series 327 and printed by
Gordon Norwood at The Roundwood Press, Kineton,
in the county of Warwick, and bound by Eric Neal,
Welford, Rugby

Made and printed in England

For Frances Clare Spurgin, O.B.E.,

and for all friends of Blockley

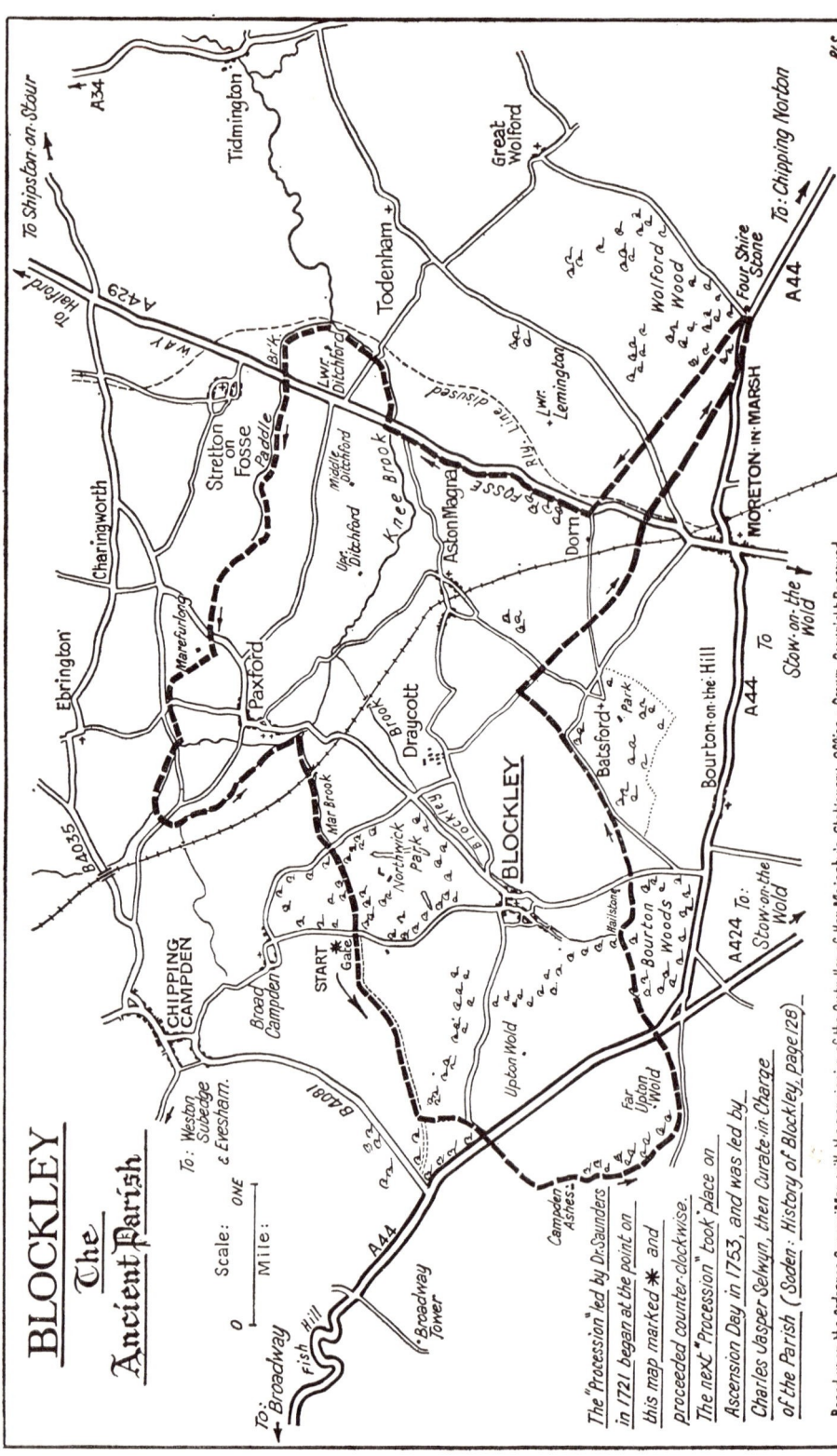

BLOCKLEY
The Ancient Parish

Scale: ONE Mile
0

To: Weston Subedge & Evesham.

To: Broadway

Fish Hill

Broadway Tower

CHIPPING CAMPDEN

Broad Campden

Ebrington

Charingworth

To Halford

To Stripston-on-Stour

A34

A429

Tidmington

Stretton on Fosse

Paddle Brk

Marefurlong

Paxford

FOSSE WAY

Lwr. Ditchford

Middle Ditchford

Upr. Ditchford

Knee Brook

Todenham

Great Wolford

Wolford Wood

Railway Line disused

Lwr. Lemington

Aston Magna

Dorn

Four Shire Stone

To: Chipping Norton

A44

MORETON-IN-MARSH

FOSSE

Draycott

Blockley Brook

Mar Brook

Northwick Park

START
Gate

Camden Ashes

Upton Wold

Far Upton Wold

Hailstone

Bourton Woods

BLOCKLEY

Batsford

Park

Bourton-on-the-Hill

A44 To: Stow-on-the-Wold

A424 To: Stow-on-the-Wold

A44

To Stow-on-the-Wold

B4035

B4081

The "Procession" led by Dr Saunders
in 1721 began at the point on
this map marked ✳ and
proceeded counter-clockwise.
The next "Procession" took place on
Ascension Day in 1753, and was led by
Charles Jasper Selwyn, then Curate-in-Charge
of the Parish (Soden: History of Blockley, page 128)

Contents

Appendices

Illustrations

Frontispiece: Manor House from "Church Gates," by *Hubert Williams*

Acknowledgments

Two names must come first in this list–those of the two 19th century curates and historians of the parish of Blockley, W. T. Eyre and A. J. Soden. Each of their books gives a vivid impression, not only of the state of the parish at the time of its writing, but also of the somewhat different ideals and values held by writers separated by a changeful half-century. Of the indebtedness of the present writer to the works of more recent contributors to our knowledge of Blockley's past the following pages will bear witness, and notably to those of Professor H. P. R. Finberg, Dr R. H. Hilton, Mr P. A. Rahtz, Dr E. A. B. Barnard, Mr A. Oswald, Miss Marjory Hollings and Mrs N. Marshall.

Over the years of his gradual accumulation of material the writer has received help generously given, and here it is gratefully acknowledged, from the county archivists at Worcester (Mr E. H. Sargeant) and Gloucester (Mr I. E. Gray and Mr B. S. Smith), the Very Rev. G. W. O. Addleshaw, the late Professor T. S. Ashton, Mr M. Balhatchet, Mr C. W. Clarke, the late Captain E. G. Spencer-Churchill, the late W. I. Croome, the late G. C. Darlaston, Dr A. B. Emden, Professor Sir John Hicks, the late A. L. Horne, Mr W. C. Lockwood, Mrs J. T. Lucas, the late J. A. O. Muirhead, the late J. H. Milton, the late Dr C. Nicholson, Mr T. G. Odling, Mrs H. E. O'Neil, Mr P. Pritchard, the late Rev. A. J. Ridler, Mrs U. E. L. Walker (with whom the project of this history originated), Mr C. Warner, Dr Graham Webster, the Rev. B. R. White and Miss N. Yoxall.

For the period since 1860 the issues of The Evesham Journal, and, more intimately, the Survey (1859) and Scrapbook (1966) of Blockley history compiled by members of the Women's Institute, have been invaluable: and the writer gratefully recalls many talks with his Blockley neighbours on the subject. The Blockley Collection in the keeping of the Antiquarian Society provides visible evidence of local pride in the past of this ancient parish.

That this history appears in print has been made possible by the generosity of certain guarantors, and, above all, by the tireless and imaginative collaboration of Mrs F. C. Spurgin, Mrs N. Marshall and Dr A. W. Exell.

Blockley through Twelve Centuries

The Blockley Antiquarian Society is indebted to Mr H. E. Mc.L. Icely for allowing us to publish his admirable work and for generously giving us the copyright, and to Mrs F. C. Spurgin, to whom the book is dedicated and without whose help it would never have achieved publication and to the artists Miss C. Compton-Smith, Mr R. A. Smeeton and Mr H. Williams.

We are grateful to Mr Gordon Norwood of the Roundwood Press for expert advice and constant encouragement.

Finally we wish to thank those who have given us the gifts and guarantees that made this publication possible, with the appreciation that there are many other friends of Mr Icely and of Blockley who would have been equally willing to help us.

Donors and Guarantors

Lady D. G. Angwin

Mrs M. Ashton

Miss C. Compton- Smith

Mr R. Cook

Major H. F. Cox

Lord Dulverton (Batsford Estates)

Mrs O. Dicks

Dr & Mrs T. E. Elliot

Dr A. W. Exell

Mrs M. A. Exell

Mr & Mrs F. R. Garrood

Mrs K. M. Goadby

Mr W. J. Heming

Sir John & Lady Hicks

Mr M. Hope

Mr & Mrs H. R. Hoskins

Mr H. E. M. Icely

Mr P. James-Carrington

Miss A. M. L. Joyner

Mr and Mrs C. Keeble

Mr W. B. Lingard

Lady Linstead

Mr W. C. Lockwood

Mr F. L. Luckett

Sir Robert Lusty

Mrs N. Marshall

Mr A. J. W. Milton

Mr S. M. Moore

Mrs H. M. Norman

Mr S. P. Pyke

Brigadier R. B. Rathbone

Sir Thomas & Lady Skyrme

Mr J. D. Speakman

Mrs F. C. Spurgin

Miss A. M. Warburton

Sir Edward Warner

Miss E. Whitford

Miss N. Yoxall

Addition and Corrections

P. xv. *Acknowledgements*. Add Mr. B. S. Halliwell

P. 21 *line* 30. For Gonscalves read Gonçalves.

Coloured plate facing p. 192. For *Tulsatilla Vulgaris* read *Pulsatilla vulgaris*. *Photo by Lord Dulverton*

Preface

This enthralling history, written over a quarter of a century, is dedicated not only to me but to all friends of Blockley.

Mr Icely was born in Canada in 1884. Having been on the staff of Bromsgrove and Loretto, he was Reader in Education at Oxford and was enormously inspiring and practically helpful (even to supplying a blackboard!) in setting up a school for evacuee children at my home at Rodneys in 1939.

In 1945, when Dame Janet Campbell left Bishop's Barn, Mr Icely retired to Blockley and lived here for over fifteen years to our great benefit. The life of the village, past and present, was one of his major interests and he brought many distinguished friends to enjoy its unique character.

He saw in the life of the village a microcosm of experience and he applied his acute feeling for the past and his capacity to communicate with his contemporaries to this study of it.

The results of his twenty years of academic work in Oxford are constantly acknowledged by practising teachers today who avow that his personal care and interest were determining factors in their lives. He has devoted the same care and interest to the village and people of Blockley — from counselling to crosswords. The pictures in the History are largely of Mr Icely's selection and the Drawings and Appendices are our tribute to his text.

I have specially to thank Dr Exell and Mrs Marshall for invaluable help in writing and indexing as well as launching the History through the Press. I would also thank countless people for ideas and information and also those who made drawings or head-pieces or wrote appendices, and, above all, bore being constantly badgered by me with equanimity, especially: Mr C. Barter, Miss Buxton, Major Cox, Mrs Dicks, Lord Dulverton, Dr Eason, Dr Exell, Lady Fisher and the late Archbishop, Mr Flaherty, Mrs Goadby, Mr Hughes, Mrs Marshall, Dr Owen, Mr Smeeton, Mr Hubert Williams, also descendants of William Warner, many officers of the Gloucestershire County Council, the Record Offices, University and other Libraries, Christie's Ltd., and the Editor of the Evesham Journal.

It is a hundred years since the last history of Blockley was published — how can we properly thank the author except by treasuring this fascinating volume?

F. Clare Spurgin
Boveton Hill, Blockley, 1974

Introduction

WITH VERY SLIGHT modifications,[1] the bounds of the ancient parish of Blockley have remained unchanged throughout its history. Two descriptions of them which were recorded long ago define them as they were until the present century, and perhaps add some suggestion of landscape to the bare topographical detail of the map.

The first is a record of the beating of the bounds some two and a half centuries ago. The writer was Dr. Erasmus Saunders, then vicar of Blockley, and, as this history will show, a notable antiquary:

> 26 May, A.D. 1720, being Ascension Day, a Procession was made ab[t] ye outbounds of y[e] Parish according to y[e] ancient costom, beginning at y[e] gate leading to Broad Campden Hill and so up ab[t] y[e] Upton Olds and without y[e] hedge ab[t] Burton wood to y[e] stile out of Hailstone into y[e] Wood, so to Burton Hill & between Battsford & Dorn as far as y[e] Four Shire Stone, and then back between Lemington & Dorn & Aston, and between Lemington & Ditchford, and between Stretton & Ditchford, and between Charingworth & Paxf[d], and between Ebrington & Paxf[d], and between Broad Campden & Northw[k], y[e] principal persons of y[e] s[d] Parish with y[e] Minister & Churchwardens attending y[e] same.
>
> ER:SAUNDERS, Vicar.

These boundaries coincided with those of the manor of Blockley, of which the parish was the ecclesiastical counterpart. An account of the manor bounds made in 1647 on the occasion of its confiscation by the victorious Parliament after the Civil War

xvii

will therefore serve equally well for the parish. Here the circuit has a different starting point and it runs clockwise, the 'fields' alongside which it marches being the wide arable fields, the common open fields, of the adjoining villages. Morton Henmarsh is the original spelling of Moreton-in-Marsh, Everton is Ebrington today and Tadmin is Todenham—one catches the local pronunciation of the time in the obviously phonetic spelling:

"Beginning at the four shire stone near Morton Henmarsh, extendeth to Dorne including the same, and from thence to Battsford field, and so along to Campden Ashes taking in Upton Old within this manor, and thence to Broad Campden field side; so to Everton field side, and then along by Charingworth grounds to Stretton fields including the two Ditchfords within this manor; and so by Tadmin fields, and from thence to the four shire stone where it began: including within this circumference these several hamlets, viz: Blockley, Northwick, Paxford, Aston, Draycott, the two Ditchfords, Dorne and Upton Old, all which are parcels of this manor of Blockley and are in their circumference about twelve miles".

That was a countryman's estimate of distance. The map shows that it is well over twenty! Of these eight hamlets encircling Blockley five have dwindled. Northwick indeed remains, but in different shape, partly owing to emparkment between the 16th and 18th centuries, and partly through the erection in the park during the second World War of buildings to house first an American military hospital, then German prisoners of war and finally a Polish expatriate settlement. The other five have, since the end of the Middle Ages, shrunk to farm status, but the plan of the dwellings, barns and roadways of the ancient hamlets of Dorn, Upton Wold and the Ditchfords are to be seen in the humps and hollows on the surface of the fields, and the site of Upton Wold is now in process of scientific excavation.[2] The parish of Blockley must indeed hold something of a record in deserted villages.

From west to east the parish stretches for over six miles from the limestone uplands about Campden Ashes and Upton Wold, along the lias clay valley of the Blockley Brook, across the Knee

Brook, and so over the low rise of Ditchford Hill to the Paddle-brook, which with the Fosseway marks its north-eastern angle. Out of either steep flank of the upper course of the Blockley Brook, and more particularly the northern flank, a remarkable number of springs are thrown out along the line of the outcrop of the impermeable clays of the Upper Lias. The spring-line is high up the southern side of the valley, and Park Farm and Pasture Farm are sited on two of the streams which emerge from it. On the northern side the spring-line is, owing to the tilt of the underlying beds of older rock, very much lower—indeed, as the Russell Spring shows, it comes in places down to the level of the village itself, and two clusters of its springs—at the foot of the Warren and in the Coneygree behind the post-office, emerge only a few feet higher. The Coneygree streams unite to form the Colebrook, which once drove the wheels of three silk mills and is today linked with the water supply of the district. The Blockley Brook itself with a never-failing head of water from its springs once turned the wheels of eight other mills, and the thrashing sound of them must have been constantly in the ears of the village folk. All are silent now,[3] but the Blockley springs have been the 'liquid history' of the parish over many centuries back to Domesday, when twelve mills were recorded within the manor.

Blockley was known for its springs in Shakespeare's day, perhaps to Shakespeare himself when he returned to Stratford. His fellow Warwickshire poet, Michael Drayton, certainly knew them, for they are the most conspicuous feature in the account he gives of the Cotswolds in his poetical description of England, *Poly-olbion*, published in 1613.[4] That poem is based on details taken from William Camden's recently published *Britannia*, but seeing that Camden makes no mention of Blockley and that Drayton was a constant visitor at Clifford Chambers, it seems reasonable to assume that the latter wrote from personal knowledge of our village. Not that he was topographically exact in his knowledge, for his printed sketch-map of the district (Plate I) shows 'Blockley Springes' flowing into the Evenlode –'bright Enload' as he calls it–and so ultimately into the Thames: and his lines describe Blockley as near of kin to that river:

And being near of kinne to that most springfull place,
Where out of Blockley's banks so many fountains flowe
That cleane throughout his soyle proud Cotswold cannot showe
The like: as though from farre his long and many hills
There emptied all their veines, wherewith those founts he fills,
Which in the greatest drought so brimfull still doe float,
Sent through the rifted rocks with such an open throat,
As though the Cleeves consumed in humour; they alone
So crystalline and cold, as hardneth stick to stone.

[1] Dorn and the narrow tongue of land reaching to the Four Shire Stone were transferred to the parish of Batsford in 1935. The whole of Blockley parish was transferred from Worcestershire to Gloucestershire in 1931.

[2] Trans. B.G.A.S., lxxxv (1966), article on *Upton, Glos.* 1959–64, by R. H. Hilton and P. A. Rahtz.

[3] One, at least, still survives, and till recently was put to use, at Northwick Mill Farm.

[4] Song xiv.

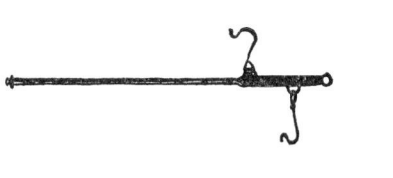

CHAPTER ONE

Romano-British Prelude: Dorn

ALL BUT ONE of the place-names in the ancient parish of Blockley are of Anglo-Saxon derivation, and its continuous history properly begins with the Saxon conquest of Britain. Dorn, with a name of Celtic origin and a history stretching back at least four centuries before that conquest, stands apart in our record. Yet the name survived the Saxon onslaught and there was a hamlet of Dorn till far on in the Middle Ages. That in itself is no proof of continuity of occupation, of a transformation of the Romano-British settlement into the Saxon hamlet without a catastrophic break at the time of the fifth century conquest of the area. But it does, perhaps, suggest that at least something survived on the spot to link its later history with its Roman past. If, as a historian of our day[1] has written, "Roman cities and villas are an alien interlude, the imagination is the more strangely stirred when we come on the bases of Mediterranean colonnades scattered on Northumbrian moors and mosaic pavements buried deep in Cotswold woods." We may have to regard Romano-British Dorn as a separate interlude in the history of the parish, but it cannot be irrelevant to it.

The site of Dorn has been known as an ancient settlement for centuries. Thomas Habington visited it perhaps about 1620 and wrote that "this Dorne, a place some tyme of especiall note, is nowe obscur'd."[2] In 1695 Erasmus Saunders, soon to become vicar of Blockley, but then curate of Morton Henmarsh (Moreton -in-Marsh to us), reported to the Keeper of the Ashmolean at Oxford his recent acquisition of:

10 or 11 more Roman Coins found at Dorn and I also had a Roman Brick wch I was the more inclin'd to take because it is filletted about with a sparkling substance about a halfe inch thick wch perhaps is an adhesion of ashes vitrify'd in the furnacing of them. . Many of them are ordinarily dug by the Gardener.[3]

All the eighteenth century revisions of Camden's *Britannia* describe the site. This is from 1731:

> The country people have a tradition that Dorn was formerly a city, and many old foundations that have been dug up there with an abundance of Roman and British coins commonly found by the husbandmen, and the lines in which the streets ran being still very discernible. . shew that a colony of Romans must have resided here.[4]

Ever since then coins and potsherds turned up by the plough on the Dorn farms have found their way into private collections, and usually into oblivion. Dr. Saunders was not the only vicar of Blockley to collect them; an attorney at Stretton was reported in 1789 to have many more. Soden in his careful account of the site in 1875,[5] and Dr. Haverfield's report of a store of some 170 coins at Dorn Farm in 1901,[6] show how the wastage went on. Even the larger casual finds have not been safe. Two *stelae*, three feet high and carved in relief with figures that may have been *genii*, were last heard of sixty years ago in an Eastbourne shop.[7] How much was squandered when the railway cutting was dug close by the south-west angle of the site in 1851 can never be known.

Theories about the nature of the Roman settlement at Dorn have till recently been vague. Haverfield could only guess, in default of excavation, that it might have been a villa or a wayside village connected with the Fosse, which today runs about 300 yards east of the site. But we now know that it was neither of these things. Aerial photography and ground reconnaissance by Dr. St. Joseph of Cambridge have lately shown that it was a town of some ten acres in area with a parallel street system, all enclosed within rectangular ramparts, and that it was actually on the Fosse, the original course of which was just outside the eastern rampart of the town.[8]

Of excavation there has been only one case since Haverfield

wrote over sixty years ago. In 1937–39 the late Colonel R. K. Morcom of Bromsgrove privately organized a dig at a point in the south-west angle of the town. His notes have recently been analyzed and edited by Mr Adrian Oswald of the Birmingham Museum.[9] At the upper level was the floor of a corridor house of late date—the pottery found in association with it was of the late 4th century and some coins were of the 5th century. Fragments of coloured plaster and some coarse *tesserae* showed that some of the walls were decorated and at least one floor paved. Two feet below this building was a much earlier floor of clay and gravel covered by wood ash, suggesting that the building had been destroyed by fire. Pottery and coins at this level were of the 2nd century, and Mr Oswald finds evidence in some of the potsherds of even 1st century occupation. The most interesting finds were at this early level—two large steelyards (for weighing) and an ornamental iron cauldron hook or turnspit.

This evidence, so far as it goes, suggests that the little town of Dorn dates back at least to the earliest years of the Fosseway. It has been suggested that it may possibly have been built as one of a series of forts along the line of the Fosse between the Devon border and Lincoln.

That raises the larger question of the date and original purpose of the construction of the Fosseway. The view now most commonly held is that in their conquest of the island the Roman legions swept westward and northward rather easily through the more populous agricultural and low-lying country in the south and east. The hard core of British resistance between 44 and 51 A.D. was in Wales under Caratacus, and the more forested and difficult terrain on which the invaders looked down when they reached the Jurassic escarpment, of which the Cotswolds form the highest section, gave scope for raiding forces of the Britons to disrupt the communications in rear of the Roman columns as they pushed on to the Welsh marches and beyond. It was for this reason that perhaps about the year 47 the Fosseway was constructed as a defensive boundary manned on a block-house system with forts at intervals along its course.[10] That Dorn may possibly have been such a military station is a theory which perhaps gets some support from its site on the most vulnerable route through the Cotswold barrier—its choice for the modern

3

railway suggests how vulnerable it must have been. The name of Dorn may be called in evidence too, for it is thought to be from a Celtic root *duro*, meaning fortress.

And yet, when all this is said, the theory that the Fosse was built in the course of the Roman drive towards the Welsh marches and to serve a military purpose remains unproven. It has been held that it may not have been till the time of Hadrian (c.120) that it was constructed. There was no Caesar to leave us an account of the second Roman invasion of Britain, and the fragmentary notices of it in contemporary writings contain little or nothing on the campaign in the midland parts of the island. Archaeology gives no conclusive testimony yet. Certainly nothing has so far been found on the site of Dorn to suggest military occupation, and it seems that the same can be said of the whole stretch of the road from Leicester to Cirencester. If the earthwork just outside Moreton-in-Marsh through which the present road to Batsford passes is a Roman fort and connected with the Roman conquest of the Cotswold area[11]—and here again we have no certain proof—it seems unlikely that another fort only half a mile away would be established at Dorn. The question can be answered only after the Dorn site has been comprehensively excavated.

Other questions about the little town would be answered too. The abundance of 4th century coins and pottery found on the site suggest that it may have been prosperous, perhaps as a market on the highway for the wool and other products of the North Cotswolds, in that period. We do not know its fate when the Saxon invaders came—perhaps along the same highway, which must now have given an easy approach to raiding bands from the North Sea. Excavation may perhaps give some hint of how far it was destroyed.[12]

[1] G. M. Trevelyan; *Autobiography and other Essays*, 107.
[2] Habington: *Survey of Worcestershire*, ii. 33 (W.H.S.).
[3] Bodleian Library, MSS Ashmole 1817 A.
[4] Cox: *Magna Britannia et Hibernia*, vi. 240.
[5] Soden, 115–8.
[6] V.C.H., *Worcestershire*, i. 221.
[7] *B.G.A.S.* lxxxi. 194–5. Soden gives drawings of both stones. One of them is illustrated in this chapter.

[8] *Journal of Roman Studies*, li. (1961), 132–3.

[9] *B.G.A.S.* lxxxii, 18–24.

[10] *Archaeological Journal*, cxv. 49 ff. 'Roman Military Advance under Ostorius Scapula' by Graham Webster.

[11] *Ibid.* cix 23 ff. 'The Roman Conquest of the Cotswolds' by B. H. St J. and H. E. O'Neil.

[12] See p. 6

CHAPTER TWO

Saxon Blockley

THERE IS NO knowing exactly when or how the Anglo-Saxon conquerors of Britain came into the North Cotswolds. They were unlettered and left no chronicle of their own; and, for reasons that can be imagined, their victims left none either. Such few facts as we have of the dark two centuries that followed the departure of the Roman legions—say from 400 to 600—were recorded by Bede or in the Anglo-Saxon Chronicle long after. The Saxon conquest was no organized series of campaigns, as the Roman conquest four centuries earlier had been, but a succession of tribal movements spread over a long period and held back as they got further west by stout British resistance under a leader who became a legend as King Arthur. It was not till 577 that Ceawlin, king of the West Saxons, drove a wedge between the Britons of the Devonian peninsula and those of Wales by his victory of Deorham near the head of the Bristol Channel. That must have opened the South Cotswolds to Saxon settlers from Wessex.

It was probably by Angles, not Saxons, that the North Cotswolds were occupied. From landings on the east coast they may have come either by way of the Thames and Evenlode valleys, or if the Humber or the Wash was their point of entry, by way of the Fosse. Dorn lay in their path either way and can hardly have escaped devastation from their war bands. It was perhaps here that the first English settlers in the Blockley valley found the starting point for their pioneering ventures. From Dorn the eponymous Blocca and Paecc, if there really were invaders so

6

named and if Blockley and Paxford were named after them, could well have made their way with their kinsfolk to settle by our local streams on the marlstone clearing of Blockley and the pre-glacial gravels of Paxford, and there built their farmsteads.

A Saxon burial site, discovered in 1924 on the brick-field near the former Blockley railway station, must date from the earliest period of settlement in the area. From it were unearthed five skeletons beside which were found a metal shield boss, two iron spearheads, an iron knife blade and a number of glass or amber beads. It was a case of pre-Christian burial, for the church forbade the interment of such grave-goods with the dead. These pagan worshippers of Woden were perhaps very early Paxford folk—possibly of the 7th century.[1]

That was the period in which the North Cotswold area and the Saxon settlers in it were absorbed into the kingdom of Mercia after the victory of Penda, its ruler (632–54), over the West Saxons. It became part of the province of the Hwiccians, which comprised, using later names, all Worcestershire and Gloucestershire with part of Oxfordshire. The old name survives in Wychwood (*huicce wudu*, in a 9th century Saxon charter), and the high ground of our own parish about Far Upton Wold is called the Hwiccian Hills in one of the 10th. About 680 Archbishop Theodore created a bishopric of the Hwiccians, later to become the see of Worcester. But it was much later than this that Blockley was converted to Christianity; much later, indeed, that it became a village.

As late as 730 there would seem to have been no significant settlement on that scale here. In his illuminating analysis of a charter of that date concerning Batsford (*Baecceshora*, then) Professor Finberg interprets the boundaries of that estate, which in the charter is granted to Wilfrith, then bishop, and the church of Worcester, in a way that makes this clear. He renders the Latin phrases as follows:

> On the south it includes a great part of the hill; on the east it is enclosed by the king's highway; on the north it is girt by flowing waters; the west bounds it with certain marshes.[2]

These are all features of the landscape still. The hill must be the upland above Bourton-on-the-Hill, and the highway can only be the Fosseway. A mile west of Batsford there is a water-logged flat where the Blockley Brook levels out after a short drop from the spring which is its source, and that, no doubt, is the marsh of the charter. But it is the phrase *fluviales undae*, or 'flowing waters', forming the northern boundary, which takes us into Blockley and its history. They can only be the Blockley Brook to its junction with the Knee Brook and thence the Knee Brook to the point where the Fosseway crosses it. This wide arc took in the whole southern flank of the Blockley valley—a good third of the later manor and parish of Blockley—and included Dorn and the sites of Aston Magna and Draycott. It excluded the site of the village of Blockley, but ran along the edge of it—and the boundary of Batsford in 730 could hardly have been brought right up to the site if there had then been a village of Blockley on it.

It is in a charter of 855[3] (*Plate 5*) that we first find a mention of Blockley, though in a context which implies that it was then a place of some standing. It was a grim year for the kingdom of Mercia, for the Danish raids were at their height and one of the war-bands was ravaging the upper Severn valley.[4] To fight the invaders, or more probably to buy them off, the Mercian king needed money or treasure, and some was forthcoming from the bishop of Worcester, whose diocese was directly threatened, in return for grants of land in the Coln valley, near Cirencester and at Block-ley.

> I, Burgred king of the Mercians, for the redemption of my soul. . . grant to my faithful bishop and friend Ealhun the donation of this privilege namely the minster which is called Bloccanleeh (*monasterium quod nominatur bloccanleeh*). I will exempt it from the feeding and maintenance of all hawks and falcons in the land of the Mercians and of all huntsmen of the king or ealdorman, except only such as are in the province of the Hwicce; likewise also from the feeding and maintenance of those men whom in the Saxon tongue we call *Wahlfaereld*, and from lodging all horsemen of the English race and foreigners. Bishop Ealhun gave to me 300 silver shillings as an acceptable price, that these privileges might be the more freely enjoyed thereby.

The bishop thus became owner, with the customary rights of

lordship implied by the archaic formula in the text, of the *monasterium* in Blockley and of the land which was its endowment close to the village. His Batsford estate was thus extended beyond the brook which had been its boundary.

The phrase '*monasterium quod nominatur bloccanleeh*' in Burgred's charter does not mean that there was a house of cloistered monks in Saxon Blockley, or indeed in any other period, in spite of the old village tradition that there was. The *monasterium* in Blockley which is referred to here was a semi-monastic community of secular priests, deacons and clerks in minor orders sent by an early bishop of Worcester to convert and minister to the still pagan uplanders of the North Cotswolds. There were at this time many such missionary communities in western Christendom. Such bodies in Saxon England were called minsters, and it is by this word that *monasterium* must here be translated.[5] The minster at Blockley was no doubt a small one—perhaps a presbyter or two, a deacon or two, and a few other brethren (*fratres*) in minor orders, any of whom may have been married and separately housed. Their living will have come from an endowment of land for houses, gardens and farms, all of which would require servants to work them. It must have been their first care to mark off a site for a church set in a graveyard, and there is good reason to assume that it was the site of the churchyard we know today and that our church stands on the spot where the original Saxon 'minster' was set up.

No trace remains of that first Blockley church, but there does survive a legend which attaches to it. The story was told, over a century after the event—if it ever was an event—by William, the monk of Malmesbury, in his Life of St. Wulfstan, [6] who was bishop of Worcester from 1062 to 1095, the one pre-Conquest English bishop to retain his see and the respect of the Norman rulers.

(The Bishop) had come just after Easter to the place called Bloccelea and on the octave of the feast, being about to say Mass, he was grieved to see all the ornaments on the altar in a state unworthy of the sacred rite—the candles out of shape and set in common household sconces, the altar cloths foul with the dirt of ages. He thereupon bade a young server beside him to run quickly to convey his displeasure to the man whose fault it was in his cell.

But this man, who often had taken advantage of the clemency of the gentle bishop fell into a rage and boxed the ears of the boy. Bearing the marks of his punishment and in tears the lad returned to his lord, The evidence of such insolence from one of his servants moved the bishop to anger, as his change of countenance plainly showed, but he kept it close in his heart and proceeded with the solemn rite in quietness and silence.

But there was a miracle. At the very moment when anger rose in the mind of the bishop in the church a sickness overcame the body of the servant in his cell, He fell to the ground, his breathing all but ceased and he swooned away, so that he lay as one at the point of death . . .

Needless to say there was a happy ending. The good bishop forgave the wrong-doer and all was well. So the story runs, and it is the only faint trace we have of something, however elaborated in the telling, which may have happened in Blockley's vanished Saxon church

The area of rough upland country over which the Blockley minster staff carried out their mission was vast and travel over it difficult. Chapels, each of them subordinate to the minister, the 'mother church', must have been established in the principal settlements of the area. As time went on certain ecclesiastical dues became customary—church scot, tithe, mortuaries and the like—and some or all of these were payable from the chapelries to the mother church. It could happen that some of these claims on the daughter churches lasted on after the time, in the 11th or 12th century, when they became parish churches in their own right and the old minster no longer had pastoral responsibility for their people, but was itself a parish church just as they were.

We find here a clue to the extent of the wide 'minster parish' over which the earliest Blockley clergy did their missionary work. Throughout the Middle Ages the rectors and vicars of Blockley exercised the right of sepulture over the parishes of Batsford, Bourton-on-the-Hill, Moreton-in-Marsh and Stretton-on-Fosse. The history of this claim and its exercise will be given on a later page,[7] but the names of the parishes must surely indicate the extent of the wide tract of country which was the original 'minster parish' of Blockley.

The build up of the great Blockley estate, later to be called a manor by the Norman lawyers, from its Batsford nucleus remains to be described. It had taken in Blockley and its neighbourhood by 855, as has been shown. Northwick was added within the next century, being among the possessions of the bishop of Worcester recorded in the well-known charter of King Edgar in which he created the Hundred of Oswaldslow in 964. Upton Wold, after a dispute as to its ownership between the 'church of Worcester' and the abbey of Winchcombe, was adjudged to the bishop, subject to a life interest of one Wullaf, in 897. The area of the Ditchfords accrued to the bishop before 1052, when a certain Wulfgeat was granted a three-life lease of it. Paxford was added last of all. Professor Finberg[8] has pointed to its protrusion north-westwards from the northern boundary of the parish and to its treatment as a separate estate in 13th century manorial surveys. The earliest known lease of it by the bishop is dated about 1120.

Long before this Batsford had been taken from the bishop by the infamous Edric Streona in 1016, as the monk Heming of Worcester Priory recorded, and Domesday Book gives Batsford as a separate three-hide manor held in Edward the Confessor's reign by a thegn named Brismer.

---

[1] *Worcs. Arch. Society*, iii. 128. 'Saxon Finds at Blockley' by E. A. B. Barnard.
[2] H. P. R. Finberg: *Gloucestershire Studies* (1957), 5–11.
[3] Birch: *Cartularium Saxonicum*, no. 488, translated in *Eng. Hist. Documents* i. 486.
[4] Another exactly contemporary charter, translated in E. H. D. 485, states that "the heathen were then in the region of the Wrekin people".
[5] See two papers by G. W. O. Addleshaw: *The Beginnings of the Parochial System* (St Anthony's Press, York, 1970) and *Pastoral Organization of the modern Dioceses of Durham and Newcastle in the time of Bede* (*Jarrow Lecture*, 1963).
[6] William of Malmesbury's *Vita Wulfstani* was based on an account of the bishop by his chancellor, Coleman.
[7] See especially p. 19-20
[8] *Op. cit.* 5.

CHAPTER THREE

Church & Parish in the Middle Ages

N O DATE CAN be given for the creation of the parish of
Blockley as defined today, as distinct from the wide 'minster
parish' of the missionary phase of the church. We know
from the Domesday survey of 1086 that "a priest who has one
hide" was a tenant of the manor of Blockley. It may be that he
was rector of the parish of Blockley, which certainly in years to
come had the same boundaries as the manor, and that the 'group
ministry' of earlier days had by then ceased to be. But precise
evidence on these matters is lacking.

We can be rather more certain about the replacement of the
old minster church building by the oldest portions of the church
we know today. The architectural features suggest that it took
place about 1175. The founder of the new church must have
been the bishop of Worcester of that date, as lord of the manor.
All over the Cotswolds the Norman landowners, now in the third
or fourth gneration from the Conquest, were building churches
on their estates, their recognition of their duty in this matter being
perhaps sharpened by the martyrdom of Archbishop Becket in
1170.

The new church was no mean building, as befitted an episcopal
foundation, and the benefice was richly endowed and privileged.
Even now, after the decay and refurbishing of eight centuries,
the church retains enough Norman detail to suggest what it must
have been like when fresh from the mason's hands. With the lord's
hall or hospice adjoining it—no doubt on the site of the present
Manor House—it must have dominated the humble dwelling

houses (many with small farmyards) along the village street. In plan it consisted of a chancel, generously proportioned, an aisle-less nave and a western tower, both nave and tower being much lower than they are today. Much of the original stonework of the of the chancel survives—in the columns of the chancel arch, the round-headed windows (two of them now blind owing to later building) on the north side, much of the fine corbelling which must have supported the barrel roof of timber, and the aumbries on the north side of the altar, which may have served as the Easter sepulchre in pre-Reformation days. Outside, the flat pilaster-like buttresses and the much-weathered 'rope' moulding under the east window (which itself is a 19th century feature) recall the original Norman design, however much they have since been restored. The rarely used south door into the nave, with the mitred head on its western jamb to remind us of the quality of the church's founder is original, so far as its wide outer arch is concerned, but the infilling to accommodate a smaller door is 16th century work. All that is left of the original tower seems to be the lower portion of the newel stairway.

It was a rich benefice. Assessed in the *Taxatio* of Pope Nicholas IV in 1291 at about 37[1] annually it was worth half as much again as Campden and over three times as much as the more than average livings of Ebrington and Mickleton. The parish was no gainer from this. Having so rich a prize in his gift the bishop made Blockley one of the benefices regularly used to remunerate high diocesan officials, the incumbent being given leave to absent himself from the parish on condition that he appointed a sti-pendiary chaplain to carry out the parochial duties. Worse still, the power to appoint the rector might pass to the Pope, who exer-cised the privilege of 'providing' to a benefice when its incumbent ceased to hold it, whether by death or resignation, while he happened to be in Rome, and these papal 'provisors', generally foreigners and usually Italians, drew tithes and other dues from English parishes which they never visited as their wage for their functions in the Roman *curia*. Blockley suffered quite exceptionally from this hated custom, and between 1294 and 1332 no less than five rectors, one Italian, two French and one Portu-guese, were papally provided. The bishop of Worcester then ended the practice for Blockley by appropriating the benefice for himself and his successors. This did not end the absenteeism from the parish, but it did secure that privilege for Englishmen. Of the nameless priests who, for what was probably a pittance, did the work for which these absentees were paid, we know nothing at all.

RECTORS OF BLOCKLEY

Except where otherwise stated, all were collated to the benefice by the bishop of Worcester, as patron.

c. 1240 Vincent de Abergavenny.
He was also Archdeacon of Worcester.

1269   Lucien de Cormeilles.
A relative of the bishop, Godfrey Giffard.[1] His family home was in Brittany and he may not have been in holy orders. He held the benefice *in commendam*, drawing the revenues pending a permanent appointment.

c. 1272 Gregory de Caerwent.
A canon lawyer, and used by the bishop for diocesan administration. Probably called to Rome for similar work in the papal court, for he died there in 1279.

1280 Philip de Crofta (Croft).
Owing to the death of the last rector in Rome the nomination of his successor lay with the Pope, who passed it to the Archbishop of Canterbury, Peckham. This invasion of his own privileges was resented by Giffard, especially when Croft acted on a mandate from the court of Canterbury in connexion with a sequestration within the Worcester diocese.

1291 William de Grinefeld (Greenfield).
A relative of Giffard and only in minor orders. He passed on to the rectory of Stratford-on-Avon, where he was ordained deacon. He ultimately became Archbishop of York.

1294 Peter de Escot, a member of the bishop's household.
After his institution Bishop Giffard learned that Escot, when he applied for ordination, had suppressed the fact that he was of illegitimate birth. It was a grave canonical offence and involved trial at Rome. The bishop duly sent him there, though reluctantly and with letters testimonial in his favour. Unhappily Escot died in Rome before trial. The bishop thus again lost the right to collate to Blockley.

14

1295 Bartolomeo di Ferentino.

Papally provided, he was presumably an official of the Roman curia and quite unknown to his English parish.

1310 Benedict de Paston.

Another papal nominee—this time by Pope Clement V who had lately moved the pontifical court and residence to Avignon-Benedict was a pluralist and much occupied in diocesan work, so that it is likely that his residence in Blockley was fitful. He was nevertheless, for Blockley, the most important of all these early rectors.

Paston, his home, is the village in the north-east corner of Norfolk which was also the home of the family which, in the next century was to leave in the 'Paston Letters' so vivid a picture of English life then. Benedict may well have been an earlier member of that family. At Oxford he became M.A. by 1302 and in due course proceeded to doctorates in Civil and Canon Law, thereby qualifying for high administrative office in the Church. He found a powerful patron in Walter Reynolds, who became bishop of Worcester in 1308 and at once appointed him Official of the diocese (with functions like those of a diocesan Chancellor today) and in 1310 made him Vicar-General for some months during his own absence from England on a mission to the pope on the king's behalf. It was, no doubt, while there that Bishop Reynolds secured Paston's nomination to the then vacant Blockley benefice. He later, on becoming Archbishop, continued his patronage of this able priest by appointing him Auditor of Causes in the consistory court of Canterbury. One could have wished for Master Benedict a more worthy patron, for Reynolds was a worldling and far too much at ease in Edward II's disreputable court. And it is hard to think the better of Benedict himself for adding to his cure at Blockley a canonry of Exeter in 1313, the rectory of Harvington (near Evesham) in 1316 and a canonry of Beverley in 1322.

Yet the church in Blockley owed him the project of a chantry—the endowment of a priest to serve daily at an altar dedicated to the Virgin Mary. He had not been rector for more than a year or two before he obtained from the bishop the grant of forty days indulgence "to all who shall give a helping hand to the maintenance of the priest who celebrates daily the mass of the Blessed

15

Virgin in the church of Blockeleye". A parishioner, William de Dichforde, responded with a gift of land in that hamlet. In 1320 a far larger benefaction of land in Blockley and Northwick—a supplementary gift was made four years later—came from Ralph de Baketon, rector of Coln Roger. Bacton, today's spelling of Ralph's home, is only a couple of miles from Paston. Ralph was no doubt a relative, or at any rate an old friend, of Benedict. He must surely have owed his Coln Roger living to Benedict's influence with the bishop. The close relationship between the two men is confirmed by an entry in Bishop Cobham's register dated 1320 granting the pair a year's leave of absence from their parishes, and it seems likely that it was during this interval together that Ralph's endowment of the Blockley chantry was arranged. It consisted of some 40 acres of land and two houses, one of which was for the personal use of the chantry priest. Thus the parish church gained an addition to its staff of priests, and it may be that the need thus created for a Lady Chapel led to the building not long after of what is now the north aisle of the church.[2]

In 1326 Benedict de Paston left England to become a chamberlain at the papal court. There he died in 1330.

Three papal presentations to the Blockley benefice followed in the next two years—and the parish certainly saw none of the nominees, all foreigners:

1330 Armand de Roseto, a Frenchman, He died before he could be instituted.
1330 Gerard de Pristinio, also French, who resigned on becoming a bishop.
1332 The bishop of Oporto, presumably a Portuguese. He was the last of the papal provisors to Blockley.

VICARS OF BLOCKLEY

In 1332 the pope gave official approval to the appropriation by the bishops of Worcester of the office and emoluments, subject to deductions detailed below, of Rector of Blockley. The practice of the appropriation of benefices by their patrons was so common at this period as to constitute a serious abuse. Monasteries with livings in their gift were the worst offenders, the profits from the transaction usually going into the funds of

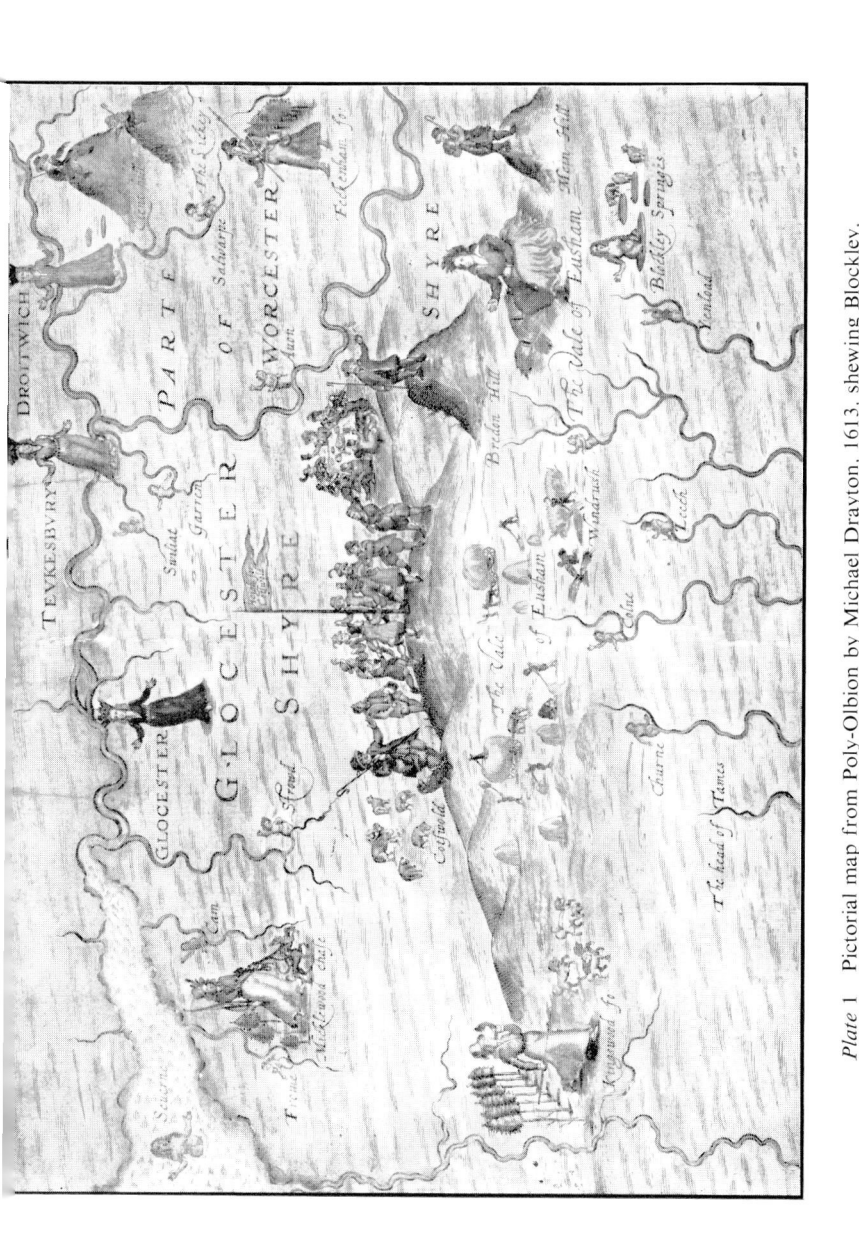

Plate 1   Pictorial map from Poly-Olbion by Michael Drayton, 1613, shewing Blockley.

Plate 2   Dorne and Bachford: map, 1662.

Plate 3 Portion of Enclosure map of Aston Magna, 1733, (chap. 10), reproduced by courtesy of Lord Dulverton

Plate 4   Field Map, 1955, compiled by R. Belcher and Margaret Ruestow, (*née* Garrard.)

Plate 5 Copy of the Charter of A.D. 855, giving the Manor of Blockley to the Bishop of Worcester. (chap. 2) (*Photograph by courtesy of British Museum*)

Plate 6   Brass, Worthyn.

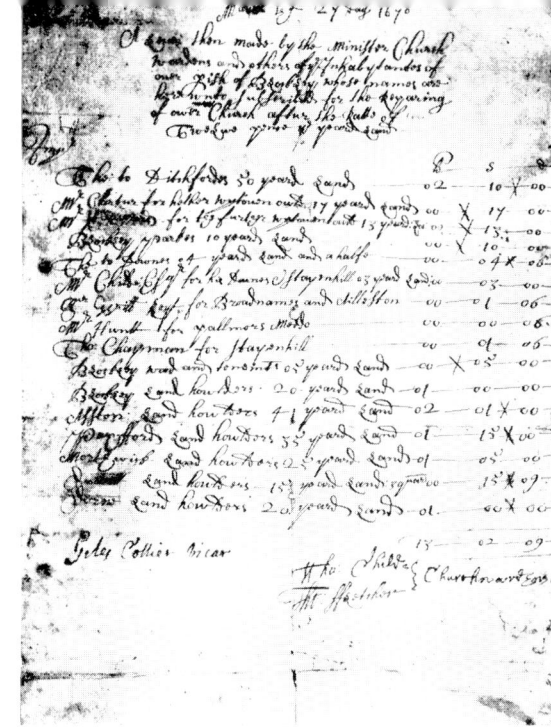

Plate 10 Lowe's Mill, 1886 (now Malvern Mill), from a painting by Mrs Annie Warner, when a pupil at Miss Judson's school. (*Photograph by courtesy of P. Pritchard*)

Plate 11 The Gleaners; Mrs Silas ("Trotty") Eastbury of Rose Row and helpers c 1905.

the community, and so being lost to the work of the church at large. That disadvantage did not apply when the impropriator was the bishop of the diocese.

There were obvious reasons which led to the appeal by Adam de Orleton, bishop of Worcester in this year 1332 for the appropriation by himself and his successors of the Blockley benefice. For nearly forty years they had been deprived of the patronage of one of the richest livings in the diocese—and consequently of means for payment of the stipend of one of the high officials in its service. The nomination by the pope of so many aliens to the rectory must often have left the parish in charge of ill-qualified chaplains. Pending the formal transfer of the benefice and the settlement of permanent provision for the care of the parish, the bishops 'farmed' the rectory. Thus in 1340 Bishop Bransford commissioned Master John, rector of Hinton-in-the Green and farmer of Blockley church to exercise rectorial functions, including the exempt jurisdiction attaching to a 'peculiar'. This bishop was an outstanding administrator, and Master John was, no doubt, well chosen for the temporary oversight of the parish. On grounds such as these there could be nothing but gain if for the future the bishop became rector and appointed as his vicar–the word means deputy or substitute–an Englishman and one well qualified for the work of a parish priest.

When the Pope approved the transfer of the rectory of Blockley to the bishops of Worcester it was because of the insufficiency of their revenues, and in particular of the great repairs needed in the manor of Blockley "on account of the age of its noble buildings" and the bishop's "frequent journeys to London on business of the diocese and the realm." The appropriation of the benefice was approved subject to the proviso "a perpetual vicar's portion to be reserved." In other words, the future vicars of Blockley were to have a permanent living settled on them and to be no longer subject to the will of the rector for their stipend and tenure of office.

The settlement was made by Bishop John Thoresby in 1352.[3] By it the bishop was to take the glebe, the 'great tithes' of corn and wool, Peter's Pence and some minor payments. The vicar was to have the manse hitherto occupied by the parish priest and an adjoining house "called Mosthous", with a curtilage of twenty acres round them—the site, we must conjecture, of the present vicarage, though its grounds have greatly shrunk since then. He was to have all offerings at the great festivals in the parish church and its chapels, including the one on the fair ground, together with all those made in the church porch and churchyard, All the 'little tithes' went to him: on hay (except from the lord's demesne), underwood, lamb's wool, calves, pigs, poultry, milk, cheese and honey. Church-scot, the ancient due in kind on fruit and corn due on St. Martin's Day, was to be his; and mortuaries which gave him the right to the second-best beast on the death of a householder in the parish. It still made a good living—and a growing one.

One clause in the settlement made the bishop of Worcester, as rector, responsible for "the burden of building, supporting and repairing the said church." That raises the question of the date and circumstances of the building of the north aisle with its piscina (at some time brutally shorn in half to make the pillar into which it was built, conveniently flat). The altar beside that piscina must have been the one at which the chantry priest celebrated the daily mass, and the aisle must have been the Lady Chapel.[4] Was this chapel built by the bishop at this time to mark the change in the nature of the benefice? And did he, at about the same time, build the sedilia beside the high altar? Both appear to be 14th century work, and we shall presently see that there were developments in the case of the chantry at this period.

That so little is known of these developments and that the list of the earliest vicars is so deficient is due to the grim disaster of of the Black Death, the first epidemic of bubonic plague, which coincided with them. The pestilence was at its height in Worcestershire in the summer of 1349. In the next six months 67 vacancies had to be filled in the 138 benefices of the diocese, and that Blockley was one of these is evident from the fact that in August John Bavent was collated as vicar.[5]

Further evidence of the plague in Blockley and its economic consequences lies in the state of the chantry endowment, which was "left desolate." It took two new gifts to re-establish it. The benefactor was John de Blockley, as he was known at the court of Edward III, where he was a king's clerk and important enough to be one of the two auditors for the privy purse of Queen

Philippa. From his property in Aston Magna ("Hongynde Aston") he conveyed to John Wilde, the chantry priest, in 1356[6] two houses, 54 acres of arable land, 7 acres of meadow and 4 of pasture. In 1375 he added more land, a mill and a toft in Blockley, the priest then being Henry Rose.

In 1366 John de Riddlyngton was collated as vicar, and it is not till well on in the next century that we can take up the list.

But one event in the interval may be recorded. In March 1395 the bishop, Henry Wakefield, old and for long a sick man, died in his Blockley manor house on a journey home from a session of Parliament. We can be sure that the people of Blockley saw the beginning of the solemnities that followed in their church before the body of the dead bishop was conveyed to the cathedral at Worcester for burial. He was the second bishop to die in the house. Walter de Cantilupe, the friend of de Montfort, ended his days there in 1246.

The list of vicars can now be taken up:

1419 Richard Culey, who died the same year in Blockley.

1419 Walter Aston (or Eston). A Fellow of Trinity Hall, Cambridge. Having a degree in Civil Law he was qualified for diocesan administration—always a sinister portent for the parish. In his case the diocese he served was that of Hereford, and he held the papal licence to be absent from all his benefices, including Blockley, for the purpose. In 1421, on becoming a canon of Hereford, he vacated his Blockley living.

1430 John Kemmis was vicar at this time, and in this year he was licenced to be absent for study, no doubt in Canon Law, at a university, after which he took up administrative work in the papal curia at Rome.

1433 John Skiffington collated to the benefice.

1440 William Clerk. He too was given leave of absence for study at a university with permission to 'farm' his Blockley benefice. But there is reason to think that he may not have been absent for long. In 1441 he resisted an attempt by his namesake, John Clerke, rector of Stretton-on-Fosse, to break free from the hardship caused by the ancient claim of the vicar of Blockley to bury the dead of Stretton in his churchyard and take the customary dues. The bishop refused Stretton's appeal for relief made on the ground that "their mother

19

church of Blockley was far distant and that in winter they were not able because of floods to carry their dead thither."[7] That is why a later 15th century rector of Stretton, William Lombarde, was buried in Blockley church. Moreton-in-Marsh made their appeal direct to the pope in 1512, pleading hardship caused by "the intervening hills, especially in winter" and gained their wish. So did Bourton-on-the-Hill in 1542. But the parish registers show that Batsford were still burying their dead in Blockley churchyard at the end of the 17th century.[8]

William Clerk seems still to have been resident in 1454, in which year he conveyed a house and land "near Partriche Hill"—perhaps a variation of the earlier Altrichesdon, the Blockley Downs of today[9]—to his brother, Thomas.

1455 John Balle. An Oxford M.A., to which university he soon returned as head of a hall of residence.

1462 Philip Worthyn came to Blockley as vicar after serving for five years as head of an Oxford hall—possibly on exchange with Balle? That he was resident in his parish of Blockley seems evident from the fact that he resigned another benefice which he had held in plurality in 1472 and that he was buried in the chancel under the fine brass, in which the figure is shown in academical robes and the epitaph recalls his dignity, his learning and his piety. (*Plate* 6)

The architectural evidence gives ground for thinking that the chancel arch and the doorway inserted under the original Norman arch of the south entrance to the church may date from his time, or from that of his successor.

1488 William Neele. (*Plate* 8)

He was an Oxford M.A. and fellow of Merton College until his collation to the Blockley benefice. Though he held other livings simultaneously for short periods, including North Cerney from c. 1491 to 1498 and Bourton-on-the-Water for the last year of his life, there is nothing to suggest that he did not reside at Blockley, and, as his memorial brass[10] in the chancel perhaps implies, eventually die there. As already suggested, he may possibly have had some share in structural changes in the fabric of the church. A deed has survived among the Northwick papers in which is recited the conveyance by him of a house and some land to one Henry Harthill of Blockley.

1. Giffard's mother was a de Cormeilles heiress.
2. See p. 18
3. The document is given in full by Soden 25-7.
4. See p. 16
5. Reg. Bransford, ed. R.M.Haines, 426 (W.H.S.)
6. Patent Rolls, 30 Ed.III, ii. 345: also ibid. 82.
7. Dugdale: *Warwickshire* (1730 edition) 599.
8. Soden 24.
9. See p. 42
10. Now on the wall of the sedilia, A rare, possibly unique, type of memorial brass. It shows a priest vested in a cope and *kneeling*. When so vested he is normally shown standing.

The fragment of a third brass by the vestry door is all that remains of a memorial of William Lombarde, rector of Stretton-on-Fosse, for whom see p. 20

Eyre, p.8., shows that it was intact in 1827, when he wrote. It probably suffered when the chancel was restored a few years later.

Note. For details in this chapter the following works have been consulted:-

W.H.Bliss: *Calendar of Papal Registers relating to Great Britain and Ireland* (1893).

Episcopal Registers (published by W.H.S.):-

Giffard, ed. J.W.Willis Bund.

Reynolds, ed. R.A.Wilson.

Cobham, ed. E.H.Pearce.

Bransford, ed. R.M.Haines.

R.M.Haines: *Administration of the Diocese of Worcester,*1300-50. (S.P.C.K.)

A.B.Emden: *Biographical Register of the University of Oxford to* 1500. (O.U.P.)

Notes BLOCKLEY AND THE PAPACY

On p. 16 MrIcely recounts how the Bishop of Oporto, in 1332, was the last Rector of Blockley to be provided by the Pope.

As this work was being printed, through the kindness of Sras. Maria Leonor Gonscalves and Maria Benedita of Lisbon, additional information of interest, mainly from Fortunato de Almeida, *'Historia da Igreja em Portugal'*(1930), has come to light.

It appears that for a few years Blockley played a humble part on the European stage in the struggle between Church and State for temporal power. In 1325 Dom Vasco Martins was elected to the bishopric of Oporto by the Pope against the wishes of the King of Portugal, Dom Afonso IV, and of the Câmara of Oporto. Quarrels began over jurisdiction and after roiting which endangered his life the bishop fled to Avignon where Pope John XXII was in exile. The King ordered D. Vasco to return to his See which he refused to do, whereupon the king sequestrated his revenues in 1331. The Pope replied to this by giving him the benefice of Blockley in 1332. D. Vasco returned to Oporto in 1335 on the orders of Pope Benito XII and the king restored the 'Revenues of the Mitre' in Oporto to him.

He did not, however, return to Blockley to the See of Worcester at the date as we know (p. 17) that he had farmed it to the Rector of Hinton-in-the-Green in 1340. D. Vasco died in 1344 and that was probably the date of the restitution to Worcester, the next firm date being 1352, the date of Bishop John Thoresby's settlement (p. 17) when Blockley had definitely been returned to Worcester.

CHAPTER FOUR

The Medieval Manor of Blockley

1086-1600

THE ACCOUNT OF the manor of Blockley contained in the Domesday Book was drawn up in 1086 for the information of King William and his Norman administrators. It is a dry statistical summary, in severely contracted Latin, of the bishop's tenants in their several classes and of the taxable assets on the estate.

The Bishop of Wirecestre holds BLOCHELEI. There are 38 hides that pay geld (*tax*). Of these there are in demesne 25½ hides, where are 7 ploughs: and there are a priest who has 1 hide and 4 radmen who have 6 hides, and there are 63 villeins and 25 bordars who have between them all 51 ploughs. There are 14 serfs and 12 mills worth 52 shillings less 3 pence, and 24 acres of meadow. The woodland is half a lewa (*league*) in length and width. It was (*in the time of King Edward the Confessor*) worth 16 pounds: now 20 pounds.

Of this manor Richard holds 2 hides at DICFORD (*Ditchford*) where he has 1 plough: and there are 2 villeins and 1 bordar and 2 serfs with 1 plough. There are 4 acres of meadow. It was and remains worth 30 shillings.

Ansgot holds 1½ hides of the land appropriated to the villeins and has 1 plough with 1 bordar. There are 3 acres of meadow. It was and is worth 15 shillings.

To the said manor is attached (*jacet*) 1 hide at IACUMBE (*Icomb*) apportioned to the support of the monks (*of Worcester*).

Stephen the son of Fulchered holds 3 hides at EILESFORD (*Daylesford*) where he has 2 ploughs and a priest and 6 villeins with

5 ploughs and 4 serfs and 1 bondwoman. There are 20 acres of meadow. It is and was worth 3 pounds

Hereward holds 5 hides at EUNILADE (*Evenlode*). There are 2 ploughs and 9 villeins with 2 ploughs and 1 serf. And there is a mill worth 32 pence.

These last three outlying estates were attached to the manor of Blockley for administrative purposes only. Their holders owed fealty to the bishop and attendance at his court leet at Blockley. Icomb seems to have dropped out of the connexion quite soon, but the constables of Daylesford and Evenlode were appointed, and the representation of these villages duly recorded, at the annual sittings of the manorial court at the Crown Inn as late as 1769.[1]

The special mention of Ditchford in the Domesday record may mean that it was sub-let to Richard and so had, for the time, the same status as Evenlode and Daylesford. It is possible that Paxford was not a member of the manor at the time of the Domesday survey,[2] though it seems to have been an estate of the bishop very soon after, as a lease of it granted by Theulf, whose episcopate lasted from 1115 to 1123, attests. There must be some significance in the facts that Paxford is referred to as a manor in Bishop Gainsborough's Register in 1304, and that it was separately surveyed in Bishop Giffard's great inquest into his manors in 1299, though it was there described as *hamelettus*. The puzzle is made no easier by the explicit inclusion of Paxford among the members of the manor of Blockley in King John's Book of Fees in 1208. Dorn was another special case. An entry in the Evesham Abbey copy of the county entries in the Domesday Book had a marginal note, " de hoc manerio tenet Urso v hidas in Dorne": of this manor (of Blockley) Urse holds five hides in Dorn. Urse D'Abitot, the Conqueror's formidable sheriff of Worcestershire, preyed on ecclesiastical owners of land, as the monks of Evesham well knew from their own experience, and the saintly Bishop Wulstan was perhaps not the man to stand up to him. The Dorn estate passed to the Beauchamp family, into which one of Urse's daughters married, and the name D'Abitot, variously spelt, occurs in taxation rolls and other official documents in lists of Dorn residents down to 1356 at least.[3] Dorn is not mentioned in the survey of the manor in 1299, and it must be assumed that the bishop drew no revenue from it, but only the fealty of its owner and his representation in the court leet.

It will already be clear that any deductions from the Blockley record in Domesday must involve guesswork. There need be no doubt about the outstanding size and value of the manor. Campden, by comparison, had lost a third of its value since 1066 and had less than half Blockley's number of plough teams. If we assume that the radmen, villeins and bordars were heads of households averaging four persons each, and that the priest and the serfs are to be counted as individuals, Blockley manor had perhaps a population of about 400, whereas Campden had little more than half that number. Against that must be set certain apparent drawbacks. The hidage figures show that the lord of the manor of Blockley kept two-thirds of the productive assets in hand as his demesne: Campden, with a more distant, if not necessarily more liberal, lord in the Earl of Chester, enjoyed a far higher tenantry share of the manor's resources to provide a basis for its later prosperity. Blockley, moreover, had very few 'free tenants' (*liberi tenentes*), exempt from all services except a money rent, fealty and attendance at the lord's court. The priest was one of them, and the only four others were the radmen—riding men, with the duty, perhaps, of providing a mounted escort for the lord and his officials and conveyance of his briefs and the like. Three of the greater tenants, including Reginald Daistune (*of Aston*) and John de Norwyke, are still recorded as radmen a century later.[4] There is, lastly, the recording in the Domesday entry of the occupation by one Ansgot of land normally reserved for villeins—the Latin word *villani* means villagers and conveys no hint of the modern sense of the word. In all this there is little to suggest that Blockley people of the 12th and 13th centuries were especially privileged under an ecclesiastical lord of the manor.

Two centuries later, in 1299, Bishop Godfrey Giffard ordered a survey of all the episcopal manors and from it we get a detailed and in some respects still recognisable picture of the Blockley community and its organisation. The first part of the survey gives an account of the land and other resources which the lord kept 'in hand' and, through his agents, the steward of the manors and the local reeve or bailiff, managed himself. The second gives a

24

nominal roll of each of the five categories of the tenants of the manor with details of the dues and services owed by them to the lord for their holdings. Those who know Blockley today may be able to identify some of the references in the summary of this seven century old survey. It includes Paxford, though this was in fact surveyed separately, and all the other hamlets except Dorn.

DEMESNE LANDS AND OTHER RESOURCES KEPT IN HAND

1 Arable land of 785 acres, 220 of them in Paxford. Part of it was perhaps a compact home farm and part distributed among the strips (or 'lands') of the open fields among those of the tenants. The bishop's park, though not cultivated for cereal crops, must no doubt be included here. It covered the present grounds of the Manor House and Park Farm—with extensions to be presently noted.[5] The earliest communal open fields seem to have been Great Hill to the west of Blockley village—roughly the land of Dovedale Farm today—and Little Hill on the west side of Bourton Hill Road. The survey makes it clear that half the land lay fallow each year.

2 Water meadows for hay, of which the lord kept 27 acres in all, 16 of them on the flatter Paxford ground adjoining the Knee Brook. The Blockley meadows were on land between the Blockley Brook and the road to Draycott.

3 Pasture for 110 cattle and some 1600 sheep. The Blockley cow pastures were on the ground known today as Pasture Farm. The sheep were on the uplands—none therefore in Paxford—and the survey names these as Northcumbe, Huptone and Altrichesdon— today, respectively, the Northwick Hill-Holt Farm area, Upton Wold on both sides of the Moreton-Broadway road and Blockley Downs. Lord and tenants must have shared all these pastures.

4 All the woodlands—mainly of course those today called Bourton Wood, but formerly called Blockley Wood and including that part of it to which early 19th century romanticism gave the name of Dovedale. The tenants of the manor had certain rights in these woods. They could run their pigs there on payment of pannage— a charge of a penny or a halfpenny according to the size of the animal: and they could collect fallen boughs and brushwood for similar payments to the lord; haybote for the repair of hedges, housbote

for their dwellings or for firewood. 'Wooding' was still a privilege exercised in the 1940's.

5 Two gardens near the lord's residence on the site of today's Manor House. One, called Bertonehay in the survey, must be Barton Hill, the field on the north side of Pasture Lane.

6 Three mills—all water mills, for wind mills were a later invention. One, a corn mill, was probably on the site of the Old Mill, being right in the village and accessible for tenants bringing their grain for grinding, subject to the lord's deducted share. The other two are named. One, called 'frenismulne' was a fulling mill and must be the 'French Mill' which a lease of 1703 locates at the bottom of Snugborough Lane and of which a building survives, the third, called 'Peomull' must be Pye Mill in Paxford.

7 An annual fair, granted in the 13th century to Bishops Walter de Cantilupe and Godfrey Giffard. It followed the corn harvest, when purses were fullest, lasting for the fortnight round Michaelmas. It provided for the shopping of the whole area. It was held on the Warren, where a chapel was built, served by the parochial clergy, to meet the spiritual needs of the crowds there assembled. There was too a court for the summary trial of dishonest traders and visiting malefactors—the court of pye powders, as it came to be called from the dusty feet (*pieds poudreux*) fresh from the fair ground. The fair was a valuable perquisite for the lord of the manor. Stallage, the fee payable by stall-keepers, the fines from wrong-doers and other receipts brought in £4—no small sum in 1299.[6]

Before passing to the second part of this survey of 1299, the various classes of tenant and their services and payments due to the lord in return for their holdings, some account may be given here of one essential service for which all, from the highest holder of a knight's fee to the humblest cottager, were liable. This was 'suit and service in the lord's court'.

At least once a year the steward of the lord's manors held this court in Blockley. Its business was twofold: to try minor offences and to regulate and record such matters as changes of tenancy, breaches of custom or contract, seasonal operations in the common fields and the like. A sworn jury, listed in the court roll under the title of the 'homage', brought up or 'presented' the matters requiring judgment or decision. The proceedings were democratic, even to the extent of decisions concerning 'customary' tenures[7] being left to the members of the court and sentences for offenders to two 'affeerors' appointed by them. Two descriptions from the Blockley court rolls may illustrate all this—both from the 16th century, but like enough to medieval practice in this unchanging sphere of action to serve our purpose.[8]

At a court leet held in Blockley in December 1575 by the lord's steward, Sir Robert Throckmorton, thirteen tenants were sworn as the homage—several with long-lasting Blockley names: Fletcher of Paxford, Mansell of Stapenhill, Dyde of Draycott, Eden of Blockley. There being no offenders to present, but only communal affairs to regulate, the proceedings were strictly those of a court baron. The homage presented "that the common pound stands open through a defect in one of the gates. Also they order that each man shall serve the office of hayward (*hedgekeeper*) for six months when it shall come to his turn on pain of forfeiting ten shillings. And otherwise they say all is well. They present that Henry Dobbyns cottager did fealty to the lord and was admitted tenant and that Thomas Hunckes esquire and Robert Hunckes gentleman surrendered to the lord three virgates of land within the fields of Northwyke, whereupon the lord by his steward granted all the premises to Richard, Alice and John Freman and they were admitted on payment of 40 shillings and their fealty was respited until the next court."

Another side of the business of the manorial court may be shown from a still earlier extract from the court roll, recording the acts of a sitting in April 1520:

"the homage present that William Mill has foraged his animals in the meadow of the tenants in Paxford against the rules—fine 12d. Also they present that Edward Stwt tethers his horses in the pasture there against the rules and that he has cut down one le Crabtre without leave: therefore he forfeits his tenement. Thomas Mill who held of the lord 2 messuages, 2 virgates of land and appurtenances in Paxford has died. Whence there falls to the lord for a heriot one cow Ruby and one mare to the value of 20 shillings. Thereupon Robert Stevyns came to the court and took as tenant from the lord all the said messuages and lands to hold to himself and his heirs according to the custom of the manor for the usual services and he pays to the lord a fine of 20 shillings and does fealty."

A copy of that extract from the court roll henceforth constituted Robert Stevyns's title to the tenement. In later times such lease-holders were called copyholders.

THE TENANTS: THEIR LANDS AND SERVICES

The second part of the manorial survey of 1299, to which we now return, gives the various classes of tenant, with a nominal roll of each class and details of the services due:

First came the holders of knight's fees—military tenures. They were seven in all and included Richard of Evenlode, Milo de Hastinges of Daylesford (ancestor of Warren Hastings), John Dabitot of Dorn, Robert de Clipstone of Northwick. Their duty was to provide an armed and mounted man for the king's army and pay scutage, when called upon. To the bishop they owed fealty and 'suit and service' in his court.

Second to these came seventeen Free Tenants, holding land varying from a hide to a virgate, subject only to a money rent and court service. Peter, the priest at Aston, paying 8s. annually, was the hardest hit. Six of the seventeen had holdings in Paxford—a high proportion.

The third class, that of the Customary Tenants (*consuetudinarii*) holding by custom of the manor and jealous of the slightest varia-tion from it, was the most representative of them all. Their tene-ments consisted of a dwelling house with a small yard or homestall as its back side, certain definite lands or strips in the common fields, a fixed share of the meadow and 'common of pasture' for a stated number of cattle and sheep. There were twenty customary tene-ments in Blockley, ten in Upton Wold (though these were to dis-appear within a century as will later be related), twenty-one in the Ditchfords, thirteen in Aston, five in Draycott and eight in Paxford. Their services due to the lord were:

A quarterly rent of five shillings.

Six days of ploughing yearly.

Up to six days of carting—three at the hay harvest and three at the corn harvest.

Three extra days of boon-work (bedrippas or reapings) at the corn harvest, in which the man's whole household except his wife and his shepherd must take part, if called upon.

Special permission before his sons could leave the manor or his daughters marry.

Some of the customary tenements carried special services. Thus John West held three virgates (or yardlands), for which he had to carry briefs for the bishop anywhere within the bishopric at his own expense or outside its bounds at the expense of the lord. He must further escort the collector of rents, be present at the shearing of the lord's sheep and take charge of the wool, and do a limited amount of ploughing and carting on the demesne.

Two or three of the customary tenants in the 1299 list were exceptional. The abbot of Bruern, a monastery near Kingham, held of the bishop a tenement at Shesnecot (*Sezincote*) for which he owed two doddoks of oats on St Martin's Day; and 'the whole hamlet of Draycote' owed 8½d. and 8 hens yearly in respect of special rights on the waste of the manor.

The fourth class of tenant was that of the *enchelondi*, small holders of up to half a virgate. John *porcarius*, the swineherd, heads the list of eight in Blockley—there were five in Draycott and six in Paxford. Their services to the lord were heavy, including two days manual work of any kind ordered by the bailiff in any week throughout the year and in the winter threshing of forage for four oxen.

Last and humblest of all were the cottagers (*cotmanni*), twenty-seven in all, each holding a patch of ground and owing the heaviest and most menial service of all. Thus, Walter Doggetayl had 'to keep the kord's residence clean against his coming and make up the fire while he is present, and act as caretaker and keep the grass in the courtyard in order. He must carry in three loads of straw for the beds and make these up, and he must work in the brew-house, and may take the grain of the ale for his trouble.' Adam aten Assche—beside the ash-tree, Nash to us—held his hovel and vegetable patch in return for looking after the lord's curtilage and maintaining its fences, gathering and cleaning the produce from the lord's gardens, and helping in the kitchen.

The task of the bailiff in organizing the work on the demesne out of all the bits and pieces detailed above must have been an impossible one but for the early introduction of money payments by the tenants in lieu of their actual labour. This seems to have begun quite soon after the Domesday survey, and throughout the Blockley schedules of 1299 each *operatio* is given its money equivalent, enabling the bailiff to collect, if he thought fit, a fund out of which he could pay regularly hired men, while the tenants, freed from their manual liabilities, could cultivate their own land. An example may be quoted:

> John Germayn of Ditchforde holds one virgate of land. . . . He must plough one acre for the winter sowing (or pay 3d.), must harrow it (½d.), weed it (3d.), reap it (3d.), rake it together and bind it (3d.), and carry to the lord's barn (½d.), where he shall be given from it one fair-sized sheaf.

So much, then, for Bishop Godfrey Giffard's lawyerlike survey of his manor in 1299. It fell conveniently in the period not long before the catastrophe of the Black Death brought trouble and change in the countryside, and it may serve as the makings of a picture of medieval Blockley. As the population very slowly grew more land had to be cleared for cultivation—any such clearing of the waste was called as an assart and each newly ploughed addition to the common fields was a 'furlong' to be divided into strips or lands. Winterway furlong was one such extension and the whereabouts of another, called Long Hedge furlong, may account for the former name of what is now Park Road. Till well on in the 19th century this was Edge Lane. Old leases make it clear that there was a long hedge where the houses in Park Road now stand. Another and later set of assarts formed the Lower Field, part of which is today land of Sheafhouse Farm.

The bishops used their Blockley manor house mainly when in transit for business in London—at court or in the House of Lords, for instance. Oxford and Hillingdon, where they had another manor, were the other halting places on their way. It is easy to imagine the bustle in Blockley caused by the lord's arrival. He would come with a considerable cavalcade—chaplains, clerks, pages, indoor and outdoor servants, a huntsman, perhaps, if he proposed a day's hunting of the deer in his park, and certainly an armed escort. But as the centuries passed the lord's visits to Blockley became less and less frequent and the manor house fell into disrepair. There is evidence that it was a costly building to maintain,[9] and there were so many other manor houses for him to keep up—most notably Hartlebury Castle, which eventually became his sole residence within the diocese. The death in 1394 of Bishop Henry de Wakefield in the Blockley house as he was returning from Parliament in Westminster cannot have helped to keep it on the itinerary. By 1500 it was ruinous, and during the century that followed the bishops put their Blockley demesne lands out to 'farm' on long lease.

The bishop's Park was the first of his Blockley lands to be so alienated. This must be distinguished from his residence and its 'curtilage', which roughly covered the present grounds of the Manor House. The Park included the land of Park Farm, all Bourton Wood (then called Blockley Wood) and the Warren. It was let for a term of sixty years to one John Halswell in 1523, subject to the proviso that the lessee must keep the number of deer up to 100 and maintain the stock of fish in the stanks (ponds), and must not fell the larger timber trees. The lease changed hands many times before the sixty year term was up. About 1550 William Sheldon, the Worcestershire magnate, bought the unexpired portion of it and assigned it, perhaps in payment for some service, to his friend and agent William Childe of North-wick, who promptly sold it to one Baugh for £170. Before the term expired, John Stephens of Bourton-on-the-Hill became its owner, until the bishop re-entered into possession in 1583. He then 'disparked' the grounds, dividing them into the enclosed fields we know today. Five years later, in 1588, Bishop Edmund Freke negotiated another lease of a much more comprehensive kind with a very exalted purchaser—Queen Elizabeth herself.

Before continuing with that part of the story we must turn to the matter of the ruined manor house and its grounds—"all those messuages, Barnes, Stables, Dove houses, Edifices and Buildings, being parcells of the Site of the Mannor or Parsonage[10] of Blockley", as the lease of 1588 put it. This became the leasehold property before 1539 of Richard Palmer[11] of Bourton-on-the-Hill, builder of Bourton House there and of the tithe barn, which bears his initials and the date 1570. He may well be the builder of today's Manor House, or at least part of it, on the site of the former residence of the bishops in Blockley. With that site went certain other property within the manor: the ground which today is Churchill Close and Mill Close, the Coneygree (behind the Post-Office) and certain acres in or near Draycott and Aston Magna. The Palmer family held all these properties for nearly a century.

We now turn back to the sweeping and surprising changes resulting from Bishop Edmund Freke's transaction with the Queen in 1588. She wished to reward her physician, a Spanish Jew named Roderigo Lopez, and for the purpose she took a ninety years lease of the whole of Blockley Manor, which she at once assigned to him. It was a strange thing to happen in the Armada year of all years! Lopez lost no time in turning his windfall into cash by selling the lease within a year to one of the Throckmortons—though not before he had sub-let certain parts of the demesne lands, including the Park, to Blockley people. These Lopez leases, as they were called, gave much trouble to the lord of the manor in whom the freehold was of course vested because of their carelessly drawn terms. Lopez himself, however, soon passed out of Blockley's history, for he was executed for treason in 1593. Because he was a Jew and because his accuser was named *Antonio* Perez and because his spectacular intrusion in Armada year into a village so near Stratford[12] must surely have been news for Shakespeare, it has been suggested that the character of Shylock may possibly be his monument. If so, Blockley has had its moment of contact not only with majesty but with high drama as well!

In thus 'farming' his manor the bishop remained in full possession of his title as its lord and of possibly greater profits than direct management of the estate would have brought to him. The tenants, too, kept their rights and the custom of the manor was unchanged. But the old relation between lord and tenant had become less close than ever as the manor of Blockley entered on the 17th century.

THE CUSTOM OF THE MANOR

A sworn statement describing the 'Custom of the Manor' was made before the Parliamentary Commissioners who, in June 1647, surveyed the manor in preparation for its sale after the abolition of the bishopric, resulting from the king's defeat in the Civil War:

The Custom of the Manor of Blockley is, and time out of mind hath been that the Lord for the time being hath usually granted to the Copyholders there the Customary and Copyhold Lands for one life in possession and three in reversion. And that the Widow of every Copyholder dying seized of any Copyhold or Customary Lands, Messuages or Tenements shall have and enjoy the same during her life, if so long she keep herself sole and unmarried. And that the Executors of every Tenant dying seized of any Customary Lands or Tenements shall have the same for one year . . . which is called the Deads Year. And that a Herriot is due to the Lord upon the death of every Copyholder Tenant dying seized of a Messuage or Tenement, viz: the best Beast or for want thereof the best Good.

---

[1] Court Rolls.

[2] Finberg: Gloucestershire Studies 5.

[3] Worcs. Lay Subsidy Rolls, 1275 and 1327 (W.H.S.) and Pat. Ed. III ii. 499.

[4] Red Book, iii. 314.

[5] See p. 31

[6] In the 18th century it had become a hiring fair for the employment of farm and indoor labour, and was held on the waste ground above what is now Blockley Court.

[7] See note on The Custom of the Manor at end of chapter.

[8] The two following extracts were deciphered at the county Record Office through the kindness of Mr Irvine Gray.

[9] See p. 17

[10] The bishop was 'parson', i.e. rector, of Blockley, as well as lord of the manor.

[11] The date is taken from the Muster Rolls of that year, for which see p. 37. The name there given is Robert, not Richard.

[12] He was also given the manor of Tredington, a village even closer to Stratford.

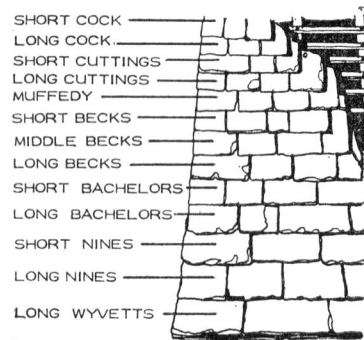

CHAPTER FIVE

SHORT COCK
LONG COCK
SHORT CUTTINGS
LONG CUTTINGS
MUFFEDY
SHORT BECKS
MIDDLE BECKS
LONG BECKS
SHORT BACHELORS
LONG BACHELORS
SHORT NINES
LONG NINES
LONG WYVETTS

The Hamlets: 1086-1600

ASTON MAGNA

TILL ABOUT THE middle of the 16th century it was called Hanging Aston, variously spelt. This meant Aston-on-the-Slope—the slope which runs down from the modern village street to the mid-Victorian church below. Little remains today of the medieval village on this hill-side, but, in a dwelling house close by the modern church there survives a good part of the chancel arch of the little Norman chapel which once on this spot supplied its spiritual needs. A lease of 1604 gives clues to the dates of both the secularisation of the chapel and the changing of the village name to its modern form:

> ... (the sale) to William Wack of Aston Magna alias Hanging Aston of a parcel of waste on Aston lately enclosed unto the late chapple there by one Richard ffletcher ... and the Dwellinge house of the sayd Richard.

The chapel was in fact sold in 1549 as a result of the Chantries Act.

A short way south of this spot is another relic of ancient Aston—a dry moat, within the circle of which there may have stood the great house of the village. The principal landowner in Aston in 1166 was 'Jordanus destone', Jordan of Aston, who held three hides there of the bishop on military tenure. The Adam de Aston of the survey of the manor in 1299 may have been a descendant, to whose three hides was added a mill called Spina, which may possibly be the Bran Mill of today.[1]

The estate of Adam de Aston seems to have passed to his three

34

daughters in equal shares—and so, in law, to their husbands, John Chester, John Bagge and John Wattes. Bagge and Wattes are named in the lay subsidy roll of 1327—Chester is not, and he may not have been then resident in Aston; but all three men contributed to the aid levied by Edward III in 1346 for the knighting of the Black Prince, and by 1450 all three portions of the property had been united under the ownership of a Chester descendant.

Henry Bagge, presumably son of John, was a witness in 1353 to a transaction in which "John de Blockleye clerk in the town of Hongynde Aston" became owner of some property there,[2] part of which, a year later, he received a licence in mortmain from the king to bestow on the chantry of St. Mary in Blockley church. In the enrolment of this licence he is described as a king's clerk—that is, one employed in the royal service in London. It is tempting to think that he was a Bagge—but such guesses are idle.

All the evidence suggests that Aston was a prosperous community. Its hidage rating was high—twice that of any of the other hamlets: and its total contribution to the lay subsidy of 1275, over 100s., was exceeded only by Blockley, where the bishop paid nearly two-thirds of the total. This may well be what attracted the Freeman family, originally of Ebrington, to the place and to the neighbouring hamlet of Batsford—a proprietary association which was to endure till the 20th century. The two brothers, Thomas and William Freeman, acquired property in Blockley—mainly perhaps in Aston Magna—and in Batsford, respectively early in the 16th century. Thomas became steward of the manor of Blockley in the 1520's, was succeeded by his son John,[3] who married into the Warmestrey family of Worcester, and was in his turn succeeded by William Freeman of Blockley and Aston, who died in 1634 and whose tomb in Blockley church is mentioned on another page.[4] It was his second son, Edward, barrister-at-law of Gray's Inn, who befriended Vicar George Durant in his distress after the Civil War.[5] But this is carrying our story far beyond the date limits of this chapter, and the later developments which ended in Aston Magna becoming the property of the Freeman-Mitford family of Batsford must be left for a later page.

THE DITCHFORDS

Upper and Middle Ditchford were comparable in size of population with Draycott and Dorn at the beginning of the 14th century. The manorial survey of 1299 lists 21 customary tenants in Middle Ditchford, paying in rents and services over £15. Johanne Kenwych held the estate of the bishop in 1275, and his family were still in posession in 1428, when it passed by marriage to Robert de Clynton. Perhaps it was he who turned it into a sheep run, for it was later in this century that John Rous, a priest of Warwick, included in his chronicle history of England a list of 58 villages in his area which had lately been depopulated for this purpose, and the list included "the three Dishfords".

Upper Ditchford is shown by the Lay Subsidy roll of 1327 to have been very similar to Middle Ditchford in population and in its contribution to the Exchequer. After its depopulation the estate passed for a time into the hands of Thomas Freeman, steward of the manor in the 1520's. In 1550 both Ditchfords were sold by Bishop Heath to William Sheldon, as part of a transaction recorded on another page which included Blockley Park.

DORN

The passing of the Dorn estate out of the bishops' ownership (though not out of their suzerainty) and into that of Urse d'Abitot and his Beauchamp descendants until the middle of the 14th century, has been described on an earlier page.[6] Between 1356 and 1478 it was held, perhaps on leasehold tenure, by a succession of owners named John or Thomas de Blockley, the first of them being presumably the Aston Magna benefactor of the chantry in Blockley church.[7] A century later, in 1583, a Throckmorton held it[8]—he held a Lopez lease of the land of the bishop's 'late disparked park' a few years later and was in due course implicated in the Gunpowder Plot.

By this time the hamlet must have been largely depopulated. The Lay Subsidy rolls of 1275 and 1327 give the names of twelve and sixteen taxpayers for Dorn respectively, more than those for Draycott and Northwick, but fewer than those for Aston and Paxford. They include, incidentally, a Ricardus Capellanus, relics of whose chapel survive in some farm buildings today. But 1327 would seem to mark the high point of the hamlet's population, and we can perhaps guess that the 14th and 15th century owners ousted the people to make room for their flocks, as had happened in the Ditchfords and, perhaps, in Upton Wold. The Muster Rolls of 1539, giving the quotas of men called up to serve in the king's army against the northern insurgents in the Pilgrimage of Grace give the following numbers for the parish of Blockley:

Blockley and Upton le Olde	20 men
(Robert Palmer and Richard Walgrove 2 Harness)	
Draycote and Northwicke	8 men
Paxforde and Dorne	9 men
Hangyngeston	4 men

The figures are not easy to interpret, but they suggest a significant drop in the Dorn population.

In 1662 the owner of Dorn and Dorn Heath was Sir Robert Pye of Faringdon, Berks, and a map of the property,[9] some 500 acres (partly in Blockley parish and partly in Batsford), may indicate that he bought it in that year. His family held it till 1767, when Henry James Pye, the first Poet Laureate and, as such, not highly regarded by the critics of his time, sold it to Thomas Edwards Freeman of Batsford. It thus passed into the Batsford estate—and was in our time to become part of the parish of Batsford, as recorded on an earlier page.[10] See *Plate* 2.

NORTHWICK

It was so named because it stood to the north of the main village, Blockley, just as Aston stood to the east and Upton was up the hill. Northwick ceased to be a village community, located about Northwick Mill, when emparkment by the Childes and Rushouts cleared away the houses in the 17th and 18th centuries.

It became part of the bishop's lordship some time before 964, when the mention of it in King Edgar's land charter 'Altitonantis' confirms an earlier grant. The Northwick estate was held of the bishop as a knight's fee by Roger de Norwyke in 1152. His direct line ending with two heiresses, the property was divided between their two husbands, one of them being Roger de Draycote, and the other a remoter suitor (1227). A century later the two halves were reunited when Thomas de Clipstone married into the family and became the bishop's tenant for the whole Northwick estate. Half a century later it came to another heiress, who in 1383 married John Childe, a Northwick man whose family had long been coming up in the world.

Thus began three centuries of Childe squirearchy at Northwick, though it was broken for half a century in Tudor times, as will appear. So Childe succeeded Childe, Thomas, described as 'gentilman,' some time before 1426, Edmund in 1459, and in due course William, who married Anne Hunckes, who came of an important Gloucestershire family, in 1520. This was the occasion of a gift to the couple from the bridegroom's father of a small rent charge on his Northwick estate—a detail worth mentioning only because the principal witness to the deed of gift was the vicar, Dr. Robert Haldesworth. It must have been almost the last appearance of that inveterate absentee in the parish, as a later page will show. William Childe had for some reason to part with the property in 1530 to his wife's brother, Thomas Hunckes. He and his descendants held Northwick for the next half-century. During this period the eldest son of William and Anne Childe prospered, becoming the friend and agent of William Sheldon of Beoley and Weston, the receiver of royal revenues in four counties, notable for being the first patron to introduce the art of tapestry into England, and, all in all, a power in the land. His purchase of the lease of Blockley Park in or about 1550 has already been recorded. Later he acquired the Ditchfords. He may well have helped his friend Childe to buy back from the Hunckes intruders the family property in Northwick in 1583. The older parts of the Northwick mansion are no doubt of his building. There he passed the last years of his life, serving the county as magistrate and twice as high sheriff. His memorial in Blockley church, showing a kneeling figure in armour, now bears no name, but we know from Nash that the words 'Gulielmus Chylde armiger, 2 Nov. A.D. 1601, aetatis 80' were inscribed above the head of the figure. The unceremonious removal of the Childe monuments from the east end of the aisle to make room for those of the Rushouts no doubt accounts for the loss. His is not a name to be forgotten in Blockley.[11]

PAXFORD

Before the middle of the 14th century two families, holding free tenures of the bishop, were most prominent in this community: the Legers and the Silvers. Both owed military service and scutage, when called for, and suit and service in the manorial court in Blockley and the hundred court of Winborotree. They duly paid the feudal aid of 1346, but by 1358 the virgate called Lyggers, the Leger holding, passed to the collegiate church of Westbury-on-Trym, near Bristol, where too the bishops were lords of the manor; and the Silver land, after brief possession by John Weleye, one of the Campden wool merchants, soon went to the same college of priests. The Chantries Act of 1547, by which such ecclesiastical colleges were dissolved, brought these lands into the market, and they were bought by Sir Ralph Sadleir, who promptly sold them to an armigerous family called Fletcher. For a century and a half the Fletchers played a leading part in the parish of Blockley, one of them being the first of the church-wardens responsible, with the vicar, George Durant, for the major reconstruction in the parish church in 1635–36. The last of the Fletcher churchwardens served as late as 1732.

The Leger family seems to have moved from Paxford to Block-ley. The ground now occupied by Northwick Terrace was, before the Enclosure of 1773, a customary tenement known as Leagres, and some of the out-buildings in rear were no doubt in its home-stall or farmyard.

Of other folk in medieval Paxford we have many names, especially for a fifty year period shortly before the Black Death. The lists of taxpayers in 1275 and 1327 give the limits of this period and are perhaps more reliable guides than the roll of tenants of the manor drawn up for the bishop in 1299 for enumer-ating the heads of households actually resident in the hamlet. Thus we have, leaving aside the common but uninformative patronymics—John son of William and the like—a number of occupational names: Walter faber, the blacksmith, Roger Wode-ward the forester, Roger le Bercher, the shepherd, Adam le

39

Palmer—so called because he had been on a pilgrimage to Canterbury, at least, if not to St. James of Compostella or St. Peter at Rome. Of local names, indicating where their owners lived, Paxford had several: Simon Bovetun lived above the village, John atte Grene presumably on the village green, Richard in Angulo in the 1275 list in the same house as Henry in the Hurne in 1327, both the indicative words meaning corner. Willelmus de Bosco and Thomas atte Selure, which may be corrupted from silva, may have lived by some woodland site. Walter le Reven is a nickname, like many others in Blockley parish at this period—the raven conveys its own meaning.

We can only guess at the total population of Paxford in the early years of the 14th century. There were 26 taxpayers in 1275, indicating, if these were all heads of families, a total of about 100.

UPTON WOLD

Whatever date the archaeologists now examining the site may ultimately assign for the foundation of the small village community of Upton Wold, and their findings may take it back to the period of the Roman occupation, there is every reason to think that its end came towards the end of the 14th century. It may be that the Black Death of 1349 and the second pestilence of 1361 struck down most of the people of the hamlet and that the survivors left their homes to settle on holdings which the plague had left empty in Blockley. This is the view of Dr. Hilton in his survey of the documentary evidence.[12] Alternatively, or perhaps even as an additional cause, the boom in the wool trade and the insistent demand of the wool merchants of Chipping Campden for Cotswold fleeces may have led to the depopulation of the hamlet and the throwing open of its arable fields, its cow pastures and farmyards that they might revert to grass for more sheep to crop. That is what happened to the Ditchfords somewhat later, as John Rous, monk of Warwick, recorded in his chronicle history about 1450. Whatever the cause, Upton Wold after 1400 appears in manorial documents only as 'pastura', and it loses its separate identity as a hamlet, being thereafter reckoned as part of Blockley.

Any estimate of the hamlet's population must be guesswork, and some of the tenants recorded in 1299 were certainly not resident. But, assuming that they sublet their holdings, each to one family, the twelve 'customary' tenancies of a virgate or yard-land and the three cottage holdings in Upton suggest a total population of about 60.

The documentary evidence seems to point to one prosperous peasant family of long standing in the hamlet. The Book of Fees drawn up for King John in 1208 records that 'Henry son of Henry in Upton holds one virgate.' In 1299 Gilbert de Upton is first in the list of customary tenants there and evidently the headman. He may have been the son of 'Gilbertus in angulo', Gilbert at the corner, mentioned in the tax roll of 1275, and father of John Gilbard in the tax roll of 1327. In 1340 a William Gilbert repre-sented Upton before the tax assessors of the shire, and in 1346 a John Gilbert was assessed at a twentieth part of a knight's fee for his contribution towards the feudal aid levied by Edward III when the Black Prince was knighted on the field of Crecy—and what perhaps links this chain of family entries together is the express statement that the tenement on which John paid his aid was 'the land which Henry the son of Henry de Upton formerly held.' The Gilberts may thus have seen Upton Wold through all its most prosperous years right to its very end.

Other names of Upton folk in 1299 may be mentioned. Milli-cent, widow of Richard Wodeward—the successor, perhaps, of William 'forestarius' of Upton who is recorded in the taxpayers' list of 1275—was a virgater owing all the services of a customary tenant. Nicholas Boveton must have lived up the village street, and Walter '*ad fontem*', by the stream, at its bottom, Of the three *cotarii*, cottagers, two were shepherds, as might well be expected in that limestone sheep-run. Shepherds must have outlasted all other folk in the hamlet. Significantly the only cottages that have remained on the site were named Lamb Cottages.

Throughout the 14th and 15th centuries wool production brought much profit to the lord of the manor. Dr. Hilton, quoting a manorial survey of 1384, has shown that Blockley was then the shearing and fleece packing centre for all the flocks on the bishop's manors, and that a large barn near the 'rectory' as the bishop's residence in Blockley was named after the appropriation of the benefice, was then built for the purpose. It is tempting to think that the site of the barn was where Sheafhouse Farm now stands. Earlier records spell it as Sheephouse. That year over 3000 sheep were shorn in Blockley, 1110 from the Upton Wold pastures. The nearness of the great Campden wool market, then at its peak, was the ruling factor in all this. William Grevel, 'the flower of the wool merchants of England', was himself the purchaser of the Blockley wool clip that year.[12]

From the middle of the 15th century the bishops seem to have discontinued their direct concern with wool production. They then let the Upton pastures to a grazier from outside the manor named Bleke, who later bought the episcopal flocks as well. Robert Handy became the lessee in 1474, and John Hornyold in 1512—the latter being the manager of all the estates of the see of Worcester which then was held by absentee Italian prelates.

By then all Cotswold flocks were dwindling and the Campden wool market was in decay. In 1549 Bishop Heath, soon to be deprived for his opposition to the doctrinal changes of Edward VI's reign, parted with the Upton Wold property to John Dudley, Earl of Warwick, on long lease. The property is thus described in the deed of transfer:

> the pasture called Upton and Upton Old—(*corresponding to the later names of Hither and Far Upton Old?*), the close of pasture on the south side of Blockley Wood adjacent to Upton Old— (*apparently above Troopers Lodge*)—another pasture called Abrygedowne next the park there— (*on the far, or east, side of Park Farm, now Blockley Downs*)—and another adjacent to it called Lytell Downe, and all other the bishop's lands in Blockley lately in the tenure of John Hornyold. (Patent Rolls 3 Ed. VI, p, 254)[13]

The execution of Warwick, then Earl of Northumberland and Protector of the realm, by Queen Mary brought Upton Wold into the possession of the Crown. It was sold to two Staffordshire partners, Gifford and Biddulph in 1560, and by them let to Ralph Sheldon, son of William Childe's friend and patron, who had held Blockley Park a few years before, in 1588. Sheldon acquired the freehold in 1608,[14] and sold it in the following year to John Carter, who settled it on his son William—"savinge and exceptinge all those pastures lyinge together neare to . . . Blockley parke called by the names of Abrige downe and little downe."[15] Thus it was that Blockley Downs became a separate estate and before long was acquired by the Freemans of Batsford.

We can only guess who built the fine Cotswold dwelling house so long known as Hither Upton Wold. It may have been John Carter. But a case can be made out for Ralph Sheldon. The deed which gave him the freehold contained this passage:

> "the saide Ralphe Sheldon his mannor of Upton Olde . . . and his lands tenements meadows leasowes pastures and hereditaments situate in Uptone Olde aforesaid."

This list suggests that he had converted what had once been all pasture land into a comprehensive use covering arable, hay and live stock: and the separate mention of a manor can well imply the secondary meaning of the word—manor house.

[1] The Lay Subsidy Roll of 1275 includes among the Aston taxpayers one Johanne de Brodemille. See p. 171 for another theory about the moat.

[2] Close Rolls, 29 Ed. III, 82, cited, as is the reference which follows, V.C.H. Worcs. iii 265 ff. in the authoritative article on Blockley, which is here freely used.

[3] John Freman of Blockley lent money to Henry VIII in 1523 for the war against the Scots.

[4] See p. 66

[5] See p. 60 For Freeman pedigree of this period see Harleian Miscellany of 1938 (Visitation of Worcs.), cited V.C.H. as above.

[6] See p. 23

[7] See pp. 18-19

[8] See p. 32

[9] I am indebted to Mr B. S. Smith, county archivist, for this reference.

[10] See p. xvii (n.1)

[11] The monument of his son, also called William, shown with his wife, both kneeling, was moved and hidden from view behind a pillar when the Rushout memorial bay was added to the church by the first Lord Northwick in the 1790's. The marble statuary commemorates the latter's grandparents, his parents and aunt, Lady Northampton. Her bust is the work of Rysbrack.

[12] See reports on *Upton, Gloucestershire* by R. H. Hilton and P. A. Rahtz in BGAS lxxv (1966) 70 ff. and lxxxviii (1969) 74 ff. Dr Hilton's historical section in the first of these reports has been freely drawn upon by the present writer.

[13] Abrygedowne is presumably the Altrichesdon of the 1299 survey of the manor (p. 25). It seems to be the Partriche Hill of 1454 (p. 20) and the Partridge Hill of the Parliamentary survey of 1647. That it is to be identified with the Blockley Downs of today, already so called in the Enclosure Award of 1773, is strongly suggested by the occurence of the name Little Down attached to a field at the eastern end of Blockley Downs in the Tithe Map of 1843.

[14] Close Rolls, 6 Jac. I, xvii, no. 23, cited by V.C.H.

[15] N.P. lxviii/II.

CHAPTER SIX

In Tudor Times 1510-1627

THERE IS NO record of how the people of Blockley took the religious changes imposed on the nation in these years, but we catch glimpses of the reaction of some of the clergy. Of the general unease and suspicion there is evidence enough.

1510–56 Robert Haldesworth (or Hallsworth),[1] Vicar.

His 46 years tenure of the benefice set a record by the calendar, but he spent hardly any of them in or near Blockley.

The son of a wealthy Halifax merchant, who left him a considerable fortune, he matriculated at Lincoln College, Oxford in 1487, took his M.A. and was ordained priest seven years later, and then proceeded to the degrees of Doctor of Theology and of Canon Law. About the turn of the century he went to Rome for further study, which led to yet another doctorate, that in Sacred Decrees. It was a very notable academic career, qualifying him for high administrative office in the Church.

In Rome these were the years of the Borgia pope, Alexander VI, and of a worldly court and society which destroyed the spiritual authority of the Holy See. It is difficult not to see in Haldesworth's later career some reflection of the intrigue and acquisitiveness amidst which he passed these Roman years of his life. In the course of them he came under the patronage of a high official of the papal *curia*, Silvestro dei Gigli. This man, strangely enough, was then bishop of Worcester, the first of four Italians 'provided' by the Pope in succession between 1497 and 1534, to hold this English see, which none of them visited. In

44

1507 Gigli appointed Haldesworth to the office of Chancellor of the diocese, and two years later to that of Vicar-General.[2]

As wages for his diocesan duties Dr. Haldesworth was presented to several benefices, notably Blockley in 1510, and Hampton Lucy in the Warwickshire part of the diocese. Each was worth over £50 a year—and that at a time when £20 constituted a good living. In 1521 he acquired one far richer and far distant from Blockley—that of Halifax, his native town, and it was there that he henceforward made his home. It is on record that he was in Blockley some time in or about 1535[3] but apart from other possible rare visits to his southern parishes he left the care of them to chaplains to whom he allowed some frugal portion of the tithe and other dues which he pocketed. The most certain quality known of him is that he was a miser.

Before his departure to Halifax in 1521 he seems to have resided in Blockley, and it is more than likely that some of the existing features of the vicarage were of his making—notably, perhaps, the inner doorway at the back of the building which was the original front entrance opening on to what was then an open space with what was until recently the Bell Inn, but then was the lately built dwelling house of the Waldegrave (or Walgrove) family, on the opposite side. Certainly he was responsible for some internal alteration on the upper floor, as is made clear by the following deposition made by a cousin of his years later before the king's justices in York at a time when Dr. Haldesworth was in sore trouble. What the trouble was will be explained later: the facts detailed in the deposition refer to the quieter years before his migration to Yorkshire. It is one Allan Hay who is recounting a conversation which took place, say about 1520, in Blockley Vicarage:

> I was with Master Doctor Hallsworth my cousin at his Vicaridge of Blockley in the county of Worcester, and then and there the said doctor walked with me all about his vicaridge, and let me see all his building there made by him. And so walking we came to one stair head among many chambers, and there the doctor said, Cousin, I have cast my vicaridge of a new fashion into divers partitions, for here is round about us a dozen doors, and one stair serves them all. Then I said, Sir, you have been at great charge in building here. And Master Doctor answered me again. Cousin,

I am no loser by this building, for in pulling down one old wall I found three hundred pounds in gold and money. So would I had many such buildings in hand.

A tale of treasure trove, from which we learn that the vicarage was not new in Haldesworth's day and must have housed such medieval vicars as Neele and Worthyn at least. It also brings out the doctor's obsession with money and his practice of hiding it about his house and garden—for later evidence will suggest that the three hundred pounds which he here found was probably of his own hiding.

In 1534 King Henry VIII secured from Parliament the passing of the Act of Supremacy, declaring the king of England to be Supreme Head, under Christ, of the Church in England. The shock to all who looked to the Pope for such authority led to deep unsettlement all over the country and the hunting out by spies, who were responsible to Thomas Cromwell, of upholders of the papal claim against that of the king. One Christopher Jenny was Cromwell's agent in Yorkshire, a hotbed of such disaffection as the Pilgrimage of Grace was presently to show, and Dr. Haldesworth, vicar of Halifax,[4] soon came under suspicion and had Jenny at his heels. That is how he came to stand trial at York for the offence concerning treasure trove at Blockley long before. Not content with this, Jenny, in March 1535, ferreted out a more relevant indiscretion by suborning one of the doctor's former serving men, and in a letter to Cromwell about local suspects he wrote:

> . . . And, Sir, Dr Holdesworth vicar of Halifax is likewise accused by one that was sometime his servant, which words, if they be true, sound either to treason, or else to such effect that he deserveth imprisonment for all his life. For the words ben very shameful: By my priesthood and Saint John Baptist, quoth he, I have lost yearly by my mortuaries now taken from me by the king's act of Parliament . . . four score marks, and by my troth, William, if the king reign any space he will take all fro us of the church, all that even we have. And therefore I pray God send him short reign.
>
> I have bound the said vicar and his accuser by recognizance to appear before you and my lord Chancellor in the next term. The

said vicar is said to be a man of great substance and that he deceived the king at his valuation.[5]

Again we note that obsession with money, which made Dr. Haldesworth think more of King Henry's raid on the wealth of the Church and clergy by means of the Mortuaries Act of 1529 and the *Valor Ecclesiasticus* of 1534 than of his attack on the Pope. He duly faced trial in the Star Chamber Court, and it may have been his early legal training which allowed him to escape with only a fine, which he complacently described as "not past the half of my livelihood for one year." But the experience may have accounted for his discreet aloofness from the fray when the Pilgrimage of Grace roused so many Yorkshiremen around him in 1536.

Meanwhile, Jenny, still looking for evidence of treason, had been prowling round Blockley as well. Here he found an informer in John Jenkyns, a priest and presumably put by Dr. Haldesworth in charge of some part of the parish. But it was not his vicar whom Jenkyns wished to incriminate, but rather his colleagues, William Cave, priest of the chantry since 1502, and Martin Cave, his brother, perhaps the chaplain at Aston Magna or Paxford.

The said Sir John Jeynkes[6] deposes that about three years past Sir Marten Cave leaning upon the churchyard wall said to him that though he prayed for the king and took him as supreme Head for fear he could not find it in his conscience to do so. He told him this was treason and reported it to Master Saunders, a priest at Winchcombe, who advised him to open the matter and came to Blockley and preached the Royal Supremacy. He declared Cave's words in Ric. Walgrave's house in the presence of Ric. Tucker and John Wever and to Master Wyttney, who said he would help him to have Cave punished and to Thomas Hunckes gent, who examined him about it last hay harvest.

Deposes also that going to Campden to pay the tenth to one Tyndale receiver Sir William Cave, kinsman of Sir Marten, grudged paying for his chantry in Blockley and cursed the makers of the act and afterwards said there would never be a good world in England while the king lived. One William Broderer of Blockley kinsman of the Caves threatened him for calling them traitors. Hunckes and

Dr Hallysworth vicar of Blockley attempted to make peace between him and Broderer.

About last Michaelmas Thomas Hunckes prevented the inhabitants of Northwick from contributing to the cost of the men who went to serve in the wars against those of the north when desired by Thomas Freman bayley of the lordship of Blockley.

Corroboration of this was forthcoming from Richard Walgrave, whose deposition is worth quoting if only to show how variously the name Jenkins could then be spelt!

A year ago Sir John Geynkynnes told me of Cave's saying. I said Cave was worthy to stretch a halter and advised him to open the matter further.

When charged before the magistrates. John Grevell of Campden and William Sheldon of Weston, William Cave defended himself in these words:

Where Sir John Jenkes says I grudged at the payment to the collector at Campden, I deny it plainly. For John Lytster, Thomas Freman and others were present with others mo, which by reason should have heard as well as he. And I deny saying we should never have the other world while the king lived, as Jenkes swore by God's blood that I did.

Here, the echoes of Blockley dissensions come sharply to us across the centuries. Was the absentee vicar present there out of a sense of duty—or because, coming fresh from his Star Chamber trial in London,[7] he knew that informers were about? He knew Thomas Hunckes, who had become owner of the Northwick estate since 1530, for he had been one of the trustees when the Hunckes family first acquired an interest in the property at the time of the marriage of Thomas's sister, Ann Hunckes, with William Childe in 1520. Richard Walgrave's house was just opposite the vicarage, and was to become the Bell Inn when the Walgrave family died out early in the 18th century. It is interesting, too, to find a Tyndale acting as collector of the king's 'tenths' at Campden within a year or two of the death at the stake in Louvain of William Tyndale, translator of the New Testament, a Gloucestershire man and surely a relative. "Those of the North" were the rebel champions of the monasteries,

Plate 12   Northwick Picture Collection. John Rushout and family by Thomas de Critz. c. 1643, showing John, his son John (1629-47) his second wife Elizabeth with either Anne or James; Catherine and Abigail. (*Photograph by courtesy of Christies*)

Plate 13 The Old Mill, 1956

Plate 14 Sir John Rushout, painted by Sir Godfrey Kneller in 1715. (*National Portrait Gallery*)

Plate 15 Blockley Church in 1788; engraving by T. Bonnor.

Plate 16 Joanna Southcott engraved by Henry Sharp.

Plate 17 Alice Seymour and Mary Robertson, biographers of Joanna Southcott, in Rock Cottage garden.

Plate 18   Martha Reynolds, *née* Smith, fore-woman in her father's silk mill, 1815.

Plate 19
B. Belcher, drawn by grandson, Richard Belcher. (*Photograph y courtesy of the 'Evesham Journal"*)

Plate 20 Handy Family at rear of Powell's Row. Kate Shepherd, *née* Handy on left, her father Charles Handy, former child silk-worker and railwayman, on extreme right.

Plate 21 Henry Robbins, former child silk-worker, and R. B. Belcher, a "village Hampden", 19th century Liberal Nonconformist. Cart made by R. R. B. for H. R. to peddle goods.

Plate 22 First Ordnance map, 1801; this section published 1826.

Plate 23 Rev Charles J. Middleditch. Baptist Minister, 1865-71.

Plate 24
Rev H. Bromfield,
Vicar 1855-78

which just then were being dissolved and plundered by King Henry. We know from another source, the muster rolls of that year, that "Draycote and Northwicke juxta Blokley" were under orders to furnish eight men to serve in the king's army against this Pilgrimage of Grace.[8]

William Cave must have cleared himself of the charge of disaffection on this occasion, for he was still priest of the Blockley chantry ten years later, when royal commissioners visited the parish to report on it with a view to its dissolution in accordance with the Chantries Act of 1548. This may well have been for the ordinary parishioners the first clear sign of the changes in their accustomed worship now looming ahead. It meant the end of their 'morrow mass priest' and his early service at the altar of the Lady Chapel. The three commissioners visited the church in February 1548 and reported as follows:

The Chantrie of owre Lady within
ye Parishe Churche of Blockeley

Benedict Paston sometyme Parson of Blockeley and Raffe of Brockdon (*sic*) priest did ordeyne and founde the said Chauntrie. . . and gave unto a prieste to mynyster and saye masse there certeyn lands and tenements, the Kynges licence firste obteyned. After that, because the said Lands . . . were not sufficient for the fyndynge of a Priest, John of Blockeley Clerke gave other Lands to the same, as by his Deede dated the Mundaye after the assumption of owre Lady Anno Dni MCCCLVI may appeare

The yerely valewe accordyng to this Surveye £7 16s. 6d.

Rents payd unto the bishop of Worcester 13s. 8d.

Tenthes payd yerely to the Kynges majestie 11s. 1½.

In thole £1 4s. 9½d.

The clere yerely vallew £6 11s. 8½d.

which bin imployed to the Mayntenaunce of a prieste there and the reparation of the Houses belongynge to the same. The said Chauntrie is wythin the Parishe Churche of Blockeley and no parishe Churche of ytself. The valewe of the Ornaments accordyng to an Inventorie £1 14s. 8d.[9]

The chantry was dissolved, the priest William Cave, described as "of the age of lxiiij yeres, competently learnyd and of honeste conversation", was allotted a pension of £5 a year, and the chantry lands with "the cottage or chamber called the Chayntry prestes Chamber and a little Garden adjacent"[10] were sold to two speculators in such 'Augmentations' in Crown property.

Yet another blow fell on the parish at this time—the closing and disposal of the ancient chapel at Aston Magna. The transaction was enrolled on 20 July 1549 as follows:

> For 1057[1] 11s. 1[d] p[d] in the Augmentations by Richard Feld and Ralph Woodwarde in ready money ... the late chapel of Hanging Aston in the parish of Blockley.[11]

These two speculators in church property soon found local purchasers and the chapel was converted into two cottages, separated by the Norman chancel arch, most of which still remains.

We do not know if these abrupt changes in the amenities of his parish brought the absent vicar to visit it, if only to reorganize for the future. There is no evidence that it did, or that he ever saw Blockley after 1538. An order from the bishop, John Bell, in April 1540 called on the curate then in charge of the parish, Simon Pope by name, a former monk, to appear at Worcester as Haldesworth's proxy "to show his title and plurality"[12]—fair evidence of the scandal of his absence.

He was in fact paying a penalty for it in the rough times through which he was passing in his Yorkshire vicarage. He was much involved in a feud between two local magnates, one of whom sent his minions to plunder the well-stocked vicarage. Dr. Haldesworth's depositions following that outrage show how old habits in the disposition of his property about the house and garden had grown on him.

> (They) in forcible manner repaired unto the said vicarage of Halifax, being riotously arrayed with swords, bucklers, daggers, staves and other weapons invasive, and put me in jeopardy of my life, and violently took from me my purse then hanging at my girdle, wherein was contained five or six pounds in gold and silver, and also cut out of my sleeve a purse wherein was contained 17 or 18 pounds in gold ... The malefactors took into their possession the keys of the chambers, parlours, and chests ... and unlawfully took away all the silver plate, coin, napery, bedding, books, apparel,

stuff of the household, evidence of lands, obligations, indentures and many other chargeous writings.

Somehow he weathered the religious changes under Edward VI and Queen Mary, in spite of complaints against him, not least about his preaching—or the lack of it. On a day in 1556 the old man was in his vicarage, then dilapidated, as we may believe he was himself, when a last gang of thieves burst in and murdered him. His bones lie under the Holdsworth Chapel, built by himself in an aisle of the parish church of Halifax for this purpose.

1556-60 INTERREGNUM AT BLOCKLEY

Blockley was without a vicar for the next four years, and, having lost its chantry priest and perhaps a chaplain for Aston Magna as well, must have seemed a flock without a shepherd. The news of Dr. Haldesworth's death reached the bishop of Worcester late and in a garbled form, as is clear from the wording in his register recording the nomination of his successor, "Hugh Jones vice Roberti Holdesworth decessum *per mortem naturalem*"

Hugh Jones seems never to have been instituted. We may guess why. Queen Mary by now was sick: she died in 1558 on the same day as the archbishop, Cardinal Pole. The bishop of Worcester, Richard Pate, a 'Papist' with no hope of continuance in office when the Princess Elizabeth became queen, may well have found no opportunity to admit his nominee at Blockley. Before resigning his see Bishop Pate did in fact take some strange measures by way of rewarding friends, and he assigned certain of the livings in his gift for the next presentation to some of them. That accounts for the discreditable affair of John Freeman, who was nominated to the vicarage of Blockley by Thomas Coxe and Humfrey Kings, two of the lucky friends. Freeman was in fact instituted, but by proxy and at Canterbury, where the Dean, because the vacancy in the archbishopric had not yet been filled, performed the ceremony. Shortly afterwards the Worcester see was filled by the appointment of Edwin Sandys. He soon discovered that the elaborate chain of substitutes and proxies in Freeman's nomination and institution to Blockley concealed a fraud: the man was not even in holy orders. The new bishop promptly deprived him, and collated Thomas Wilson, who had been one of his companions in exile at Frankfort during their 'Marian' exile, to the living.

1560–86   Thomas Wilson, Vicar

He was a Cambridge scholar and theologian, confirmed in his sternly Protestant views during his sojourn in Germany. We cannot doubt that the act "primo Elizabethae (1558) for the Uniformity of Common Prayer and Service in the Church" was under him uncompromisingly observed in the parish of Blockley and that the people soon became reconciled to the Second Prayer Book of Edward VI with the slight revisions now required. If there were any recalcitrants, as there were at least among some of the gentry thereabouts—the Gunpowder Plot was hatched not far away—they soon disappeared. Before a century had passed the Blockley churchwardens reported at the bishop's visitation that there were no known Roman Catholics in the parish.

That Dr. Wilson was a resident vicar is suggested by the entry in the parish registers of the baptism of one of his children in 1567. But after 1571, when he became Dean of Worcester, the parish must have been served mainly by curates.

1586–1627   Henry Daniell, Vicar

The years of his long ministry covered the stirring exploits of the Elizabethans, the issue of the Authorized Version of the Bible—the copy still preserved in the church may have been bought in his time—and the great days of Shakespeare, who may, like Drayton, have known the countryside and been seen by Blockley folk. They covered, too, the period of the consolidation of the new order in the Church of England. That Henry Daniell passed them faithfully in residence in his Blockley vicarage is attested by the careful entries in his own handwriting in the parish registers. He and his wife were buried within the church.

The annals of the parish from his time are few. Three events may go on record. The first, a little surprising perhaps, was the grant of the royal pardon in 1594 "to Robert Palmer of Blockley for the crime of highway robbery." This can hardly have been the Robert Palmer who had lately taken up residence at the Manor House, part of which, at least, he may have built as we know it on the presumed site of the former bishops' residence: it was perhaps the prank of a madcap son of the house. The second was the death in 1601 of the principal layman of the parish, William Childe of Northwick. His monument within the church, was moved to its present position beside the north door by the Rushouts when they created their memorial bay over the family vault at the eastern end of the north aisle in 1795.

The third event was the visit of a notable Worcestershire antiquary to the church, Thomas Habington, on a date between 1610 and 1620. A wealthy Catholic and recusant, suspected probably unjustly of complicity in the Gunpowder Plot, he had been restricted by the court to movement within the limits of the county. He spent his remaining years in the compilation of his 'Survey of Worcestershire'.[13] and it was this task which one day brought him down Greenway Hill from which he caught the still visible view of the church, then with a lower Norman tower, which prompted his note about "this fayre churche which humblethe it sealfe allmost to the botome of the hylles"—a fair sample of his elaborate spelling. He describes the three memorial brasses in the chancel,—"on the north syde on a blewe marble stone ingraven in brass the resemblance of a Pryst in a habit (*Lombarde*) . . . On the other syde is a Pryst with a Cope (*Neele*). In the mydele of the Chauncell the likeness of a preyst praying (*Worthyn*)." The only other monument then to be seen was that of William Childe mentioned above:

> In the east end of the Northe Ile is raysed somewhat high on the wall the portraiture of a man all armed savinge his heade and hands bare kneelinge and prayinge under an Arche betweene towe pyllars and Pyramides with this superscription over hym: Gulielmus Child Armiger 2 Novemb. An. Do. 1601 aet. 80. He searved thys Shyre tyyse as Shyreefe and long in Commission of the Peace: he leaft a fayre estate and issewe whose name and bloud nowe sitteth on the benche of Justice for thys county of Worcester.[14]

[1] In Yorkshire the name seems normally to have been spelt Holdesworth.

[2] For details of his many benefices see Emden: *Biographical Register of the University of Oxford to 1500.*

[3] See p. 48.

[4] For a full account of his life as vicar of Halifax see Lister: *Life of Dr Holdesworth* (Halifax Antiquarian Society Papers, 1902). For this reference and other Holdesworth information I am indebted to Mrs S. T. Lucas of Aberdeen.

[5] The Valor Ecclesiasticus of 1534.

[6] 'Sir', translating the Latin title 'Dominus', was then used (as in Shakespeare) for clergy and others who were not 'Masters'—of Arts.

[7] See p. 47

[8] See p. 37

[9] P.R.O., E. 301–61.

[10] Patent Rolls, 3 Ed. VI (1549).

[11] *Ibid.*

[12] For this reference I am indebted to Mr C. W. Clarke of Evesham.

[13] Ed. John Amphlett. (W.H.S. 1895).

[14] The inscription has not survived the moving of the monument to its present position from its original place at the east end of the aisle to make room for a Rushout memorial.

CHAPTER SEVEN

Laudian and Puritan: Years of Strife

1628-78

THE STORMY MIDDLE half of the seventeenth century was spanned by the ministries in Blockley of two vicars, George Durant and Giles Collier—the one a high churchman, the other a Puritan. Because contemporary records from this stage onwards in our parish history become much more accessible, the contrast and conflict between them are revealed in some detail and show in a village setting something of the bitter controversies which were then tearing the nation apart.

1628-47 George Durant, Vicar

He came of a Worcester family, graduated from Balliol College Oxford, and was 27 years of age when, after having served for two years as rector of the small Surrey parish of Newington, he came into residence as vicar of Blockley. William Laud had lately become bishop of London and a power in the Church: Durant was one of the clergy who responded to his influence. Under him, for ten or a dozen years at least, Blockley seems to have known something of the drive and discipline which Laud sought to enforce over the whole Church of England. Trouble enough was to come of that, and George Durant was to have his share of it.

But that lay in the future. In spite of political storms in Parliament and the rumblings of sectarian controversy up and down the land there was quiet and contentment in England during the first ten years of King Charles's reign, and especially in the

55

countryside. These were the years of 'the King's Peace,' when England, while central Europe was quailing under the savageries of the Thirty Years War, seemed to be, in Clarendon's phrase, the garden of the world. George Durant came to his Cotswold vicarage at a time when builders must have seemed to be everywhere at work—on manor houses, on grammar schools, on farm houses and barns, the very stuff and substance of the Cotswold landscape. The recent leasing of demesne land in the manor of Blockley had added new proprietors to the long established Childes of Northwick and Freemans of Aston Magna. The Palmers were lately settled in their new mansion on the old rectory site, the Carters in theirs on Upton Wold, and there were less affluent newcomers in Blockley Park—Park Farm to us—and Stapenhill.

Durant must have found his church the more shabby for all the new building in the parish. The long distracting years in which the Reformation had worked itself out had left churches everywhere in sad decay. He lost no time in setting masons to work on the fabric. In 1630 a new south porch was built in a mixture of Gothic and Renaissance style—the work, no doubt, of local craftsmen. With its incised sun-dial, its builder's emblem and the Blockley names of that year's churchwardens, William Dide and Thomas Widdowes, it provides a not unworthy approach to the ancient doorway into the church. And, because it has in the past been the scene of much secular business as well as of liturgical procedures, it carries echoes of an older Blockley, as the mean Victorian porch on the north side never can. It was rarely used, rarely even seen until recently, when it housed an exhibit of Blockley antiquities during the Arts Festival of 1971.

Five years later a much larger work was undertaken: the addition of a clerestory and the raising of the roof of the nave. The dates incised on stone give the dates, 1635 and 1636, together with the initials of the churchwardens of the day, Andrew Lydall of Blockley, Arthur Fletcher of Paxford and Thomas Freeman of Aston Magna. Probably, too, several of the traceried windows of the nave are insertions of the Durant period—those with dripstones terminating in the diamond-shaped pattern to be seen in the clerestory. However that may be, the church in Durant's time was given an exterior very like that which we know today, and it is with good reason that a high modern authority[1] has taken it as typical of the Laudian revival.

These were costly undertakings and most of the expense was no doubt met by the levy of church rates by the vicar and his parish officers, the product of which must have been increased by the accession to the parish of land holders of substance, as already noted. Because the money was obviously raised and the projects carried out, we may take it that Durant had the support of his people. Worcestershire was, in fact, a high church stronghold and the gentry of the Blockley area were firm for Church and King. But there was a strong Puritan minority too, and there was an omen of future trouble, could he have but known it, in the baptism in Blockley church shortly before George Durant's coming of an infant from Draycott. This was William, son of John and Margaret Warner, christened on 8 July 1627. He was in due course to serve as captain in Cromwell's army and, after the monarchy and the established Church had been restored, to become a Quaker and emigrate to North America, where he bought a piece of land in the Delaware valley—he called it Blockley—adjoining the site on which William Penn two or three years later founded Philadelphia[2] (The name is preserved in Blockley Neurological Hospital formerly called the Blockley Almshouse. The pioneer woman doctor, Elizabeth Blackwell, spent time working here in 1848, during her medical studies.)

Other evidence of a Puritan minority in the Blockley congregation in Durant's time will presently appear.

Trouble came upon the parish in 1637 with what must have been its worst epidemic of bubonic plague since the Black Death.[3] In the margin of the parish register opposite the entry of the burial of Anne Walden on 22 November of that year Durant wrote the words "Init. pestis" and he marked with the letter 'p' all the deaths from plague that followed, 26 in all, the last falling exactly three months later. Five died in the Walden household. December was the worst month with thirteen plague burials, and on the last day of January there were four funerals in Blockley church. The vicar and his curate, William Tymmes, between them took 53 funeral services in this grim year, against an average in that decade of 30.

A more personal trouble befell Durant in 1639. He had unwisely become surety for one of his brothers in the matter of a loan, which was in default. Unable to meet his obligation, he had to suffer distraint and during divine service on a Sunday morning the sheriff's officers forcibly entered the church and read an official warrant forbidding the payment of tithe to the vicar until the debt had been paid. It may be that there was a sectarian motive behind this outrage, for the strain between the parties in church and state was now near breaking point: certainly the incident must have weakened his authority as vicar.[4]

A still more violent episode three years later, a few months before the Civil War began, puts all this beyond doubt for us. Robert Chapman of Stapenhill was constable for that year, 1642. On Easter Monday he had occasion to go round the village on official business and a quarrel seems then to have arisen between him and Mr Durant—and to have been carried a good deal further when, later on, Chapman was riding home on the way towards Paxford. It ended in a formal complaint against the vicar to be heard by the magistrates at the Midsummer Sessions at Worcester. Part of the indictment may be quoted:

ffirst the said George Durant doth beare causeless mallice towards the said Robt Chapman and in expression thereof upon Easter monday last after the said Robt Chapman having bene at Blockley aboute the kings ma^{ts} affaires for levying a leune[5] for the kings provision and retourning homwardes about an hower within night the said Mr Durant aboute a lands length of the said towne of Blockley did lye in waite and then and there pulled the said Robt Chapman from his horse and pulled him downe into a dytch and soe hurt and bruised the said Chapman that he was all gore and did spitt blood and alsoe pulled a greate deale of haire from the said Chapman's head.

Item that the said Robt Chapman for feare of being mischiefed by the said Mr Durant was inforced to crye out for help, whereupon two p'sons rann in, to one of whome the said Durant offered his fist, and then the pettie constable was sent for, at whose cominge and apprehendinge the said Mr Durant he againe threatened the said Robt Chapman to doe violence to his p'son and that he would not leave him for longe as he was worth a groat and would trample upon his skirte soe longe as they two lived in Blockley p'ishe together . . .

We have no account of this incident from Mr Durant, and no record of the hearing of the case—if, indeed, it ever was heard, for in those weeks before the fighting began the justices must have had more serious matters to concern them. What does emerge from the story is that there was opposition in the parish to the vicar, that feelings ran high and that trouble lay ahead for George Durant.

That autumn the Civil War began. Blockley, like Worcestershire in general, was for the king—but not unanimously or without some backward glances. As the war went on, and the king's armies in the north and the south-west were put out of action, the road from the royal headquarters at Oxford to Worcester, which was the collecting centre for men and stores from the Welsh marches and Ireland became more and more a bone of contention. It was no accident that the last battle of all in the Civil War was fought along it—and so partly within the bounds of Blockley parish. During the two years before that, both sides in the fight took an uncomfortable interest in the neighbourhood. There were Parliamentary garrisons at Gloucester to the south and Warwick to the north. But to loyal Blockley the king's troops were much closer at hand, and those which were quartered in the great manor house built only a score of years earlier adjoining Campden church by Sir Baptist Hicks were the terror of the countryside. Years later Lord Clarendon, the royalist chronicler of the Civil War still remembered their commander, Sir Henry Bard, "the licentious governor of Cambden House, who exercised an illimited tyranny over the whole country, and took his leave of it by wantonly burning the noble structure where he had too long inhabited."

As vicar of Blockley, Durant was exposed to special attention from Bard and his "cormorants", as one indignant victim called the troopers, and we may guess that his hot temper, already noticed, did not help him. He was indeed sorely tried. In the autumn of 1644 his wife, Elizabeth, died after giving birth to their eleventh child—and he was left with ten surviving children, the eldest not more than eighteen. Not long after Colonel Bard sent him a requisition for a horse and a sum of money "for the King's cause,"—no doubt, not for the first time. Durant had the temerity to refuse, whereupon "the Governor of the Garrison

59

threatened me with imprisonment and sending a partie of horse to take me from my house in the night."[6] That was more than he could face, and he "made an escape" and took refuge with the other side for the next seven months, much of the time being spent with Colonel Edward Freeman, of the Batsford family of that name and a barrister of Gray's Inn who was serving in the Parliamentary forces. Freeman later stated under oath "that George Durant Vicker of Blockley freely of his owne accord sent in a very able horse to me beinge in armes for the Parliam[t]. And allso sent in the fund of 21[li]. for the use of the State upon the publiq faith . . . And (this deponent) hath oftentimes received intelligence from him also of the strength of the Kinges party, whereby the better to avoid them . . . and was present when it was proved upon oath that the said Mr Durant sheltered and protected the Parliament soldiers from the Kinges fforces."

This singular interlude in Durant's ministry came to an end with the fall of Worcester and the end of the war. In April 1646 he returned to his parish, a few weeks after the disturbed night of 21 March, when Blockley must have heard something of the tumult of the running battle on the hills above, as Sir Jacob Astley in his desperate bid to reach Oxford with the last available reinforcements for the king tried to fight off three pursuing Parliamentary armies. It all ended at dawn in the market-place of Stow-on-the-Wold with the surrender of the king's forces and the old and weary Sir Jacob sitting on a drum which the Parliamentary soldiers had brought up to him, pronouncing his epilogue on the Civil War: "Gentlemen, ye may now sit and play, for you have done all your work—if only ye fall not out among yourselves." Many stragglers from that fight must have come down into Blockley village that night, two of them so wounded that they never left it. The parish registers record the burials on 30 March of "Edward Norman, a Summersett-shire man, shott at Stowe-fight," and on 3 September of "Captaine Phillip Gyttens"—not a Blockley name.

That the vicar was an absentee from his parish in this time of crisis looks very like dereliction of duty—and it was so taken by his Puritan critics, of course. That he had given information and shelter to the "enemy" can more easily be condoned, for this was no alien enemy, but rather a group of his own neighbours, to spare whom from the attentions of Bard and his troopers may well have seemed to him no more than common humanity.

The inevitable reckoning came within a very short time of his return to the parish. The victorious Parliament had set up county committees to deal with "scandalous, ignorant or insufficient, ministers." He was summoned to Worcester for examination[6] but seems to have satisfied his judges on that occasion. But one official of the committee was not content to leave it at that—a lately ordained young Puritan from Pershore with a zest for witch-hunting and a more particular interest in the living of Blockley, where he seems already to have had friends. This was Giles Collier. He saw to it that a further hearing of the Durant case was held in April 1647. This time the Committee ordered "that the vicarage of the parish church of Blockley be sequestered from Mr Durant," and that, in view of "a petition preferred from the said parish on behalf of Mr Giles Collier, the said vicarage and the parish thereof shall from henceforth stand sequestered to the use of the said Mr Collier who is required forthwith to officiate the cure of the said church as Vicar and to preach regularly to the parishioners thereof, and that he shall have for his paines the vicarage house and glebe lands."[7]

So George Durant lost his living. But he did not leave without a struggle. He appealed to the central Committee for Compounding at Westminster for a review of his case. It was not heard till the summer of 1650, and it led to nothing. But the delay may have enabled him to remain in his vicarage till that date—a possibility supported by the fact that Mr Collier did not pay dues for the benefice till 1650 and that the first entry of the baptism at Blockley of one of his children occurs in the register for 1651. When George Durant did leave Blockley he had to be evicted. "He was dispossess'd by a party of horse who dragged his children (whereof he had ten then living and most of them very young) out of doors; and the neighbours out of charity put them into a poor cottage in the same town and relieved them, where a sister of the ejected minister was put to nurse them; for their own mother had died a little before."[8]

The next years were more difficult than ever for the dispossessed clergy who could not conform to Presbyterian church order and worship in place of the now prohibited episcopal government and the Book of Common Prayer, to which they were pledged. Many of them, living in hiding, continued to exercise a clandestine ministry for the faithful. There is evidence that George Durant was at Sezincote just after his removal from Blockley, and it may be that he was reported to the authorities for action of this kind. Whatever the reason, he spent his last few years in Newgate prison with other clergy, all confined "for the King's cause." A copy has survived of an appeal signed by eight of them, Durant's name being the last, which must have been smuggled out of the prison in the hope of raising money for the employment of legal counsel for their defence. It reads:

> Wee humbly beg Pardon for this bold Address, and if that which excuses all may be our Advocate, Necessity will not be silent untill it hath obtained both your Money and Charity to us, whose Names are subscribed. Our Case is sad, havinge drunke more than an ordinary Draught in that Cup of Calamity, wch hath gone round from the Nobility and Gentry to the Clergy, amongst whome we reckon ourselves. (Will you) please to contribute, by sending what you please to Mr John Agar a lawyer at his house in Holborne over against Grays Inn, and you shall have the Prayers of Eternall Day in Heaven of Yr Humble Servants.[9]

Poor George Durant seems never to have been released. The last record of him is the entry of his burial in the registers of St. James's Church, Clerkenwell, not far from Newgate, on 24 June 1657.

Giles Collier—'Intruded' as Minister, c. 1650: nominated as Vicar by the Crown, 1661. Died 1678.

Giles Collier was born at Pershore in 1622. At 15 he matriculated at Oxford, and it may have been as a servitor that he was entered at New Inn Hall. Servitors were poor undergraduates who helped to pay their way through their course to a degree by performing more or less menial duties in the service of the seniors of the college—or, worse, of gentleman commoners, rich undergraduates. If that was indeed Collier's status in the not very reputable Hall, the memory of which survives to day only in an Oxford street name, it might possibly go some way towards explaining the aggressive qualities which earned him so much dislike as time went on. Any young Puritan growing to manhood in such circumstances might well leave Oxford with a chip on his shoulder and a grudge against dissolute royalists. But such speculation has no firm basis.

He took his B.A. in 1641, and was ordained by the Bishop of Worcester in or about 1645, becoming rector of Aston Somerville, ten miles from his native Pershore. After the downfall of the King's cause "he closed with the presbyterians . . . took the Covenant . . . and was a busy man[10] when he was made an assistant to the commissioners of Worcestershire for the ejection of such whom the godly party called scandalous, ignorant and insufficient ministers and schoolmasters." How Collier carried out these unpleasant duties and how they brought him to Blockley vicarage in or about 1650 has already been recorded.

Of his ministry at Blockley during the Commonwealth years we have little information. There was no bishop—Dr Prideaux lived privately in a village in his diocese till 1650, when he died—and the Book of Common Prayer was banned by Parliament. It was replaced by a formulary called *The Directory*, which laid down the lines on which services were to be conducted, but left the details and most of the words to the minister's choice. In 1654 the celebration of marriages was taken out of the hands of the ministers and became a purely civil ceremony before a magistrate. Banns—or more precisely 'notices of intended marriage'—could still be published in church, but several of those recorded in the Blockley registers were announced in the Evesham or the Shipston market. The registers, even, were taken out of the ministers' hands and kept by an elected 'Register,' but at Blockley the choice of the congregation fell on William Tymmes, who continued his impeccable entries till 1655—so far, at least, as concerned baptisms and burials. Marriages were not so easily dealt with, as they called for a magistrate's certificate,[11] and many were evidently celebrated secretly by Anglican clergy who had private access to churches in the neighbourhood.

We have little evidence of how Giles Collier was received by his Blockley parishioners. That there were some among them to whom his new ways may have been congenial has already been noted. But there is ample proof of Anthony Wood's assertion that his accession to Blockley was deplored by loyalists in the

63

neighbourhood whom he had much displeased. Wood might have added that no one disliked him more than his own principal parishioner, Thomas Childe of Northwick, as our story will soon make clear. But so long as the Cromwellian regime lasted his enemies had perforce to bide their time.

One of them, Edward Fisher, lord of the manor of Mickleton, clashed with him in 1655 in a theological controversy. He published in London a lively attack on the sabbatarianism, which Collier as a Puritan vigorously proclaimed, holding that the Jewish Sabbath and the Christian Sunday required similar observance. To Fisher's 'A Christian Caveat to the Old and New Sabbatarians' Collier replied with a pamphlet entitled 'Vindiciae Thesium de Sabbato, or a Vindication of Certain Passages on the Morality of the Sabbath, to which they were subjected by Edward Fisher, Esq.' Mr Fisher, a good Church and King man from Brasenose College and one of the Inns of Court, replied and it took a counter-blast from Collier to make sure of the last word.

At least one instance is on record of his sternness with sabbath breakers who disregarded his admonitions. He wrote in 1663 to the diocesan registrar calling for sentence of excommunication on an offender after judgment in the Consistory Court: "We have a Tucker at Blockley who hath several times been warned and yet will not amend, but keeps his mill going on Sundays. The next time the Apparitor comes this way, pray send a citation to him. His name is William Bartlet."[12] It was, perhaps, no less the Puritan in him that made him ready to relax the observance of Lent— as is shown in another letter to a diocesan official which he sent in 1660 by the hand of a Blockley butcher: "I am troubling you at the request of this bearer who is a Butcher here at Blockley, and seeing there be many in this great Parish that will need Dispensation for eating some flesh in Lent and consequently need a Butcher to kill it for them, my desire is that you will be pleased to direct and further him in getting a Dispensation."[13]

With the restoration in 1660 of Church and King, Giles Collier's principles underwent a change. Like many another intruded minister he was ready to accept the new Act of Uniformity restoring the Book of Common Prayer, and in 1661 he petitioned the Crown for the regularisation of his status as incumbent of the benefice, which owing to the still unfilled see of

Worcester was in the gift of the Crown by lapse.[14] The shortage of clergy was extreme after the fifteen year gap in ordinations, and Collier, in spite of his record, got his nomination. In August 1662 he rode to Worcester, accompanied by "Samuel Fowler, M.A. Schoolmaster at Blockley," and both there subscribed to the Act of Uniformity.[15]

That schoolmaster, an Oxford graduate at that, calls for explanation. He was usher, or assistant master, to Mr Collier— for whom he no doubt acted also as curate—in the private school for 'tablers' or boarders carried on in the Vicarage. The range of small dormitories for the boys still remain in the attic there. Its curriculum was that of a grammar school, and it produced at least one pupil to be read of in the *Dictionary of National Biography*. This was William Derham (1657–1735), F.R.S. and author of several works on what he called Physico-Theology, in which he sought to harmonize religion and natural science. He was a meteorologist, he wrote notes on the death-watch beetle, on wasps and on bird migration. His Boyle Lectures in 1711 before the Society went into twelve editions and were translated into several languages. Two other titles, *Astro-theology* (1715) and *Christo-theology* (1730) show his continuing interest in his chosen field of study. His son, also William, became President of Trinity College, Oxford.

The school obviously prospered till the end of Collier's life and its profits no doubt account for the considerable purchases of land in the parish which he was able to leave to his widow. But it was also the cause of some friction. Thomas Childe, of Northwick, his principal parishioner, was the vicar's constant enemy, and the records of the bishop's Consistory Court between 1664 and 1674 abound in citations and counter-citations between them and include one conditional sentence of excommunication against Childe and another charge against him of disturbing Divine Service between 9 and 11 on a Sunday morning. The quarrel then was about seats in the church. Childe claimed seats on benches for his no doubt considerable indoor and outdoor staff—in addition to his family pew in the centre of the nave. The vicarage family pew was in the chancel, but the vicar's school pupils overflowed elsewhere—and the Northwick housekeeper and her fellow-servants suffered. One of the stone monuments in the church—the Freeman tomb—also suffered, as will presently be shown. There was another quarrel about the right of way which ran, and still runs, along the west boundary of the churchyard from the vicarage gate to the post-office square. Childe had in some way obstructed this, and the vicar in 1672 cited him to appear in the bishop's court for trespass in the churchyard, claiming also that he and his predecessors had time out of mind used the road as a horse and foot way from the vicarage to the king's highway.

A description of the interior of Blockley church in Collier's time has come down to us, and from no less a visitor than the Oxford antiquary, Anthony Wood. Among his few friends was Francis Sheldon of Weston Park (some seven miles east of Blockley) and on Michaelmas Day 1675 the two men came to Blockley. In his journal under that date Wood listed the monuments in the church, including the three brasses in the chancel, and the Childe memorials in the north aisle as they then stood—"William Child cut in armour at the upper end . . . William Child and Elizabeth his wife fairly cut in marble kneeling and Marie Ann wife of William (*he should have written Thomas*) Child now living. These monuments still remain, though unceremoniously displaced by the Rushouts when they built their family vault and set the statuary above it at the end of the 18th century. Wood describes one other monument, which Giles Collier himself had recently been treating with even less ceremony and of which the only remnants today are the stone figures of two ladies in Jacobean dress kneeling forlornly on the floor at the bottom of the tower. This was the table tomb of William Freeman of Batsford, who died in 1634 and whose recumbent effigy with his two wives— the ladies just referred to—kneeling at his feet lay on top of the tomb. Wood's account of it shows that the tomb originally lay east and west close to the pulpit but "they have now turned it to north and south for boyes to sit on just opposite to the Pulpit. . . Their Memories here are quite woren out." Those 'memories' (or inscriptions cut in stone under the figures) must have been obliterated by the boots of the fidgety boys, who certainly cannot have slept during the sermons, and the boys were surely from Collier's school. Squire Childe seems to have had reason to complain of the seating arrangements in church!

The 'gentry' of course sat in greater comfort. The Carters of Upton Wold had their family pew built in Collier's time. On the wall just to the left of the chancel arch there stands today the memorial of Edward Carter, Esquire and Professor of the laws of England, who died in 1667, and of Mary, his daughter, who died later at Bath where she had gone for a cure. That monument was erected just above the enclosed pew which Edward Carter obtained the bishop's licence to build in 1664—together with an undertaking that it should remain for the use of his heirs so long as they continued in his mansion in Blockley for ever. From the definition of the area in the church assigned for this pew we get a hint of the appearance of that part of the nave at that period:

> The seat here related is scituate as followeth. It butts northward towardes the North Isle, southward towardes the seat now in the possession of Nicholas ffletcher of Paxford, westward towardes Mr ffreemans Tombe, eastward towardes the Chancell.

That the condition of the fabric at this time left something to be desired, and especially of the chancel itself, we have evidence in the 'presentments' of the churchwardens at the visitation in 1663:

> We present and complaine of the ruinessnesse . . . of the Vestry and Chancell, the repairing whereof belongs to the Ld Bishop of Worcester Rector and Lord of the Mannor, by means whereof the most diligent care cannot keep the Church in that cleanlinesse and and decencie as becometh the House dedicated to the solemn worship and service of God.

This document is in the vicar's handwriting and it had its effect inasmuch as the complaint, after repetition in the presentments of the following year, disappears from the Visitation records. Giles Collier kept his churchwardens up to the mark in regard to the upkeep of the nave and tower, the cost of which fell on the parishioners, and there are records of two levies of a Church Rate in his time. Thus on 27 March 1676 at a meeting of the Vestry there was "A Leune (*levy*) then made by the Minister Churchwardens and others of the Inhabitants of our Parish of Blockley whose names are hereunto subscribed for the Reparing

of ower Church after the Rate of Twelve pence the yardland."
There follow, over the signatures of Giles Collier as Vicar and of
Thomas Childe and Thomas Fletcher as churchwardens, the
several assessments on the land holders in the common fields
of Blockley, the Ditchfords, Aston, Paxford, Northwick, Draycott and Dorne, and on certain named leaseholders of enclosed
land—Mr Carter for Hither Upton Old assessed at 17 shillings
for 17 yardlands, Mr Harward for 13 at Further Upton Old,
Mr Childe Esqr for parts of Blockley and Stapenhill, Thomas
Chapman (plain Thomas to indicate his lower rank) for the rest
of Stapenhill, Sir William Keyte (of Ebrington) for Broadnams,
which adjoins Paxford, and Ailleston which today is Hailstone
Farm, and finally Mr Hunt (of the Manor House) for Pallmore
Meadow. The total sum raised was £13. 2s. 9d., no small sum in
those days, especially when it followed a similar levy of two or
three years earlier. *Plate 7*. There can be little doubt that Giles
Collier left his church in good repair.

What may well have been the last letter he wrote[16] brings us
nearer to him than any of these formal matters. It is dated from
Blockley, 27 June 1678, and addressed to that wise and learned
scholar Dr. John Wallis, Fellow of the Royal Society, Savilian
Professor at Oxford and friend of Wren, Evelyn and Pepys. He
had evidently recommended Collier's school at Blockley to a
lady for her sons:

To the Reverend Dr Wallis at his house in Oxford

Reverend Sir,

About a fortnight since Mrs Crosse desired me to send a note of
Disbursements for the children and for the half yeares Teaching
and Tabling. I was absent the weeke after the Letter came and had
not opportunity to make answer thereto. Not knowing whether
she may be in Towne still, I give you the trouble of this, and it is
to desire you please to order the payment of the money which is
due to Mr Taylor my Assistant who will wait upon you the later end
of this weeke in it and deliver an Acquittance. He takes his Masters
degree this Terme and so will need it. The children are well and the
rest of the family now through Gods mercy, after a long time of
sicknesse upon us and a sad breach by the removing of my two
younger daughters from us by the small Pocks. Tom Crosse had it

but was preserved and returned to perfect health, as several other young gentlemen and my eldest daughter, blessed be the Lord to whose grace I commend you and yours, desiring an interest in your praiers, and remain,

Sir,

Y^r assured Servant,

GILES COLLIER.

Within a month of writing this letter Giles Collier died—of the disease, no doubt, which had removed his daughters. A year later Thomas Childe of Northwick also died—the last of the Childes of Blockley, as was shortly to appear. The two men, enemies for so long, may have composed their differences before the end, for Childe served as churchwarden more than once after 1674. For the parish their deaths marked the end of an era.

[1] The late W. I. Croome of North Cerney and Cirencester.

[2] For a full record of the Warner family see pp. 215-19.

[3] The Burials Register records an epidemic of plague in Blockley, in 1597 and there were no doubt other visitations.

[4] J. Noake: *Worcestershire Nuggets* (1889), 353.

[5] Leune, now obsolete, means levy.

[6] P.R.O., SP 23/G 81. A petition by Durant to the Committee for Compounding at Westminster, August 1650.

[7] Bodleian Library, MSS Bodley 324.

[8] Walker: *Sufferings of the Clergy* (1714), cited Soden 63.

[9] Bodleian Library, MSS Tanner 60/61, f. 55.

[10] Anthony Wood: *Athenae Oxonienses* III. 1171.

[11] One example is inserted in the Marriage Register.

[12] Worcs. Record Office, Diocesan Records, Churchwardens' Presentments.

[13] A tradesman's token has survived from this period, perhaps a fellmonger's. On the obverse in inscribed "Thomas Warner" over a pair of Shears: on the reverse is "Of Blockley 1667" (from information by B. G. Cox of Evesham).

[14] P.R.O., SP 29/12/68.

[15] Worcs. Record Office, Diocesan Subscription Books.

[16] Bodleian Library, MSS Add. D. 105.

CHAPTER EIGHT

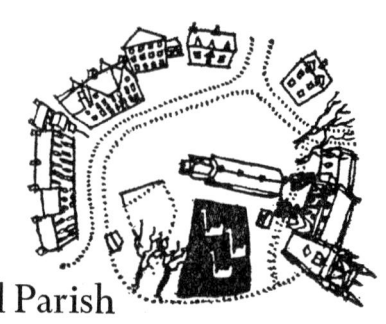

Changes in Manor and Parish

1650-1700

ALL WARS HASTEN change, civil wars perhaps not least. As the storms of the mid-century gave way to the domestic calm of the age of Anne and the Georges, there were new stirrings in the life of the parish.

The victory of the Parliament in 1646 ousted the bishop from his manors as well as his See. Orders came down from the new rulers that the manor of Blockley was to be surveyed with a view to its sale. The survey was carried out in 1647 and the manor was sold a year later to a certain William Combe for just under £1400—a bargain he was not to enjoy for long.

The survey,[1] in its full account of the copyholders, lease-holders and freeholders on the manor, reflects unfavourably on the intrusion of one John Castle into the rent-roll of the manor as the result of negotiation on the bishop's behalf by his son Matthias Prideaux. Castle thereby acquired a score of cottages, some miscellaneous parcels of land, the stewardship of the fairs and, worst of all, Blockley Wood. This, during the war years he seems to have plundered,

> The woods the surveyor wrote, "have been much spoiled and de-cayed of late by one John Castle, who hath cut down at least 35 acres and sold it, which in our judgment was worth 70[1]. Likewise the said John Castle did take into the said Woods great store of Cattle, which did crop the young springes to the great hinderance of the growth of them.

There was possibly political feeling in all this. Perhaps Castle gave his money for the king's cause. It is certain that his leases were renewed after the Restoration.

This we know from another survey, ordered by Bishop Morley in 1664. This Restoration Survey, like the Parliamentary Survey of 1647 though in somewhat ampler form, is rich in the detail it gives of the persons and places in the parish at that time.

Another and a more profound change for the parish was the departure of the Childes from Northwick after their three centuries of squiredom there. In 1682, Thomas Childe having ended his days in the Oxfordshire home to which he had retired, the Northwick property was sold for £14000 to Sir James Rushout, and a new regime began for Blockley, which was to last another three centuries.[2] *Plate* 12.

James Rushout was the son and heir of a wealthy Flemish immigrant from the textile centre of Roulers, near Courtrai, who settled in London and was naturalised in 1635. There he greatly prospered in that trade. He later made a second home, and no doubt a second business—there were many Flemish settlers in the textile trade in Essex—at Maylards, near Hornchurch. It is significant that there were silk throwing mills in that county producing threads for the broad silk woven in Spitalfields well before the end of the century; and it may well be that Sir James Rushout, when he inherited his father's estate and moved to Blockley, brought with him an interest in this branch of the family trade. He greatly added to his fortune by his marriage with Alice, the heiress of Edmund Pitt of Harrow-on-the-Hill, which became the principal seat of the Rushout family for the next three generations, gave its head much property there, the patronage of the living and an almost hereditary right to a place on the governing body of Harrow School.

James Rushout must have known something of Blockley long before he settled there. He had been a member of Parliament for Evesham since 1661, with Thomas Childe of Northwick as one of his constituents. It may be, though this is pure conjecture, that his wife knew the place of old, for her first husband had been one Edward Palmer. Was he related to the Palmers who for over a century had lived in the Manor House in Blockley? More likely, perhaps, it was his textile interests which drew him to the Cotswolds, famous textile country, and to Blockley, well known for its water mills. For his coming to Blockley was very soon followed by the creation of the first of the Blockley silk throwing mills.

The process of 'throwing' consists of washing the fibres of raw silk and spinning them into threads for the weavers to handle. It was the ribbon weavers of Coventry who took the product of the Blockley mills. The earliest known Blockley throwster was Henry Whatcott, who died in 1718. A three-life lease to Edward Whatcott in 1688 of a tenement called Gaunts which included "a Water Mill used as a Spinning Mill"[3]—it is Blockley Court today—gives us the clue to the site of Whatcott's mill. Was Sir James Rushout the moving spirit and patron of the enterprise?

The third change to be noted was more impalpable. It lay in the quality and social standing of the clergy. About this time there began a greater infusion of the younger sons of the gentry, as then reckoned, into their ranks. The reasons may not always have been creditable—agriculture was flourishing, and tithe with it: but the consequences were not altogether bad. Certainly the fires that burned in George Durant and Giles Collier were replaced by an ardour very real, if less devouring, in Samuel Scattergood and Erasmus Saunders. There were visible results of the change. These 18th century divines, often brought up in ampler households and larger comfort than their predecessors, were apt to enlarge and adorn their rectories, and we shall see that Dr. Saunders added to the accommodation and amenity of his vicarage at Blockley. They mixed more, too, in county society and liked to sit on the bench, as two later vicars did. That must have involved some loss of ease in their relations with their parishioners.

That the bishops of Worcester, as lords of the manor, began more than ever to withdraw from their responsibilities is certain, and as their interest lessened, so the squires of Northwick took on more of a likeness to squires of Blockley itself. In 1698 Sir James Rushout acquired the leasehold of Blockley Parks—the Park Farm of today. A year later he bought the leasehold of the Warren, Blockley Wood, which a later Rushout called Dovedale, and "Ayleston," which is now Hailstone Farm. But the grand acquisitor was his son Sir John, as will appear in due course.

There were three vicars of Blockley in the score or so of years here under review—

Francis Phipps, Vicar 1679-81

It seems doubtful if he resided. The only known record of his time, the certificate of the due execution in church of an act of penance imposed by the bishop's court on an erring woman parishioner, was signed by "Will. Toms, Minister," presumably the curate in charge.

Samuel Scattergood, Vicar 1681-96

He was the son of Antony Scattergood, Canon of Lichfield, and extracts from two letters[4] written by his father may illustrate the pious, cultured and affectionate family from which this good vicar of Blockley sprang. The first is in answer to a letter from Samuel, then a young Fellow of Trinity College, Cambridge, in which he had apparently complained of some lack of affection shown to him. The father answered:

> You have no great reason to charge me with too little kindness to you and too much to your sister. My Mouth would have made a larger Apologie, but now my Penne shall onely tell you that though I love all my Children very tenderly, yet you alwayes have had and yet have an equall share in my affection ... My kindness to you shall still encrease and nothing bee thought too dear for you that is in the power of
> > Yr very loving Father
> > A.S.
> Mr Hayes, I hope, by this time hath got two Bibles bound for me. If so, take one for y^{r}self and send the other hither. God keep you and bless you, dear Son.
> > Ap. 2. 1677.

The second letter is dated 19 April 1681, just after Samuel and his wife were installed in their vicarage at Blockley:

> Most dear Son,
> > I was very glad to hear that in a piece of a day you and your wife got well to Blockley, for I hope it will bee an easy dayes journey for mee when I shall give you a visit. We have sent you the goods you left by Samuel Walton and wish you a good settlement in y^r house and (wch is better) in the affections of y^r people. I doubt not but you will do y^s duty worthily amongst them and gain double honour

from them. The great Shepherd gratiously bless both Shepherd and Flock . . . God grant wee may be still watching for the Masters coming. Dear Son and Daughter, the good Lord keep you.

Y^r very loving Father

Antony Scattergood.

The parish registers under the year 1685 record the baptism of "Martha d^r of Mr Samuel Scattergood Vicar and Elizabeth his Wife." Martha never forgot her birth-place, for in her will over half a century later she bequeathed to the town of Blockley the sum of £100 to be disposed of as the Minister and Church-wardens think best for the benefit of the poor—and the Scatter-good Charity has ever since been so administered.

Recorded annals of Samuel Scattergood's ministry in Blockley are scanty. He must periodically in every year after 1883, when he succeeded to his father's stall in Lichfield cathedral as a residentiary canon, have been absent for some weeks in order to carry out his duties there. That no doubt accounts for the signature of "Samuel Marshall, Cur^{te}" on a certificate for the public recantation in church on a Sunday in 1687 by a Paxford woman of a slander on two others "contrary to good manners and Christian charity." It is possible that Mr Scattergood found other things to complain of in his country parish. In one of his published sermons[5] he complained of the lack of "an humble, reverent and decent behaviour" in church in these words:

We (blame) the prophane and graceless deportment of many (especially of the vulgar sort of People) in our Country Churches now-a-dayes, that are so far from worshipping God with a bended Knee, that they will not vouchsafe so much as to uncover their Heads before Him, but most irreverently and impudently sit them-selves down upon their Seats and put on their Hats even in the very Face of the Lord of Hosts, as if they came into His House rather to defie Him than to adore Him.

If this is a reflection on the Blockley congregation, it may be that something of the Puritan antipathy to any form of ceremony still survived from Giles Collier's time.

All the other evidence suggests that the parish was ruled well by Vicar Scattergood. Year after year at the Visitation held at Evesham by or on behalf of the bishop—Blockley, as a "peculiar," was not subject to the archdeacon's jurisdiction—the churchwardens report all well with the fabric of the church, the poor worthily relieved, and (with rare exceptions) "nothing presentable" in the way of scandalous behaviour. In 1683, however, the vicar had to certify that he had published in church sentence of excommunication on Edward Warner[6] "for not appearing upon lawful summons before the Ordinary to answer articles for not goeing to Church and for not receiving the Sacram[t]."

He took to his last Visitation a written statement which had been specially ordered by the civil authorities and which will have a sequel in a later chapter:

> The totall Summe of the Assessm[t] for the Poor of the Parish of Blockley for the last year (1695) was one hundred and twenty pound, two shillings and eight pence, and *communibus annis* (in average years) it is higher.

That was written by him in October 1696. He died before the end of the year and was buried under the chancel.

Thomas Turner, Vicar 1696-1700

That the Church still exercised its penitential discipline before the whole congregation is shown by what occurred during service on a Sunday in 1699. It was the penance of one William Edwards who had been convicted by his own confession in the Bishop's court of immoral conduct:

> He shall come to the said Church at the Tolling of the Second Bell into Morning Service and shall stand in the Porch of the same having a white Sheete over his wearing Apparel and holding a White Rod of an Ell long in his hand and shall ask Forgiveness of all that pass by him, and the Second Lesson being ended he shall be brought into the said Church by the Parish Clerk and be placed in the middle Ally near unto the Minister's reading Desk, where he shall stand, covered as before, all the time of Divine Service and Sermon, and immediately after the reading of the Nicene Creed he shall make an humble Confession of his Fault saying after the Minister . . . (*There follows the form of words to be used*).

The parish registers record the baptism in 1699 of an infant who was later to be a pioneer in the history of engineering and earn the title of "Father of Steam Navigation" for his design for the propulsion of a boat by steam.When tested on the Avon the experiment failed, but the design was the basis for later advance. The entry reads "Jonathan son of Thomas Hull of Aston and Mary his Wife, 17 December." Two successive entries in the burials register for 1697 are the first pair of a tragic sequence of losses which befell the Rushout family. "The Lady Alice Rushout of Northwick was buried on 17 February" and her husband, Sir James, followed her only a fortnight later. In 1700 Vicar Turner himself was buried.

---

[1] Eccl. Comm. 43962.

[2] For a full account of the early years of the Rushout family in England see Norah Marshall: *Blockley and the Silk Trade* 2–4 (1972, privately published).

[3] N.P. XLVII/I 5.

[4] Antony Scattergood was residentiary canon of Lichfield and rector of Yelvertoft, Staffs. from where he wrote. He had been fellow and chaplain of Trinity College, Cambridge, was a distinguished theologian, and collaborated with Sancroft in seeing the 1661 Book of Common Prayer through the press.

[5] *Fifty Two Sermons upon several Occasines* (*sic*) i. 73. There is a copy in the parish chest.

[6] See p. 120

Diagram of Hull's Steamboat (*from a race pamphlet published by him, 1737*)

CHAPTER NINE

MORS IANUA VITÆ
E.S.1716

Erasmus Saunders and his Times

1700-61

DR SAUNDERS THE central figure in this chapter, was curate of Morton Henmarsh when Mr Turner was vicar of Blockley, and became curate of Blockley under Turner's often absent successor. He has already been quoted in these pages as an amateur archaeologist on the Roman site at Dorn in the year 1695. Four other letters of his[1] to the same correspondent, Edward Lhuyd, Keeper of the Ashmolean Laboratory (now the Old Ashmolean) at Oxford reveal more of his scholarly interests—the deciphering of Roman inscriptions, the excavation of an urn and a stone chest in Wales, and requests for books to be purchased for him from Oxford booksellers. "Let me know," he writes, "whether it is too late to put in a subscription for Camden,[2] and what may be the price of Mr Rays Stirpium Britannicarum Descriptio." He commends visiting scholars to Lhuyd, one Gilio from Italy and a French 'abbot'—presumably an *abbé* —who is vouched for "by Mr Lloyd my Lᵈ of Worcester's son." This was in 1701, and William Lloyd was then his vicar at Blockley.

William Lloyd. Vicar 1700-05

He was at best a part time vicar, for his father, the bishop, used him for diocesan duties and soon made him Chancellor. But he seems to have lived in the vicarage and we know from the

78

Diary of Francis Evans,[3] the bishop's secretary, that the bishop was an occasional guest. There was one week-end in high summer in 1701 when on the Sunday "my L ᵈ preached and administered the Sacrament there. In the afternoon his Lo ᴾ confirmed abᵗ 400 persons" and followed it up on the Monday by confirming 500 more at Shipston and Stratford. Such mass confirmations were customary then.

Two years later Evans was again in Blockley in very different weather. The great storm of late November 1703, which rarely escapes mention in writings of that time, caught him on his journey there. It left a great swathe of destruction a hundred miles wide from the West country to the Wash, cutting down the Eddystone lighthouse, levelling houses in Bristol, killing the bishop and his wife at Wells, unroofing Ely cathedral and all but destroying the fleet under Sir Cloudesley Shovell in the North Sea and so deciding the fate of Marlborough's armies in a night. Here is Evan's account:

1703 Nov. Th. I went from Oxon to Honington in a dreadful stormy day.

26 Fri. I went thro' a most violent wet storme thence to Blockley, passing the waters (*the Kneebrook by Paxford?*) wᵗʰ great difficulty, and that night happen'd the most violent storme that has been known in the memory of man in this kingdom.

27 Sat. I went from Blockley to Shipston in a very stormy day and going thence to Honington in the night, being dark and the ways deep, crossing a rut my horse fell upon me but by the assistance of two p'sons that were on the road I got from under him.

The storm must have raged down the Blockley valley that Friday night and squarely smitten the church tower. Three years before the churchwardens had reported at the visitation that "the Tower hath a great Cracke in it." In 1701 they presented that it was "well amended," but the old Norman structure must surely have received a mortal blow during the wild days of the storm. The sequel was not long delayed.

There were changes, too, in the interior of the church. As rector the bishop was responsible for the maintenance of the chancel and Bishop Lloyd had frequent opportunities for inspecting it. In 1702 he "ceiled and beautified the chancel." That can only mean that he had the timbers of the roof covered with a flat plaster ceiling such as the nave unhappily still has. The chancel no doubt lost this beautification during the extensive reparations in 1831.

Both the Lloyds were disliked in the diocese, and the bishop as time went on withdrew more and more to his study at Hartlebury to write on biblical subjects and on the shortcomings of the Popes, leaving the affairs of the diocese in the hands of his son. He had had his moment of fame once, as one of the Seven Bishops whose trial had toppled James II, but Whig though he was, the Whig Macaulay was moved to call him a half-crazed fanatic. One good deed at least cannot be denied him—for on 13 August 1705 he collated Erasmus Saunders to the benefice of Blockley.

Erasmus Saunders, Vicar 1705-24

He was born at Clwyd, Pembrokeshire, in 1670, matriculated as a member of Jesus College, Oxford, in 1689, and took the degrees of M.A. in 1696, B.D. in 1705 and D.D. in 1712. Just after becoming vicar of Blockley he was made rector of Helmdon, some 30 miles away in Northamptonshire: and later still, he was made a prebendary of St. David's cathedral. But though to this extent a pluralist, and in other fields wide ranging in his interests—most notably as a scholar—he stands out in a the long list of Blockley vicars for his piety, his devotion as a parish priest and his enlightened views on church reform.

His ideas and ideals are set out in three of his published sermons and in a study of "The State of Religion in the Diocese of St David's . . . and the Causes of its Decay" (London 1721). These causes he finds in the ignorance of the clergy, including their ignorance of the Welsh language: and that he puts down largely to their extreme poverty, which is to be attributed to the wholesale impropriations of rectories in earlier centuries by bishops or monasteries. "Let us reflect a little upon the pitiable circumstances of these Men. The Advice of Friends, and some distant Prospects of Encouragements, with the Honour of being the Ministers of God and His Gospel, and the Desire, we hope,

Plate 26 Augusta, widow of the third Lord Northwick, c. 1902. (*Photograph by Chapman, Sirret & Co., Blockley*)

Plate 27 Capt. E. G. Spencer-Churchill in the saloon, Northwick Park, 1955 (*Photograph by courtesy of the Evesham Journal*)

Plate 28 Northwick Park: Lord and Lady Northwick with some of the out-door staff, 1884.

Plate 29   Aquatint of Lake in Northwick Park by the Hon. Anne Rushout, c. 1805.

Plate 30   Meet of Fox-hounds in front of Northwick Park, showing picture gallery on right.

Plate 31 Northwick Park Picture Gallery, 1954. (*Photograph by courtesy of Christies*)

Plate 32   Church and Vicarage, 1956. (*Photograph by courtesy of P. Pritchard*)

Plate 33 Henry Sale.
(verger; 1863-1953)

Plate 34
Charles Wilcox
of Rose Row sowing
with a fiddle.

Plate 35　Party in Northwick Institute, 1931. (*Photograph by courtesy of Butt Studio*)

Plate 36　Bowling Club supper. From left, Major Cox, Mrs F. Davey, Mr F. Davey, Mr H. E. Mc.L. Icely, Miss P. Cox, Miss Danilina, Mr H. Franklin and Mr. H. Butler

of promoting His Service and Glory . . . These, we may suppose, are commonly the Motives, that lead Men on so boldly to take upon them this most Aweful and Tremendous Function."

In July 1712 he was selected to preach the Act Sermon before the University of Oxford, having that day been admitted to the degree of Doctor of Divinity, Political feeling was running high just then, not least in Tory Oxford, Saunders chose as his subject, "The Divine Authority and Influence of the Pastors of the Christian Church" and he had the courage to attack those of the clergy who mixed party politics with their pastoral duties.

> However profitable, or however fashionable, it may be to be bigot-ted and espous'd to Parties, I am one of those who think it our Unhappiness and our Shame, that it is so . . . To lay and compose, and not to animate unnecessary Contentions, is, I think, the proper part for those who are the Messengers, are the Agents, of the Prince of Peace . . . May all of us in our Parochial Cures be faithful in the Performance of what we have undertaken. May we at all times remember the Dignity of our Functions, and how distinguish-ing that Purity and Holiness ought to be, which is expected in such who are the Embassadors of the great God. May we be diligent in preaching, catechizing and exhorting, both in public and in private. May we shew that Sincerity in our Reproofs, as will make it appear that we are set above Secular Views, are above Flattery and Dissimulation, and so steady as not to recede from our Duty by Compliance with Sinners of the highest Quality.

These were brave, as well as edifying, words for a country clergyman to address to that presumably learned, often world-ly, and almost wholly clerical congregation.

He was in demand as a preacher before other public authori-ties. In 1720 he preached the Assize Sermon at Welshpool, and in December 1721 on a day appointed as a national fast in thank-fulness for the escape from the epidemic of bubonic plague which that year had raged on the continent, he preached before the House of Commons in St. Margaret's, Westminster. Sir John Rushout, then member for Malmesbury, no doubt suggested his name to the Speaker. His discourse on "the Dangers of abus-ing the Divine Blessings, shewing that National Calamities are the sure Consequences of Publick Iniquities" was marked by his usual grave sincerity and plain speaking. This visit to the capital seems to have moved him to enter into the Burials register when he got home notes, as always in Latin, on two public events—the dissolution of the Septennial Parliament "votorum omnium suffragiis" and the "negotium vulgo dictum South Sea." It also seems to have impaired his health, as will appear later in this chapter.

All his entries in the registers are as methodical as they are learned. Two of his earliest were of the burials of Lady Arabella Rushout and of her husband, Sir James, who died within two months of each other—recalling the almost simultaneous deaths of the first Sir James and his wife only eight years before. And, to fill up the cup of this family's misfortune, the death of their son, a third Sir James, followed in 1711, only six years later. He was only ten years old.

This brought the title and the property at Northwick and Harrow to John, the boy's uncle, (*Plate* 14), then aged 26. For the next 14 years he made his home at Harrow, leaving the mansion at Northwick, then apparently falling into disrepair, to his sister Elizabeth—she must have earlier acted as guardian of their young nephew. Sir John does seem to have paid occasional visits to Northwick, however, and it is said that Addison was a frequent guest there.[4] We get a glimpse of Mistress Elizabeth Rushout in a lease of 1726, by which she handed to Sir John, who was clearly thinking of residence at Northwick at last, "a Stable and Coach-house at Blockley Church Yard Gate." This was the gate on what is now the Post Office square and Elizabeth had had the stable and coach house built there in 1709—in which to put up the horses and the family coach during the time of service in church. Late in the 19th century these buildings became the stables of the Bell Inn, and they later housed the fire engine, when Blockley had its own volunteer brigade. In 1729, being then aged 44, Sir John Rushout married Lady Anne Compton, the daughter of the Earl of Northampton, a political colleague of his, and Northwick became their usual home. The house was largely reconstructed to designs by Lord Burlington soon after this.

Sir John Rushout's political activities are hardly relevant to the history of Blockley, but they have their background interest. He sat continuously in the House of Commons for over half a century, ending as 'Father of the House.' As a young man he was concerned in at least two duels. He was a Whig, but strongly opposed to Sir Robert Walpole—which earned him some waspish epithets in Horace Walpole's letters,[5] of which 'old dishcloth' was a breezy example! He served for a year (1743–44) in the lucrative office of Treasurer of the Navy, as a member of Carteret's administration, and even Walpole found no fault in him there. He lived to be 91, and Nash, the historian of Worcestershire, who visited him at Northwick a year before his death, wrote that "his memory, good humour and politeness being in their full bloom, old age seemed to him rather an ornament than a burden." Dr. Saunders can have known him only in his earlier and wilder years and may conceivably have had him at the back of his mind when, in the sermon of 1712 already quoted, he spoke of the duty of the clergy to make no exception of 'sinners of the highest quality' in their reproof of backsliders. But for the later vicars and the parish Sir John must have been an honoured figure, as he was over the county.

Two inventories[6] of household contents made after the deaths of the respective owners help towards a picture of what Dr. Saunders must have seen when he visited his parishioners. One of them, taken at Northwick in 1705, reflects an opulence which is not representative. The others, listing the goods and chattels of Robert Warner in 1709 and Sarah Warner, his widow, in 1713 may stand for the more comfortable of the ordinary households.

Robert Warner of Blockley[7]—he must be distinguished from the Draycott Warners, whose attitude to the established church cannot have been to Dr. Saunders's taste—was a dyer, who was tenant of the fulling mill known as French Mill on the Blockley Brook.[8] He was also, like all the more prosperous parishioners, a farmer holding lands in the common fields and pasture rights for his beasts. His goods therefore fell into several categories:

Personal and household goods—

Wearing apparel and money in his purse Two	£12
Joynt Bedsteeds and Bedding thereto belonging, two Chests, one hanging Press	£10
One Bedsteed, two Beds with all Sheets and Blankets.	£10

Two little Tables two Joynt Chaires five Joyn
Stooles one little Cupboard one Clock one Gun
two Pistols two Spits one pair of Andirons Fire
Shovels and Tongs with other Lumber   £5
Eight Chaires one Table   £1
Materials for Dyeing—
Two parcells of Archill (*a lichen*)
About two hundred weight of black Madder
Thirty pounds of Indigo
                etc. etc.   Total value   £119

Farming Items—

In Barley Wheat and Pulse	£13
Six Cowes, one Heifer, two Calves	£19
Three Horses with their Tackle to them	£17
Hay in the Rickyard	£10
Hay and Grass in the Park Ground	£10
Forty Sheep and Lambs	£12
Four Piggs	£2–10s.
Muck in the Yard	£1
Timber under a Hovel	£5
The Timber in the Orchard	£1–16s.
and at the Saw Pitt	£8
All the boards and Planks in the Kalendar house and dwelling house	£6
Timber in the Mill pond	£10
Three hundred of Cheese	£2–14s.
The Pewter	£3
The Brass	£2–10s.
Nine Barrels one Messfat one Tub one Cheese press with all other Lumber)	£3
Debts owing upon Bond and Book	£128–3s.–1d.
Desperate Debts	£40
The Total	£465–0s.–1d.

Between the Rushout opulence and the yeoman's sufficiency
of Robert Warner there was in the parish, and always strong in
support of Dr. Saunders, that group of smaller landed proprietors earlier mentioned—the Carters at Hither Upton Wold, the
Martyns at Far Upton Wold, the Crofts of the hamlet of North-

wick and others. With their generous help Erasmus Saunders started the charities, which have notably benefited generations of Blockley people, by himself building the village school, today used as a county library, which is just inside the north gate of the churchyard. That was in 1713 and the top half of the Latin inscription on the north front of the building records the gift.

Erasmus Saunders S.T.P. Vicarius Ecclesiae
Scholam condidit A.S. MDCCXIII

There would seem to have been an earlier school building which this new one replaced. In his will,[9] drawn up in 1723, Saunders included this clause:

Item, I confirm the Grant I have already made of the new School-house built in Blockley to be a Charity School for the Use of the said Town and Parish of Blockley for ever, upon condition that according to the Agreement with the Right Reverend William Lord Bishop of Worcester the old School-house shall remain for the Use and Benefit of the Vicars of Blockley for ever.[1]

The old school had already attracted a benefaction. In 1711 Mrs Jane Croft of Northwick—perhaps residing in the house now called Wellacres—died and by her will devised the yearly sum of £3 10s. "charged on all my enclosed grounds called Broadnams situate in Northwick" to be disposed of by the vicars and churchwardens for ever "for the cloathing of six poor children yearly that are taught in the Charity School lately erected . . . and for the buying of Bibles for the said poor children.'[10]

Another bequest must have been at Dr. Saunders's disposal for the maintenance of the old school. Mrs Mary Carter of Hither Upton Wold died in 1700 leaving £100 to be invested and its annual interest to be laid out "for teaching poor children at Blockley and for buying books for the poor." As she mentioned no school, we may assume that the old school did not exist at that date. Though the principal sum of this bequest was realised by the parish officers with the consent of the parish in 1741 and then used to build the parish workhouse, an annual payment of £4, equivalent to the original interest on the investment, was made towards the school by the churchwardens until the 1950's, when the local educational authority became responsible for its maintenance.

Two other bequests added to the new school's endowments in Dr. Saunders's time. Francis Martyn of Far Upton Wold in 1713 left £100, but the sum seems never to have been invested and an annual sum equivalent to the interest was paid by descendants of Francis Martyn instead. The charity lapsed altogether long ago. In 1723 Goddard Carter of Hither Upton Wold, son of the Mary Carter above-mentioned, charged his estate there for ever with the duty of providing £10 a year "to teach poor children living in the parish of Blockley to read, write and something of arithmetick." Sir John Rushout became liable for this payment when he bought Upton Wold in 1765, and his descendants after him.

To these educational charities must be added two more, also established in Dr. Saunders's time, for the benefit of the poor of the parish. Richard Perkins in 1710 bequeathed £400 to be invested in land, the yearly rent from which was to be laid out "in clothing poor, old, impotent, industrious and honest people, who regularly attend the service of God in the parish church of Blockley." Just over £380 of this was spent in the purchase of two closes of land in Mickleton. The odd £20 was left with the Court of Chancery and never used for the benefit of Blockley. Canon Houghton, as vicar, made an attempt to recover this sum with the accrued interest in or about 1900, but without success. The other bequest was a further charge of £10 on the Upton Wold estate made in the will of Goddard Carter in 1721 "for clothing the poorest old people of the parish of Blockley."

Some of the credit for this remarkable flow of charity may fairly go to the vicar who set the example. A stone on the wall of the Vicarage garden beside what was obviously a gateway into the churchyard—its fitting on which the gate used to swing was removed from the wall only a dozen or so years ago—bears the inscription 'Mors Ianua Vitae E. S. 1716' (Death the Gateway to Life. E.S.) His initials are also carved on the panelling of the north wall of the chancel, which must have served as the backing of the vicarage pew which was no doubt his gift to the church. The pulpit, too, may perhaps be of his time—the wall just there suggests that there may once have been a two- or three-decker of which the present pulpit once formed the top stage. And it is not impossible that he may have to share with his church officers responsibility for the plaster ceiling of the nave. That he bore the cost of the first two of these seems to be indicated by his initials. It is at least appropriate that the wall tablet which his son Erasmus[11] erected to his memory in 1771 should stand above the pulpit. The claim on it that "by the piety as well of his life as writings he endeavoured to promote religion and virtue", seems amply justified by all that we know of him.

This inscription adds that "by his prudence in secular affairs he improved the value of this living." That he was a good man of business is indeed suggested by many of the documents in his hand which have survived. His entries in the parish registers are a model and they include a list of the rectors and vicars of Blockley as compiled by his distinguished antiquarian friend, Brown Willis. His beating of the bounds of the parish, already recorded in these pages, is further evidence of a similar kind. There exists in his hand a terrier of church lands in Blockley as they stood in 1714 which shows eleven 'lands' or arable strips in the common fields of Draycott and a meadow, shared with Ebrington parish, close by. Which, if any, of these was added to the resources of the church by Saunders's prudence, we cannot say.

His visit to London and the sermon he preached before the House of Common in December 1721 have already been recorded This winter journey seems to have affected his health. He wrote from Blockley in late February to another antiquarian friend, Bishop Kennett of Peterborough:

My Hon^d and Good Lord,

I humbly beg pardon that in all this time I have not sent y^r L^{dp} the Account of Impropriations wch I promised, but having had a fit of Illness that lasted ab^t six weeks since I came from London that made me listless to the doing of anything, Y^r L^{dps} Goodness therefore will, I hope, excuse me for that Omission.

(*There follows a list of impropriated benefices in the dioceses of St David's and Hereford*).

The late B^p Lloyd of Worcest^r was a considerable Benefactor to severall Vicaridges of which mine is one and enjoys an Improvem^t of near 30^1 by virtue of his donation.[12]

There is some evidence of a loss of grip even before this date, for the church tower was again giving serious cause for concern and Dr. Saunders seems to have done nothing about it. In 1719 the churchwardens reported at the visitation that "We present that the Tower of the Church is out of Repair." In 1721 and 1722 they repeat the complaint. Two years later the bishop, John Hough (the man who had been elected President of Magdalen College in defiance of James II), himself visited Blockley on his way to Oxford. While there he scribbled a note, which has survived in the diocesan records, to his secretary at Hartlebury Castle:

> In the Tower of Blockley Church is a very dangerous Settle and they take no care. I doubt, of it. Pray let an Order be drawn—'Whereas Information has been given . . . It is therefore ordered that the Churchwardens do immediately take advice of skillfull workmen and report to the Court.' 'Tis said when it falls it will break down a great part of the Body of the Ch. wch perhaps may be prevented by a timely taking it down.

Before action could be taken Erasmus Saunders had died. He seems to have left the care of the parish to a relative, Francis Saunders, as curate, and it was while he was staying with Edward Lloyd, his wife's brother, at Aberbechan, Montgomeryshire, that he died of apoplexy. He was buried in St. Mary's Church, Shrewsbury, on 5 June 1724. In a long Latin inscription on his tomb there it is claimed that in Blockley "in his ministrations and care of souls he was faithful, unwearied and prosperous." Few of the country clergy of the time can have better deserved that epitaph.

His will, drawn up fifteen months before his death but even then mentioning his 'frailty,' suggests a piety which is far more than a matter of testamentary phrasing. "I wish to set my house and the little affairs I have in the world in the best order I can . . . I desire that my Body may be buried in a Christian manner. I would rest my Ashes, if my Wife pleases, near the place where she intends to have hers laid." He leaves small charities for the poor of Moreton Henmarsh as well as of Blockley. To his sons he left a surprising amount of property, Erasmus, the eldest inherited an estate which his father had bought in the parish of Ashchurch, near Tewkesbury: the other four—William, Edward, Thomas and Samuel Tobias shared the freehold property which he had acquired in Blockley parish. This was Walgroves which included a house (now the post office), its grounds and a mill, and a further score of houses or cottages, some adjacent to the Warren, some near the "Town Elm," "two houses, a Barn and Gardens below the Church Yard Hill" (which surely must be the top pair of the Lower Street row), together with lands in the open fields and the stewardship of the fairs. We shall see that the name of Saunders lived on in the parish as a result of these bequests.

Michael Biddulph, Vicar 1724-28

He and three vicars who followed him served as chaplains of Bishop Hough, who used the benefices of Blockley and Ripple as convenient rewards for them. The registers show that the main work of the parish was done by curates—John Price, Benjamin Field, Joseph Williams and from 1753 to 1761, when he became vicar, Charles Selwyn.

The new church tower made the short ministry of Mr Biddulph memorable. The old tower was taken down in the summer of 1725. In November of that year the vicar and churchwardens signed a contract with Thomas Woodward the Elder, mason of Chipping Campden, whereby the latter agreed:

> in consideration of the payment of Five Hundred Pounds of Lawfull Money of Great Britain before the four and twentieth day of June 1727 in the best and most compleat workmanlike manner well and substantially to erect, build and sett up a new Tower according to the platformes (*ground-plans*) draughts and schemes hereunto annexed, the foundations thereof to be sunk to such depth, the walls to be made to such thickness, and the buttresses likewise. The whole outside of the Tower to be built with good, new and sound freestone, and neatly done with good axe work, and sett in the best workmanlike manner in the same kind of building as the new Church Porch . . .[15]

Comparison of the tower doorway with that of Durant's south porch will show how faithfully Woodward carried out that last undertaking. His belfry windows are copies of those in the tower of Campden Church. He seems to have left the lower part of the old tower's newel stairway in place. Its six bells, dating from the time of Durant and Scattergood, were rehung in the new tower in 1728, in time for the coronation of King George II—when the ringers got 1s. 6d. worth of ale for their loyal greetings.

William Byrche, Ll.D, Vicar 1728-30

Well qualified as an ecclesiastical lawyer, his short stay in Blockley—if ever he did stay, for as chaplain to the bishop he probably lived in Hartlebury Castle—has left no trace. Bishop Hough soon made him Chancellor of the diocese, whereupon he moved to the living of Fladbury.

Edward Wheeler, Vicar 1730-42

Two successive curates, John Price and Benjamin Field, presumably cared for the parish, while he served the bishop as domestic chaplain. But two additions to the church fabric were made in his time. The first was a gallery stretching across the whole of the west end of the building, and involving the blocking up of a mediaeval, perhaps 14th century, window at the west end of the north aisle. The gallery was occupied during service mainly by school children, with musicians and singers in the front seats.

The other addition was the parapet over the south wall of the chancel. It bears the much weathered inscription, "This Battlement over ye Chancel was erected at ye voluntary expense of ye Honble Colonel Hunt, Anno D^{ni} 1738". His death shortly after marks the end of his family's long tenure of the Old Rectory—the Manor House today.

Richard Congreve, Vicar 1742-61

He served Bishop Maddox as chaplain. That he was often absent from his Blockley parish is obvious from a note he made in the Burials register: "From September 24 1743 to Lady Day following Mr Field made few or no entries of Burials, and these seven now made are from the Informations of the Churchwardens." Mr Field shortly after left the parish, and his successor as curate was impeccable in his keeping of the registers. He died in 1753, and was succeeded by Charles Jasper Selwyn, who, after serving for eight years as curate and marrying his vicar's daughter, was himself to become vicar, and a notable one, in 1761.

[1] Bodleian Library, Ashmole 1817 A.

[2] Presumably Edmund Gibson's edition of *Britannia*.

[3] Ed. David Robertson (W.H.S. 1903).

[4] Addison was his colleague as M.P. for Malmesbury.

[5] Ed. Toynbee (1903): i. 241, 394, ii. 175, iv. 134, v. 399.

[6] The Northwick inventory is among N.P. at Worcester and was published in Evesham *Journal* of 18 May 1940 and following issues. The Warner inventory is in the Birmingham Public Library.

[7] He was churchwarden in 1686 and 1687.

[8] Lease of 1684 among N.P.

[9] A copy of the will is in N.P.

[10] Soden 75.

[11] He was vicar of St Martin-in-the-Fields.

[12] B.M., Lansdowne MSS 988.

[13] The contract is in N.P. For the Woodwards, master builders of Campden, see *Architectural Review*, March 1948.

Some Blockley Families & Their Links

note S.T. = Silk Throwster

Erasmus Saunders D.D.
Vicar of Blockley
d. 1724

Henry Whatcott
S.T. d. 1718

Maria W.   Giles W.
           S.T.

Samuel Knight m. 1714
S.T.
from Campden

William Saunders
Vicar of Thornby

Edward Saunders
see Enclosure Award

John Robinson
of Gloucestershire, Merchant
fl.c. 1750

James Smith
m. Sarah Checkley
of Aulersperry, Northants.

Joseph Ayston m. Martha Knight
S.T. from 1747 to 1781
originally from Southwark

Ann m. 1743
Thos. Spilsbury

A daughter
Samuel Spilsbury

Saml Spilsbury
S.T.

Alicia
m. Smith
of Stratford-le-Bow

Helen S.
m. John Wade
farmer of Aldighland

Philip Robinson

Elisha Smith
Baptist Minister & Grocer &c.
1754 - 1819

Caroline S.
m.
Thos. Smith
of Campden

Thos. Ayston
S.T. d. 1811

Caroline, Sarah
married in turn to
Edward Banbury
S.T. Colebrook Mill

C. Edwin Smith
S.T. Mill Close

Robert Smith
m. Miss Payne

Very Revd. Dr. Payne-Smith
Dean of Canterbury

Edward Robinson
of Overbury Paper Mill
b. 1791

Maria S.
b. 1793

m.

Crescens S.
1789 - 1836
S.T. m. Maria Malpas
of Worcester

James Smith
1792 - 1862
S.T. m. Esther Cannon
of London

Other Issue

Hannah
m.
Thos. Higgins
Builder & Churchwarden

Thos. B. Higgins
Builder fl. 1860

George Cannon Smith
1819 - 1888
S.T. m. Maria Horne
of Moreton in Marsh

Thomas Horne Smith
1863 - 1946

Elisha Smith Robinson
Alfred Robinson
Joint Founders of E.S. & A. Robinson
of Bristol, Paper Manufacturers

Maria — Martha
married in turn to
Joseph Reynolds
of Slaughter

R.B. Belcher
1816 - 1901

James S.
b. 1857

George Cannon Smith
b. 1860

Esther Elizabeth
m. Rev. James Dunn,
Baptist Minister

A daughter
m. —— Knight

Rebecca Mary
m. Wm. Fairfield

Edward Robinson
Donor of the Village Hall
1925

J.V. Reynolds, J.P.
of Rapsford

J.W. Reynolds

Ellen R. m. Charles Belcher

Edward Belcher

Richard Belcher
Printer

Charlotte E.
Belcher

Agnes
m. Arthur
Joyner

Olive
d. 1968
m. —— Amolison

Wm. H. Fairfield   Rifka Mary

Sir Foster
Robinson

Col. H.G.K.
Robinson

Katherine
Robinson

E.S.G.
Robinson

All Benefactors, St. George's Hall, 1957

Charles Belcher
Sculptor

Agnes Joyner
b. 1890

Esther
m. A. Lewis

CHAPTER TEN

Georgian Blockley: Silk Mills & Enclosures

1725-1830

OUTWARDLY THESE WERE years of growth and fairly wide-spread prosperity, though with ominous stirrings in the social and economic structure of the nation in the later decades, which had their repercussions in our parish.

THE SILK MILLS

The beginnings of the silk-throwing industry in Blockley under Henry Whatcott near the end of the 17th century have been described on an earlier page.[1] The trade prospered, and by 1824 when it reached its peak, there were eight mills along the Blockley Brook and its Cole Brook tributary, employing some 300 women and children on the factory floors, and up to 3000 working in their homes within a ten mile radius of the village. That an average sum of £400 a week was then being paid in wages to these workers is proof enough of the importance of the industry in the life of the Blockley folk of this period. The trade had, no doubt, its ups and downs, Changes in women's fashions,[2] and competition from the superior silk ribbons from France smuggled across the Channel despite the protective ban on such imports, were bound to have some effect on the demands made by the Coventry weavers on the Blockley throwsters. But up to 1824 the mills grew steadily in number.[3]

Henry Whatcott's original mill passed in 1718 to his son Giles. It remained in his descendants' hands till near the end of the century—a rental of the manor in 1795 records Henry Whatcott as the occupier of a silk mill on ground called Gaunts and Sneevelands, names which repeat those of the first Henry's tenement.[4] But the family was then dying out and must have been hit hard by two deaths in 1791, when the burials were recorded of "Edward Whatcott aged 19 drowned by accident" and "George Whatcott junior aged 41." By the turn of the century Martin Westmacott had taken over the Whatcott mill. When Eyre compiled his census of the parish in 1827 he found only one bearer of the old name left, that of "George Whatcott, labourer."

But the Whatcott strain was not confined to that first mill. Henry Whatcott's daughter Maria married Samuel Knight of Campden in 1714. He shortly after built a silk mill on the Cole Brook in what was then known as the Lord's Orchard. Its shell survives today as part of the range of houses called Mill Close. He later, when its long occupation by the Hunt family ended, took up residence in the Manor House, which thenceforward was to house the owners of the mill so long as the silk trade in Blockley lasted.

Samuel Knight had three daughters, each of whom made marriages of significance in our story. The eldest, Martha, married a newcomer to Blockley, Joseph Peyton, who had been a stationer in Southwark. He, with Edward Whatcott as partner, a grandson of the original Henry, took a long lease on the Coney-gree, the rising ground behind the house, the post-office of today, which became his dwelling house. This ground contained a cluster of springs which there united to form the Cole Brook, on which there already stood a fulling mill. This was converted by the two partners into a silk throwing mill in 1747[5]—making a third in this sequence of dynastic throwstership. It survives today, vastly changed, as the pumping station.

The Coneygree formed part of the ancient tenement of the manor known as Walgroves from the family which had held it since the 15th century. The death in 1712 of Thomas Walgrove, the last of the line, led to its break-up. The family mansion became the Bell Inn and a most notable feature in the life of the village. The rest of the property was bought, as freehold, by the vicar, Dr. Saunders, and it was from his second son, William, that Joseph Peyton leased the Coneygree and his mill. The two men were brothers-in-law, William Saunders having married another of the Knight sisters.

The third sister married another newcomer to the parish, Samuel Spilsbury. He succeeded to his father-in-law's mill in the Lord's Orchard and to his home in the Manor House, and was was followed in both by his own son, also named Samuel. It would seem, though positive evidence is lacking, that Knight's other son-in-law, Joseph Peyton of the Coneygree Mill also took a share in these properties, though without moving into them. Peyton died in 1761 after a fall from his horse, leaving his son Thomas and his daughter Martha, still young children, as his principal heirs, while his partner, Edward Whatcott continued to run the mill till his death in 1772. Thomas Peyton must then have taken charge. He, in 1785, handed over the mill-house (today's post office) to his sister Martha on her marriage to Elisha Smith, the Baptist minister who is the subject of a later chapter, and moved to the Manor House to join his cousin Spilsbury—and perhaps to share with him in the ownership of the Knight mill. Thomas Peyton and Samuel Spilsbury died within a few months of each other (1810–11), and were succeeded in both mill and Manor House by Crescens Smith, the elder son of Elisha and Martha—and a great-grandson of the original Henry Whatcott!

In following up the dynastic tradition from Henry Whatcott, we have done some chronological injustice to the Franklins, for it is on record that in 1747, the year when the Coneygree mill was opened, a Franklin was already in the business. In that year "John Franklin junior, Silk Throwster" signed a bond for £40 indemnifying the parish officers against any risk of his failing to meet certain liabilities. That seems to prove that the Franklin mill was the third in order of foundation. Its location is something of a puzzle, but there is evidence that it was perhaps on the Blockley Brook closely adjoining the original Whatcott mill. A deed in the Gloucestershire record office, dated 1763, is concerned with a loan raised by "Edward Franklin of Blockley, Silk Throwster" on the security of a water mill situated on ground called Grants (which we may take to be a clerical error for Gaunts) and Cotland called Sneevelands. The deed further states that this property was bounded on the east by Whatcott's Close, on the west by Collier's Close (on which a century later Admiral Collier was to build Blockley's first police station) and on the north by "The Green" on which the statute (fair) was annually held on Michaelmas Day for hiring Servants. The site is obviously the Blockley Court of today, for Gaunts and Sneevelands are the names locating Henry Whatcott's mill.[6] It may be that the western block of Blockley Court stands on the foundations of this Franklin mill. Tradition in the village had it that each of the blocks had a water-wheel and that one of them either never worked or worked for a short time only—and it is likely enough that the head of water cannot have been equal to the demand on it from two wheels so closely sited.

Whatever the facts about this may be, the Franklins certainly moved some time after 1763 to another site, and there is ground for thinking that it may have been to the Coneygree—perhaps when Thomas Peyton left the mill house there in 1785. The evidence for this is contained in the title deeds to the whole property, mill and mill-house, when James Smith, the second son of Elisha and Martha, acquired the freehold in or about 1830. This document (now among the Northwick papers) reads, ". . . also all that Silk Throwing Mill . . . lying near the said Messuage (*now the post office*) formerly in the possession of John Gibbs, afterwards of John Franklin, and then of Henry Franklin." Doubtless the Coneygree was the scene of the drowning of Charles, another of John Franklin's sons, in 1781. Henry Franklin still held the mill when Eyre took his census in 1827.

Another of John Franklin's children, Lucy, through her marriage in 1800 to William Russell, formerly of Broadway, takes this story to yet another of the silk mills, part of which survives today in the house we know as Malvern Mill. We do not know when the Russell Mill was first built—or by whom. It may possibly have been founded by the Robert Strong, silk throwster, whose burial is recorded at the age of 58 in 1780. Lucy Russell was widowed early in the 1820's, but continued to operate the mill for a score of years. It is to her that the village owes the Russell Spring "from the living rock" by the road side opposite her mill.

Two more silk mills founded within this period remain to be

recorded. The earlier of the two was probably Stanley's mill at Snugborough—subsequently named Sleepy Hollow, since the actor Fred Storey used it as the location for filming a version of Washington Irving's *Rip van Winkle*. Robert Stanley, of an old Blockley family, was its owner in 1820, and Richard (his son?) when Eyre wrote in 1827. Its name today is The Old Silk Mill.

The other can be dated more exactly. It was Stratton's mill on the Cole Brook a short way before it flows into the main stream. All that remains of the mill today is a remnant of the footings of the structure on part of the lawn of Colebrook House, the lawn being, in fact, the filled-in site of the former mill pool. The mill and its mill-house (now, much enlarged, Colebrook House) occupied part of the ancient tenement called Slatters, of which Lower Brook House, the modern name, was the dwelling house. In the entry about Slatters in the rental of the manor taken in 1795[7] there is no mention of a mill, but a note on this added in 1799 shows that "a Messuage, Silk Mills and four tenements" covering some two acres of the Slatters ground were then in being. Anthony Stratton, new to the village, was the throwster, and he was succeeded in 1811 by his son, John, in 1811. But John Stratton did not last long—two disreputable entries about him in the parish records may have had something to do with this—and in 1817 he sold the lease to Edward Banbury, who also had a mill at Winchcombe and was to play a large part in the life of Blockley for many years.

The silk industry in Blockley reached its highest point of prosperity in the early 1820's.[8] But 1825 brought a sudden check. The prohibition of imports of silk from France was suspended, as part of Huskisson's policy of freer trade. The British producers were henceforth protected by no more than an import duty of 30% *ad valorem*—with the result that in Blockley piece wages fell from 16d. for a pound of spun silk thread to 12d. By 1850 three of the eight mills that were working in 1830 had closed. Far worse was to come.

THE LAND AND THE ENCLOSURES

The silk mills and the industrial problems which they involved were obviously beyond the scope of the manorial organisation—

and hastened its replacement by the newer type of local government, which since Tudor times, and especially since the passing of the great Poor Law of 1600, had been developing over the country. The county magistrates in their Quarter and Petty sessions worked, under this system, with the parish vestries and their elected officers in the manner illustrated in the following chapter. But in Blockley, apart from Aston Magna, one vital part of the daily life of the people remained under manorial regulation till 1773—the land and its cultivation under the ancient communal system. A look must now be taken at the working of the ancient system in its last decades in Blockley. The court rolls give us the picture.

The court baron met usually in November. By some accident the actual scrap of paper on which the summons to attend was scrawled by the bailiff in 1755 has survived. It was obviously copied from an official specimen handed down from year to year, for its correct terminology could never be the work of so unready a writer as Joseph Brown, a cobbler by trade, plainly was.

NOTICE is hereby given to all Tenants and Inhaibitants that the Court Leet and Court Baron of the Right Reverend Father in God Isaac by Divine Permission Lord Bishop of Worcester is to be holden for the Lord of the Mannor upon Tuesday the second day of Nov[r] next by ten of the Clock in the Forenoon at the Sign of the Crown in Blockley when the Tenants and all that owe Suit and Service are Required to attend.

JOS. BROWN Bayliff.

These extracts from the rolls entered by the lord's steward or bailiff who presided are typical of the 18th century order of things:

We order that on the first of June 1764 and not before every Landholder may stock the Cow Common with three Cows to the yardland and no more.

We order that all Landholders within the Manor shall before the first of May next ring their Pigs and nob their horned Cattle.

We present that the Mounds dividing the Common Fields and Common Pastures presented at the last Court as Deficient to keep the Cattle from straying have not been made good. To be amerced (*fined*) ten Shillings if not made good by Christmas.

Presented Nicholas ffletcher and Richard Baylis his man for reskewing a parcel of Sheep from the hands of Thomas Wheatcroft and William Harris who were driving them to the Pound, which we mearce them the some of six shillings and eight pence, that is to say six shillings the Master and eight pence the Man.

We present Thomas Wigget for not Scouring a Ditch at Maphale, Amerced two pence, and one Shilling if not put right in a Month.

Thomas Martin of Paxford hath dug up the Highway to Hanging Aston by carrying away Gravel. To fill in and amerced twenty shillings if not done at once.

We order a View to be made by the Jury before March next in the Common Field of Blockley to set out each persons Land and to set up meer Stones at the butt ends of the Lands of each person with the two initial Letters of the Owners name on such meer Stones. Owners not setting up such Stones before the first of May to be pained thirty shillings.

This last order arose out of the difficulty caused by the frequent poaching of land during the ploughing season. This was easy because the strips were separated by no more than very narrow unploughed balks, and nothing could have been easier than a judicious manipulation of the meer-stone[9] to add verisimilitude to the intake. Sometimes mischief or malice led to more wholesale trouble. The court of 1750 reported:

Part of the Meer Stones have been dug up by Persons unknown to us, and although diligent enquiry hath been made by the Steward in open Court in order to have the Offenders herein severely punished, they cant be discovered.

The Blockley landholders and the fieldsmen who had the duty of supervising the open fields no doubt said Amen with special fervour to the versicle "Cursed is he that removeth his neighbour's landmark" if they were present at the Commination Service on the following Ash-Wednesday!

We hark back a little, to 1675, and to personalities already met with in these pages, for a case before the court of disputed ownership of land held on long lease within the manor—Lopez leases, in this case, a constant source of trouble,[10] but complicated here by the memory of old unhappy political hatreds. The parties to the dispute which the court baron had to settle were Sir William Keyt of Ebrington, son of the gallant Captain Hastings Keyt, who, as his monument in Stow-on-the-Wold church records, was killed *ex parte regis* in the battle that ended the Civil War in the square just outside:[11] and Giles Collier, vicar of Blockley, ex-Puritan and Parliamentarian. The court roll gives in full the evidence of two aged men of the village, who quoted what their fathers had told them about these Lopez leases of the Armada year and about who owned this, that or the other strip in Winter-way or Barton Hill furlongs, which were the subjects of this dispute. They told of ale house gossip and of how Mr Thomas Walgrove "with his whimsicall tricks" tried to cajole them into testifying against the vicar. But both stoutly denied the claim of the alien Keyts—of Ebrington by rights—and the vicar won the day.

So did a descendant of his who appeared before the court in 1756 to answer a complaint of a different nature. Edward Collier lived in the house which then stood on the site, perhaps on the foundations, of the one today called Rodneys. A newcomer to the village, Colonel Dickens, had lately taken possession of the adjoining Porch House.[12] The story is given in the court roll:

> Complaint made by Melchior Guy Dickens against Mr Collier of this Manor that he had stopped an old underground Drain of the said Mr Dickens running through the yard of Mr Collier, and mounding had been erected between Mr Dickens Garden and Mr Colliers Yard. The Jury took a View this day and adjudge that the said Drain is not an old and accustomed Drain, but that it was made at the time Mrs Martin erected a Brew-house adjoining to Mr Dickens house, and we adjudge that the Wall complained of stands on the old and accustomed Foundation.

So once again the stranger in the case came off second-best!

THE BLOCKLEY ENCLOSURE ACTS

The open field system came to an end in Aston Magna in 1733 and in the rest of Blockley parish in 1773—and with it ended all but a remnant of the business of the manorial court. Much of the land had long before been "made several"—that is, had been fenced off from the "commonable" fields, meadows and pastures of the manor and developed into separate compact farms. Such were the larger "old enclosures" listed in the Blockley enclosure award: "the two Upton Olds, Stapenhill, Blockley Warren, Blockley Downs and Blockley Park." But there still remained commonable and unenclosed land to the extent of 2300 acres in Blockley, Draycott, and Paxford, and 900 acres in Aston Magna. That it was inefficiently farmed under the ancient communal system has perhaps become clear from the court rolls just quoted. The principal land holders in the parish accordingly united to promote parliamentary legislation for the compulsory enclosure of these commonable acres. The process involved a detailed professional survey, made under the supervision of three commissioners, based on which allotments were to be made which should, "Quantity, Quality and Situation considered," be "contiguously laid" to form compact holdings equivalent in value to the hitherto scattered holdings of the freeholders or long leaseholders concerned. The allotments of land carried with them responsibility for fencing the compacted holdings. This involved in our area dry walling on the limestone and 'mounding' on the clay—the latter being set with the hedgerow plants which have so enriched the countryside since the open field centuries. The enclosure awards also defined the routes and widths of the public roads, bridle roads and footpaths within the parish, and quarry sites providing material for their maintenance.

The Aston Magna award of 1733 divided the commonable acres among five owners. Richard Freeman of Batsford received 60% of the land awarded, stretching on either side of the road to Batsford from the borders of Draycott to those of Dorn, as the equivalent of his dispersed yardlands and his long lease from the bishop of the rectorial tithe of Aston Magna. Elizabeth Robins came second with some 18%, adjoining the Fosseway. Elizabeth Wise took 11% continuing southward from that allotment, and John Charles a similar share along the Knee Brook to the north. This was good land and in the mid-Victorian period of high farming the tenants who then tilled it prospered greatly, the Pursers, John Marshall, Joseph Camden among them. The ample tombs of some of them in Blockley churchyard bear witness to that.

The commonable lands of the rest of the parish were enclosed just forty years later. By far the greater part of the allotment to be held in severalty in the Blockley and Draycott areas went to Sir John Rushout. As lessee of the rectorial glebe and tithe, and of 14 yardlands within the manor, he was awarded just under 600 acres—some 60% of the total award. In Paxford, where representatives of the Fletcher family were still the principal tenants of the manor, Margaret and Elizabeth Fletcher received 70 acres as lessees of the rectorial tithe, and their cousin John Pott—a Londoner, who makes no other appearance in these annals—another 270 acres for the 10 yardlands he had inherited: the whole making up 40% of the Paxford allotment. All rents due to the bishop as lord of the manor before the award remained unaffected: the lease holders took their liabilities from their previously scattered holdings to their new compact ones with them, But the new holdings were freed from future liability for tithe, whether to the bishop as rector or to the vicar for his tithe of hay.

As compensation for this the vicar was allotted 47 acres in Blockley and 45 in Paxford. The other allottees in Blockley were Thomas Wilkes, who took 127 acres for his leases of Porch House and Slatters with 2¾ 'yards of land' that went with them. Edward Collier came next with 86 acres, partly taken out of Winterway and Dewberry Furlongs where they adjoined the homestall and grounds of his house (on the site of Rodneys) and partly on land which today forms part of Hailstone Farm. Edward Saunders, grandson of Erasmus, having inherited the 2 yardlands that went with Walgroves, was allotted land on the Hill above Town (Boveton Hill) just across the road from the Coneygreen. He also shared with Joseph Peyton's widow 66 acres in the former Lower Field, where now is Sheafhouse Farm. Only three others received allotments—and the ordinary villagers none at all, apart from their share in the improvements in the width and surface of the roads. The quarry set aside for their maintenance can still be seen at the corner behind Upper Terrace.

The other beneficiaries at Paxford were Thomas Roberts, whose family came second in standing only to that of the Fletcher clan, Thomas Heydon, William Newitt, who was later to become a strong supporter of Elisha Smith, and the two brothers, Francis and John Wheatcroft.

With all the land now concentrated in compact parcels and later divided into farms, as we now know them, the parish soon took on the look familiar to us today.

---

[1] p. 73

[2] Beads and feathers sometimes ousted ribbons in popular taste.

[3] The authority for this Blockley industry is *Blockley and the Silk Trade* by Norah Marshall, to whom I am indebted for much help.

[4] See p. 73

[5] Peyton took the oath of fealty at the court baron of that year.

[6] See p. 73

[7] Eccl. 43956.

[8] Marshall op. cit. 9. Martin Westmacott's detailed account is there given in full.

[9] Meer, from O.E. *gemaere*, means boundary.

[10] See p. 32

[11] See p. 60

[12] Porch House is not mentioned in the 1664 survey of the manor and was presumably built after that date. Elizabeth Martyn of Far Upton Wold occupied it during her widowhood from 1713 to 1747, when Col. Dickens took it over. He was still there in 1779, when his son, a clergyman, was buried in Blockley church. Soon after it passed to Thomas Wilkes. Rodneys seems to have been built by Edward Collier on the foundations of an older house which was once the property of his ancestor Giles Collier. His sons, Richard, vicar of Upton Snodsbury (very much *in absentia*) and Edward (later Sir Edward and Admiral, R.N.) shared it after his death in 1794. Sir Edward's last command was H.M.S. Rodney. (1749).

A COLLIER PEDIGREE

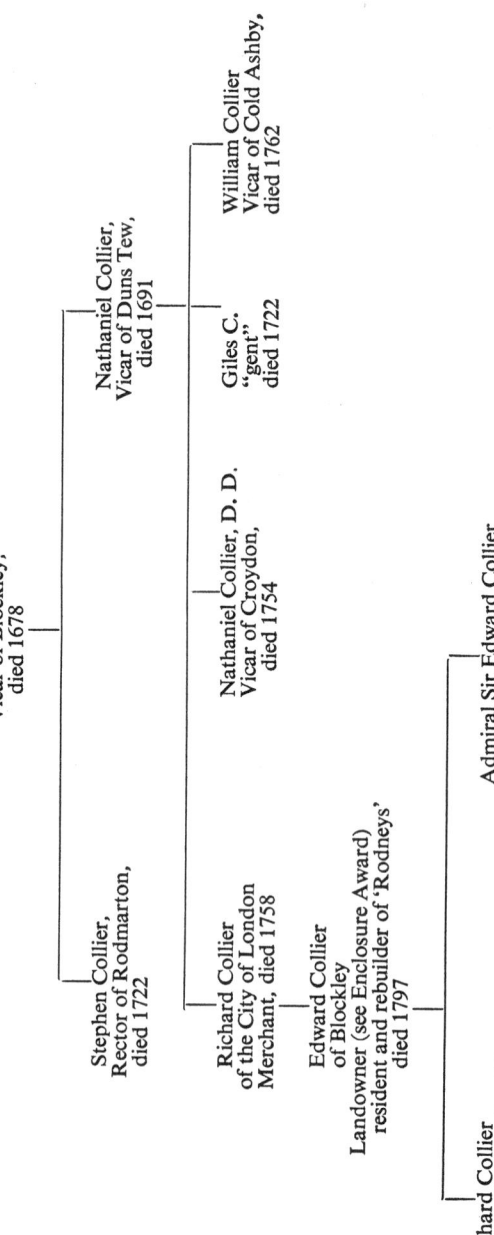

Giles Collier
Vicar of Blockley,
died 1678

Stephen Collier,
Rector of Rodmarton,
died 1722

Nathaniel Collier,
Vicar of Duns Tew,
died 1691

Richard Collier
of the City of London
Merchant, died 1758

Nathaniel Collier, D. D.
Vicar of Croydon,
died 1754

Giles C.
"gent",
died 1722

William Collier
Vicar of Cold Ashby,
died 1762

Edward Collier
of Blockley
Landowner (see Enclosure Award)
resident and rebuilder of 'Rodneys'
died 1797

Richard Collier
Vicar of Upton Snodsbury
but resident at Rodneys
1778–1828
died without issue

Admiral Sir Edward Collier
K.C.B., J.P., D.L
permanently in residence
at Rodneys from 1849
1763–1872
(for full details see
Soden, pp 97–99)
died without issue

CHAPTER ELEVEN

Georgian Blockley II: The State of the Parish

1725-1830

I T WAS STILL in a 'sequestered vale' and 'far from the madding crowd' that Blockley passed these changeful and resounding years of the nation's history. But they could not leave the parish quite unchanged in their passage. There must surely have been some increase in literacy following Dr. Saunders' foundation of the village school, some widening of outlook and of skill as the silk industry developed, some alteration in social and economic relationships with the passing of the communal system of agriculture. The French wars of the period may have had little direct impact apart from the militia service to which some in the parish were called, but their effect on prices, especially after the unsettlement caused by the enclosures, and on moral standards in general, is reflected in the local records.

The figures for population moved markedly upwards during the period. For three centuries after the Black Death growth in Blockley was certainly slow—perhaps to no more than 800 or so. But now a change began, and with growing interest in the subject statistics appear. Prattinton, the early 19th century Worcestershire antiquary, records a total of 288 families in the parish in 1757, and some 300 in 1776, both returns being sent by the clergy to the bishop. If we take the usual estimate of four persons to a household, that shows a growth from about 1150 to 1200 in the twenty years. Growth became more rapid in the next half-century, as the figures from the first four national censuses show:

1801	1569 persons
1811	1654 . . .
1821	1890 . . .
1831	2015 . . .

The census made in 1757 includes the figures (in terms of families) for each of the hamlets, as does the detailed census made in 1827 by the curate, William Thomas Eyre, for inclusion in his 'Guide'. Both are given in terms of persons in this table:

	1757		1827
Blockley (with Upton Wold)	688 (est.)		1300
Aston Magna	172	,,	251
The Ditchfords	20	,,	53
Dorn	16	,,	52
Draycott	108	,,	215
Northwick	36	,,	58
Paxford	112	,,	158

The increase in Draycott looks startling: the households in Dorn and the Ditchfords, with seven and six families respectively, were beyond average large.

The main reason for this increase was obviously the growth of the silk industry. But another was the rudimentary welfare service administered by the parish officers under the Poor Law system. A rich collection of their records has come down to us in the parish chest and these, together with the parish registers, reveal the energy which went into the humanitarian efforts, so typical of the latter half of the 18th century, of the Blockley clergy, churchwardens and overseers of the period. Two vicars presided over this social work, not only as chairmen of the vestry, but also as magistrates of the county bench.

Charles Jasper Selwyn, Vicar 1761–1794.

He came of a notable Gloucestershire family, was a member of Christ Church, Oxford, and had served as curate of Blockley under his father-in-law, Richard Congreve, as recorded on an earlier page.[1] He was a pluralist, being also incumbent of a small Gloucestershire living (which can rarely have seen him) and the holder of a prebendal stall in Salisbury cathedral. But he was officially recorded as[2] being "constantly" resident at Blockley—a term which implies only occasional absences—and his copious and careful entries in the registers and Poor Law papers reveal his care for the welfare of the parish. The foundation of the Blockley Benefit Society just two years after he became vicar must be ascribed to him. His monument in the chancel commemorates "his Christian zeal as a Minister, his unshaken integrity as a Magistrate and his exact observance of every social duty"—qualities borne out by all the evidence we have. It was his friend, Thomas Edwards Freeman of Batsford, who wrote this tribute, and it is in Batsford churchyard that he lies buried.

William Boughton, Vicar 1794–1831

A member of Oriel College, Oxford, and a magistrate, he was continuously resident in the parish and perhaps lived closer to his people than his more amply beneficed predecessor. He came to his ministry just as the long war against France and a period of lawlessness and lowered morality were beginning. It was a Nonconformist versifier who in 1888 looked back to the memory he left as a man "by all revered, by each one loved, by no one feared," and as one who used his money and his counsel to help his people. His curate, William Thomas Eyre records his great improvements to the vicarage, which seems to have taken its present shape in his time.

Under these two vicars the parish vestry and its officers administered the Poor Laws, as the following pages show.

Public health was not yet a matter with which the vestry directly concerned itself. It took the cholera epidemics of the mid-19th century to make sanitation a matter for urgent action But infant mortality and small-pox—the great killer, especially of the young—emerge from the parish registers as having been of deep concern to these two vicars. Of a total of 1380 burials recorded in the second half of the 18th century 304 were of infants—not far short of one in every four born. And small pox was a constant scourge.—till Jenner by his discovery of vaccination early in the 19th century cut the figures dramatically. That the clergy were in two minds about the drastic device of inoculation from diseased persons is obvious from the careful note made by Selwyn and Boughton as to whether death from small-pox followed inoculation or occurred in a natural way. The visitations from the disease were constant. It was often brought by 'travelling men' searching for work. Thus in 1769 a discharged soldier died of it on reaching the village and within three months there were eight other deaths from the disease. Vicar Selwyn recorded thirteen epidemics and buried 51 victims. The total incidence of the disease cannot be estimated, as we have no figures for those who recovered. Yet, in spite of all, those who could survive early childhood in 18th century Blockley had a good chance of reaching old age. The burials for the year 1808 illustrate the trend, though perhaps too emphatically: a total of 30 buried, of whom 13 were under ten, and 10 averaged seventy-seven years of age.

The problem of the poor and their relief was a constant care. Those who took to the roads and passed through the parish gave little trouble. The Churchwardens' Accounts, now unhappily missing but quoted by Soden, record payments of a shilling or less in 1719 to "Tho. Williams having a loss att sea," "to poore slaves," to "men taken by ye Turks"—Algerian pirates in the narrow seas, perhaps, if the tale was true—to "a poore wid. loss by fire," and so on. The real trouble arose when poor applicants claimed that they had a "settlement" in the parish and therefore a right to maintenance by it. The Elizabethan Poor Law of 1600 had imposed this duty on the parishes, and later legislation had required paupers to establish their right to this benefit by proving to a magistrate that they had a settlement in the parish through birth in it, or serving apprenticeship in it, or having served one of the parish offices, or paid the parish rate at some time. The magistrate's summary of the tale told him when the applicant was examined gives us a clear and unsentimental picture of what it could then mean to be poor. There is a special reason for beginning with the examination of a man who sought, not to remain in Blockley, but to leave it for the more raffish attractions of the metropolis. The special reason lies in his name, Richard Durant. Was he a descendant of George Durant, the vicar of Civil War times, or of his brother?[3] The fact that he had in his wanderings found his way to Blockley, perhaps for the fair, and decided to make a stay, suggests that he may have been. He was examined by Sir John Rushout and Vicar Selwyn, whose certificate was as follows-

4th Jan. 1779. The Examinant on his oath saith that he was born. . . in the Parish of St George's, Bloomsbury, that in the Year 1745 and for some Years before and after that time he rented a Publick House known by the name of the Prince of Oranges Head at the corner of White Gate Alley. . . in Spitalfields at ten pounds per ann. Rent. He thinks, whilst he occupied the said House, he did pay the Parish Rates . . . He well remembers that during the Rebellion of the said Year 1745 he was called upon to serve in the Train Bands. He further saith that since he quitted his residence in the Parish of Christ Church, Spitalfields he had lived in different places, travelling about the country with a mountebank, till he came to Blockley where he now resides. But he solemnly affirms upon his oath that he has never done any Act whatsoever to gain any Settlement elsewhere, since the Settlement he gained at Christ Church aforesaid.

The magistrates duly made an order for the man's removal to Spitalfields, and the parish constable no doubt saw that Blockley was rid of him forthwith.

A Removal Order and Pass (requiring the officers of parishes on the way to the destination of the pauper to give her food and shelter overnight) was issued by the Mayor of the city of London in 1791 in respect of Hannah Reynolds and child "apprehended as a Rogue and Vagabond, wandering abroad, lodging in the open air, and not giving a good Account of herself." It was addressed to the parish officers of Blockley "to receive and obey." The mayor's certificate was as follows:

"upon Examination taken before me it doth appear that the last legal Settlement of the said Hannah is in the Parish of Blockley. She on her oath saith that her husband Thomas Reynolds, who was impressed into the Sea Service, was born in the Parish of Blockley and hath not since his birth obtained a subsequent Settlement.

	The Mark of
J. Boydell	X
Mayor	Hannah Reynolds"

There follows on the Pass a list of the stopping places on the ten day journey in charge of a succession of parish constables, ending with one at Shipston-on-Stour, who conveyed "the within named vagrant" to Blockley, and took a receipt from Charles Jasper Selwyn, as magistrate.

A study of the Removal Orders preserved in the Blockley parish chest, which comprise 114 Orders from, and 97 Orders to, Blockley, gives some idea of the traffic in human misery on the roads of 18th and early 19th century England. It was not eased by the zest with which the parish officers were prone to dispute orders to receive paupers and to show that they were not to be put upon. Papers concerning fourteen disputed cases between 1722 and 1818 survive among the Blockley records, nine of them being lost when they came before the bench and all of them apparently leaving the parish out of pocket! Blunt letters, too, were often exchanged:

One who describes himself as a "friend unknown" writes to "The Churchwardens and Overseers of the Parish of Blockley in Worcestershire":

> Chepping Wycomb Bucks Feb yͤ 18th 1747.
> Gentlemen,
> Mary Hulls a Parishioner of your Parish and had a Certificate from you (*acknowledging responsibility for her maintenance if necessary*) has removed into this Burrow and our Offercer will not let her stay here with her four Children without a new Certificate. Att her request I send this to inform you except you send her your Certificate and that pretty soon too she and her Children will be sent by an Order to your Parish, as her Husband left her poor. If she is sent she must be a considerable charge to you. If you please to give your Certificate, yͤ sooner yͤ Better, for our Offercers will not be easy long.

It was common for parish officers faced with the possibility of having to support women with illegitimate children to compel the fathers, if they could be traced, to marry and so assume responsibility. On a day in October 1813 the father of one such young man, trying to save his son from a 'knobstick wedding' (so called because they were attended by the churchwardens with their staves) came from Charlbury with a letter from his solicitor in which the Blockley officers were threatened with reprisals if they proved obdurate. "If you refuse," the letter went, "I shall take such steps against you as will make you sensible of your error."

Sometimes there were less sophisticated letters of appeal or complaint—or, as in the following case, of both! A cordwainer wrote from Oxford in 1831:

Gentlemen,

I wrote to you about a Month since and I am surpris'd that you was not Condescending enough to send me any answer thereto. It was relative to my poor distressed Mother in Law, Mary J., who, poor dear soul, is now bedridden or totally (as we may say) confin'd to bed thro' a paraletic Stroke which is an awful thing, tho' it pleased the divine Disposer of all things to inflict so severe a Calamity on her. I always thought we was living in a land of Humanity. I am surpris'd at the Conduct you Gentlemen has shown to a poor unfortunate old Woman who lies unable to help herself, tho her spirits are good thro' (as I said before) the affliction of the Divine being . . . She wants Assistance from you and Assistance she must have and that immediately too, for I have applied to a higher power, two respectable Gentlemen of this Parish. Therefore Lett not Apathy nor Negligence nor Cruelty reign in your Bosoms no longer.

If the Blockley officers were sometimes slow to move, they were certainly not cruel. It is only fair to say in their defence that Mary J. had in her younger days lived in the parish workhouse with her six children. Let one more case out of the rich choice from the parish chest serve as an illustration. A not very reputable family called Lively, not long resident in Blockley, consisted of a mother and her five children. The husband had absconded, and the parish officers with the approval of Mr Boughton, the vicar, suspecting that some of the children were born out of wedlock, were sparing in their grant of poor relief. They were goaded into more lavish provision through the intervention of an Evesham magistrate, and then—it was January 1813—prompted perhaps by the vicar they took the imaginative step of sending one of the children, William, who was blind, to the recently founded School for the Blind, the earliest of its kind in England, in Liverpool. The boy remained there at the cost of the parish till 1817, when he was returned to Blockley with a favourable report on his conduct and the following recommendation: "He is a good basket maker, and can make all sorts of twine, cart-ropes, etc. He will be able to maintain himself with your assistance in setting him up. He is also a tolerable organist." That faded document was brought to life for the present writer in 1951 in a conversation with the aged verger, Henry Sale, born, bred and honoured in Blockley, who told of Sunday School treats in the 1870's in Northwick Park, always attended by a blind old man called Bill Lively, with his fiddle to accompany the children's songs and dances.

Another, and less edifying, footnote to the Lively story is the hunting down and arrest by the parish constable of the elusive head of the family. It cost the parish £2. 10s. in July 1813 to fetch Thomas Lively from Welford-on-Avon, to lodge him and a man to watch him at the Bell Inn—in the attic and chained by the leg—and finally to convey him to Worcester for custody and trial.

A statement of facts prepared by the Blockley churchwardens in 1748 for the briefing of their attorney in a disputed settlement case gives some idea of the cross-purposes of the parties and the helpless bewilderment of many of the paupers with a vital interest in the upshot. Mary Robins of Paxford, an unmarried woman employed as a servant at Oddington (near Stow-on-the-Wold), returned home in May 1745 and gave birth to a child there. The Blockley officers sent her and the child under a removal order back to Oddington on the ground that she had gained a settlement there by residence—and for three years the Oddington officers made no protest. At the end of January 1748, however, an Oddington churchwarden unceremoniously conveyed the pair to Paxford and left them. For some reason, perhaps because her parents would not keep her, she went to Blockley and to the recently built workhouse there—it was erected by the gateway to the Vicarage in 1740 and remained till it was replaced by Milton's store early in the present century. Finding the door unlocked, Mary Robins left the child inside and stole back to Oddington. The Blockley officers promptly obtained a warrant for her arrest, went on 2 February to Oddington to take her, found that the Oddington officers had sent her away to Dayles-

Plate 37 "Jockey" Bennett aged 82, on his post round of the hill farms (10 miles) 1951, with Sully, Jimmy and Whiskey. (*Photograph by courtesy of the Evesham Journal*)

ate 38 Spring Hill Ox Team visiting Stratford-upon-Avon with Chris Spiers and William Taylor.

Plate 39 Fire Brigade, 1939; *from left,* Bert Figgures, George Mayo, Conrad Warner, Harry Ledbetter, Mr Stinchcoombe, Harry Brotherton, Roland Wiggins *Back row;* Tom Mayo, Ralph Pain, Bert Timms.

Plate 40 Blockley Band, 1956, wearing uniforms given by J. Collier, Ltd. (*Photograph by courtesy of R. E. George*)

Plate 41 21st Birthday Party at Rodneys, 1952; including Jane MacMillan (*née* Spurgin), Michael and Hilary Spurgin, Clare Spurgin, Mrs Pearce, Mrs Goadby, Sir John and Lady Hicks, Mr and Mrs Elliot and family, Rev. and Mrs Ridler and John, Brig. Coldstream and Patrick, Mr and Mrs Yoxall and Anne, Mr and Mrs Muirhead, Mr and Mrs Smeeton and family, Maj. and Mrs Cox and Tim, Mrs Margaret Turner, Dr. and Mrs Shaw and family, Miss E. Buxton, Mrs Bayley (*née* Clarke), Judge and Mrs Kirkhouse-Jenkins and Mary, Bruce Griffith, Muriel Hueffer, Susan Skurray, Imogen Dodd, Richard Gibbons and Colin Clayton.

Plate 42
Prisoner-of-War Camp,
Bourton Hill;
painting by
C. Compton-Smith.

Plate 43 Opening of Council Houses, Springfield, c. 1947; first to be built in reconstructed stone. *Group including:* Chairman of N. Cotswold R. D. C., Mr W. C. Lockwood; Mrs C. Spurgin, Chairman of Housing Development; Serg. Maj. Heath, Chairman of Parish Council; architect Thomas Bateman; Clerk to R. D. C., W. G. Knight; Surveyor to R. D. C., G. E. Knight; Blockley representative Mrs Lingard, and tenants Mr & Mrs Macgillivray.

Plate 44 Edward Belcher carving Coronation emblems for Council Estates, 1953

Plate 45   Over-60 Club Presentation to police Sergeant Wall on his departure to Australia, c. 1956. Group, including Committee members, *from left*; Mr A. Savidge, Dr Frank Haine, Miss Hardy, Mr R. Belcher, Sergeant Wall, Mr E. Purser, Mr J. Milton, Mrs N. Marshall, Mr G. Nobes, Mrs A. Mitchell, Dr Jean Haine, Mrs A. Yoxall, Mr W. Bailey.

Plate 46   Brownie Pack Christmas Party, 1954; *including:* Carol Hawtin, Jennifer Taylor, Maureen Hanrahan, Janet Wheeler, Brenda Green, Sheila Jackson, Sheila Taylor, Christine Macgillivray, Mary White, Josephine Bates, Janet Cadle, Dinah Jackson, Anne Bates, Sheila Arrowsmith, Sheila Heritage, Janet Dyer, Pamela Claydon, Sandra Keeley and Mrs N. Marshall.

Plate 47 Blockley Football Team, 1950-51 Season, Winners of the Gloucestershire Minor Cup. *Back Row:* M.Collumbine, A. Mayo, R. Mayo, B. Mumford, W. Cadle, B. Waite, A. Dicks, D. Godson, R. Warner, C. Smith. *Front Row:* M. Beasley, C. Harvey, R. Taylor, D.Mayo, F. Cother.

Plate 48 Miss Clare Stanley, a Founder Member, cutting the cake at the W.I.'s 50th Birthday Party, June 1974, with Committee members Mrs Wheeler, Mrs Kryssa, Mrs Williams, Mrs Figgures, Mrs Cook, Mrs Flaherty, Mrs Gill, Miss N. Aston, Mrs Gasside, Miss M. Stanley and Mrs Button. (*Photograph by courtesy of the Evesham Journal*)

Plate 49 Fossils from the neighbourhood of Blockley.

A. An ammonite, *Liparoceras naptonense* Spath from the Lower Lias of the Blockley Station Pit (BNHM., C 73505, coll. *Hugh G. Owen*)

B. An echinoid, *Clypeus mulleri* Wright from the Inferior Oolite near Blockley (BMNH., E 76427, coll. *Adam F. White*). *Photographs by Mr* P. J. Green of the British Museum (Nat. Hist.)

ford, obtained another warrant (necessary because Daylesford was in another county), only to find when they went there to execute it that she had returned to Oddington, where the authorities had put her in the lock-up to prevent her fetching the child back there. Not to be beaten, the Blockley officers secured a removal order for the conveyance of the child to Oddington, but were there refused access to the mother. An offer from them to pay a shilling a day for the support of the child if only Oddington would keep it till the case was settled, was refused—and the party returned with the child to Blockley. It was now the end of March, and the churchwardens applied for and got a removal order making Oddington responsible for both mother and child. Oddington appealed to Quarter Sessions against this—and it was for this that the briefing, with which this complex paragraph began, was intended.

The cost to the parish of this rough system of poor relief rose steeply as the years passed. In Blockley it stood at £120 in the year 1695, as Vicar Scattergood recorded:[4] in 1795 it was £748. That was the year when Berkshire magistrates, sitting at Speenhamland, set a new standard by tying the rate of relief to the price of bread and the size of family, whether legitimate or not. That helped to bring the Blockley poor rate to £1291 in 1815 and £1670 by 1830. Three years after that the Poor Law Amendment Act put a brutal stop to the process, and under the Shipston Board of Guardians, created by this measure, the Blockley ratepayers were greatly eased. It was far otherwise for the Blockley poor, for whom hard times were to come.

They had indeed suffered from the enclosures of 1773. There is evidence of this in the prompt formation—in 1774—of the Blockley Association for the Prosecution of Felons. A copy of its rules, as revised in 1816, shows that its members—farmers and silk throwsters mainly—subscribed to a fund from which rewards were to be paid to informers able to give evidence against offenders. The rewards ranged from £10 in cases of highway robbery or arson and £5 for horse or sheep stealing to 10s. for the theft of turnips, potatoes cabbages and fruit. The members added this warning:

If any Alehouse keeper resident in the Parish of Blockley shall be known . . . to entertain any disorderly Person or shall suffer any

113

tippling on the Sabbath-day, and more especially during the time of Divine Service, which practice we conceive to be the fundamental cause of the very many offences committed, it is our determined resolution to report him to the Acting Magistrate . . . that his house may not be licensed in future.

Both vicars, Selwyn and Boughton in turn, were treasurers of the Association, and were no doubt concerned in the drafting of that clause. The offenders brought to book were not in fact dangerous criminals. They were usually women stealing turnips or men stealing corn—no doubt for their starving families.

Of the general decay of morals, however, there is evidence enough. Illegitimate births, which were comparatively rare and sternly reprobated before the 18th century, multiplied as war followed war, homelessness and vagrancy increased, and 'permissiveness' spread. The Blockley parish records include the papers of some 80 affiliation cases between 1745 and 1831, the years of the Napoleonic wars showing up worst. But the entries in the church baptismal register, in which the clergy were unsparingly blunt in their note of 'base born,' give a more complete record. The percentage of illegitimate births rises in relentless progression.

Of the infants baptized in the third quarter of the 18th century one in every twenty-four were recorded as illegitimate: in the fourth quarter the figure was one in twelve: and in the first dozen years of the 19th century, with the war against Napoleon at its height and the Speenhamland example most potent, it was one in eight. And even that leaves the unbaptized out of the account.

There were reparations in the parish church in Mr Boughton's time—possibly in response to the challenge from the Baptist revival under Elisha Smith. English parish churches as depicted in 18th century illustrations often present a disorderly array of privately designed family pews amid much humbler woodwork. Most of the greater Blockley households had their own accommodation in church. The Northwick pew was in the centre of the nave, the Upton Wold pew stood under the monument of Edward Carter, who had erected it a century and a half before,[5] the Porch House pew was in the north aisle together with seats for the Northwick servants—"hideous structures", as Soden described them in his history of the parish—and there was a Ditchford high pew elsewhere. In 1797 a start was made on this jumble. William Long of Blockley erected 72 feet—perhaps five or six pews—of seating with "mouldings and raised panels" on the bench ends. These may be the pews still in being at the back of the nave. In 1804 Richard Hulls of Campden gave an estimate of £35 10s. "for erecting a Range of Pews in the middle of Blockley Church," eight in all, "to be completed fit for the inspection of any Workman." He had, in fact, greatly to exceed this estimate "owing to the great Advance in Deals"—timber from the Baltic was not reaching England owing to the Napoleonic blockade. Thomas Figgures, himself a builder, was a churchwarden in some of these years—aptly enough.

It was in 1804, too, that an even greater charge was incurred. The old tenor bell in the tower had to be replaced by a new and heavier one from the great Gloucester bell-founding firm of Rudhall. Abraham Rudhall had recast the 3rd bell in 1729. The gross cost for taking down the old tenor bell, supplying and erecting a new one of just over 15 cwt. together with a clapper of 31 lb. and leather baldrick to hang it with, was £131, reduced by credit for the metal of the old bell to £50. That the new bell rang for Trafalgar is likely enough.

One of Mr Boughton's parishioners one of whom he probably had doubts, was Joanna Southcott, (*Plate* 16) 'the prophetess', who was given a home in Rock Cottage between 1804 and 1814 by one of her adherents, Miss Townley. With her hostess and her maid as amanuenses she compiled many voluminous 'writings' and there, sealed, nailed and corded in a 'great box' they were kept for a time after her death in London in 1814. Rock Cottage was destroyed by fire in 1971, and many Southcott relics with it—and sadly their faithful custodian Mrs A. M. Veysey-Stitt with them. But there remains a visible reminder of the cult in the tombstone at the west end of the churchyard of William Troup, a Blockley man and a Southcott believer, who had served the Prince Regent as a Page of the Back Stairs (or valet) for several years. There is a story that he once induced his master, while in the neighbourhood, to visit Joanna in Rock Cottage—a bizarre confrontation indeed, if it could be true! The Prince did in fact pass through the parish along the Worcester highway in September 1807 for a visit to Ombersley.

In 1816 John Rushout, the second Lord Northwick, succeeded to the Northwick estate. He was unmarried and well known as a virtuoso and antiquarian. He had spent years in Italy studying and collecting paintings—he was at Naples in 1799 when the royal family, accompanied by Sir William and Lady Emma Hamilton, were obliged to escape from an invading French army to safer quarters in Sicily. They sailed in Nelson's flagship, and Rushout was in the party. He was constantly on the move between his houses at Cheltenham, Harrow and Northwick, where he built the picture gallery. It was he who constructed Five Mile Drive,[6] and 'landscaped' the Dovedale Plantation, with its ornamental cascades along the brook, as it flowed among the beeches, firs and larches of his lordship's planting. Was the name, suggested by the call of the ring-doves haunting the valley, coined by his sister, Anne Rushout? She too was artistic —her sketches of Northwick Park show that and her love of the place clearly enough. A friend in 1808 sent her a finely bound copy[7] of his poems to her—the poems perhaps not quite a match for the binding—with this nostalgic inscription:

> At Northwick Park, my little book,
> You in your turn will have a look!
> And as you range, with curious eye,
> Its rich and tranquil scenery,
> Will you not wish—altho' so faint
> Your colours be—again to paint,
> And rival with your mimic hues
> The matchless grace of Anna's views?
> Will you not say, "Ah me! it grieves
> To find, sweet Park, in all my leaves
> No mention of thy calm delights,
> Thy sober, soft and soothing sights,
> Thy hanging woods and sloping lawns,
> Thy thousand deer and sportive fawns,
> Thy lakes, thy river and thy rills,
> Thy calm home-scene and distant hills!

There is more of such versifying in Eyre's *Guide to Blockley*, published in 1827, after he had lived in Blockley for seven years as curate. A man of immense energy, he found time to compile his 'guide', to make a detailed census of the entire parish, and to go on then to publish a vigorous attack on the bill about to be discussed in Parliament in 1829 for Catholic Emancipation. This was addressed to the Householders and Electors of Blockley. In it he urged them to join in a petition to the king to prevent the grant of political power to Roman Catholics by dissolving Parliament and taking the sense of the country on "the breaking in upon the Protestant Constitution of 1688". He was incensed by the fact that some Manchester Unitarians had petitioned Parliament in favour of the bill:

> I have been accustomed to consider you as Christians, and I have too much confidence in the soundness of your faith to suppose that you would permit Jews, Turks and Infidels to make laws for you which must seriously affect your civil and religious liberties . . . .

Recalling the submission to the Pope of King John and King James II, he hints at dire consequences if the bill is passed:

> I am not one of those who expect on the passing of the proposed bill to see the Host carried about our streets and people falling down to it. I am not one of those who expect to see . . . human sacrifices offered on the altars of Popery. Yet I have but a poor opinion of human nature at all times, particularly when deserted by God for inexcusable apostacy, and I will not conjecture what may happen before another quarter of a century has rolled over our heads . . .

> Men of Worcestershire! Your country is indignant . . . and the rising spirit of free-born Britons is rapidly expressing its digust at the indecent speed with which this Bill is hurried through the House of Commons.[8]

There can be no doubt that "Church and King!" expressed William Eyre's sentiments and that Mr Peel's liberal tendencies were not for him.

But he did know his parishioners, as an analysis of the census which he made can show. Some account has already been given of the silk trade in the parish, and this chapter may end with a glance at the other occupations in which the Blockley folk of 1827 were engaged. Farming and its ancillary trades must come first. Since enclosure the two great landowners of the parish had split up their broad acres into separate farms, and there were now 32 farmers in the parish, mostly tenants of Lord Northwick or

Lord Redesdale of Batsford. The grain which they produced could be ground by any one of six millers in the parish, William Hobbs at the Old Mill (*Plate* 13) the best known. There were six fellmongers and four woolcombers in Blockley to deal with the hides and fleeces of their livestock. Building perhaps came next, with a score of masons, another score of carpenters—one of these, incidentally, keeping a Sunday School for the teaching of the three R's at Paxford—and five slatters, most of them in the Figgures family. Of other trades in the parish there were four families of blacksmiths, three of weavers, two of tailors and five of cordwainers or bootmakers. And trade then was good.

[1] See p. 91
[2] See *Bishopric of Worcester, 1782–1808, 49* (W.H.S.).
[3] See p. 55
[4] See p. 76
[5] See p. 67
[6] The 1" Ordnance map of 1828 shows the Drive in course of construction. I am indebted to Mr J. P. Nelson of Sedgecombe for this reference.
[7] The late Captain E. G. Spencer-Churchill kindly put this and other Northwick material at my disposal.
[8] There is a copy of this pamphlet in the Evesham Public Library.

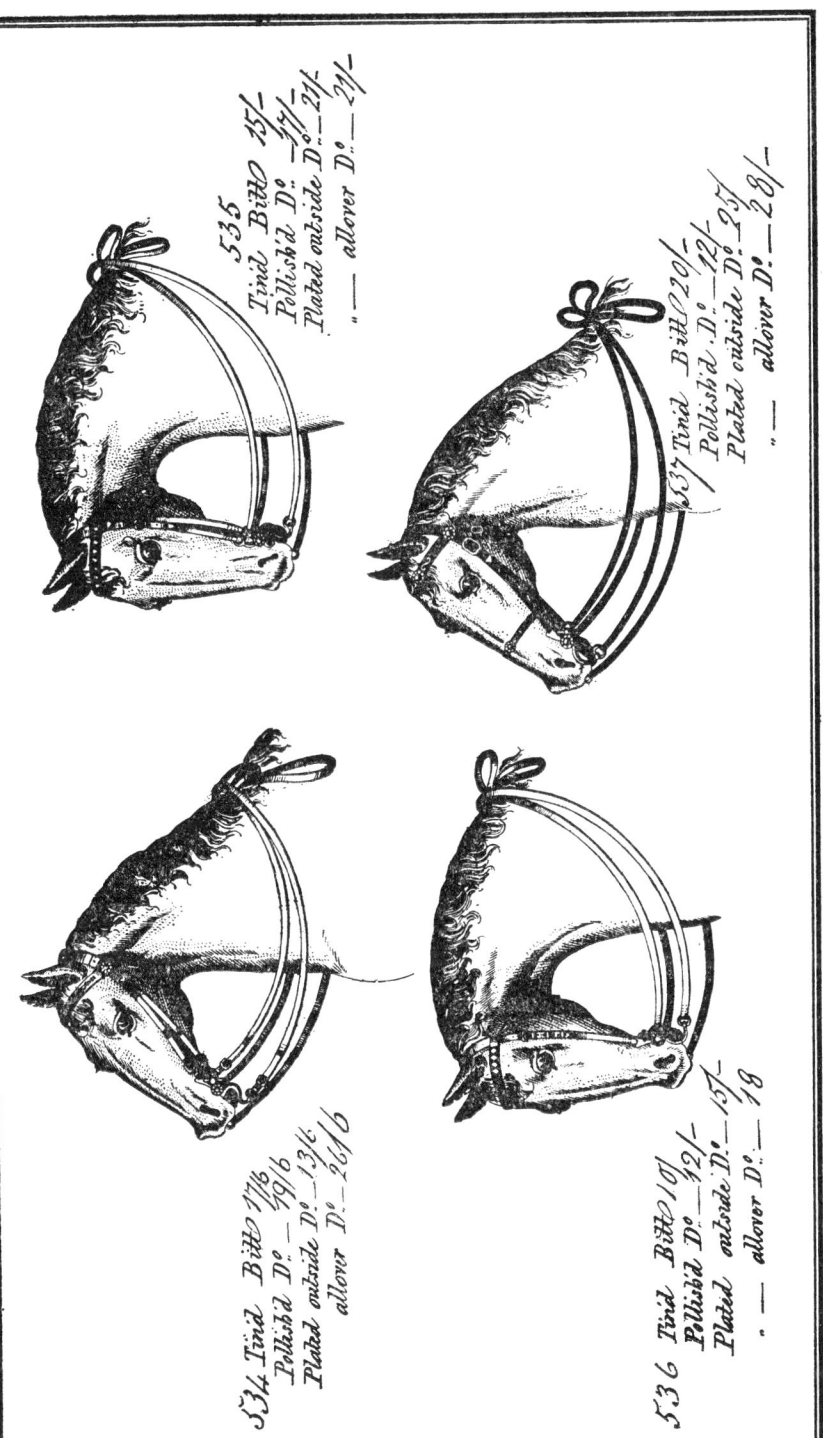

535
Tind Bitt 15/-
Pollish'd D?. 17/-
Plated outside D?. 24/-
   allover D?. 27/-

537 Tind Bitt 20/-
Pollish'd D?. 12/-
Plated outside D?. 25/-
   allover D?. 28/-

534 Tind Bitt 17/6
Pollish'd D?. 19/6
Plated outside D?. 13/6
  allover D?. 26/6

536 Tind Bitt 10/-
Pollish'd D?. 12/-
Plated outside D?. 15/-
  allover D?. 18

Page from saddler's trade catalogue, found behind wainscotting in High Street, 1965.

CHAPTER TWELVE

Noncomformity in Blockley: Elisha Smith

1660-1820

WHEN GILES COLLIER reverted to the Established Church after the Restoration there were some of his parishioners who could not, in conscience, follow him. He had to report to the bishop at his visitation in 1664:

> There are some few Persons in the Parish reported Anabaptists and some others Quakers, that hold not communion in the publique Worship of God amongst us. But in regard we are not utterly without hope of their amendment, we present not their names.

Only two years before, in 1662, the Year of Ejectment, when the Clarendon Code was in process of being enacted, a group of Baptists was 'formed into a church' in Chipping Campden — perhaps by Thomas Knight—and a year later, in 1663, a group of Quakers, including Edward Warner and John Norris of Blockley, bought the site in Broad Campden for the erection of the Friends' Meeting House there.[1] Vicar Scattergood's pronouncement in 1683 of the bishop's sentence of excommunication on Edward Warner, a relative, of course, of William Warner of Philadelphia, has been recorded on an earlier page. Dr. Saunders in 1710 entered in the church baptismal register the names of five Quakers—*tremuli* was his quaint Latin rendering of the word— and of a wife and husband, Elizabeth and James Wigget, "converted from the errors of the Anabaptists." These were defections but they prove the continuance of Nonconformity in the parish. The early records of the Baptist church in Chipping Campden are scanty, but Peter Payton, then minister, in 1729 made a list, which has survived,[2] of the 43 full members. It contains six Blockley names and two from Paxford. The first of the Blockley names is that of Mary Knight, a relative, surely, of Samuel Knight, the silk throwster, and so a precursor of the future attachment of so many of his colleagues in the trade to the Baptist Church.

The religious apathy during the middle decades of the 18th century, which moved the Wesleys and Whitefield to the missionary campaign, affected the churches of every denomination, and by 1780 the Baptist congregation in Campden had dwindled. That year it received a visit for a few weeks from a theological student from Bristol. He had been sent to gain practical experience as part of his training for the ministry. He was later to serve as minister there for many memorable years. His name was Elisha Smith.

He is, indeed, remembered for much more than this—as an apostolic evangelist, who carried his message all over the North Cotswold countryside. He founded the Baptist church at Shipston-on-Stour and served it as minister for eleven years, while all the time serving his church at Campden as well. Those Sunday journeys of his over the uplands in winter and summer alike, sometimes on foot and sometimes on horseback, in order to conduct services in both his churches, have become legendary. He was a leading spirit in the founding of other churches, notably at Stow-on-the-Wold; and the Oxfordshire and East Gloucestershire Baptist Association was inaugurated, largely at his instance, in his Shipston church. A truly prophetic figure, his influence reached far afield.

Yet he must be claimed as a Blockley worthy. It was in Blockley that he married and made his home, was most easily accessible as pastor, and earned his living from day to day in the general store in which he served the whole village and shared in its life.

Elisha Smith was a Northamptonshire man, born in 1754. He grew to manhood in the village of Paulerspury, near Towcester. The county and the year of his birth were significant, for they brought him into touch, as he grew up, with three of the leaders of the Baptist revival of that period. At Northampton he sat at the feet of John Collett Ryland, who in due course furthered his entry into the ministry; he knew and was counselled by Andrew Fuller, then minister at Kettering, whose book, *A Gospel worthy of all Acceptation*, was published in 1785, the year of Elisha's ordination as minister at Campden; and at Paulerspury he attended the school kept by the father of William Carey, the future missionary and Orientalist, whose boyhood friend he was. Elisha drew his early inspiration from a rich source. And here it is pleasant to note two coincidences. Ryland, his first mentor, was actually born at Lower Ditchford and went to school at Moreton-in-Marsh; and Fuller's son, Andrew Gunton Fuller, became Baptist minister in Blockley and took the first services in its new Chapel in 1836.

Elisha's father, James Smith, a wool comber and later a boot manufacturer in a small way, was a decent man, but rash and easily taken in as a man of business. That, to Elisha as a young man, was a matter of grave concern: failure in the affairs of life signified divine judgment, James, moreover, treated his children with great reserve, so that, as his son wrote, "they rather feared than loved him." For his mother, Sarah, Elisha felt a deep affection, and the comparative poverty to which her husband's fecklessness reduced her in old age was another count against him. Always sincerely religious, she joined the Baptist church at Towcester early in the 1770's. Her influence in her son's life was profound.

His progress towards his ministry of the Gospel is shortly described in an account he wrote of his life. It was at Coventry, where he was working as a shop assistant in 1774 that, influenced by the preaching of the minister there, Mr Butterworth, his mind was made up. "I broke off from all my loose companions, and forsook my play at crickett, coits and dancing, the former of which I was particularly fond of . . . I joined the company of several young persons whose example was a blessing to me. We met every morning for prayer in which with great confusion I sometimes engaged." In September 1776 he took the first necessary step. "I gave in my experiences to the church at Towcester and was baptised by immersion." Not long after he obtained employment at Northampton to receive instruction from J. C. Ryland, and in August 1778 he was admitted to the Bristol Academy, Ryland's old college, where he studied classics, logic and divinity, mainly under the tuition of Caleb Evans. This was one of the best known of the Nonconformist Academies founded to provide higher education for those shut out of Oxford and Cambridge by the Clarendon Code. Elisha studied there for three years. As a theological student he was sent in 1780—and here we come back to the point at which, earlier in tihs chapter, we broke off our account of the Baptist church in Chipping Campden— to serve in a lay capacity at Shipston-on-Stour and Campden for a few weeks of practical experience.

A letter to him from his mother at Paulerspury and dated September 1780 belongs to this time, and, but for its length, could well be quoted in full. It is addressed "To Mr Elisha Smith, at Mr Lines, Carpenter, at Shipston, Worcestershire, by Way of London." It is concerned mainly with church affairs at Towcester, but its special purpose is given in these words:

> Ordinance Day is appointed for tomorrow fortnight, and we should all be glad if with any Propriety and without disobliging your People you could be there . . . I would send one of the mares to meet you at Banbury, which will in some measure save some expense in Horse hire. We all think it would be less expence to you to keep a horse than to hire, and would have you consider which will be most prudent, as I hope the old mare will soon be very usefull and make you independent of others. Many Friends desire their love to you, particularly William Carey.

Of his trial weeks at Shipston and Campden Elisha wrote: "There I found, though many things were discouraging, my mind inclined to fix among them. Accordingly on July 3rd 1782 I was ordained at Shipston, having previously joined them into a church, professing their belief of the duty of Believers' Baptism, but admitting other true Christians into their communion." He also served the church at Campden, though not formally chosen to be its minister till 1785. He had lodgings in both places. "I boarded sometime at one place and sometimes at the other for the conveniency of both. On my marriage, Jan. 26 1785 I fixed wholly at Blockley."

The Blockley woman whom Elisha married was Martha Peyton, one of the daughters of Joseph Peyton, the silk throwster whose purchase of Walgroves and establishment of his mill there was recorded on an earlier page. The marriage gave the Smiths their home, for Martha's brother, Thomas Peyton, who had succeeded to the mill on their father's death, elected to live in half the Manor House—the other half being occupied by his cousin Samuel Spilsbury, who by that time had inherited the mill (now Mill Close) which his grandfather, Samuel Knight had founded, Martha Smith thus came into her father's old home (now the post office), and she and her husband Elisha spent the rest of their lives in it, no doubt as tenants of her brother. His marriage had another and more important consequence for Elisha and for the church he served: it brought them both into close touch with the circle of silk throwsters, with the result that in the mid-19th century six of the seven mill owners in Blockley were leading members of the Baptist community there.

To earn a living for himself, his wife, and their five children, Elisha Smith had to engage in business, and for some time his enterprise did not prosper. "My mind," he wrote in 1803, "has been deeply occupied in worldly concern owing to an engagement in pottery, of which I was totally ignorant. Like other new objects it has taken away too much of my thoughts, but having embarked I was anxious until I had completed my undertaking— and have happily been carried through difficulties and dangers." Pottery was, in fact, only a branch of his business, which was primarily that of a grocer and druggist. A brief account of his life by one of his descendants[3] adds the characteristic comment on his business difficulties, that his main anxiety was "lest the issue might bring disgrace upon the cause of Christ. He was fearful lest his great trials were a divine judgment . . . for engaging in business at all." Once these difficulties were solved, his business prospered exceedingly.

There is a link, paradoxically enough, between his village shop and the great paper manufacturing firm of E. S. and A. Robinson of Bristol. The initials of the senior partner and founder of the firm stand, in fact, for Elisha Smith, the man himself being Elisha's grandson, and according to the tradition in the firm, his apprentice. "Some of the Robinsons of today hold that it was the infusion of Smith blood that gave the family the fire and energy which it had before lacked."[4] In token of this the scales used by Elisha in his Blockley shop were, until they were destroyed in an air raid over Bristol in the second World War, a cherished heirloom in the head office of the firm.

Most of the accounts of Elisha Smith lay stress on his kindness to young men, and to the case of the young Elisha Robinson may be added that of John Mann, son of the Baptist minister at Moreton-in-Marsh, whose memoirs[5] relate the part played by Elisha in his choice of a career in medicine. John, aged about 16, was apprenticed to a Leamington printer. One Saturday he took home a specimen of his work—a play-bill. Elisha happened to be calling on John's family, his familiar friends. "As soon as he cast his eyes over this bill he lifted his hands and exclaimed with great fervour: 'John Mann print play-bills! That will never do. He must never go back to such a place as this.' " And John Mann never did.

Dr. Mann, writing seventy years after Elisha's death, gave a vivid picture of the sturdy old Puritan. "In my mind's eye I can still see him in his brown wig, in his frock coat and with his pipe in his mouth. He was so affable that he shook hands with almost everyone to whom he spoke. His fervour was aided by the deep bass of his oracular voice and the weight of his judgment, He was the Baptist minister at Blockley. I never heard him preach, but his kindness and sympathy as a pastor fixed him in the hearts of all. I spent many pleasant hours in his company. I remember when at one time my father felt that his small income at Moreton was insufficient for his necessities and he consulted his friend Elisha about looking for some other place. His reply was characteristic: 'Bread is given thee and water is sure; be content, Brother Mann, and wait for a clear call from Providence.' Honourable and unspotted remained the character of old Elisha to the end of his life."

As pastor, he stood by the principles laid down by his teachers, Ryland, Caleb Williams and Andrew Fuller. He held and exacted strict moral standards, but like them he rejected the high Calvinism of John Gill and his disciples. "As a preacher," we learn from an obituary account of him, "he was judicious, affectionate and experimental. He was not inordinately attached to systematic theology, but he plainly loved and faithfully preached the glorious doctrines of the Gospel." All the accounts of him stress his friendly, tranquil disposition. One of his friends from Bristol

Academy days, James Hinton, minister of the New Road Baptist Church in Oxford, wrote of the Blockley community of which he was the inspiration: "Seldom has primitive Christianity been better exemplified than in this beautiful and sequestered village." His own choice for a text for the sermon at his own funeral can perhaps best give a sense of his spiritual attitude. It was from the 5th psalm: "And let all them that put their trust in thee rejoice: they shall ever be giving thanks, because thou defendest them: they that love thy Name shall be joyful in thee."

In all the occasional brief comments on his ministry that survive from Elisha's own hand there is only one which, in contrast to his habitual cheerfulness, betrays some dejection of spirit. It was written in 1794. At the time his business affairs were going awry, he had just resigned his pastorate at Shipston and undertaken Sunday afternoon services for the newly founded church at Stow-on-the-Wold, and it would seem that the recently appointed vicar of Blockley, William Boughton, was giving cause for complaint—the only complaint against clergy of the Establishment that appears in Elisha's writings. There was, on the other hand, cause for satisfaction in the building of the meeting house (today the Village Hall) at the top of Bell Bank.

> We opened our Meeting-house the 30th May last. What success the Gospel may have I know not; I sometimes fear the spirit of the World is advancing and religion is low. The enemies of the Gospel have been violent this year, and the scandalous reproaches of the Holy Church party against Dissenters are a means of trying the faith and zeal of many . . . This is one cause why we have had but few join with us here. I fear the cause is our indifference and conformity to the world. . . My field-day work is large. Have engaged to supply the people at Stow, but know little of the state of their souls. Do not see much of the increase of religion among my people at Campden. It is a day of small things.

There was indeed much to concern all over England in those last years of the 18th century—demoralisation arising from unbridled industrialisation, political unsettlement, wartime lawlessness, the faulty working of the Poor Laws, and, most relevantly, the decay of religion. Blockley did not escape these things. But for Elisha Smith cheerfulness soon broke in again, and the records of his church at Campden tell of the proceedings at the fortnightly meetings of its members, at which candidates seeking admission gave accounts of their spiritual state, and, if accepted, were formally received into the fellowship, signed the covenant on which they undertook to model their lives—all which was later followed by their baptism in the mill-pond at Pye Mill in Paxford. How well their minister knew them can be seen in the entries he made in the church records when members of the fellowship died. Two may be quoted, partly because they reveal something of the man himself, and partly because they bring our story back to Elisha's own family circle. The subjects of his comments were the sister and brother of his wife, Martha, the former being the wife of Thomas Figgures, a very active churchwarden of the parish church of Blockley in 1802, 1806 and 1811—a fact which no doubt accounted for her non-membership:

20 March 1806 died Mrs Hannah Figgures. She never joined us as not being able to attend at Campden. Her life was exemplary. I never thought highly of her religion, though had a good hope she might be sincere.

Mr Thomas Peyton died in a fit of apoplexy by himself in Bourton Wood. He joined our church in 1798. He retained his regard for infant baptism, but always was candid, and seemed most pleased with Baptist ministers.

Of his wife he wrote in 1807, when he was at the happiest stage of his ministry:-

I am fully pleased with her, conscious of her good temper, persuaded that she fears God and keeps up family worship. I find myself inclined to share her care and increase her joys. By so doing I can better serve my friends at Campden. I had a wish to introduce the Gospel at Blockley, and by business to be able to continue my labours in these parts. I am thankful the Lord directed me in mercy to person and place.

Ten years later he was to enter in the records of his church in Campden:-

Died 7 Nov. 1817 Mrs Martha Smith, the affectionate wife of E. Smith, after a long illness which she bore with great patience.

127

Some months before this his own health had begun to fail. To lighten his load he took his second son James into business partnership, the eldest son, Crescens, being already installed as owner of the Spilsbury silk mill (Mill Close) and resident in half of the Manor House. But Elisha was not to survive his wife for long. He died of heart failure on 29th March 1819, in the 65th year of his age. He lies in the Meeting House Yard at Campden, the burial ground of his church there and is commemorated by a cenotaph in the churchyard of the Baptist Chapel in Blockley.

[1] See J. P. Nelson: *Broad Campden*, 15–8, (privately printed, 1971).
[2] I am indebted to Mr R. R. Smith for a copy of this list.
[3] The late A. G. Reynolds. His manuscript account was lent to me by the late R. B. Belcher.
[4] Bernard Darwin: *Robinsons of Bristol*, 1844–1944.
[5] John Mann: *Recollections of my early and professional life*, (privately printed, 1887).

CHAPTER THIRTEEN

Victorian Blockley: An Age of Vicissitudes

1830-1901

THERE WAS PROSPERITY in the parish during the early Victorian years, even in the 'hungry forties', but grievous poverty in the latter half of the queen's long reign. The census figures tell the story all too clearly. The population of the parish rose from 2015 in 1831 to 2596 in 1861—an increase of $22\frac{1}{2}\%$. From that high point it fell to 1812 in 1901—a drop of 30%, which brought it below the level at which it had stood when George III died. The cause lay in the national policy of free trade. which hit both main industries of the parish—the silk trade abruptly in 1859, and, in more gradual fashion, farming from the middle 1870s onwards. By the end of the century Blockley was something like a distressed area.

But the earlier years were full of promise. The farmers prospered in their lately enclosed acres. And in the silk trade the forebodings of Martin Westmacott and William Eyre were not borne out. All the mills were active. James Smith, long established in his father's shop, bought the freehold of the whole Walgroves site,[1] including the mill in the Coneygree, in or about 1830. New plant came into operation in 1840, when the Good Intent was taken over by the Stanleys of Snugborough,[2] and in 1843 when Edwin Smith enlarged his works, as an incised stone on the south end of Mill Close still shows, Richard Belcher found the village prosperous when he came to settle in it in 1847, and John Noake, who visited it in the early 1850's, wrote that "there were eight silk mills at work, trade being in a very flourishing state."

Suddenly the bubble burst. In January 1859 a commercial treaty between Britain and France allowed the entry of French silks into this country free of all duty. It meant immediate ruin for the Coventry ribbon weavers who were left with unsaleable stocks for the coming season on their hands. The Blockley throwsters, though they must have known that the trade was doomed, struggled on for that year, but in August 1860 the newly founded Evesham Journal reported: "All the mills have been still the greater part of the summer. The condition of the village may easily be imagined." Noake, after a second visit, wrote in 1868:[3]

> From the very depressed state of the trade in the last few years the mills have been either shut up or worked only occasionally, and then only half time. The mill belonging to Mr Stanley is being converted into a paper or cardboard factory, and there is great fear that the silk trade will never again be prosperous. The manufacturing of men's linen collars by sewing machines has been lately introduced by a London firm and is employing nearly a hundred women.

The cardboard factory was in the Good Intent Mill which was let for the purpose by Isaac Stanley to a stranger from Birmingham. Much of the building and its highly combustible contents went up in flames on a December night in 1866, for which the tenant, who had started the fire for the insurance money, served a long term in prison. Two incidental details illustrate the hardships suffered in those hungry years. One of the witnesses in the case, in explaining how he came to see the incendiary at work, said that he had passed by Bourton Wood, where he had seen two men with a dog crossing a drive. Poaching was a natural alleviation for a hungry family. And the same motive may be assumed for the furious anger of a crowd from the village who nearly lynched the accused man. He had not only lost them jobs, but had destroyed good food by wrecking an orchard. There was to be a worse riot a few years later—and for much the same reasons.

The 1830s saw the end of a far more ancient Blockley heritage —its feudal link with the bishops of Worcester as lords of the manor. By an act of Parliament in 1836 all episcopal manors were vested in a body of Ecclesiastical Commissioners. The bishops had long parted with their Blockley lands. The title of lord of the manor now passed to the Commissioners together with such shadowy legal rights as had survived. The court baron continued to meet at intervals, but in 1856 the 'homage,' meeting as always in The Crown, and having no business to transact, decided to meet no more. It was a thousand and one years since King Burgred's grant of the lordship to the bishop.

Church affairs in the parish present a new, and perhaps a sharper, interest in this period owing to the foundation of the separate Baptist Church in Blockley. For this we have to go back to the year 1820. Elisha Smith out of loyalty to his Campden church had kept Blockley within that organisation, but after his death his sons, Crescens and James, with Edward Banbury, Robert Stanley and others, largely silk throwsters and business people, met in the Bell Bank meeting house and formally recorded: "On Lord's Day, 24 September 1820, we gave each other the right hand of fellowship and subscribed a form of Covenant." They thereby bound themselves to strict observance of the laws of God, and to receive into their society "all those who shall appear to have received the Lord Jesus Christ into their hearts, whether baptised in infancy or upon profession of faith." Sixty persons signed the covenant that day, seventeen of them with their 'mark.' They appointed Daniel Wright as their first pastor and Crescens Smith as the first deacon of the new church. At a very early hour on a Sunday in the following May "four persons were baptised in the mill pond attached to the Silk-mill of Mr C. Smith, a convenient place having been fitted up for the purpose."[4] Few other records have survived from Daniel Wright's ministry of fourteen years, but the church surely prospered. Unhappily, such evidence as there is does not suggest that relations with the parish church were easy. William Eyre's entry in his census of 1827 of "Daniel Wright, dissenting teacher" is slighting, to say the least; and Miles Coyle, who became vicar in 1831, stood aloof from all men.

Andrew Gunton Fuller, the second minister (1834–38), bore a name honoured in Baptist history[5] and during his short pastorate lived up to it. The number of full church members rose to 109, a new meeting house was opened in Paxford in 1835, and

1836 was *annus mirabilis* indeed. It saw the opening of the new chapel and its burial ground in the High Street, a building praised by that amateur of churches, John Betjeman, as a worthy example in the tradition of English Nonconformity. Unhappily illness compelled Fuller to resign after two more years.

Then followed ten years (1838–48) of stern discipline under under the Rev. T. Smith from Ireland and the Rev. A. M. Stalker from Aberdeen. Days of humiliation were imposed, beginning with a service at 6 a.m. A Draycott member was expelled "for getting into worldly company at unreasonable hours and free drinking." One from Blockley "found guilty of dishonest work in a job of draining on a farm" was suspended for a period. Yet the numbers continued to grow. In 1848 there were 120 full members and church attendance on a Sunday in the various parts of the parish could reach a total of 400.

The influence and resources of the silk throwsters, all but one of whom were church members, lay behind all this. It was they who established a 'British School'[6]—so called because it received a small grant from the undenominational British and Foreign School Society—in the Bell Bank meeting house in 1845. By 1850 they had the help of that important newcomer, Richard Belcher, in the provision of larger accommodation. At his suggestion, to his design and largely through the work of his own hands, a new British School was built on to the rear of the High Street chapel. The new school was opened in 1852. It was to have a life of less than twenty years, though the building was later put to other good uses.

Changes in the pastorate were frequent, but the church was fortunate in its mid-century ministers. Edmund Hull (1850–55) was a strong man and a fine preacher. He was followed by Joseph Wassall (1855–64) from Birmingham, florid, forceful, impulsive and influential with working men. He later emigrated to Massachusetts, where he became a Unitarian. Both these men had Mount Pleasant—today, in enlarged form, we know it as Arreton —as their manse. Under them the full membership of the church reached its peak. But it was not for its good that it depended so much on the silk throwsters for its resources, and with the collapse of their fortunes the numbers fell and the British School was closed before 1870.

At the parish church there were no such frequent changes of ministry and a single vicar, Miles Coyle (1831–55), outlasted five ministers of the Baptist church. Too little evidence remains for us to form a fair judgment about him. An anonymous local versifier in 1888, looking back on the past, wrote dismissively of him:

> When Boughton died Miles Coyle came in
> And everything went poor and thin.

It does not seem to have been a happy incumbency. But it was no fault of his that it began with a law suit and the eviction of a drunken schoolmaster from his quarters in the school building by the churchyard entrance. The vestry had begun these proceedings before his arrival, but the new vicar, as owner of the freehold of the churchyard, had to take over the unpleasant responsibility and it was three years before the affair ended with the imprisonment of the schoolmaster because he could not meet the costs of the case. The parish had to foot the bill.

The school unhappily became a bone of contention between the vicar and Lord Northwick, who had in 1826 met the cost of its restoration and enlargement, as is recorded in the inscription on the front of the building. The quarrel was over the appointment of the new schoolmaster and it smouldered throughout Mr Coyle's time in Blockley. Both men insisted on appointing the master—and two masters accordingly ruled under the same roof, the vicar's man presumably in the old Saunders schoolroom below and Lord Northwick's nominee in his new room upstairs! The vicar administered the school charities and must have been legally in the right, but the ease with which his successor, Henry Bromfield, ended the dispute and its absurd consequences is proof enough of Mr Coyle's lack of tact.

There is other evidence of that lack. Few of the fifteen curates he appointed stayed longer than a year or so. He was at odds with the members of the vestry, the meetings of which he must often have missed—or so it would seem from the entries in the minute-book of 1853 when the churchwardens and overseers of the poor were instructed to write to the vicar demanding a meeting with him to discuss the management and distribution of the parochial charities. He must obviously have kept these matters in his own hands. It is significant that Richard Belcher was one of the over-seers that year. It was not the first time—or the last—that he clashed with the establishment. He took the lead in killing the ancient custom of levying Church Rates for the upkeep of the fabric and services of the church. The vestry, after failing to carry one such levy, seems to have allowed the custom to lapse after 1850.

Few changes in the fabric and furnishings of the church appear to date from Mr Coyle's time. The south porch of George Durant's time was restored in 1847—clear evidence that it was still used as the entrance to the church. The font, too, was moved to its present position, and there is some evidence that the Scripture texts painted on the walls date from these years.

Far more important in the church life of the parish was the building in 1844 of the new church in Aston Magna, the gift of Lord Redesdale of Batsford. Two years later he endowed it with £3500 in 3% Consols, which he later added to, and in 1853 he gave a parsonage house and 5 acres of glebe. This was not a sufficient endowment for an independent benefice, and Aston Magna remained a chapelry of Blockley parish still, though served by a resident curate. After Mr Coyle's departure its en-dowment was increased by Mr Bromfield's surrender of a por-tion of his tithe, and Aston Magna became a separate ecclesi-astical parish with the curate-in-charge, the Rev. E. F. Chamber-layne, as its first vicar, (1868).

Great changes in Blockley's communications with the outside world began in this period of the reign. The Penny Post of 1840 which followed a scheme by which letters were carried by coach to a sorting office in Moreton-in-Marsh at a charge varying according to the distance covered, and thence brought to Blockley and Campden by a postman at the cost of another penny, was the first of them.

The railway came to Blockley in 1853. Parliament had author-ised the building of the Oxford, Worcester and Wolverhampton line—"Old Worse and Worse" to its later critics—in 1845. George Rushout, nephew and heir of Lord Northwick was a director of the company, and the great Isambard Brunel as engineer was soon busy in the area planning the route. From 1850 onwards a rough horde of 'navvies' descended on it and were the cause of alarm for the next three years, especially after the 'battle of the Campden Tunnel' between rival gangs. The Crown and the Bell would have nothing to do with them, and the Railway Inn was founded to cater for them. Another visible survival from those days is the half-dug cutting at Aston Magna, where heavy rains in 1852 softened the clay and caused a land-slide towards the excavation, taking some cottages with it. The line had to be resited lower down. The first train ran along it on 16 June 1853. Just a year earlier the section of the line from Stourbridge to Evesham had been opened—to the sound, we read, of church bells, cannon and cheers all the way as the train passed from station to decorated station. So it must have been on that day at Blockley, where "about 2000 people were hos-pitably entertained," as Soden records. The company that built the line was soon obliged to sell it to the Great Western Railway.

The parish roads had suffered under the hooves of cart-horses and the wheels of wagons carrying heavy material for the con-struction of the railway. Richard Belcher, then among other offices, the elected surveyor of highways, saw in this an oppor-tunity for their thorough overhaul. He got money from the rail-way company by way of compensation for damage, more money from the sale, authorised by the vestry, of the parish quarries, and still more from the proceeds of a 3d. rate voted for the pur-pose. That vote could hardly be refused by the vestry, for Mr Belcher had saved it some hundreds of pounds in 1852 by personally, with some amateur help, working out a new and more productive rating assessment for the parish. With these resources it was possible for him, serving as waywarden or surveyor year after year, to put all the parish roads in order between the fences set out for them by the Enclosure Award of 1773, which had allowed 60-foot widths for major roads, like that to Evesham, Paxford, Campden or Bourton-on-the-Hill, and 30 feet for 'private' roads like Pasture Lane. In 1863 Blockley, on Belcher's motion, ceased to be a 'highway parish' and became a member of the Moreton District Highway Board, on which he served as the parish representative.

The visible memorial of Richard Belcher's work as waywarden for Blockley is the guard-rail provided for the safety of the user of the high footways in parts of the village, Before his time these ran along the top of high earth banks sloping down to the carriage way, which was thereby greatly narrowed, especially in the High Street. His reminiscences give this detail:

There were six footpaths several feet above the level of the horse-road and without any fence. Many dangerous accidents were occurring. I took them in hand, one each year, and completed them all with substantial iron posts and rails. I economised outlay during summer and autumn and set the unemployed to work in January and February. I was ably supported by the Vicar, who obtained voluntary contributions in aid of the rates. Widening narrow parts, draining, the pumps and the springs, all had attention.

Blockley owes much to this man of action of Victorian days. And it owes at least as much to the vicar, Henry Bromfield, whom he so often and so warmly claimed as his friend and ally, together with George, Lord Northwick, who succeeded to the title in 1859.

With a fast rising population—it increased by over 450 between 1841 and 1861—the parish needed much new building, and it was in this period that the houses in what is now Park Road were erected along the headland of the old Long Hedge Furlong. It is not difficult to see how the road came to be called Edge Lane till near the end of the century—it was little more than a footpath and much encroached on by the householders. It became the way to Campden only after Lord Northwick at his own expense converted the precipitous Dark Lane—Northcombe Bank (or Breakneck Hill) route into a viable carriage road by the building of the viaduct in 1870.[7]

The memory of this third and last Lord Northwick should be kept green in Blockley. His uncle, John Rushout, had done much for the amenity of the parish and for its education. But he was far more at home in his Cheltenham picture gallery or in London, at the Athenaeum or the rooms of the Society of Antiquaries, than on his country estate. The new Lord had been a captain in the Life Guards, and had then sat for 22 years in the House of Commons as member for Evesham and East Worcestershire before succeeding to the title, after which Northwick became his real home—with Harrow in second place. He married in 1869, when he was 48, Augusta Elizabeth, widow of Major George Warburton. It was a marriage so happy that it earned them an honorary Dunmow Flitch, duly certified by Somerset Herald. Richard Belcher, who certainly had nothing of the flunkey in his make-up, wrote of him that "he was one of the gentlest and most placid natures I have known. He was eccentric, but just, considerate and reliable in all his dealings."

The third member of this Blockley triumvirate of the 1860s and 1870s was the vicar, Henry Bromfield, "our worthy old vicar" to Richard Belcher, a Nonconformist through and through. He was collated to the living in 1855 and served his cure till 1878. A country clergyman of the school of Charles Kingsley, manly—'muscular Christianity' was a call of the day—peacable, approachable, compassionate, devout, he brought harmony to the life of the whole parish at a time of much hardship. Sectarian differences were forgotten. What could be better evidence of that than this excerpt from a school-girl's letter to her brother, Charles, who was at a boarding school in Somerset?—they were the children of Mr Belcher, and the occasion was a Baptist entertainment in the British School on a December evening in 1861:

> The soirée began at 5 and the clock struck 11 as we left the new school for home. The singing was so good. . . Mr Bromfield was in the chair, Papa made a very good speech, and Mr Mills the curate read from Longfellow so very nicely. J. Herbert recited some droll poetry, and our minister Mr Wassall made a speech too. The people roared and clapped and encored most tremendously. Everyone seemed pleased with every one else. . . It was one of the most glorious meetings I was ever at.

With Mr Wassall's successor, Charles James Middleditch (*Plate* 23) minister in Blockley 1865-1871, Mr Bromfield was even more intimately associated. They were colleagues on the parish vestry, the vicar as chairman, the minister as vice-chairman. Henry Sale, (*Plate* 33) for many years verger of the parish church, used to tell of a memory of his, perhaps dating from 1870, when he was seven, of his father coming home in Lower Street for supper after working in the churchyard and saying that the vicar and Mr Middleditch, walking arm in arm to a vestry meeting, had stopped to tell him how well the churchyard looked after he had scythed it. "There was," said Mr Sale, "a very good spirit in the village in those days."

There was a special reason for cheerfulness in the parish just then. An entirely unforeseen revival of the silk industry had been caused by the suspension of French competition under the impact of the Prussian invasion in 1870 and the fall of Napoleon III. It was a brief revival for the Blockley mills, a last flicker before the end, but we can draw again on Mr Sale's memories for a glimpse of a happy interval:

In 1871 I was eight and I went to work in Smith's mill (*now Mill Close*) for half the day. The twopence a day I earned helped to pay my school fees of 3d. a week. I had to go to the mill and light seven fires in time for them to be ready by six o'clock. Then I went home to breakfast of porridge and kettle-broth, hot water and brown sugar, and then I went to school from 9 to 12. In the afternoon I worked in the mill from 2.30 to 5 or 6, and after I was nine years old I got two shillings a week for it. It was good for me to do all this and I liked it, but I was a little afraid of seeing Mr Spilsbury's ghost that haunted the mill.

Mr Walker, the manager of the mill, was very musical. In those days the Birmingham Evangelical Society would come and have meetings in Belcher's field (*now Churchill Close*) and under the elms there we would sing Moody and Sankey songs. Mr Walker used to say: "Now byes and wenches,"—he called boys 'byes' because he came from Winchcombe way—"if you are good and work well, we'll have some music." Then he would take his viol, and the boys and wenches would sit in rows under the elms. We sang very well.

Those few twilight years of the silk trade in Blockley did indeed leave rather wistful memories for many of the mill workers. They recalled how work for the day always ended with the singing of an evening hymn. The rhymester already quoted[8] remembered how:

It was a blithesome merry rout
When from the mills the hands came out.
Ill fared it then with passers-by.
If they attempted jokes to try.

But the bustle of the mills quickly died away. France recovered from her war losses and was sending her silk goods into England so soon that Soden, writing in 1874 recorded that only two mills were then working, Edwin Smith's and George Stanley's at Snugborough. Smith's mill struggled on to the mid-1880s, but only spasmodically—if William de Morgan's account of a visit he paid to the village in 1880 with William Morris is correct in its statement that "the mills were all empty and decaying." It is only too certain that by 1885 the Blockley silk trade was dead.

In fact not all the mills were empty. Some were put to other uses. The one in the Coneygree, then owned by George Cannon Smith, James Smith's son, was partly occupied by a London firm which manufactured collars and shirt fronts. Soon two more of the mills were turning out piano frames—at Snugborough and at the former corn mill which is today called Milldene, where John Acock produced complete pianos as well, "proper tinakalorums" as an old village owner of one of them put it. The old Russell 'Malvern Mill,' which had produced no silk yarn since the 1850s, was used for wood sawing, threshing corn and, in season, cider making. Westmacott's was producing ramie fibre,[9] used for rope making and certain kinds of weaving, and later turned over to soft soap. The Good Intent, after the fire there, ground gorse and furze for the fallow deer in Northwick Park. All were stopgap enterprises with no future in them.

Epidemic disease from time to time added to the misery of many families in the parish. Prejudice, surviving from the earlier inoculation days, led to the neglect of the new safeguard of vaccination, and consequently to outbreaks of small-pox. A very severe epidemic in 1876 coincided with the collapse of the silk trade and drastic steps were called for. The vicar, Mr Bromfield, and Mr Belcher were members of the Board of Poor Law Guardians, and the latter gave this account of their action:

The outbreak put me to the utmost exertion of my strength to combat it. I and the Vicar were the only persons bold enough to visit the patients. We raised a fund of £45 to aid the grant from the Union. We engaged three excellent trained nurses, the best I ever knew. The Vicar's wife was ever ready with advice and aid. Our sanitary officer was a worthless dotard. During my absence one hot day he burnt the beds, blankets and everything in the house (*of a man who had died*). The deadly smoke carried the infection all around and many new cases ensued. Just as we hoped the spread was checked one woman who was sickening ran away from waiting on her sister back to her home at the other end of the village. Now a great contention arose. The lower end would not have her back. I called together a meeting at 9 o'clock. A builder was one of us. I put it to him to turn all his men on the work of building a hospital, and by 10 o'clock we had our fugitive woman safely housed with another patient and a nurse to attend them. It was a wooden structure in the middle of my field. The plague was stayed.

Cholera, because it was a newer and more deadly plague, was even more feared. There was a tragic outbreak in 1854, causing 21 deaths in the parish, 14 of them in a single week. It was, incidentally, followed by small-pox in the following year, making a discouraging welcome for Henry Bromfield (*Plate* 24) then just taking over his new parish. Cholera made the country acutely anxious about sewage disposal and water supply, and the minutes of the vestry meetings from 1860 onwards are full of local evidence of that anxiety, Paxford being a special cause for concern. A wide-spread epidemic of cholera in 1866 raised anxiety to fever pitch, though the disease did not, in fact, reach Blockley. Mr Bromfield, who had led the discussions on the subject, was for some reason absent from meetings of the vestry at the height of the crisis and for six months the chair was taken by the vice-chairman, Mr Middleditch, and occasionally by Mr Belcher. But it was Lord Northwick who finally set fears at rest by another of his massive benefactions. In 1868 he bore the whole cost of a complete sewage system for Blockley.

Sickness and unemployment have bulked large in this mid-Victorian period of the parish history, but there were alleviations, as will be later described. Here we may notice one of them which went wrong in the troubled 1870s, when so much else was going wrong. The parish had two Friendly Societies, founded to provide relief for their members in time of sickness, disability and death. The Blockley Benefit Society, founded in 1763 and usually called the Old Club, was originally, no doubt, one of Vicar Selwyn's plans for social welfare. The New Club, more formally named the Victoria Friendly Society, evidently got its title in 1837, the year of the Queen's accession, though Eyre's account of it shows that it was in full operation at least ten years earlier.[10] Both clubs raised their funds from members' subscriptions of 16s. a year and from volunatry support of a more substantial kind from honorary members. Both were actuarially unsound, for old and young alike paid the same subscription and drew the same sickness benefit of 6s. weekly for indefinite periods. Both improvidently subsidised their annual 'feasts' in Whitsun week—to the disquiet of the clergy, who were closely associated with the cause. Earlier in the century the New Club had amassed funds enough to purchase the Crown Inn and to build in its yard a room large enough for its gatherings; but in 1870, as Soden anxiously noted, its annual income was about £100, while its expenditure was £150. Two years later it was compulsorily wound up, the Crown was sold and the balance of its assets divided between the members. The Old Club lasted a little longer, but its accounts for 1868, showing receipts of £149 and expenses of £185, of which £26 were for the feast, explain why neither Friendly Society survived.

The Blockley Riot of March 1878 was the most sensational symptom of the privation and frustration of that time. The mills were shut, farming was now feeling the effects of freely imported grain from America, the small-pox outbreak of a year or so before was not forgotten—and now a new provocation arose. Poaching in those hungry times was a compulsive resource—and it had suddenly become more than ever difficult. A watchful keeper in Bourton Wood and a zealous police sergeant in the new Lower Street station became a sore trial. Richard Belcher's account is telling:

> Two innocent young men fled from the village and never returned because they had picked up a rabbit which they found in a snare. Another was arrested for picking up three partridge eggs which had been placed on the bare ground by the keeper. Yet another who was charged with poaching was put to the expense of £8 for a lawyer and a cartload of witnesses to establish his innocence. Oliver B. was stopped on his way home by a bough blown off a tree, which had obstructed the traffic for many days. He took the bough into his trap and openly put it into his garden. Our zealous policeman obtained a warrant and B. was locked up in the police cell for two days and nights and then committed to Worcester Sessions, where he was acquitted.

The trouble exploded on a Saturday night—after a morning

when several Blockley men had been charged by Sergeant Drury before the magistrates at Shipston. It was not wise of him to choose that evening for a visit to the Crown to see that all was in order. The moment his head appeared above the settle just inside the door someone flung a quart pot at it. He fled, pursued by a mob which grew as doors along the High Street opened to let others join it. The rout tore through the churchyard and down into Lower Street where he just managed to lock the door of the police station on the furious pack. Here the Evesham Journal can take up the story:

> The mob thereupon commenced to strip the wall on the opposite side of the road of stones which they threw at the house, smashing all the windows, sashes and bars. They next pulled up the wrought-iron palings, threw down the stone buttresses on each side of the gateway, tore up rose-trees by the roots ... and burst open the door. On getting into the room where Drury was concealed with his wife, the rioters seized him, struck his head with a blunt weapon and dragged him into the street, where some took running kicks at his body and others jumped upon his chest and stoned him. ...

His life was saved by some newcomers on the scene, a Stanley and a Figgures among them, and he was taken into the Keyte household for urgent medical care. Not all the blame for this violence can be put to the discredit of Blockley men, for there were strangers in the drunken crowd, woodmen brought into the district to fell trees at Spring Hill. But it was Blockley men only who had to appear for trial at the Mid-summer Sessions at Worcester—and it was, predictably, Mr Richard Belcher who took up the cudgels on their behalf in the columns of the *Journal* after the trial. He had good reason, for the ringleaders had escaped arrest.[11]

Henry Bromfield's ministry ended just as these things happened. Something of its character may have emerged from the incidental references already made to him. It is time for a more substantial account of it.

There were noteworthy developments in parochial organization under him. His part in the hiving off of Aston Magna as an independent parish has been described. Paxford also had reason to feel that his generous influence was at work when, in

1866, a Baptist, Richard Reynolds of Paxford House, gave the site for a new building (to which he later added a bell, belfry and clock) to be used for Anglican worship on Sundays and as a Church school on weekdays. The actual building was the gift of Mrs Gilbert Elliott, then resident there. There is something to stir the imagination in the ecumenical spirit here shown. His easy relations with his curates give another aspect of his friendly ways. One of them, Alfred Soden, pays quiet tribute to his vicar more than once in his history of the parish. Another, incidentally, Henry Fisher, who served under Bromfield in the 1860s, should go on record as the father of a future Archbishop of Canterbury, Lord Fisher of Lambeth.[12]

In 1867 a new Girls and Infants School was opened in what was then called New Lane. The site was given by Admiral Collier and the cost of the building, which was outstanding for its period and remains in full use today, was met by public subscription, the landowners of the district and the vicar himself being the largest contributors, by bazaars in the parish and by grants from Church institutions. This left both floors in the school in the churchyard for the teaching of boys.

The interior of the parish church was given a very new look about this time. We know from a schoolboy's letter that in February 1861 they were scraping the walls of the church and had found on them a picture of 'his Satanic Majesty', perhaps in a fresco of the Last Judgement, and other paintings. Soden confirms this:

> During the late alterations fragmentary portions of ancient fresco paintings were discovered on both walls and arches in several layers, indicating that they had been painted at different periods. They were too much mutilated and the material too friable to justify any attempt to preserve them.

The 'anti-scrape' Society for the Preservation of Ancient Buildings unfortunately did not then exist to give expert advice. Another of Mr Bromfield's improvements was more happily conceived. In 1868 at his own expense he repewed the north half of the nave and four years later he organized a public subscription for new seats on its south side. We may not find them very comfortable today, but the change from the unseemly jumble of old high pews, as Soden notes, must have been all to the good. In that same year 1872 Lord Northwick met most of the cost of restoration of the north aisle and then replaced what Soden calls the 'hideous structures which lately occupied it'—they included the Porch House pew—and replaced them by the oak seating we know today.[13] A pleasant little glimpse of the Northwick household entering church to occupy it is given in a reminiscence of Mrs Gould, a Herbert before her marriage:

> I remember going to church on Sundays and seeing Lord and Lady Northwick enter, followed by their retinue of servants, all in correct order of precedence. Lord Northwick did not kneel to say a prayer on entering church, but stood and murmured into his top-hat. It was a weekly delight to the children (in the gallery).

Lord Northwick also presented in 1860 the first organ used in the church. We know its place on the south side of the chancel by the absence of one of the ancient clusters of corbels, which was chiselled away to let the organ stand flat against the wall. We may gather from this that Mr Bromfield was the first vicar to have a choir,[14] and that it occupied the front of the gallery, for the seat on the north side of the chancel, with the initials of Erasmus Saunders carved above it, was the Vicarage pew. Herbert Barnes remembered that:

> Mr Bromfield was a man of means and drove about the parish in a carriage and pair. Sometimes he would come to the choir practice, which was held in the school, and he always brought a basket with wine and cake for the choristers.

Cricket in the village owed much to him. Those mid-Victorian years saw the foundation of clubs all over the country. Fred Herbert looked back in 1887 on Blockley's part in it:

> A club was first formed in 1840. I remember seeing some of the Westmacotts, Charles Hobbs (of the Old Mill), John Herbert and others play in what was called Hobbs's Park. In 1851 a few of us joined in forming a new club. We met in the street on a summer's evening and framed some rules—
> Each member to pay one shilling on entering.
> Each member to be in the playing field on Monday and Thursday evenings before 7 o'clock or be fined 1d., or 2d. if he be not there by 8.

Plate 50 Astral Electricity Works, now Mill Close, 1889. *(Photograph by Lord Edward Spencer-Churchill)* Nigel Warburton and Charles Barter on the steps of Astral Works, 1888.

Plate 51   Joyner's Stores, c. 1890 with advertisement (*below*) of illumination by electricity from the Astral Works.

Plate 52 Milton's Stores, c. 1900 (subsequently Ford's and then Balhatchet's) with Edward and William Milton. On left, Blockley Workhouse, built 1740.

Plate 53 Balhatchet's Christmas display, c. 1908, with Dashwood Albert and Thomas Dashwood Balhatchet.

Plate 54   Sirrett's photographic shop, c. 1905 and Chapel gates.

Plate 55   Upper High Street, c. 1922.

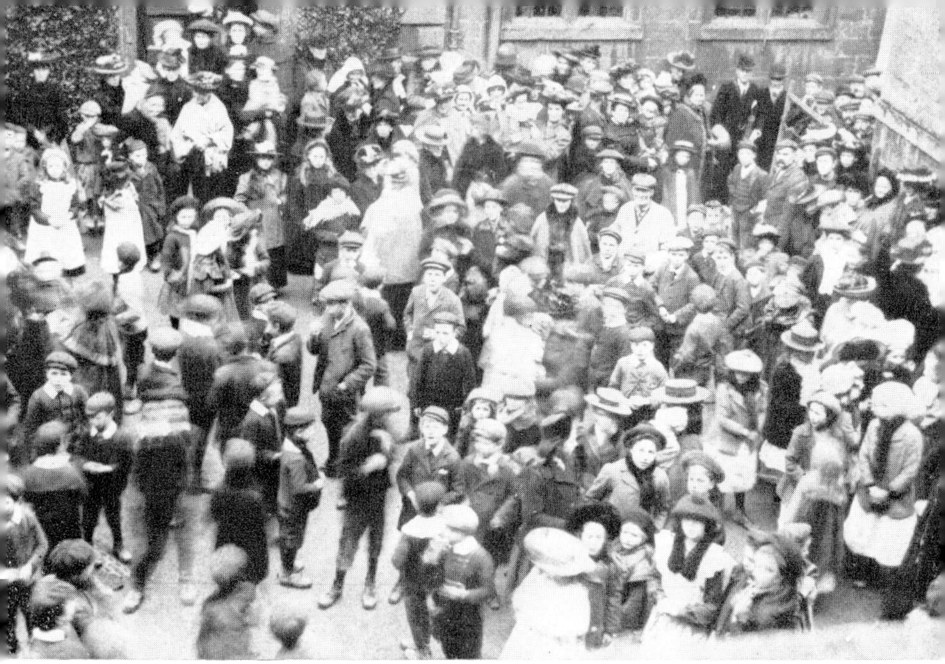

Plate 56 St. Thomas' Day celebration at Northwick c. 1903. (All children were given one penny.) *Photograph by Chapman of Blockley.*

Plate 57 Funeral of victims of 'bus accident, 1924, (*Photograph by Mayo, Blockley*)

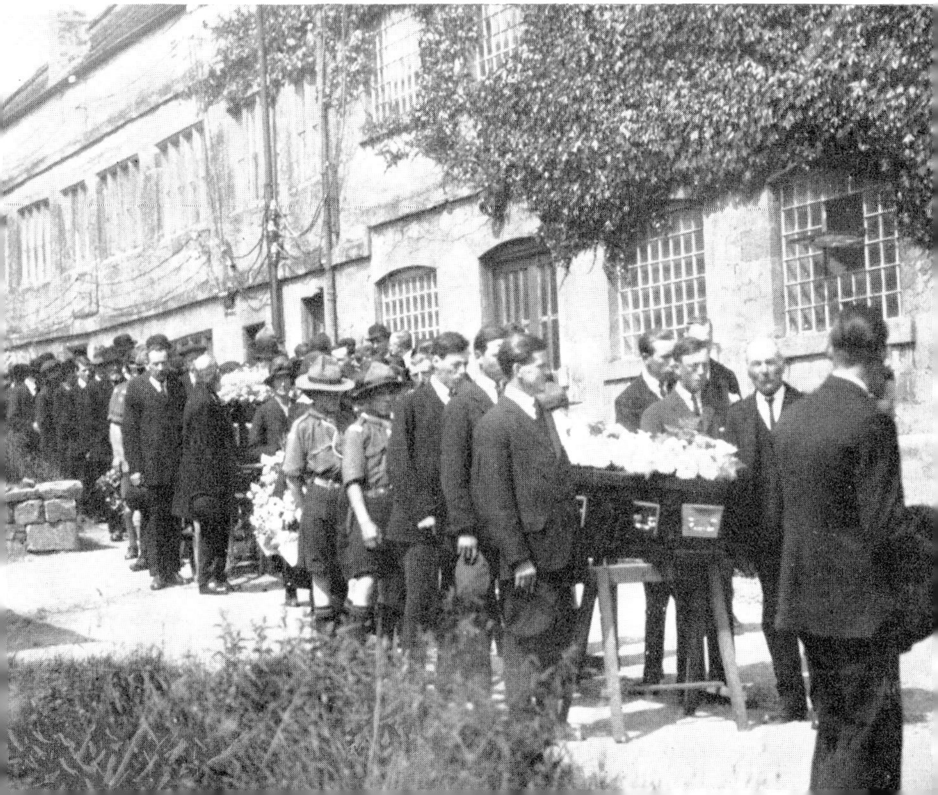

Plate 58   Pain Family group, including Mr & Mrs Hopes, Laura Pain, grandfather William Pain, Conrad Warner and his mother.

Plate 59   Diamond Jubilee Tea Party, 1897, Dovedale End.

Plate 60 Aerial map, 1953, showing flow of the stream. (*Photograph by permission of Aerofilms Ltd.*)

Plate 61
The High Street
in 1900 . . .

. . . and in 1974,
showing traffic
congestion.

Other fines were 2d. for leaving before play ends: 1d. for smoking during play: 1d. for lying down during play: $\frac{1}{2}$d. for every oath uttered.

Our greatest difficulty was to know where we might play. My cousin Josiah Herbert went to London and bought a bat made by Pilch and Martin, famous makers, but we had to put up with gutta percha balls and home-made wickets.

In 1855 the Rev. H. Bromfield came as our vicar, and he, with his son, soon put the club in a thriving condition. His curate, the Rev. E. O. Tyler, also greatly improved our play. We began playing matches and beat Evesham. Now we can boast of a stately vessel which may honestly be called The Invincible.

It seems, indeed, that it was Blockley's unanimous verdict on Henry Bromfield that, to use a phrase put into the mouth of one of his villagers by Thomas Hardy, "he was a good man and he did good things."[15] His grave a few yards to the northeast of the church lies, true to his character, among those of his people —as unobtrusive as the window in the chancel which they set up to his memory.

His successor was Canon E. J. Houghton, who ruled the parish for forty-one years, 1878–1919. He was scholarly, vigorous and devoted to his calling—an impressive figure, not, perhaps, easily approachable, as his predecessor had been. He had not been long in the vicarage before he roused the wrath of the village by putting a stop to the ringing of the Five O'Clock Bell from the church tower—a standing custom devised for the rousing of workers from slumber, and tolerated, though it cannot have been enjoyed, by earlier occupants of the vicarage. The vicar was deaf to all protests, whether from his church-wardens, one of whom resigned, or the vestry, or the authors of printed broadsides, such as one which read:

HERE LIES FOR EVER DUMB
until the Day of Disestablishment
when it will arise in all its beauty
THE 5 O'CLOCK BELL
cruelly murdered by its Guardian and Custodian
after 800 years of humble but valued
service to the Parish.

145

The sheet went on to impute 'cold priestly hate' as the vicar's motive. Here was sectarian bitterness—and all within two years of Mr Bromfield's departure. Richard Belcher shared in it, and, indeed, spelled it out in his memoir:

> Every morning at 5 o'clock a bell had been rung to rouse men who had the care of horses and cattle. It was a great convenience, and dated back perhaps to the Conquest. The bell had been hated by the High Church clergy as a desecration of their consecrated tower. It was stopped against the wish of the whole parish. A great uproar ensued and another riot seemed to be impending. The vicar was so alarmed that he sent for eight police from Worcester. He was caricatured in small bills, for which there was an immense sale. From that time he has been constantly disturbing the parish with his innovations.

The vicar, of course, had his way in the matter of the bell, but he had his reverses. In 1894, as part of its great reform of Local Government which had begun with the creation of the County Councils six years before, Parliament abolished the civil functions of the parish vestries and set up the Parish Councils which we know today. The vicar had been chairman of the vestry *ex officio*. But the first elected chairman of the new Blockley Parish Council was his enemy, J. C. Reynolds, magistrate, farmer, Baptist, great-grandson of Elisha Smith—and son-in-law of Richard Belcher. Mr Reynolds had succeeded to the property of his uncle, Richard Reynolds, in Paxford, but not to his generous church views. He clashed with Canon Houghton on many a battle field— in the columns of the Evesham Journal, once even in a law court. But it was as a manager of the Blockley and Paxford church schools that Mr Reynolds, under the chairmanship of the vicar, clashed most bitterly. The Education Act of 1902 had made it possible for 'Voluntary' or 'Church' Schools to be aided from the rates, and a fury of protest had exploded from Nonconformists all over the country which fanned sectarian strife to white heat. As compensation for receiving public money the Church had to receive on its boards of school managers members representing the new local authorities, and it was as representative of the Blockley Parish Council that J. C. Reynolds now faced the vicar, who resented his presence. Reynolds lost no time before demanding great improvements in the accommodation and amenities of the Boys' School in Blockley and the Infants' School in Paxford—and with very good reason, as the school inspectors proclaimed year after year, until they were obliged in 1904 to 'blacklist' the Boys' School and threaten its replacement by a Board School if improvements, to be paid for from church funds, were not forthcoming. The vicar resisted every inch of the way, and the death of Mr Reynolds in 1905 removed his one implacable local adversary. But the inspectors, the County Council and the Board of Education had the last word, and in 1910 Canon Houghton gave up the unequal struggle. Lady Northwick, who since her husband's death in 1887 had been the owner of the estate, came to the rescue. She gave a site for a new boys' school on Colonel's Piece and met nearly all the cost of the building. She took in exchange the old school premises in the churchyard. The Paxford school was closed, and the children were transferred to Blockley.

We catch a glimpse of Blockley church in the autumn of 1888 in a note made by a visitor to the village. It chanced to be a rather special occasion:

> ... Sunday passed quietly away with two visits to the parish church, with eloquent sermons from the gifted vicar, the Rev. E. J. Houghton. In the evening the church was lit for the first time with the electric light, and it was certainly interesting to see one of the latest discoveries of modern science introduced into a village sanctuary ... [16]

It was indeed. Blockley may well have been, as it has always claimed, the first English village to be so lit. It had the water power for the generation of current in some now disused mills. It had, too, a newcomer with the means, the outside experience and the quickness of mind to take up new ideas in Lord Edward Spencer-Churchill. Himself a younger son of the Duke of Marlborough, he had married the daughter of Lady Northwick and her first husband, Major George Warburton. They were then living in Dovedale House with their young son Edward George Spencer-Churchill. That Lord Edward was the prime mover in bringing electricity is suggested by the facts that three of the directors of the company providing the service, of which he was chairman, were relatives of his wife, or himself, that the first dynamo to be installed was close to his own house, and that his brother, Lord Randolph Churchill, had perhaps set the example in his London house—a publication of 1885 refers to that in a phrase which shows that Blockley was not far behind even London: "His house is one of the few which possess the electric light."[17] Other mills were brought into service for additional power, and the illumination of the Church, which had also a light on the tower for a time, was no doubt made possible by the main installation in the lately closed Smith's Mill. The whole system was taken over and modernised by the S.W.S. Power Co. in 1931, and became part of the national grid after the second World War.

The Baptist church in Blockley suffered a heavy loss of resources through the collapse of the silk trade, and by the 1880s the membership had fallen to 56. The foundation by Mrs Judson of her Malvern House boarding school for girls then brought reinforcement, and there was some revival in the 1880s under the Rev. J. Dann and the Rev. E. G. Lovell, two able and devoted ministers. But Mr Lovell had to leave in 1897 with half his yearly salary of £80 still owing to him, and the school moved in the same year to new premises at Malvern. Nevertheless the church, though it lacked resources, had strong leaders in men like R. B. Belcher, J. C. Reynolds and James Joyner, and in the Rev. H. Rolfe a minister (1898–1902) who served it well and was greatly loved for his friendship and pastoral care.[18] The death of Richard Belcher in 1901 marked an epoch in its history. There is a story, which one would hope to be true, that Canon Houghton visited him shortly before he died and that the two men made their peace together.

This chapter of ups and downs may perhaps end on that note— and so, not inappropriately, on a cricket field. It is the story of a match played by the Blockley Cricket Club in or soon after 1901, as it was remembered many years later by Arthur Reynolds, son of the J. C. Reynolds familiar to us in a less peaceful context. Coming from such a source, the story is the more significant:

> I only vaguely remember the Canon himself playing, but I do very clearly recollect this team:
> Jack, Cyril and Arthur Houghton.

J. Draper and C. Barter, partners in the electric lighting of the village,

C. F. Cholmondeley and A. W. F. Norton, curates,

Harry Evans (an immortal) and Harry Leadbetter, his bowling partner,

J. C. Reynolds, useful all-rounder and wicket-keeper,

Harry Smith, carpenter,

Joe Barber, stone mason,

Charles Figgures, a mighty slogger.

Of these players, Arthur Houghton was my hero.

I recall one incident which would amuse any old or young cricketer–

A summer afternoon, not a cloud in the sky. The wickets pitched as usual on the slope (*of the Cinquefoil*), and the pavilion in its old place with scorer and members watching the game. To the left a tent or two, one of which was the Vicar's. To the right a small party of villagers, including Joe Barber, drinking beer from a small barrel. A cry of 'How's that?' rent the air, and a batsman was seen walking towards the pavilion, well and truly out according to the umpire.

Watching from the pavilion, I observed Joe Barber leave his friends and, with a glass of beer in his hand, walk across to the umpire, ostensibly to give him a refresher, when up rushed a fieldsman, one of the Houghtons to wit, and knocked the glass out of the intruder's hand. After which he ran across to the beer drinkers and began to give them a piece of his mind. Rude remarks were at once made to him, and the players came over and milled round, until at last peace was achieved by the intervention of Mr Cholmondeley, the curate, a good and delightful character.

News of the row went round the village in no time. A meeting of the club was called for that night, at which my father, though not playing that day, was asked to attend. (He) proposed that Joe Barber be called in and heard. This was objected to, but finally carried. In the end he apologised, and that was the end of a beautiful summer's day long ago.

[1] The freehold had remained in the possession of the descendants of Dr Erasmus Saunders ever since he acquired it.

[2] Marshall, *ibid.* 12.

[3] *Guide to Worcestershire* (1850), 68.

[4] The bottom step of the ladder by which they went down into the water was still to be seen in the 1950's.

[5] See p. 122

[6] Peel's Factory Act of 1844 required employers of children to provide at least two hours of schooling for them daily.

[7] Before that date the normal route to Campden was by way of Paxford Lane (now Station Road) and Sedgecombe.

[8] See p.133

[9] Marshall, *ibid.* 15. The W.I. Survey of the Last Hundred Years in Blockley (1958) gives a detailed account of the village industries. See also Soden 15–7.

[10] Soden wrongly gives 1837 as the year of its establishment.

[11] An amusing account in dialect of this really ugly scene, as told by an old lady who saw it as a child, is printed in *The Countryman* (Winter 1961), pp. 784–6. See also Appendix p. 230

[12] For this and for much other detail of Blockley lore I am indebted to Mrs Clare Spurgin. In a letter to her the archbishop recalled that it was during his Blockley curacy that his father became engaged to his mother, a daughter of the rector of Wyck Rissington. . . "I am sure that as a curate there my father was what he always remained–active, alert minded, friendly, conscientious and scholarly–always respected but without much merely 'popular' appeal. It was not called for then."

[13] Soden, 37.

[14] The pitch-pipe with which the clerk in earlier days gave the note to the congregation is now in the Blockley collection of antiquities.

[15] in *The Woodlanders*.

[16] Hereford *Times*, 3 Nov. 1888.

[17] Quoted by Osbert Sitwell in *Left Hand, Right Hand*. The filament bulb had been invented only two years before. See also Appendix 235-6

[18] He was the founder of the Blockley Women's Meeting, a lasting village institution.

CHAPTER FOURTEEN

In this Century of Change

THE DEATH OF Queen Victoria at the dawn of the new century marked the true end of an epoch. It calls for no great effort of imagination to picture the effect on a rural community still largely static, inward looking, respectful to the traditional authorities, no more than partially literate, of such new inventions or institutions, all falling within a few years before or after that crucial date in 1901, as the 'safety' bicycle, the Daily Mail (1898) and the popular national press which it inaugurated, the earliest motor cars, Marconi's 'wireless' experiments, Parish Councils, Old Age Pensions (1908) and the national insurance against ill health and unemployment which soon followed. All these opened up new vistas of cultural and social change. And then, in 1914, the great catalyst of a World War came to precipitate the transformation.

Edwardian Transition (1901–11)

No great outward change was to be seen in Blockley during this decade, but there were restless stirrings which came to the surface most notably in the controversy about the boys' school earlier referred to.[1] Poverty was grievous still, with agriculture in the doldrums and the make-shift industries in the derelict silk mills closing down. It was mainly to provide employment that Lord Redesdale in 1901 promoted the establishment of the Gloucestershire Brick Co. at Aston Magna, a lasting boon. Captain Spencer-Churchill for the same purpose set up the Northwick Brickworks at the Station, after World War I: purpose-made bricks from there were used for Battersea Power Station, Taunton Town Hall, and many other well-known buildings. The Butler Saw Mills at Draycott, too, were flourishing. Squire and parson still commanded respect. Lady Northwick, with help from her daughter and son-in-law, Lord Edward Churchill, exercised benevolent sway over her tenants, and her carriage was often to be seen outside the cottages and the schools in Blockley and Paxford. Canon Houghton had their firm support in the controversy about the village schools, described on an earlier page.[1] Lord Edward served as his churchwarden. Both men were Tories, and the Canon's presence at Primrose League gatherings in Northwick Park added somewhat to his critics. That probably did not greatly trouble the old vicar as he went about his parish, masterful as ever, austere, uncompromising and old-fashioned. He had his mellower qualities. A succession of loyal curates, cricketers almost to a man, helped him to keep touch with the men of the parish. Some account has been given of cricket on the Cinquefoil, and a genial memory of this side of the doings of the family at the vicarage is recorded in the memoirs of 'Freddie' Grisewood, the well-known broadcaster, a pupil there just before the first World War. His father had been one of the curates.

A thousand-year-old tradition ended in 1906, when the bishops of Worcester ceased to be patrons of the living of Blockley. The patronage passed to the vicar of Bromsgrove by way of compensation for the loss to him and his successors of the right to present to the benefice of Kings Norton, a suburb of Birmingham which fell within the bounds of that recently created see. One last link with the bishops of Worcester remained. That was broken when in 1919 the ecclesiastical parish of Blockley was transferred to the diocese of Gloucester. The civil parish in its turn became part of Gloucestershire in 1931, and Blockley was thus finally cut off from its historical roots. Of its people's reaction to the change it may be said that "Some natural tears they dropped, but wiped them soon." Solid benefits have come and the parish has been especially happy in its representation on the Gloucestershire County Council.[2]

But our narrative must return to the earliest years of the century and the doings of Blockley folk. One of the most respected of them was James Keen, of a family long established in the parish. A shoemaker by trade he was at the heart of a number of traditional organizations in the village. Soden records that he was leader of the bell ringers in 1874. In that he must have been keeping up a family tradition, for the churchwardens' accounts show that a John Keen was head ringer in the time of George II and was paid 1s. 6d. for the refreshment of the men who under him rang the peal for the coronation of that king in 1729. He was also leader of the brass band and custodian of its instruments. The band has ever since been a cherished institution, serving and entertaining the parish and, on occasion, other neighbouring villages. Before Mr Keen's day the shoe was on the other foot and, in 1861, the Victoria Friendly Society had to call on the band of the Moreton and Campden Volunteer Rifle Corps to lead its traditional march before its annual feast, a fife and drum band which was then practising under the church organist, not being, as it would seem, quite ready for the task. In its honourable history since those early years of the century the Blockley Brass Band has played its part in Remembrance Day and other national occasions, in the churches, in concerts, at Christmas time for carols. Many good Blockley names occur in the list of its members since Keen's time, but there is space to mention only one to stand for them all: that of Baden Godson, bandmaster after the second World War, and other members of his family.

Music was James Keen's grand passion—he was church organist and it is on record that on many Sundays he played in other churches besides his own in Blockley. In 1901 he found a newcomer to the village who shared his musical passion, John Milton. Together they founded the Blockley Choral Society. There had been an earlier enterprise of the sort, for a programme has survived of a concert held "in the Assembly Room of the Crown Inn for the benefit of Mr W. Warner, pianist of the Blockley Choral Society." Sacred music, drawing room ballads and comic songs made up that programme of 1866. When Keen and Milton started their Singing Class—it took the title of Choral Society five years later, in 1906, when first it took part in the annual festival of the Stour Choral Union—they had far loftier aims.

Under a succession of inspiring conductors, of whom Reginald Smeeton is the latest, the society has presented choral works grave and gay, winning many 'banners' in the festival competitions, prior to 1964 since when the Society has given ambitious concerts employing professional musicians. John Milton lived to serve it as its leading spirit, librarian and occasional conductor for fifty years.

The Miltons were newcomers who quickly made their mark in the parish in other ways. Three brothers, of whom John was the youngest, opened their High Street grocery store in 1898. Edward and John married sisters from Surrey, both of them teachers, Edith and Alberta Walker by name. The parish church as well as the schools had long and loyal service from them over many years. Another family closely bound up with Blockley life in these Edwardian times and after was that of the Balhatchets. Thomas Dashwood Balhatchet had come from Evesham in the 1870's to take over from the Herbert brothers the business of butcher in the High Street which, after a century, is still in the family. Widely known and respected, as was his son who succeeded him, in 1910, he had great influence in the life of the parish, and as churchwarden he was a loyal supporter of Canon Houghton. It would, indeed, make a long story to recite the services of the Milton and Balhatchet families to Blockley church. A Balhatchet—Morris, grandson of Thomas Dashwood, is churchwarden and organist today (1974), and Angus Milton, as churchwarden, and leading member of the choir in the mid-century, kept up a family tradition in like manner. *Plates* 52-3

Lady Northwick died in 1912. Her son-in-law had died in the previous year, and the Northwick estate thus passed to her grandson, Captain Edward George Spencer-Churchill of the Grenadier Guards. (*Plate* 27). He was to be 'squire'[3] for half a century.

Captain Churchill was a true Blockley man, having been born in Dovedale House. He was educated at Eton and Magdalen College, Oxford. While an undergraduate he made a name for himself by acquiring an X-ray apparatus—only two years after its invention in 1895 by Röntgen and before the University itself had got one. He even had to lend it to the army medical services in the South African War, in which he himself served. In later years he put his considerable knowledge of mathematics to

154

similar practical use, applying the theory of probability at the bridge table and that of geometry in the squash court. His renown as a connoisseur and collector of paintings and of ancient Greek and Etruscan antiquities made him known throughout the artistic world. He served a term as a trustee of the National Gallery, and it was fitting that some of the masterpieces of that collection including the Flinders Petrie Collection were stored for safety during the second World War at Northwick. His Blockley neighbours recall his unobtrusively learned guidance among the treasures of his own great collection and the recitals by well-known artists within the glowing walls of the picture gallery, (*Plate* 31) to which he invited music lovers from the country round. Lord Wavell often visited Northwick: Lady Wavell's mother had been a great friend of the family. He passed through from Washington to New Delhi during War Weapons Week when other guests at Northwick had no idea he was taking up the Viceroyalty of India. His book "Other Men's Flowers" ends with one of his own sonnets to the "Madonna of the Cherries" (School of Leonardo da Vinci) which Captain Churchill left to Lady Wavell. This picture was an inspiration to Lord Wavell all his life.

The parish received many benefactions from Captain Churchill. The first, shortly before the war in 1914, was the conversion of the southern portion of the Mill Close building into an Institute for the recreation and meetings of people of the village. He also had the adjoining part of the field levelled to form the bowling green, on which the club, called after his name, has ever since flourished and brightened the village scene. The Institute was unhappily destroyed by fire in 1931. The Astral electrical generating plant, which occupied the middle portion of the old mill, was closed down in the same year,[4] and the whole structure rebuilt for residential use.

The First World War, 1914–18

It was on other fields and distant oceans that Blockley's history was made in the war years in the deeper sense, and the memorials in the church (the work of the Campden artist, F. L. Griggs) and near the site of the old town elm contain the names of close on sixty who did not return. Many are the names of the oldest of

Blockley families: Cother, Eastbury, Eden, Figgures, Herbert, Hitchman, Keen, Keyte, Ledbetter, Mumford, Sale, Taplin, Turvey, Warner and Webb among them, none of these going back less than a century in the parish annals, and two at least as many as four. Among those who did return was Captain Churchill, but only after the narrowest of escapes after a grave head wound at the battle of Loos. He was in fact in his grave when a friend noticed an eyelid flicker.

The call for skilled men to remain on the farms and for younger women to serve in the Land Army kept many at home. Dovedale and Bourton Wood lost most of their standing timber. All the neighbourliness of English village life was on call. Elisha Smith's old meeting house up Bell Bank, then tenantless, was re-opened as a recreation room for troops stationed in the district and for young people under the management of ladies of the village.

It was during the war that Canon Houghton died. He had been ill for many months, his work being carried on by the Rev. Dr. Holbrooke. Here was indeed a break with the past.

Between the Wars, 1919–39

The new vicar was the Rev. A. D. Ager, curate of Bromsgrove and the first nominee of the vicar of that parish, the new patron. It was a happy appointment and during the ten years of his ministry Mr Ager was a unifying influence throughout the community. To the Baptists, then well led by their ministers and by such laymen as Charles Belcher and Henry Yoxall, he was, as Henry Bromfield had been, 'our Vicar.' He was a close friend of the ministers of those years, the Rev. Frank Smith (1921–22), the Rev. J. A. Cook (1922–25) and the Rev. Wilfred Farrar, and shared transport with them for their respective Sunday afternoon services in Paxford. With the men returned from the wars he was a respected and approachable vicar.

It fell to him to implement the measures for the better representation of the laity enacted by the new Church Assembly. The Blockley Parochial Church Council first met in 1922, with John Milton as its secretary, to be succeeded by Mrs Edith Milton later. Ager was soon joined by a curate after his own heart, the Rev. D. H. Bodley. Great changes in the fabric of the church were made in order to modernise the order of services.

The gallery at the west end was removed[5] and the organ brought from the chancel and placed there (1924). The choir was thus better accommodated in the chancel, and a new choir vestry (rather awkwardly perhaps) was screened off with oak panelling in the south-west corner of the nave. Ill health obliged Mr Ager in 1929 to exchange into a smaller parish in Wiltshire, and the Rev. Philip Jasper became vicar of Blockley in his place.

Since the beginning of the century the parish of Blockley, like most other attractive villages, had been acquiring more than ever before a new kind of resident. The traditional new settlers had come to earn their living in the place—as clergy or farmers, shop keepers, doctors or teachers. Now, more or less well-to-do folk, retired after their life's work elsewhere, or able to do it from a home in the country, or as week-end cottagers, were taking an ever larger share in village life and housing. They were not organic to the community in the way the categories just mentioned were, and they brought about a great social, economic and cultural change as time went on. The Cotswolds, so easily accessible to Oxford, Birmingham and other centres by train, bicycle or motor car, lay wide open for such people. Summer visitors before the first World War found welcome accommodation in Blockley farms in those hard times for farmers: Oxford reading parties and college cricket teams came and went: and for the would-be settler there were converted silk mills and tumble-down cottages to convert. Influential new residents included Col. Turner, retired prison governor and his American wife, author under the name of Margaret Wilson, of several well-known books, including "Daughters of India" and "The Able McLaughlins." She was President of the Women's Institute from 1942–50 and was succeeded by Miss Cecilia Compton-Smith, talented artist and creator of one of the village's most beautiful gardens.

Another newcomer was Henry Smallwood Yoxall. A Birmingham industrialist, justice of the peace, chairman of the Winson Green prison committee and leading lay Methodist in the city and its surrounding area, he brought a strong new influence to Blockley when, after many holidays with his family in the village, he settled in 1919 in the house[6] he had built on land, part of the ancient Walgrove tenement, which he had bought from Arthur

157

Joyner. His accession to the Baptist congregation has been mentioned. He knew and was known by the village, not least on the bowling green, and Major Spencer, the agent for North-wick profited by his advice.

An important village project in which, with the vicar, he took the initiative was the Village Hall. Since the war the old meeting house had again stood unused. The head of the Bristol firm of E. S. & A. Robinson, Mr Edward Robinson, responded gener-ously to the appeal from them, bought the derelict building erected by his ancestor, Elisha Smith, renovated and equipped it as we know it today, and in March 1925 formally presented it to the village by handing the key to Mrs A. Joyner, the senior of 'old Elisha's' descendants living in Blockley.

The Blockley Women's Institute began its invaluable life at a meeting held in May 1924. The objects and activities of this national movement, a war-time creation, are too well known to need detailing here. Its appeal to Blockley was immediate. It had, for example, a membership of 80 in 1958, drawn from the whole spectrum of the community. Nothing has better served to integrate the newcomers with the older established elements of the resident population. Its first com-mittee included Mrs A. Joyner, Mrs E. Milton, Mrs A. Milton, Miss Jacob of Elm House, the doctor's sister, Mrs Evans of Church Gates, widow of the author of the *Highways and Byways* book on the Cotswolds, Mrs Hardy of Arlington House, whose family was to play an increasing part in village organizations and Mrs Odling of Paxford House, who soon after formed a separate branch for that village. Striking evidence of the feeling for community which is of the essence of W.I. influence lies in two corporately compiled studies: a Survey of Blockley history over the previous hundred years (1958) and a very detailed Scrapbook describing the state of the parish in 1966.[7] *Plate 48*

The Second World War and after (*compiled by several hands*)

Fourteen names were added to the parish roll of honour, Blockley families such as Hale, Mayo, Powell and Udell among them. Many more returned to the parish with vastly widened minds. On the home front the call for national service was far more immediate, urgent and conprehensive than in the first war, and, as in the rest of the kingdom, the whole community was mobilised. Civil Defence began with air raid precautions in the autumn of 1938 and developed under the control of Mr W. C. Lockwood, lately come from Yorkshire. The parish was close by the R.A.F. station at Moreton-in-Marsh, and was fortunate to escape bombing, except for the occasion when the Worcester Lodge on Five Mile Drive was destroyed in September 1940. Years after the war ended, an unexploded bomb was found in Mill Close Pool. The volunteer Fire Brigade, which had a long history behind it,[8] was in action at Coventry on the night of its devastation, and the special constables were fully stretched. When invasion was threatened the Home Guard unit in the parish was commanded by Major Gordon Alexander,[9] another recent settler in the village. He also became chairman of an Invasion Committee, set up to co-ordinate all agencies in case of emergency. It included Mrs F. C. Spurgin, leader of Women's Voluntary Services, Mr Lockwood, the Rev. S. C. Crowe, the Baptist minister, and Sergeant A. H. Wall of the police. "Molotov Cocktails" were made, buried in the garden at Rodneys, but never used. At the end of the war, they were forgotten until rediscovered during gardening operations. A tree trunk was placed ready to block Station Road between Arreton and the Great Western Arms. Mrs Spurgin bought Rodneys (its original name) in 1939, when it was called Cotswold House, from Lady Evelyn Parker, partly to house evacuee children of friends in London and even from Egypt.

The house carried great stories of Admiral Sir Edward Collier (descended from Giles Collier, Vicar in the 17th century) who, with one leg blown off, was paid off H.M.S. Rodney in 1849, People said "he rode about his estate on a cob & was so much liked that he never opened a gate or door for himself."

With help from the Department of Education in Oxford a small school was started at Rodneys in 1939, ages up to twelve years, for children in the house and nearby. Margaret Garrard (a pupil at Oxford of Mrs Leys of Peartrees) was in charge of the curriculum under Mr Icely's guidance. She was assisted by expert helpers including, notably, Miss Nora Yoxall, whose art classes were much enjoyed, and a Belgian lady.

The children and their mothers saw the signposts mysteriously vanish at the beginning of the war as they also witnessed D-Day preparations of piles of ammunition on the roads prior to the invasion of France when the U.S. troops, stationed locally, disappeared overnight.

Many visitors came to Rodneys, even from India, Egypt, France and Nigeria, and kept the packed household in communication with the outer world, as did the constant Invasion Committees which took place in the library. Highlights were King George's review of the troops on the top road, spirited theatricals in the Village Hall, visits by foot and train to the Stratford theatre and the odd bomb.

After Dunkirk the household helped to receive utterly war-weary troops in the garden which was full of narcissi. Visiting fathers, service or civilian, often had to sleep in the apple loft which was normally used for play space. The pupils, known as "The Rods", gradually went on to local or boarding schools. They, and Margaret Garrard (later married in U.S.A.) return often to the country heritage they shared in their youth in Blockley.

A mobile canteen was kept at Rodneys, and emergency stores for the Home Guard and canteen rations were stored in the house. The Red Cross and County Ambulance Brigade had bases there. The Blockley ambulance, paid for by the village, run by Mrs Gordon Alexander, maintained by Mr Percy (chauffeur to Mr Green, M.P., of the Brown House) and driven by him and Mrs Cox (now of the Manor House), was also based at Rodneys.

For welfare the whole parish played its part. The Women's Institute was there and ready for action. The Women's Voluntary Services brought their special powers of invention and drive. Evacuees, mainly from London and Eastbourne were found billets: first aid and hospital transport was organized: blood donors were registered and their blood taken—the churchyard, when weather allowed, came into use for that, giving space, otherwise lacking in the early years of the war, for the mass treatment of patients and for equipment for their post-operative rest and refreshment: a citizen's advice bureau was set up: a mobile canteen was provided: social gatherings for troops in the area were promoted.

One considerable wartime achievement calls for detailed

description, not only because of the formidable administrative and material difficulties involved at the time, but also for its continuing benefit to the whole community ever since. This was the building of St. George's Hall, which can well be regarded as a monument of the parish effort in the second World War. The need for a large hall had long been felt, and plans for one were in being before the war began. In November 1936 a public meeting in the Crown Inn had decided to celebrate the coronation of King George VI by festivities, including an ox-roast, on the day and the erection of a large village hall. A committee to raise funds and recommend plans was appointed, with Mr Lockwood as chairman and Mrs R. M. Paintin (of Elisha Smith lineage), Sergeant Wall, Messrs. C. J. Hull, A. Savidge, D. A. Balhatchet and N. G. Hitchman as members. The Munich crisis interrupted their operations and the project was not taken up again till the middle of the war.

The energy, resourcefulness and public spirit with which an enlarged committee took up the task may be judged by two dates. It was in April 1942 that it first met—at Rodneys, the residence of Mrs Spurgin, a prime mover in the project: the completed building was formally opened by Captain Churchill, donor of the site in Colonel's Piece and of much material, on 25 September 1943.

It was all accomplished in the face of great difficulties. The war was at its crisis. Licences for building not directly required for the war effort were almost unobtainable. It was all but impossible to find either labour or material. Money had to be raised by voluntary donations and village enterprises. Everyone combined to break through the obstacles without delay. The Parish Council, which was to have the ownership of the hall vested in it, entrusted its management to a committee of twelve elected members and the arrangements for its buildings mainly to five specially qualified trustees. Mr C. J. Hull was chairman, and as secretary to Captain Churchill, was able to settle many local difficulties: Mrs Spurgin was vice-chairman, and constantly active on and off the site: Dame Janet Campbell, lately settled in the village after serving in high office at the Board of Education and the Ministry of Health, negotiated with authority in Whitehall: Mr Eric Yoxall, architect and resident, gave his services as designer and supervisor on the site: and Mrs E. Gordon Alexander was secretary. Inevitably the building in its first state was somewhat inchoate. Permission was given for the outer walls to be built of stone, all of it to be had from the debris from the bombed Worcester Lodge and elsewhere, the foundations were dug by the boys of the village. For the roof only asbestos sheeting was allowed, and for the floor a bitumastic composition, very hard on dancers' feet, had to be put up with. This last was put right as soon as timber became available after the war: the roof got its tiles in 1964. But however much it lacked at the outset, the hall came into constant and diverse use at once—for school meals, the need for which had been the crucial argument in the appeal for a licence to build, for dances, concerts, cinema shows, plays, welfare and other official purposes for which the other village hall was too small. Under wise management St. George's Hall has paid its way and was well served by Mr and Mrs Hopes (Caretakers) and Mrs Shadbolt—cook caterer. Successive chairmen have been Mrs F. C. Spurgin, Mr W. C. Lockwood, and, from 1952 to 1970, Brigadier R. B. Rathbone, now succeeded by Michael Hope. There has been a steady increase in accommodation and amenity—in the kitchen and servery, the heating system and the car park. One memorable benefaction calls for special note. Just as Edward Robinson of Bristol had given the Village Hall to Blockley a generation earlier, so, in 1957, his children led by Sir Foster Robinson, then head of the great firm, added to St. George's Hall a permanent stage and proscenium with valuable backstage facilities. All this was done in memory of their ancestor, Elisha Smith. Many villagers have good stories to tell of how they got their halls. Blockley likes to think it has one too.

After the war and its years of no building, new housing was the first need. Within a very few years the North Cotswold Rural District Council passed the thousand mark in the provision of new houses, modern in design and equipment, and fitting naturally into their Cotswold setting. The decision to continue the policy adopted after the first World War of building along Station Road and Winterway by developing the adjoining Springfield estate has made this area the most populous part of the far flung village. With Mrs F. C. Spurgin as vice-chairman, and later chairman, of the Housing Development Committee of the Council, and with Mr W. C. Lockwood vice-chairman and, from 1952 to 1956, chairman of the Council itself, it is fair to say that Blockley's representatives played a full part in this period of reconstruction.

The Parish Council, working to the limit of its statutory powers took care of the daily concerns of the parish, keeping them before the notice of higher authority when not empowered to act itself. Fortified by the local knowledge, tact and knowledge of procedure of its clerk, Mr Conrad Warner (appointed in 1946 and serving still, after nearly thirty years), and chaired impartially by re-representatives from various parts of the parish, and notably by Mr A. Heath of Paxford, Mr W. Heming of Draycott and, most recently, Mr Stuart-Turner of Blockley, the council has served the parish well. The readiness of Colonel Shakerley, as County Councillor, to attend occasional meetings to give information and advice on special post-war problems greatly helped it.

Educational changes were among the most significant of these problems. The Education Act of 1944 made the 'all-age' village school obsolete by making a severance between the primary and secondary age groups. Children who qualified in the '11-plus' examination had long gone on to Campden Grammar School: but now those over 11 who failed to qualify moved to the Secondary Modern School at Moreton-in-Marsh. It was not a satisfactory arrangement. The '11-plus' test was bad for many reasons: and the county Education Committee could not provide buildings and equipment and teachers appropriate for modern needs unless all the secondary age-group in so extensive an area as the North Cotswold district were collected into one school. Thus it was that the plan to convert Campden Grammar School into a 'comprehensive' school was promulgated in the late 1950's. It was received at first with wide-spread suspicion, but since the opening of the new Chipping Campden School in September 1964 under A. L. Jones, M.C., M.A., who had, with his senior colleagues on the staff of the Grammar School, long before won the respect and confidence of North Cotswold parents, all doubts vanished, for the transition took place with unexpected smoothness. Educational opportunities undreamed of at the opening of the century are enjoyed today by the children of Blockley and all the district round.

The removal from Blockley of all children over 11 made adjustments necessary in the now wholly primary schools there. In 1965, on the appointment of Mr E. Bishop to a larger school in the north, the boy's school on Colonel's Piece became an Infants' School under Miss C. Stanley, and Mrs D. Yoxall continued her work in the School Lane buildings, but with now the 7–11 age-group of both sexes as her pupils. The re-organization of the schools of the parish under the Education Act of 1944 was thus completed. Paxford had had its own school in the early years of the century under Miss Willcocks,[10] and Aston Magna's Infants' School under Miss Clennett and later Miss Stanley, mentioned above, was no less cherished there. A significant change in a village community is inevitable when its children go elsewhere for their schooling. But for the children the new concentration of facilities has brought incalculable advantages.

The churches in Blockley parish have had their problems and their changes to record since the war. Under the Rev. P. Jasper the parish church had immediately to incur the heavy cost of resurfacing the churchyard rights of way and the playground of the girls' school, both dangerously overdue for repair after the war years. It was ironic that very soon after this drain of its resources the church was able, as a result of new legislation, to transfer responsibility for the upkeep of the churchyard and the school to the Parish Council and the county Education Committee respectively. There was change involved, too, at the burial ground in Station Road which Lady Northwick had conveyed to the parish church in 1891. An extension to this was now required, and Captain Churchill had in fact provided adjoining land for this. The cost of draining, fencing and otherwise preparing the site was, however, now beyond the resources of the church to meet. Complicated negotiations were necessary before the church could get relief from the trust which it had in more prosperous times gratefully undertaken. But the goodwill of all parties was not wanting, and the Parish Council in due course assumed responsibility for the establishment, maintenance and administration of the new burial ground.

Another change of the 1950's was the removal of the ancient

but beetle-ridden chancel screen and the clutter of pews which left no space at the front of the nave. New electric wiring and lighting replaced the primitive equipment which, perhaps, had survived from the pioneering novelties of the 1880's. There was some gain in all this, but Blockley church deserves a more wholesale and better inspired refurnishing.

Under Mr Jasper and his successor, the Rev. A. J. Ridler (Vicar 1948–61), the first to hold the united benefices of Blockley and Aston Magna, some help in providing for the services in the three churches was given by lay Readers, of whom Mr Ivan Yoxall and Mr A. B. Woollams are especially to be remembered. The death of Henry Sale, verger for many years and one whose long life was an epitome of old Blockley at its simple best, was a signal of changing times. Canon G. Berwick succeeded Mr Ridler as Vicar in 1961 and was followed by the Rev. Malcolm Northall in 1967, assisted by Peter Newing (1966–69) and Richard Alcock (1969–73) as curates

The Baptist church had its changes too. The Rev. Sydney Crowe recalls that his first pastoral duty after taking up his ministry in 1937 was the funeral service for Mr Charles Belcher, whose name and lineage speak for the loss this betokened. In 1942 the five fruitful years of Mr Crowe's ministry ended with his appointment to an important new church in Oxford—to Blockley's great loss. Five ministers succeeded in the next twenty years, a rapid sequence which imposed on the deacons a special responsibility for maintaining continuity. In the Rev. H. B. Parris, an ex-missionary, the church had a minister of true ecumenical spirit: and what Blockley lost when the Rev. S. J. Wallace ended his too short ministry can be gathered from the importance of the London church to which he went. He was succeeded by Sister Eileen Stevenson, whose departure in 1971 was a break with the past of special poignancy, for she was the last of the long line of ministers which had begun a century and a half earlier. Mounting inflation led the Baptist Union to group their country churches, as the Anglican dioceses were doing, to economize man-power. Thus Blockley lost its resident minister, and its church records are now in the keeping of the Campden church—as in Elisha Smith's day.

Meanwhile the number of new residents constantly grew, to

the enrichment of the life and appearance of the village in many ways. Old and often derelict cottages were restored and enlarged, so that most of the debris left on the sites once occupied by mill workers was cleared away. Two resident architects, Eric Yoxall and Reginald Smeeton, and two local building firms, Messrs. Osborne & Barrett and Da Silva & Sons have left their mark on Blockley to its great advantage. The newcomers left their mark in another way—by their social, artistic and intellectual interests. New organizations came into being. There was a short-lived branch of the Historical Association, set up in 1946 and valued by the Council of that learned society as being the only village branch in the country. But it soon, on the initiative and under the experienced guidance of James Muirhead, who as a Clifton College master had organized such a club in Bristol, became the Blockley Discussion Group with wide terms of reference. It has prospered ever since, and can boast of having had as its chairman during the early 1960's the distinguished economic historian, Professor T. S. Ashton. The present Chairman is Mr Cook son of Dr. R. Cook of Home Guard fame who took (by his own request) the dawn watch at the Water Tank.

The Blockley Antiquarian Society, founded in 1961, has drawn much of its inspiration from the general interest in the social habits and industrial methods and implements of Blockley's earlier days. This has been fostered by the researches of members of the Women's Institure, of which some account has been given. With such authoritative help at hand as Professor Ashton, Dr. Arthur Exell and Mrs Norah Marshall have so freely given to the cause Blockley has been made unusually aware and proud of its own past history and the folk whose daily lives and labours were the very stuff of it. The collection of implements and other relics, which has been formed, represents many facets of it.

The Horticultural Society has a long history and makes its own special appeal to every part of the community. Its spring and summer shows and competitions in St. George's Hall and its grounds have been memorable yearly events.

The Over-60 Club dates from 1955 and was founded by a group including the two doctors, partners in every sense, Frank and Jean Haine. Its regular meetings in St. George's Hall bring many

166

helpers from all sections of the village to join the elders in their social gatherings. The Haines initiated a private scheme to supplement the existing provision for housing the elderly and the Cotswold Villages' Old People's Housing Association was formed in the early 1960's. A site in the High Street was purchased and foundation stone laid in 1968 by Miss Kathleen Robinson, a member of the family which had done so much for their old village. The building, to house twelve residents and named Orchard Bank, was opened by Lady Dowty in September 1970.

Meanwhile, great changes had been accomplished at the Northwick Homes, the Almshouse cottages bought by the family of the third Lady Northwick and endowed as a memorial to her. By the 1960's, it was evident that the building was in such a state of dilapidation that the fund was totally inadequate to bring it up to modern standards. However, the site on which it stood, including long front gardens, enabled the trustees through their secretary, Mrs Goadby, to conclude a most happy arrangement with the North Cotswold Rural District Council by which two-thirds of the land was sold to the R.D.C. On the total site, they built eight flats, of which two were handed over to the Charity Commissioners and retain their old name and almshouse status. The main block, called Buchan House, after the Chairman of the Housing Committee at that time, was opened in 1970 and has proved very popular with local residents.

The 1970's have brought other visual changes, most welcome being the removal of Blockley's ugly 'wirescape,' a legacy of the early days of electric lighting. The burial of the cables has greatly improved the village.

The greatest change of the period was undoubtedly the death in 1964 of Captain Spencer-Churchill and the departure from Northwick Park of the last of the family associated with it since the latter part of the seventeenth century. The series of sales of the art treasures caused world-wide interest and the estate did not pass into alien hands, as it was purchased by the Hon. Michael Pearson, son and heir of Lord Cowdray and great-nephew of Captain Churchill, on behalf of Whitehall Securities, a subsidiary of S. Pearson and Co. Ltd. The house and home farm were let in 1967 at a nominal rent to "The Life for the World Trust" which, under the leadership of the Rev. Frank Wilson, a Baptist Minister, rehabilitates drug-addicts. The mansion, in a sad state of disrepair and shabbiness at the death of its late owner, is being beautifully restored and re-decorated by the temporary residents and by devoted volunteers who come for periods to give their help and skills. The farm, market-garden and printing press offer other forms of work-therapy to help the young male addicts back to a normal life.

Familiar figures who have faded from the scene include George Rouse, third generation of his family to promote Blockley transport: he and his drivers, particularly Ernest Compton, who only retired at the age of 77, Frank Hemmings and "Tiny" Udell were among the village's best-known characters. Mrs Gertrude Keeble (née Hardy) was given the B.E.M. for her work for National Savings, and was very active in the W.V.S. (Her son, Curtis, is the first British ambassador to the Republic of East Germany). Thomas William ("Jockey") Bennett, after a lifetime spent among horses, began a new career at the age of 70 as a postman and continued to walk a round of the hill farms, said to be nearly ten miles, until he retired at the age of 83 in 1948. During the dreadful winter of 1947 when all roads were blocked, he volunteered to take the mail-bags to the station on a sledge. On his daily round, he was invariably accompanied by three dogs (*Plate* 37) and wound up with bread and cheese and a beer at the Red Lion. Another retirement was that in 1973 of Mrs Ivy Richardson, who had delivered newspapers for the previous 32 years: her gifts from a grateful village included a barometer. In the same year, Mr and Mrs Charles Cother retired from the Post Office; Mrs Cother's outstanding helpfulness over form-filling, pensions and allowances, had been much valued and musical tributes from the band accompanied the presentation to them both of radios and a tea-maker. One whose exit was tragic was Mrs A. M. Veysey-Stitt, owner of Rock Cottage, home of the Prophetess Joanna Southcott from 1804 to 1814, who died in 1971 in a fire which left only the shell of the historic house. With the passing of Bertie Barnes, the skilled cabinet-maker and his neighbour John Bishop, the blacksmith, two crafts were lost to Blockley in the 1960's but, gains are Mrs Moore (porcelain mender) Miss Hoskins (bookbinder) and Rodney Forss (sculptor). The closing of the Bell Inn in 1970 was much deplored, but it has been turned into flats without spoiling its outward appearance and during the reconstruction in February 1973, a number of skeletons were found beneath the floors of the Public Bar and Smoke Room. These were subsequently carbon-dated by Professor F. W. Shotton, F.R.S., of Birmingham University, as Saxon bones of approximately A.D. 840, an interesting correlation with the charter of 855.

At the end of the war, the American Army Hospital in Northwick Park was altered to provide accommodation for refugee Poles. In 1949, Mr A. Dragowski asked the W.I. President for the Institute's help in promoting good relations between the two communities. A Darby and Joan Club was opened at the camp in 1950 and thereafter many social functions were shared by this body with the Over-60 Club and the W.I., led by Miss C. Compton-Smith, President from 1950–55 and an enthusiast for cultural relations. Language difficulties were an obstacle, but a common love of music formed a meeting point for the two communities. In 1951, Mr J. Q. Evans, the Warden, established the Anglo-Polish Society, ably supported by Colonel Underka, a fine linguist who conducted English language classes. Many of the older residents were moved to a Devonshire hostel around 1957 and the place was finally vacated in 1970. Many Poles are buried in Blockley cemetery.

Since the camp was closed, several short-term industrial permits have been granted to small firms anxious to occupy the buildings on the site and the Parish Council continues to press the Planning Authority for it to be given a Change of Use into a small industrial estate to provide local employment. The Northcott Brick Works and metal pre-fabricators, the Gloucestershire Brick Works at Aston Magna, Cotswold Promotions (letter-cutters for sign-makers), Small Craft Blue Hulls, Ltd., Cotek Papers, Ltd., both at Draycott, and Cotswold Emblems Ltd., all help to create much-needed local work, as an alternative to the big distances travelled by many of the population (see appendix). Building firms continue to be the largest employers of labour, farm mechanisation having greatly reduced the numbers employed on the farms in the parish. The post-war period has seen a sharp decline in the number of shops, not unconnected with the sharp rise in car ownership and the number of week-end cottages.

Craftswomen with a reputation in the world far outside the Cotswolds are Nora Yoxall and Elsie Whitford, who have been designing and making stained-glass windows in Blockley for many years. Although their work is treasured in so many other churches, 1974 sees the first piece installed in the village, a small porch window in memory of Albert R. Neal, an American who died while on holiday in Blockley. (*Plate* 9).

Another fine craftsman was Edward Belcher, who did a number of small works locally after his retirement to the family home from a lifetime's work as a monumental sculptor. These included plaques to commemorate the Coronation of Queen Elizabeth II, on Council Housing, carved house-names and grave-stones for family and close friends. (*Plate* 44).

Blockley continues to attract men and women from the academic and professional world. James Muirhead, former Housemaster at Clifton College, was a tireless worker for village causes, particularly the Youth Club; E. R. Hughes, missionary to China until the revolution and thereafter Reader in Chinese at Oxford University: the distinguished historian and Fellow of All Souls, Sir George Clark, who lived for several years at The Hollies, and Professor T. S. Ashton, famous historian of the Industrial Revolution. Sir John Hicks took over Porch House from his aunt, Mrs Whale, who translated the works of Anatole France, Sir John, Drummond Professor of Political Economy in Oxford from 1952 to 1965, was awarded the Nobel Prize for Economics in 1972. Lady Hicks, University Lecturer in Public Finance, has done much to help emerging independent States with advice on currency problems. Sir Patrick Linstead, F.R.S., Rector of the Imperial College of Science and a distinguished chemist, came to live at Bishop's Barn; he opened the new wing at Campden School. After his untimely death, Lady Linstead became Principal of Lady Spencer-Churchill College at Wheatley; she still lives in Blockley. Sir Robert Lusty, Chairman of Hutchinson's, the publishers, bought Sleepy Hollow, which he re-named The Old Silk Mill. In addition, many distinguished overseas Juvenile Court Judges have come to know Blockley as guests of Mrs F. C. Spurgin, who became the first British President of the Association Internationale des Magistrats de la Jeunesse in 1966.

Music and drama continue to flourish. In 1971 Mrs Hebe Ashley organised a Festival of Arts centred around the church, which was honoured by a visit from the Anglican Archbishop in Jerusalem, the Most Rev. George Appleton. Exhibitions of paintings, dolls, crafts old and new, floral decoration; Handel's "Jephtha" by the Choral Society; Christopher Fry's "Boy with a Cart" by the Cinquefoil Dramatic Society and a literary evening, featuring Elizabeth Spriggs of the Royal Shakespeare Company and much local talent: all these gave great pleasure.

It is good to know that the spirit of self-help which has been very evident through Blockley's history, is not dead. The Play Areas Committee, a group of young people under the chairmanship of Mrs Fay Jeffrey, has raised substantial sums of money for playground equipment for Churchill Close and Springfield.

As this book goes to press it is learned that Mr L. Bradley, President of Shipston-on-Stour Local History Society, is preparing a paper on his researches into the so-called "castle & moat" at Aston Magna. This he believes to be a Neolithic henge or site for religious ceremonies of between 4000 and 3000 B.C., a forerunner of Woodhenge and Stonehenge. Its former name of Hanging Aston might originally have been Hengen Aston. He has found interesting tools there made from chert, a hard local stone used in areas which have no flint. He considers it to be in a far better state of preservation than many similar sites he has visited in Britain and on the Continent.

Local Government reorganisation (1974) has put Blockley (represented by S. M. Moore) into a new Cotswold District Council centred on Cirencester. This centre would surely have been familiar enough to the Romanised Britons of Dorn.

[1] See p. 146-7

[2] Col. (later Sir Geoffrey) Shakerley was elected to the County Council in 1946, later became its Chairman and ultimately Chairman of the County Councils Association. He was succeeded by Lt. Col. W. A. McLelland.

[3] The lordship of the manor being legally held by the Ecclesiastical Commissioners.

[4] See p. 148

[5] The carved oak front of the gallery was sold, and parts of it are to be seen in houses in the village today. The finely lettered charity boards were unhappily moved out of sight to the base of the tower.

[6] 'Windywold'.

[7] They have been freely drawn upon for this chapter and the previous one.

[8] That history goes back to the 18th century. In 1806 Thomas Bearcroft, parish clerk, sent in his bill to the churchwardens "for Cleaning and Oylong the Engine". A new fire engine was acquired by the parish in 1865, just in time for use at the Good Intent Mill. Other turn-outs included fires at the old post-office adjoining the gateway to the Baptist churchyard, at Dovedale House, at Milldene and at the Institute in Mill Close. A good parish tradition ended when, in 1946, the National Fire Service superseded volunteer brigades of this kind.

[9] He was known to sleep with a loaded pistol under his pillow.

[10] As Mrs Bennett, she was long to remain a respected Paxford resident and a lover of Paxford traditions.

Elizabeth R
1953

A NOTE ON SOURCES

A. MANUSCRIPT MATERIAL

Three collections are in the County Record Office at, Worcester:-

1. Records of the manor of Blockley (court rolls. surveys, presentments, etc.)
2. Diocesan records (visitation presentments, etc.)
3 The Northwick Papers (leases and other documents relating to Rushout property in the parish, etc.)

In the County Record Office at Gloucester are :-

1. Records preserved in the Blockley parish chest, including Poor Law papers, rate books, vestry minutes, etc.
2. Old leases and other papers.

At Blockley are:-

1. The registers of Baptisms, Marriages and Burials beginning in 1538 (described by Soden, pp 118-23) in the keeping of the vicar.
2. A Survey (1958) and Scrap-book (1966) of recent events in the parish, compiled by the Women's Institute, at present kept at Church Gates, Blockley Society.

At Chipping Campden are the records of the Baptist Church in Blockley.

B. PUBLISHED WORKS

1. W. T. Eyre: *A Guide to Blockley* (Evesham, 1827). It contains a valuable census of the parish at that date.
2. A. J. Soden: *A History of Blockley* (Coventry, 1875).
3. V. C. H. *Worcestershire*, especially vol. iii. 265 ff. an authoritative and fully documented history of the parish by Marjory Hollings.
4. *The Red Book of Worcester* ed. by Marjory Hollings, (W.H.S.), esp. vol. iii. 295 ff. for the survey of the manor of Blockley and of Paxford in 1299.
5. H. P. R. Finberg: *Gloucestershire Studies* (1957) and *The Early Charters of the West Midlands* (1961) published by the Univ. of Leicester Press.
6. R. H. Hilton and P. A. Rahtz: articles on excavations at Upton Wold and its history. B. G. A. S.. vols. lxxv (1966) and lxviii (1969).
7. N. M. Marshall: *Blockley and the Silk Trade* (Blockley, privately printed, 1972).

The files of the Evesham *Journal* provide abundant material.

Other references are in the notes following each chapter.

ABBREVIATIONS

B.G.A.S. for Journal of the Bristol and Gloucestershire Archaeological Society.
Eyre for his *Guide to Blockley.*
N.P. for the Northwick Papers.
P.R.O. for the Public Record Office.
Soden for his *History of Blockley.*
V.C.H. for Victoria County History.
W.H.S. for Worcestershire Historical Society.

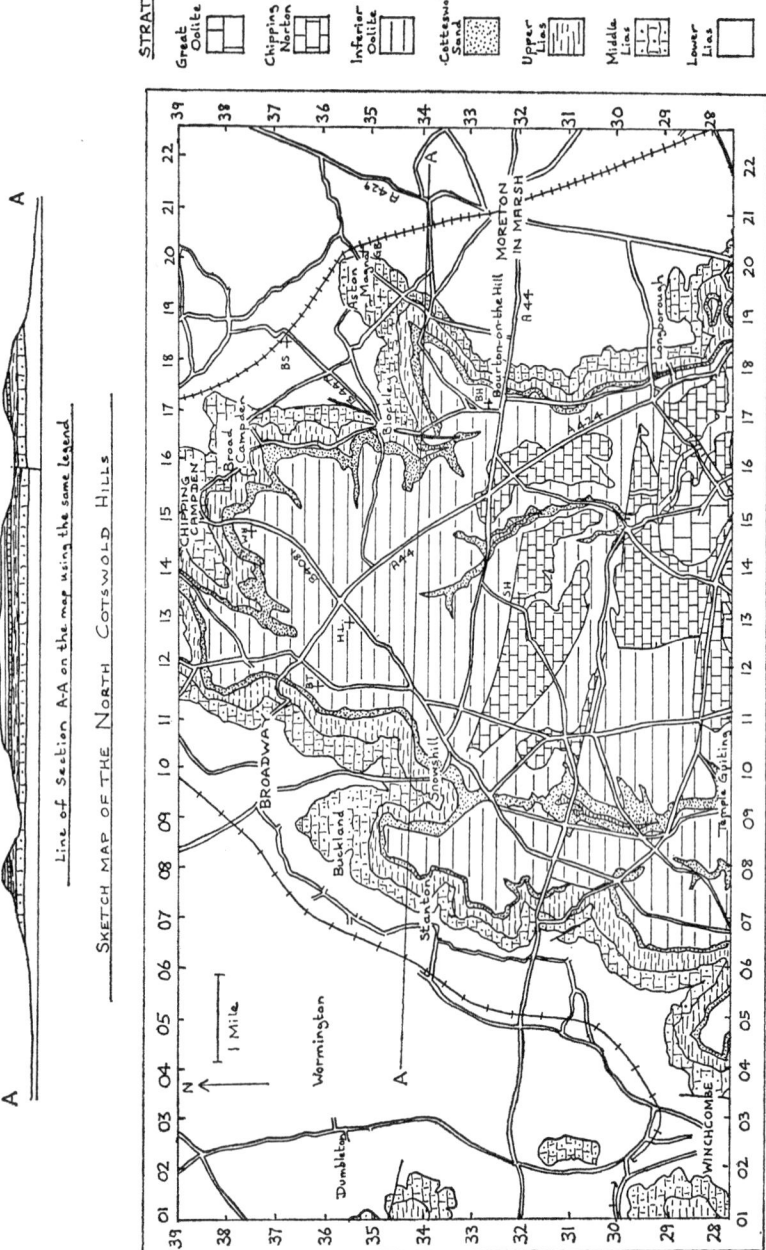

A

A

Line of Section A-A on the map using the same legend

SKETCH MAP OF THE NORTH COTSWOLD HILLS

STRATA

Great Oolite

Chipping Norton Lst

Inferior Oolite

Cotteswold Sand

Upper Lias

Middle Lias

Lower Lias

Abbreviations

BH = Bourton Hill Quarry, BS = Blockley Station Pit, BT = Broadway Tower, GB = Gloucestershire Brick Co.
HL = Hoarlands Quarry, SH = Snowshill Hill Quarry, W.H = Westington Hill Quarry.

Appendices

I. GEOLOGY OF THE BLOCKLEY DISTRICT
By
HUGH G. OWEN ph.D (LOND.) F.G.S.

The Cotswold Hills, formed essentially of Middle and Upper Lias capped by Inferior Oolite and overlying Great Oolite, terminate at their northern end near Chipping Campden and Broadway on the Gloucestershire-Worcestershire boundary. The broad plain-like valley of the River Severn to the west of the North Cotswolds is cut in the thick clays of the Lower Lias. The Vale of Evesham is largely underlain by Lower Lias clays and the outcrop of these clays sweeps round the northern end of the Cotswolds to floor the deep embayment of the Vale of Moreton in which Blockley lies. The Lower Lias gives rise to the heavy clay soil of the vales.

In the Vale of Moreton, brick and tile manufacturing has been carried on for many years and there are two good exposures today in the clays of the upper part of the Lower Lias one of which also exposes the loams of the Middle Lias. The first of these sections is situated close to the former Blockley Station (SP 182369) immediately to the south of the railway line. In the earlier literature this pit was known as Captain Churchill's claypit (e.g. Richardson 1929: 15) but is now worked by the Northwick Brick & Tile Co. The section exposed there has been described in recent years by Callomon (in Sylvester Bradley & Ford—editors 1968: 202-4). The lower part of the dark grey clay sequence contains scattered cementstone nodules, sometimes arranged in distinct courses. Fossils are of scattered occurrence, but good specimens of the ammonite *Liparoceras* are to be found, in particular *L. rusticum* Spath. This is overlain by a particularly fossiliferous bed (Bed 2), some 30 ft. above the base of the pit, termed the 'Pecten Bed' by Callomon, but also known as the 'Blockley Shell Bed'. This bed contains ammonites such as *Lytoceras fimbriatum* (J. Sowerby), *Liparoceras pseudostriatum* and various species of *Beaniceras*, together with specimens of nautiloids, many bivalves and gastropods. A similar fauna occurs in the overlying clays. The whole sequence falls within a relative-time zone characterised by the ammonite *Tragophylloceras ibex*, near the top of the Lower Lias.

The second exposure, the large pit of the Gloucestershire Brick & Tile Co., at Aston Magna (SP 198356), shows the highest clays of the Lower lias and the lower part of the Middle Lias. Unfortunately, there is at present no published detailed description of this pit although it has been mentioned by Richardson (1929: 15, 23), Arkell (1947), McKerrow & Baden Powell (1953) and Callomon (in Sylvester-Bradley & Ford-editors 1968: 204).

The Lower Lias clays fall within the next highest zone to those seen at Blockley; the zone of *Prodactylioceras davoei*. This ammonite has been found in this pit but is uncommon. When in work the grey clays near to the brick kilns, the lowest clays seen contain bivalves and species of ammonites belonging to the genus *Androgynoceras*, such as *A. lataecosta*. The clays worked in recent years lie close to the top of the Lower Lias, and contain the later derivative of *Androgynoceras* called

Oistoceras. The junction between the Lower and Middle Lias is not often clearly seen, because of the tendency for the Middle Lias to slip over the rather soapy clays of the Lower Lias. Only the lower part of the Middle Lias is to be seen in this pit. It is seen to consist of rather ferruginous loams with bands of grey silty clay. Fossils are plentiful as in the Lower Lias clays, but ammonites occur such as *Amaltheus stokesi* in the lower part and *A. margaritatus* higher up.

The top of the Middle Lias consists of a sandy limestone known as a Marlstone Rock Bed. This is not now exposed in the Blockley region but its outcrop is marked by a distinct bench feature in the topography. Above this Bed occur thick clays of the Upper Lias which, again, are not exposed.

The Cotswold Hills in the area near Blockley, Broadway and Chipping Campden are capped by Inferior Oolite. Many of the old sections recorded in this predominantly limestone sequence were described by Richardson (1929: 61–68), but most of these are no longer to be seen. However, a very good excursion guide to the best sections to be seen now is given by McKerrow, Ager & Donovan (1964: 2–4). The Lower Inferior Oolite is exposed near to the top of the hill on the A44 near Bourton-on-the-Hill (SP 169327) where the Lower Freestone and beds equivalent to the Pea-Grit are to be seen. It is also exposed in the Westington Hill Quarry (SP 146376) half a mile S. of Chipping Campden where the Lower Freestone and the very fossiliferous Oolite Marl is present. The Middle Inferior Oolite is exposed in a quarry near Springfield Lodges (SP 127358) where the Freestone here may be the equivalent of the Notgrove Freestone but fossils characteristic of that formation in more southern exposures are not present here.

At Snowshill Hill Quarry (SP 131322) the top of the Middle Inferior Oolite is to be seen and the succeeding Upper Inferior Oolite is overlain by limestones of the Great Oolite Series; all are well exposed. At the base of the section the oolitic limestones of the *Clypeus* Grit are to be seen. These contain the echinoid *Clypeus ploti* Salter, and in former years the outcrop of this Bed could be traced in the newly ploughed fields, especially above Chipping Campden, by the presence of this echinoid turned-up by the plough. Above that occurs some 30 feet of massive sandy limestone called the Hook Norton Beds which is the local representative of the Upper Inferior Oolite. There follows the lower part of the Great Oolite Series comprising the Chipping Norton Limestone (about 6 feet thick) and the overlying Sharp's Hill Beds exposed in the uppermost 12 feet of the quarry. The Sharp's Hill Beds are very fossiliferous and yield gastropods, bivalves, some echinoids, brachiopods, together with occasional corals, and belemnites have been recorded. Higher beds of the Great Oolite Series are exposed further south near Naunton. *Plate 49*

The very thick clays of the Lower Lias were laid down in fairly deep water in a major epicontinental sea which covered much of Britain and northern Europe, but shallowing occurred in Middle Lias times. By the period of the formation of the Inferior and Great Oolite Series, the sediments and fauna indicate that the sea was apparently very shallow and the water warm.

Blockley village lies close to the outcrop of the Cotteswold Sands formation overlying the impervious Upper Lias Shales. Water percolating through the overlying Inferior Oolite into the Cotteswold Sands cannot in turn penetrate further downward int othe Upper Lias, and so at their common junction springs are formed draining eastward. The bulk of Blockley's plentiful supply of water comes from this source in Dovedale though the village itself is now supplied from a tributary stream near the Post Office. A geological fault occurs near the eastern side of the village bringing the Lower Lias up against the more permeable Middle Lias, and as a result a rather iron-rich source of water is also available.

Bibliography
ARKELL, W. J., 1947 *The Geology of Oxford.* Oxford University Press.
McKERROW, W. S., & McKERROW, W. S. AGER, D. V. and DONOVAN, D. T., 1964 Geology of the Cotswold Hills. *Geol. Ass., Guides. 36*: 1–26
McKERROW, W. S. & BADEN-POWELL, D. F. W., 1953 Easter Field Meeting

1952. The Jurassic Rocks of Oxfordshire and their Superficial Deposits. *Proc. geol. Ass. Lond., 18*: 391–408.

RICHARDSON, L. 1929 The Country around Moreton in Marsh. *Mem. Geol. Surv., U.K., 217*: i-vi, 1–162, pls I-VI.

SYLVESTER-BRADLEY, P. C. & FORD, T. D., (Editors) 1968 *The Geology of the East Midlands.* Leicester University Press.

II. BLOCKLEY—GEOGRAPHICAL BACKGROUND
By
Miss E. M. Buxton m.a. (oxon.) f.l.a.

Blockley (Latitude 52.01 N., Longitude 1.45 W.) lies in the North of the North Cotswolds. The parish of Blockley includes Aston Magna, Draycott, Paxford and Northwick Park and is the second largest in the rural district of the North Cotswold It now covers an area of 7530 acres (3047 hectares). The highest point is over 925 feet and the lowest under 325 feet.

Blockley is drained by Blockley Brook. This joins Knee Brook which joins the Stour (a tributary of the Warwickshire Avon). It will be noticed that Knee Brook flows South East, the Stour flows North and then North West while the Avon flows South West. During Pleistocene times a vast lake dammed the outlet to the South and caused this rather curious direction of drainage. A small portion of the parish is in the Thames Basin; most of it drains into the Severn Basin, thus one of the main watersheds of the country passes through the parish.

The Blockley Brook rises in Dovedale in a patch of swampy ground making it difficult to point to the exact source. Fed by numerous springs and one busy little tributary descending from the Warren it increases quite rapidly in volume until the Water Board begins to pipe it away, somewhat to our detriment. Many trout are still to be found in the stream and some attractive water-plants. At one time there must have been a number of fords. One of these is still in use towards the southern end of the village. It is a long ford of great interest. Vehicles crossing the stream by it have to proceed along the river-bed for about 70 yards before emerging on the other bank. That this is possible apparently without difficulty says much for the evenness and firmness of the stream-bed. At the northern end of this ford the footpath crosses the stream by a footbridge consisting of an enormous single block of stone measuring about five feet long, three feet wide and some eight inches thick.

During the Second World War, application was made to the Ministry of Power for extra coal as the inhabitants considered Blockley to be colder than the surrounding region. Temperature records were kept to prove this. Unfortunately these are no longer available. One statistic only is still known. When Moreton-in-Marsh achieved fame on January 26th 1947 by having the absolute minimum temperature in England (–1°F.), Blockley's temperature was only three degrees higher. Rainfall records, however, have been kept since 1916. These are taken at an altitude of 450′ and show that only Chipping Campden in the North Cotswolds is wetter than Blockley. Between 1916 and 1951 the average annual rainfall in Blockley was 32.3 inches.

The population of Blockley parish rose steadily between 1801 and 1861 but declined between 1871 and 1881 and continued to do so until 1931. The decline seems to have started as a direct result of the decline of the silk industry. Between 1939 and 1951 there was a substantial increase due to the establishment of a camp for Polish refugees. Many moved into private houses but in time they moved elsewhere.

Present day industries and occupations include agriculture, brickmaking, quarrying, building and construction, boatmaking and costume jewel making. The service industries include employment in the retail trade and garages, and hairdressing. There are three local doctors. People living in the parish also work in the various light industries in the area and in public administration. Two hotels and two public houses not only provide employment but also attract visitors. A number of retired professional people and people with weekend houses also live in the village.

Employment and agriculture has declined markedly since the war owing to increased mechanization and the resultant growth in the size of farms. More than half the farms are now over 150 acres. The most important cereals are barley, wheat and oats. The acreage of grasses for silage is increasing yearly. There are twice as many cattle as sheep and there is some pig rearing. Turkeys account for nearly half the total poultry reared. Vegetables (brussels sprouts, some peas and other vegetables), and fruit (pears, plums, strawberries and some cooking apples, cherries and gooseberries) are also important.

Communications to and from Blockley by public transport are limited. Even when the station was in use, its distance from the village was a disadvantage. Moreton-in-Marsh, however, is served by the Hereford, Worcester, Paddington line. This means that not only are there frequent fast trains to London and Worcester but also to Heathrow by Rail Air link. Motor 'buses came in 1924 and now the Worcester–Victoria coach via Oxford passes near Blockley although the service is not daily and may in the future run only from Moreton-in-Marsh.

POPULATION OF BLOCKLEY AT EACH DECENNIAL CENSUS

1801	1569
1811	1654
1821	1890
1831	2015
1841	2136
1851	2587
1861	2596
1871	2450†
1881	2154
1891	2157
1901	1812
1911	1845*
1921	1778
1931	1784
1939	1817 (From statistics collected for the purpose of National Service)
1951	2905‡
1961	2395
1971	1853
† Parish	7870 acres
* ,,	7896 acres
‡ ,,	7530 acres

III. FLORA OF BLOCKLEY DISTRICT

By

A. W. Exell, o.b.e., m.a. (cantab.), Dr. Sc. (conimbr.), comendador da ordem
de Santiago da Espada, f.l.s.

This list of the Phanerogams, Vascular Cryptogams and Charophytes (the flowering plants, ferns and one species of *Nitella*) is taken mainly from Riddelsdell, Hedley and Price, Flora of Gloucestershire, 1948 with a few records (which cannot all be verified) from a list made for the Women's Institute Jubilee Book, 1965 (cited here as W.I. List) together with further records kindly given me by Lord Dulverton and Mr V. P. Hughes and a few from personal observations.

In the Flora of Gloucestershire the county is divided into seven main botanical districts (with some subdivisions). Blockley comes mainly in District 1 defined as follows:

District 1 represents a small projecting area round Chipping Campden, and is the northernmost tip of Gloucestershire. Originally it extended as far north as Clifford Chambers, close to Stratford-on-Avon, and included Weston-upon-Avon, Welford, Preston-upon-Stour, Lower Quinton, Long Marston, Admington and Dorsington, but the area is now reduced by their transfer to Warwickshire, together with Pebworth and Cow Honeybourne to Worcestershire. On the other hand the District has received an addition of an area around Blockley, extending from Upton Wold in the west to the Ditchfords in the east. The Warwickshire parish of Little Compton is included in the District, which is otherwise entirely in Vice-county 33.

District 7a, which lies to the south-east of District 1, and contains part of Moreton-in-Marsh, Bourton-on-the-Hill, Hinchwick Warren etc., also includes a small area of Blockley parish.

A special feature of District 1 is the almost complete absence of bog habitats, very little marsh and few soils of an acid nature. This is shown in a very striking fashion if we look at the records for *Scirpus* (club-rushes) and *Carex* (sedges). 29 species of *Scirpus* are listed for Gloucestershire but only one for District 1. In *Carex* there are about 43 species in Gloucestershire but only 12 in District 1 and 4 of these are confined to Warwickshire. There is in fact throughout our list a constant deficiency in marsh and water plants. On the other hand we have the advantage that Dovedale acts almost like a nature reserve for a fine assembly of species.

It seemed in preparing this list that it would be neither useful nor feasible to restrict it to the limits of Blockley parish. It has been given the heading "Flora of Blockley District" and a number of species have been included from Campden, Broad Campden, Ebrington, Bourton-on-the-Hill etc. Almost any of these species may well occur within the boundaries of Blockley parish and are liable to be found there at any time. The list does in fact give a fairly complete record for the Broad Campden and Ebrington additions. For the species given in our list but not definitely recorded for Blockley in the Flora of Gloucestershire, the nearest locality is given (i.e. Westington, Campden, Broad Campden, Ebrington, Bourton-on-the-Hill (especially Bourton Woods), Hinchwick and Snowshill). The Paxford records and those of Aston Magna add a number of species not recorded for Blockley itself and quite a lot more are added by including Broad Campden and Ebrington. But to have extended the list to all the species of District 1 would have brought in many Warwickshire species from the Avon valley which are unlikely to turn up in Blockley. Where no locality at all is given it usually means that the species is a common one expected to occur almost anywhere. The Dovedale records are given for the more interesting species because an easy walk in Dovedale is the best way to see a representative sample of our flora.

Although there is no really natural woodland in our area, which has been planted or much modified by human action, we can nevertheless see very clearly the transition from the oak-ash-elm woods of the Lias to the Cotswold beechwoods at higher altitudes on the Oolitic Limestone. On the drier calcareous soils which favour the beech the latter casts such a deep shade that it succeeds in gradually ousting the oak because beech seedlings can germinate under oaks but oak seedlings cannot survive under beech.

The list follows in the main the arrangement in the Flora of Gloucestershire but the Latin names have been brought up to date as far as possible (with the Flora of Gloucestershire names given as synonyms to facilitate reference) from J. E. Dandy, List of British Vascular Plants, 1958. The species with each genus are arranged alphabetically.

The plants mentioned by Shakespeare will mostly be found beautifully illustrated by Anne Ophelia Dowden in "Shakespeare's Flowers" by Jessica Kerr (undated).

Those who are not already expert can best identify our local plants from "The Concise British Flora in Colour" by Keble Martin (1965) in which they will find a small but accurate coloured picture of nearly all the species in our list. With enough knowledge to make a good guess at the family most of our plants can be correctly identified. The present list will be of some help by indicating which species are likely to be found.

It will be of interest to record any species not in the list and also to list for Blockley parish those which are at present only recorded from neighbouring parishes. Specimens can be pressed to confirm the identifications—but—

PLEASE DO NOT DESTROY OUR RARE SPECIES

Finally do not be surprised if you cannot find quite a number of the species here recorded. Many are based on old records and for various reasons, especially the use of weed-killers, changes in agricultural methods, felling of trees, rooting up of hedges, etc., we have undoubtedly lost much.

FLORA OF BLOCKLEY DISRTICT

PHANEROGAMIA
Angiospermae
Dicotyledones

RANUNCULACEAE

Clematis vitalba L. *Old Man's Beard; Traveller's Joy*
Named Traveller's Joy because its masses of greyish-white fruits along the hedgerows delight travellers in the depths of winter.

Pulsatilla vulgaris Mill *Pasque Flower*
Anemone pulsatilla L.
Bourton Hill Downs and formerly in Campden Parish. Probably not in Blockley Parish: if found it should be carefully preserved.

Anemone nemorosa L. *Wood Anemone; Windflower*
Common in Dovedale and often appearing in Blockley gardens perhaps as a relic of former woodland.
There is a dark mauve variety (var. *caerulea* DC.) but the blue Anemone often naturalized in woods (as at Oddington) is *A. appenina* L.

Ranunculus acris L. *Meadow Buttercup*
Said to be Shakespeare's "cuckoo-buds of yellow hue"

Ranunculus aquatilis L. *Water Crowfoot*
The Flora of Gloucestershire gives this as *R. heterophyllus* var. *submersus* (Godr.) Bab., The Water Crowfoots are very complicated.
Dovedale.

Ranunculus arvensis L. *Corn Crowfoot*
Dovedale.

Ranunculus auricomus L. *Goldilocks*
Ranunculus bulbosus L. *Bulbous Buttercup*
Ranunculus ficaria L. *Lesser Celandine*
Ranunculus flammula L. *Lesser Spearwort*
Bourton Wood.

181

Ranunculus repens L.   *Creeping Buttercup*
Ranunculus sceleratus L.   *Celery-leaved Crowfoot*
Caltha palustris L.   *King Cup; Marsh Marigold*
    Dovedale.
Helleborus foetidus L.   *Stinking Hellebore*
    Batsford.
Aquilegia vulgaris L.   *Columbine*
    Blockley Woods, 1940. Not seen recently.
Aconitum anglicum Stapf   *Monkshood*
    Dovedale.

NYMPHAEACEAE

Nuphar lutae (L.) Sm.   *Yellow Water Lily*

PAPAVERACEAE

Papaver argemone L.   *Rough Long-headed Poppy*
    Campden; Ebrington; W.I. List.
Papaver dubium L.   *Smooth Long-headed Poppy*
    Campden; Ebrington; W.I. List.
Papaver rhoeas L.   *Common Corn Poppy*
Papaver somniferum L.   *Opium Poppy*
    Campden; W.I. List.
    An escape from cutlivation.
Chelidonium majus L.   *Greater Celandine*
Meconopsis cambrica (L.) Vig.   *Welsh Poppy*
    The Warren, Blockley.
    Probably not native in Gloucestershire.

FUMARIACEAE

Corydalis lutea (L.) DC.   *Yellow Corydalis*
    A common weed in Blockley gardens and sometimes found wild as an escape.
Fumaria capreolata L.   *Ramping Fumitory*
    Campden.
Fumaria muralis Sond. ex Koch   *Few-flowered Fumitory*
    F. boraei Jord.
    Campden.
Fumaria officinalis L.   *Common Fumitory*
    Shakespeare has "crown'd with rank fumiter and furrow-weeds"

CRUCIFERAE

Cheiranthus cheiri L.   *Wallflower*
    Quarry at Bourton-on-the-Hill.
Rorippa amphibia (L.) Bess.   *Great Yellow Cress*
    Paxford.
Rorippa islandica (Oeder) Borbás   *Marsh Yellow Cress*
    Campden.
Rorippa nasturtium-aquaticum (L.) Hayek   *Water-cress*
    Nasturtium officinale R.Br.
Barbarea vulgaris R.Br.   *Yellow Rocket*
    Paxford
Arabis Hirsuta (L.) Scop.   *Hairy Rock Cress*
    Campden.
Cardamine hirsuta L.   *Hairy Bittercress*
    A common weed in gardens.
Cardamine pratensis L.   *Cuckoo flower; Lady's Smock*
    Still to be found in the churchyard. Comes into flower with the cuckoo.
    Shakespeare's "lady-smocks all silver-white"

Erophila verna (L.) Chevall.   *Whitlow Grass*
Arabidopsis thaliana (L.) Heynh.   *Thale Cress*
  Campden.
Hesperis matronalis L.   *Dame's Violet*
  Blockley. Escape from cultivation.
Sisymbrium officinale (L.) Scop.   *Hedge Mustard*
Alliaria petiolata (Bieb.) Cavara & Grande   *Garlic Mustard*
Sinapis alba L.   *White Mustard*
  Dovedale.
  Mustard is made from the seeds; Shakespeare says "his wit's as thick as Tewkes-
  bury mustard".
Sinapis arvensis L.   *Charlock*
  Var. *orientalis* (L) Koch & Ziz. is said to be the common form at Hinchwick and
  Sezincote and may well occur in Blockley Parish.
Diplotaxis tenuifolia (L.) DC.   *Wall Rocket*
  Broad Campden.
Capsella bursa-pastoris (L.) Medic.   *Shepherd's Purse*
Coronopus didymus (L.) Sm.   *Wart Cress*
Coronopus squamatus (Forsk.) Aschers.   *Swine's Cress*
  C. procumbens Gilib.
Lepidium campestre (L.) R.Br.   *Field Pepperwort*
Cardaria draba (L.) Desv.   *Hoary Cress*
  Paxford.
Thlaspi arvense L.   *Penny Cress*
Thlaspi perfoliatum L.   *Perfoliate Penny Cress*
  A rare species almost confined to the North Cotswolds. There is no actual record
  from Blockley Parish but it has been found on Bourton Downs.

RESEDACEAE

Reseda lutea L.   *Wild Mignonette*
  Campden; W.I. List.
Reseda luteola L.   *Dyer's Rocket*
  Campden; Ebrington; W.I. List.

CISTACEAE

Helianthemum chamaecistus Mill.   *Rock Rose*
  H. nummularium of the Flora of Gloucestershire.
  Dovedale.

VIOLACEAE

Viola canina L.   *Dog Violet*
  W.I. List. Doubtful.
Viola hirta L.   *Hairy Violet*
Viola odorata L.   *Sweet Violet*
  Mentioned more often by Shakespeare than any other flower.
Viola palustris L.   *Marsh Violet*
  W.I. List. Seems very doubtful.
Viola riviniana Reichb.   *Common Violet*
  Campden.
Viola tricolor L.   *Pansy; Heartsease*
  The "Cupid's flower" of Shakespeare the juice of which "on sleeping eyelids
  laid will make a man or woman madly dote upon the next live creature that it
  sees".

POLYGALACEAE

Polygala serpyllifolia Hose   *Heath Milkwort*
  Campden.
Polygala vulgaris L.   *Common Milkwort*
  Springhill.

Saponaria officinalis L.   *Soapwort*
   Bourton; Stretton.
Vaccaria pyramidata Medic
   Campden.
Silene alba (Mill.) Krause   *White Campion*
   Melandrium album (L.) Garcke
   Pink-flowered forms are hybrids with the Red Campion. White, pink and red
   can be seen growing together in Dovedale.
Silene dioica (L.) Clairv.   *Red Campion*
   Melandrium dioicum (L.) Coss & Germ.
Silene noctiflora L.   *Night-flowering Catchfly*
   Melandrium noctiflorum (L.) Fr.
Silene vulgaris (Moench) Garcke   *Bladder Campion*
   S. cucubalis Wibel
Lychnis flos-cuculi L.   *Ragged Robin*
   Said to be the "Crowflower" of Shakespeare.
Agrostemma githago L.   *Corn Cockle*
   W.I. List: it is rare and seldom seen now-a-days.
Cerastium arvense L.   *Field Mouse-ear Chickweed*
Cerastium glomeratum Thuill.   *Clustered Mouse-ear*
   Cerastium viscosum of the Flora of Gloucestershire.
Cerastium holosteoides Fr.   *Common Mouse-ear Chickweed*
   Cerastium vulgatum of the Flora of Gloucestershire.
Cerastium semidecandrum L.   *Scarious Chickweed*
Stellaria alsine Grimm   *Bog Stitchwort*
   S. uliginosa Murr.
   Aston Magna.
Stellaria graminea L.   *Lesser Stitchwort*
   Dovedale; Aston Magna.
Stellaria holostea L.   *Greater Stitchwort*
   Bourton Wood.
Stellaria media (L.) Vill.   *Common Chickweed*
Arenaria leptoclados (Reichb.) Guss.   *Slender Sandwort*
   Broad Campden.
Arenaria serpyllifolia L.   *Thyme-leaved Sandwort*
Moehringia trinervia (L.) Clairv.   *Three-nerved Sandwort*
   Draycott; Paxford.
Sagina apetala L.   *Annual Pearlwort*
Sagina procumbens L.   *Procumbent Pearlwort*
Spergula arvensis L.   *Corn Spurrey*
   W.I. List.

GUTTIFERAE (HYPERICACEAE)

Hypericum hirsutum L.   *Hairy St. John's Wort*
Hypericum perforatum L.   *Perforate St. John's Wort*
Hypericum tetrapterum Fr.   *Square-stalked St. John's Wort*
   H. quadrangulum L.

MALVACEAE

Malva moschata L.   *Musk Mallow*
   Dovedale.
Malva neglecta Wallr.   *Dwarf Mallow*
   Broad Campden.
Malva sylvestris L.   *Common Mallow*

TILIACEAE

Tilia cordata X platyphyllos   *Common Lime*
   Also known as *Tilia europea* L. Commonly planted. Not native.

Linum catharticum L.   *White Flax*

GERANIACEAE

Geranium columbinum L.   *Long-stalked Cranesbill*
    Campden.
Geranium dissectum L.   *Cut-leaved Cranesbill*
    Blockley
Geranium lucidum L.   *Shining Cranesbill*
    Broad Campden.
Geranium molle L.   *Dove's-foot Cranesbill*
Geranium phaeum L.   *Dusky Cranesbill*
    Aston Magna
Geranium pratense L.   *Meadow Cranesbill*
    One of our most beautiful species which fortunately has seemed to increase in
    recent years.
Geranium pusillum L.   *Small-flowered Cranesbill*
Geranium pyrenaicum Burm. f.   *Mountain Cranesbill*
    The Warren, Blockley.
Geranium robertianum L.   *Herb Robert*
Erodium cicutarium (L.) L'Hérit.   *Hemlock Storksbill*
    Broad Campden; Ebrington.

OXALIDACEAE

Oxalis acetosella L.   *Wood Sorrel*
    Dovedale. One of our typical woodland species but often appearing as a weed
    in Blockley gardens.
Oxalis corniculata L.
    Blockley garden weed, said to be naturalized in Campden churchyard.
    Foliage usually bronzed.

AQUIFOLIACEAE

Ilex aquifolium L.   *Holly*
    Holly trees grow very well in Blockley, fruit well and produce numerous seed-
lings.

CELASTRACEAE

Euonymus europaeus L.   *Spindle Tree*

RHAMNACEAE

Rhamnus catharticus L.   *Common Buckthorn*
    Campden.
Frangula alnus Mill.   *Alder Buckthorn*
    Campden.

ACERACEAE

Acer campestre L.   *Maple*
    Provides beautiful autumn colours.
Acer pseudoplatanus L.   *Sycamore*
    Not considered to be native but produces seedlings very readily.

HIPPOCASTANACEAE

Aesculus hippocastanum L.   *Horsechestnut*
    Not native.

LEGUMINOSAE

Genista tinctoria L.   *Dyer's Greenweed*
    W.I. List.

Ulex europaeus L.	*Gorse*
Draycott.	
Sarothamnus scoparius (L.) Wimmer ex Koch	*Broom*
W.I. List.	
Ononis repens L.	*Rest-harrow*
Ononis spinosa L.	*Upright Rest-harrow*
Campden.	
Medicago lupulina L.	*Black Medick*
Medicago sativa L.	*Lucerne*
Relic of cultivation.	
Melilotus altissima Thuill.	*Common Melilot*
Melilotus officinalis (L.) Pall.	*Field Melilot*
Trifolium campestre Schreb.	*Hop Trefoil*
Trifolium dubium Sibth.	*Lesser YellowTrefoil*
Trifolium fragiferum L.	*Strawberry-headed Trefoil*
Broad Campden.	
Trifolium medium L.	*Zigzag Clover*
Trifolium micranthum Viv.	*Least Yellow Trefoil*
T. filiforme of the Flora of Gloucestershire.	
Trifolium pratense L.	*Red Clover*
Trifolium repens L.	*White or Dutch Clover*
Lotus corniculatus L.	*Bird's-foot Trefoil*
Lotus Tenuis Waldst. & Kit. ex Willd.	*Narrow-leaved Bird's-foot Trefoil*
Dovedale.	
Lotus uliginosus Schkuhr.	*Marsh Bird's-foot Trefoil*
Astragalus danicus Retz.	*Purple Milk Vetch*
Hippocrepis comosa L.	*Horseshoe Vetch*
Campden.	
Onobrychis viciifolia Scop.	*Sainfoin*
Blockley.	
Vicia angustifolia L.	*Narrow-leaved Vetch*
Campden.	
Vicia cracca L.	*Tufted Vetch*
Vicia hirsuta (L.) Gray	*Hairy Tare*
Vicia sativa L.	*Common Vetch*
Vicia sepium L.	*Bush Vetch*
Vicia sylvatica L.	*Wood Vetch*
Dovedale. An elegant species.	
Lathyrus aphaca L.	*Yellow Vetchling*
W.I. List	
Lathyrus montanus Bernh.	*Tuberous Bitter Vetch*
Lathyrus pratensis L.	*Meadow Pea*
Lathyrus sylvestris L.	*Everlasting Pea*
Bourton Wood.	

ROSACEAE

Prunus avium (L.) L.	*Gean*; *Wild Cherry*
Dovedale.	
Prunus cerasus L.	*Dwarf or Sour Cherry*
Prunus laurocerasus L.	*Cherry Laurel*
Dovedale.	
Prunus padus L.	*Bird Cherry*
Prunus spinosa L.	*Blackthorn*; *Sloe*
Filipendula ulmaria (L.) Maxim.	*Meadowsweet*
Filipendula vulgaris Moench	*Dropwort*
F. hexapetala Gilib.	
Rubus bellardii Weihe	
Campden.	

Rubus britannicus Rogers
  Quarry at Bourton-on-the-Hill.
Rubus caesius L.   *Dewberry*
Rubus corylifolius var. **sublustris** (Lees)Leighton
  Paxford.
Rubus cotteswoldensis Bart. & Ridd.
  Dovedale.
Rubus diversifolius Lindl.
  Campden.
Rubus echinatus Lindl.
  Dovedale.
Rubus falcatus Kalb
  R. thyrsoideus of the Flora of Gloucestershire.
  Dovedale.
Rubus idaeus L.   *Raspberry*
  Dovedale.
Rubus rhamnifolius Weihe & Nees
  Aston Magna; Draycott.
  NOTE. A proper study of *Rubus* is a matter for specialists.
Geum urbanum L.   *Wood Avens; Herb Bennet*
Fragaria vesca L.   *Wild Strawberry*
Potentilla anglica Laichard   *Trailing Tormentil*
Potentilla anserina L.   *Silverweed*
Potentilla erecta (L.) Räusch.   *Tormentil*
  The species we used to call *Potentilla tormentilla*.
Potentilla reptans L.   *Creeping Cinquefoil*
Potentilla sterilis (L.) Garcke   *Barren Strawberry*
  Potentilla procumbens Sibth.
  Ebrington.
Aphanes arvensis L.   *Field Lady's Mantle*
  Aston Magna.
Alchemilla vulgaris L.   *Lady's Mantle*
  Dovedale.
Agrimonia eupatoria L.   *Agrimony*
Poterium sanguisorba L.   *Salad Burnet*
  Sanguisorba minor Scop.
  W.I. List.
Sanguisorba officinalis L.   *Great Burnet*
  Paxford to Campden.
Rosa canina L.   *Dog Rose*
  Remarkable specimens in Dovedale grow to an unusual height.
Rosa rubiginosa L.   *Sweet Briar*
  W.I. List.
  Shakespeare's eglantine.
Rosa tomentosa Sm.   *Downy-leaved Rose*
  Northwick Hill.
Sorbus aria (L.) Crantz   *Whitebeam*
  W.I. List.
Sorbus aucuparia L.   *Mountain Ash; Rowan*
Pyrus communis L.   *Pear*
  Campden; Ebrington.
Malus sylvestris Mill.   *Crab Apple*
  Draycott.
  In Shakespeare we mostly find "roasted crabs".
Crataegus monogyna Jacq.   *Hawthorn; Whitethorn; May*
Crataegus oxyacanthoides Thuill.   *Midland Hawthorn*

Saxifraga granulata L.   *Meadow Saxifrage*
    Paxford.
Saxifraga tridactylites L.   *Rue-leaved Saxifrage*
Chrysosplenium alternifolium L.   *Alternate-leaved Golden Saxi-*
    Northwick.   *frage*
Chrysosplenium oppositifolium L.   *Opposite-leaved Golden Saxifrage*
    Northwick.
Ribes grossularia L.   *Gooseberry*

Sedum acre L.   *Biting Stonecrop*
    Campden.
Sedum album L.   *White Stonecrop*
Sedum dasyphyllum L.   *Thick-leaved Stonecrop*
    Ebrington.
Sedum reflexum L.   *Reflexed Stonecrop*
    Campden.

Hippuris vulgaris L.   *Mare's-tail*
    Ebrington; Hinchwick Pool.

Callitriche stagnalis Scop.   *Pond Water-starwort*
    Aston Magna.

Lythrum salicaria L.   *Purple Loosestrife*
    Paxford.

Chamaenerion angustifolium (L.) Scop.   *Rosebay Willowherb*
    Dovedale.
Epilobium hirsutum L.   *Great Hairy Willowherb; Cod-*
                                        lins and Cream
Epilobium montanum L.   *Broad-leaved Willowherb*
Epilobium obscurum Schreb.
    Hinchwick.
Epilobium palustre L.   *Marsh Willowherb*
    Westington Hill.
Epilobium parviflorum Schreb.   *Small-flowered Willowherb*
Epilobium tetragonum L.   *Square-stalked Willowherb*
Circaea lutetiana L.   *Enchanter's Nightshade*

Bryonia dioica Jacq.   *White Bryony*

Sanicula europaea L.   *Wood Sanicle*
    Dovedale.
Conium maculatum L.   *Hemlock*
Smyrnium olusatrum L.   *Alexanders*
    W.I. List.
Carum carvi L.   *Caraway*
    Ebrington.

Sium latifolium L.	*Broad-leaved Water Parsnip*
W.I. List.	
Aegopodium podagraria L.	*Goutweed; Ground Elder*
Pimpinella major (L.) Huds.	*Greater Burnet Saxifrage*
Dovedale.	
Conopodium majus (Gouan) Loret	*Earthnut; Pignut*
W.I. List.	
Chaerophyllum temulentum L.	*Rough Chervil*
Scandix pecten-veneris L.	*Venus' Comb*
Anthriscus caucalis Bieb.	*Burr Chervil*
A. neglecta Boiss. & Reut.	
Campden.	
Anthriscus cerefolium (L.) Hoffm.	*Garden Chervil*
Broad Campden. An escape form cultivation.	
Anthriscus sylvestris (L.) Hoffm.	*Wild Chervil; Keck*
Oenanthe crocata L.	*Hemlock Water Dropwort*
W.I. List.	
Aethusa cynapium L.	*Fool's Parsley*
Silaum silaus (L.) Schinz & Thell.	*Pepper Saxifrage*
Angelica sylvestris L.	*Wild Angelica*
Pastinaca sativa L.	*Water Parsnip*
Heracleum sphondylium L.	*Hogweed*
Daucus carota L.	*Wild Carrot*
Torilis arvensis (Huds.) Link	*Hedge Parsley*
W.I. List.	
Torilis japonica (Houtt.) DC.	*Upright Hedge Parsley*

ARALIACEAE

Hedera helix L.	*Ivy*

CORNACEAE

Thelycrania sanguinea (L.) Fourr.	*Dogwood*
Cornus sanguinea L.	
Dovedale.	

ADOXACEAE

Adoxa moschatellina L.	*Moschatel*
W.I. List.	

CAPRIFOLIACEAE

Sambucus nigra L.	*Elder*
Viburnum lantana L.	*Wayfaring Tree*
Dovedale.	
Viburnum opulus L.	*Guelder Rose*
Symphoricarpus rivularis Suksd.	*Snowberry*
Dovedale. An escape from cultivation.	
Lonicera periclymenum L.	*Honeysuckle; Woodbine*

Dovedale. Midsummer Night's Dream: "so doth the woodbine the sweet honey-suckle gently entwist".

RUBICEAE

Cruciata laevipes Opiz	*Crosswort*
Galium cruciatum (L.) Scop.	
W.I. List.	
Galium aparine L.	*Goosegrass; Cleavers*
Galium mollugo L.	*Hedge Bedstraw*
Galium odoratum (L.) Scop.	*Sweet Woodruff*
Asperula odorata L.	

Dovedale. Has a sweet scent of hay.

Galium palustre L.	*Marsh Bedstraw*
Galium saxatile L.	*Heath Bedstraw*
G. harcynicum Weigel	
Galium uliginosum L.	*Bog Bedstraw*
Dovedale.	
Galium verum L.	*Lady's Bedstraw*
Asperula cynanchia L.	*Squinancy-wort*
Broadway Hill.	
Sherardia arvensis L.	*Field Madder*
Blockley	

VALERIANACEAE

Valeriana dioica L.	*Small marsh Valerian*
Dovedale.	
Valeriana officinalis L.	*Great Valerian*
Dovedale.	
Centranthus ruber (L.) DC.	*Red Valerian*

DIPSACACEAE

Dipsacus pilosus L.	*Small Teasel*
Campden.	
Dipsacus fullonum L.	*Teasel*
D. sylvestris Huds.	
Succisa pratensis Moench	*Devil's-bit Scabious*
W.I. List; Campden.	
Scabiosa columbaria L.	*Small Scabious*
Knautia arvensis (L.) Coult.	*Field Scabious*

—COMPOSITAE

Eupatorium cannabinum L.	*Hemp Agrimony*
Dovedale.	
Bellis perennis L.	*Daisy*

Love's Labour's Lost: "daisies pied and violets blue." Also in Hamlet.

Erigeron acer L.	*Blue Fleabane*
Campden.	
Filago germanica (L.) L.	*Upright Cudweed*
Bourton Downs.	
Inula conyza DC.	*Ploughman's Spikenard*
Dovedale.	
Pulicaria dysentirica (L.) Bernh.	*Yellow Fleabane*
Campden.	
Achillea millefolium L.	*Yarrow*; *Milfoil*
Achillea ptarmica L.	*Sneezewort*
Westington Hill.	
Anthemis arvensis L.	*Corn Chamomile*
Hinchwick.	
Anthemis cotula L.	*Foetid Chamomile*
Bourton-on-the-Hill.	
Chrysanthemum leucanthemum L.	*Ox-eye Daisy*
Chrysanthemum parthenium (L.) Bernh.	*Feverfew*
Chrysanthemum segetum L.	*Corn Marigold*
Campden.	
Tripleurospermum maritimum (L.) Koch	*Scentless Mayweed*
Matricaria inodora L.	
Matricaria matricarioides (Less.) Porter	*Rayless Mayweed*
Matricaria recutita L.	*Wild Chamomile*

Matricaria chamomilla of the Flora of Gloucestershire.

190

Artemisia absinthium L. *Wormwood*
Thought to be the "Dian's Bud" of a Midsummer Night's Dream.
Artemisia vulgaris L. *Mugwort*
Campden.
Tussilago farfara L. *Coltsfoot*
Petasites fragrans (Vill.) C. Presl *Winter Heliotrope*
Batsford, Naturalized.
Petasites hybridus (L.) Gaertn., Mey. & Schreb. *Butterbur*
Dovedale.
Senecia aquaticus Hill *Marsh Ragwort*
Senecio erucifolius L. *Hoary Ragwort*
Dovedale.
Senecio jacobaea L. *Ragwort*
Senecio squalidus L. *Oxford Ragwort*
Snowshill.
Senecio sylvaticus L. *Heath Groundsel*
Campden.
Senecio viscosus L. *Sticky Groundsel*
Blockley.
Senecio vulgaris L. *Groundsel*
Carlina vulgaris L. *Carline Thistle*
Bourton Woods.
Arctium lappa L. *Greater Burdock*
Paxford. Mentioned in King Lear.
Arctium minus Bernh. *Lesser Burdock*
Arctium pubescens Bab. *Intermediate Burdock*
Arctium vulgare of the Flora of Gloucestershire.
Carduus acanthoides L. *Welted Thistle*
Carduus crispus of the Flora of Gloucestershire.
Dovedale.
Carduus nutans L. *Musk Thistle*
Dover's Hill; Ebrington.
Cirsium acaulon (L.) Scop. *Stemless Thistle*
Cirsium eriophorum (L.) Scop. *Woolly-headed Thistle*
Dovedale.
Cirsium palustre (L.) Scop. *Marsh Thistle*
Dovedale.
Cirsium vulgare (Savi) Ten. *Spear Thistle*
Serratula tinctoria L. *Saw-wort*
Paxford; Bourton Downs.
Centaurea nigra L. *Black Knapweed*
Centaurea scabiosa L. *Greater Knapweed*
Dovedale.
Cichorium intybus L. *Chicory*
W.I. List.
Lapsana communis L. *Nipplewort*
Picris echioides L. *Prickly Ox-tongue*
Campden.
Crepis capillaris (L.) Wallr. *Smooth Hawkesbeard*
Crepis vesicaria L. *Beaked Hawksbeard*
C. taraxicifolia Thuill.
Broad Campden; Lower Ditchford.
Hieracium lachenalia var. **transiens** Ley *Hawkweed*
Campden.
Hieracium maculatum Sm.
Campden.
Hieracium pilosella L. *Mouse-ear Hawkweed*
There are 200 or more microspecies of *Hieracium* and no doubt a number of

these occur in the Blockley district. It is evident from the lack of records that no specialist has studied them from this area.

Hypochaeris radicata L. — *Cat's Ear*
Leontodon autumnalis L. — *Autumnal Hawkbit*
Leonntodon hispidus L. — *Common Hawkbit*
Leontodon taraxacoides (Vill.) Mérat — *Hairy-headed Hawkbit*
  L. leysseri (Wallr.) Beck.
  Dovedale.
Taraxacum laevigatum (Willd.) DC. — *Red-fruited Dandelion*
Taraxacum officinale Weber — *Dandelion*
Mycelis muralis (L.) Dumort. — *Wall Lettuce*
  Lactuca muralis (L.) Fresen.
  Dovedale.
Sonchus arvensis L. — *Corn Sowthistle*
  Dovedale.
Sonchus asper (L.) Hill — *Rough Sowthistle*
  Campden; Ebrington.
Sonchus oleraceus L. — *Sowthistle*
Tragopogon pratensis L. — *Goatsbeard*
  Dovedale.
Cicerbita macrophylla (Willd.) Wallr. — *Blue Sowthistle*
  Batsford; Stretton

CAMPANULACEAE

Campanula glomerata L. — *Clustered Bellflower*
Campanula rotundifolia L. — *Harebell*
Campanula trachelium L. — *Nettle-leaved Bellflower*
  Dovedale.
Legousia hybrida (L.) Delarb. — *Venus' Looking-glass*
  Specularia hybrida (L.) A.DC.
  Northwick Hill; Broad Campden. Perhaps now extinct in our district; should be searched for.

ERICACEAE

Calluna vulgaris (L.) Hill — *Ling*
  Westington Hill.

MONOTROPACEAE

Monotropa hypopitys L. — *Yellow Bird's-nest*
  Westington Hill.

PRIMULACEAE

Primula veris L. — *Cowslip*
  Mentioned many times by Shakespeare.
Primula vulgaris Huds. — *Primrose*
  Also a favourite of Shakespeare's.
Primula veris X vulgaris — *False Oxlip*
  Bourton Wood.
  The W.I. List records "Oxlip" but the true Oxlip, *Primula elatior* (L.) Hill does not occur in Gloucestershire. When Shakespeare refers to "Oxlip" in Mid-summer Night's Dream it is far more likely that it was the Cowslip-Primrose hybrid that he was acquainted with. The hybrid occurs very frequently when the Cowslip and Primrose are growing together.
Lysimachia nummularia L. — *Creeping Jenny; Moneywort*
  Dovedale.
Lysimachia vulgaris L. — *Yellow Loosestrife*
  Dovedale.
Anagallis arvensis L. — *Scarlet Pimpernel*

192

The Pasque Flower (*Tulsatilla Vulgaris*)

OLEACEAE

Fraxinus excelsior L.   *Ash*
Ligustrum vulgare L.   *Privet*

GENTIANACEAE

Blackstonia perfoliata (L.) Huds.   *Yellow-wort*
    Tallyho Quarry.
Centaurium erythraea Rafin.   *Centaury*
    Aston Magna.
Gentianella amarella (L.) Börner   *Field Gentian*
    Westington Hill.
Gentianella campestris (L.) Börner   *Autumn Gentian*
    Westington Hill.

APOCYNACEAE

Vinca major L.   *Greater Periwinkle*
    Garden escape.

BORAGINACEAE

Cynoglossum officinale L.   *Hound's-tongue*
    Ebrington.
Symphytum asperum X officinale   *Prickly Comfrey*
    S. peregrinum of the Flora of Gloucestershire.
    Paxford.
Symphytum grandiflorum DC.
    In gardens along Blockley stream. An alien but sometimes naturalized.
Symphytum officinale L.   *Comfrey*
    Paxford.
    The purple form (var. *purpureum* Pers.) is common in Dovedale.
Pentaglottis sempervirens (L.) Tausch   *Alkanet*
    Anchusa sempervirens L.
    Blockley, 1972
Pulmonaria longifolia (Bast.) Bor.
    Dovedale, 1942, An alien.
Pulmonaria officinalis L.   *Lungwort*
    Blockley gardens. Said to be naturalized at Campden.
Myosotis arvensis (L.) Hill   *Field Forget-me-not*
Myosotis caespitosa K. F. Schultz   *Tufted Forget-me-not*
    Dovedale.
Myosotis discolor Pers.   *Yellow Forget-me-not*
    M. versicolor (Pers.) Sm.
    Aston Magna.
Myosotis ramossima Rochel   *Early Forget-me-not*
    M. hispida Schlechtend.
    Ebrington.
Myosotis scorpioides L.   *Forget-me-not*
Lithospermum arvense L.   *Corn Gromwell*
    Northwick Hill.
Lithospermum officinale L.   *Perennial Gromwell*
    Broad Campden; Bourton-on-the-Hill.
Omphalodes verna Moench
    Alien. This was well-established but may have been extirpated by grazing.
Trachystemon orientalis (L.) G. Don
    W.I. List. Alien.

CONVOLVULACEAE

Calystegia sepium (L.) R.Br.   *Great Bindweed*
Convolvulus arvensis L.   *Field Bindweed*

Solanum dulcamara L.   *Bittersweet; Woody Nightshade*
Solanum nigrum L.   *Black Nightshade*
Hyoscyamus niger L.   *Henbane*
  Campden.

SCHROPHULARIACEAE

Verbascum nigrum L.   *Dark Mullein*
  Broad Campden.
Verbascum thapsus L.   *Great Mullein*
  Dovedale.
Linaria vulgaris Mill.   *Yellow Toadflax*
  W.I. List.
Cymbalaria muralis Gaertn.   *Ivy-leaved Toadflax*
  Linaria cymbalaria (L.) Mill.
Kickxia spuria (L.) Dumort.   *Round-leaved Fluellen*
  Campden.
Misopates orontium (L.) Raf.   *Lesser Snapdragon*
  Antirrhinum orontium L.
  Dover's Hill.
Scrophularia aquatica L.   *Water Figwort*
Scrophularia nodosa L.   *Figwort*
Mimulus guttatus DC.   *Monkey-flower*
  Alien naturalized along Blockley stream.
Digitalis purpurea L.   *Foxglove*
Veronica agrestis L.   *Field Speedwell*
Veronica arvensis L.   *Wall Speedwell*
Veronica beccabunga L.   *Brooklime*
Veronica chamaedrys L.   *Germander Speedwell*
Veronica hederifolia L.   *Ivy-leaved Speedwell*
Veronica montana L.   *Wood Speedwell*
  Campden.
Veronica officinalis L.   *Speedwell*
Veronica persica Poir.
Veronica polita Fr.   *Grey Field Speedwell*
  Campden.
Veronica serpyllifolia L.   *Thyme-leaved Speedwell*
Veronica spicata L.   *Spiked Speedwell*
  Veronica hybrida L.
  Broad Campden.
Euphrasia officinalis L.   *Eyebright*
  Now split into many micro-species.
Odontites verna (Bellardi) Dumort. subsp. **verna** *Red Bartsia*
  Northwick Hill.
Odontites verna (Bellardi) Dumort. subsp. **serotina** (Wettst.) E. F. Warb.
  Campden; Hinchwick.
Pedicularis palustris L.   *Lousewort; Red Rattle*
  W.I. List.
Rhinanthus minor L.   *Yellow Rattle*
Melampyrum pratense L.   *Cowwheat*
  Dovedale.

OROBANCHACEAE

Orobanche minor Sm.   *Lesser Broomrape*
  Ebrington.
  The W.I. List records "Broomrape" which is probably this species.
Lathraea squamaria L.   *Toothwort*

194

Verbena officinalis L.   *Vervain*
Broad Campden.

Mentha arvensis L.   *Corn Mint*
The W.I. List also records "Hairy Mint" which is not sufficient to identify it.
Peppermint may be intended.
Thymus drucei Ronn.
T. lanuginosus of the Flora of Gloucestershire.
Near Broadway Tower.
Thymus pulegioides L.
Near Broadway Tower.
Thymus serpyllum L.   *Wild Thyme*
Midsummer Night's Dream: "I know a bank where the wild thyme blows".
Lycopus europaeus L.   *Gipsywort*
Origanum vulgare L.   *Marjoram*
Dovedale.
Still used as a culinary herb as it was in Shakespeare's time: "Sweet marjoram
of the salad".
Clinopodium vulgare L.   *Wild Basil*
Dovedale.
Acinos arvensis (Lam.) Dandy   *Basil Thyme*
Broad Campden: Ebrington.
Melissa officinalis L.   *Balm*
Ebrington.
Salvia horminioides Pourr.   *Wild Sage; Clary*
Glechoma hederacea L.   *Ground Ivy*
Prunella vulgaris L.   *Self-heal*
Betonica officinalis L.   *Wood Betony*
Stachys officinalis (L.) Trevis.
Stachys palustrius L.   *Marsh Woundwort*
Campden; Hinchwick.
Stachys sylvatica L.   *Hedge Woundwort*
Galeopsis angustifolia Ehrh. ex Hoffm.   *Red Hemp-nettle*
Northwick Hill.
Galeopsis tetrahit L.   *Common Hemp-nettle*
Hinchwick.
Lamium album L.   *White Deadnettle*
Lamium amplexicaule L.   *Henbit*
Broad Campden.
Lamium purpureum L.   *Red Deadnettle*
Galeobdolon luteum Huds.   *Yellow Archangel*
Lamium galeobdolon (L.) Crantz
Dovedale.
Ballota nigra L.   *Black Horehound*
Teucrium scorodonia L.   *Wood Sage*
Ajuga reptans L.   *Bugle*

Plantago lanceolata L.   *Ribwort Plantain*
Plantago major L.   *Greater Plantain*
Plantago media L.   *Hoary Plantain*

Chenopodium album L.   *White Goosefoot; Fat Hen*
Chenopodium bonus-henricus L.   *Good King Henry*
Chenopodium rubrum L.   *Red Goosefoot*

195

Chenopodium urbicum L.   *Upright Goosefoot*
Atriplex hastata L.   *Orache*

POLYGONACEAE

Fagopyrum tataricum (L.) Gaertn.
Polygonum amphibium L.   *Amphibious Bistort*
Polygonum aviculare L.   *Knotgrass*
Polygonum bistorta L.   *Bistort*
  Batsford.
Polygonum hydropiper L.   *Water Pepper*
  Bourton Wood.
Polygonum persicaria L.   *Common Persicaria*
  Paxford.
Rumex acetosa L.   *Sorrel*
Rumex acetosella L.   *Sheep Sorrel*
Rumex conglomeratus Murr.   *Sharp Dock*
Rumex crispus L.   *Curled Dock*
Rumex obtusifolius L.   *Broad-leaved Dock*

THYMELAEACEAE

Daphne laureola L.   *Spurge Laurel*
  Dovedale.

EUPHORBIACEAE

Euphorbia amygdaloides L.   *Wood Spurge*
  Dovedale; Northwick.
Euphorbia helioscopia L.   *Sun Spurge*
Euphorbia lathyrus L.   *Caper Spurge*
  Weed of gardens in Blockley; said to keep moles away.
Euphorbia peplus L.   *Petty Spurge*
Mercurialis perennis L.   *Dog's Mercury*

CANNABIACEAE

Humulus lupulus L.   *Hop*

ULMACEAE

Ulmus glabra Huds.   *Wych Elm*
  Dovedale.
Ulmus plotii Druce   *Plot Elm*
  Campden.
Ulmus procera Salisb.   *English Elm*

URTICACEAE

Parietaria diffusa Mert. & Koch   *Pellitory of the Wall*
  P. ramiflora of the Flora of Gloucestershire
  Campden.
Urtica dioica L.   *Stinging Nettle*
Urtica urens L.   *Small Nettle*
  Campden.
Helxine soleirolii Req.
  Frequently becomes a weed in gardens and on paths.

BETULACEAE

Betula pendula Roth   *Silver Birch*
Alnus glutinosa (L.) Gaertn.   *Alder*

CORYLACEAE

Carpinus betulus L.   *Hornbeam*
Corylus avellana L.   *Hazel*

Quercus robur L.   *Pedunculate Oak*
  Frequent on the Upper Lias.
Castanea sativa Mill.   *Sweet Chestnut*
  Naturalized but not native.
Fagus sylvatica L.   *Beech*
  Climax vegetation of the Oolite Limestone. Many fine specimens in and
  around Blockley.

SALICACEAE

Salix alba L.   *White Willow*
Salix atrocinerea Brot.   *Sallow; Pussy Willow*
Salix caprea L.   *Sallow; Palm*
  Dovedale.
Populus canescens (Ait.) Sm.   *Grey Poplar*
Populus serotina Hartig   *Black Poplar*
Populus tremula L.   *Aspen*

Monocotyledones

ORCHIDACEAE

Neottia nidus-avis (L.) Rich.   *Bird's-nest Orchid*
  Northwick Park.
Listera ovata (L.) R.Br.   *Twayblade*
  Dovedale.
Cephalanthera damasonum (Mill.) Druce   *White Helleborine*
  Cephalanthera alba (Crantz) Simonkai
  Broad Campden.
Epipactis helleborine (L.) Crantz   *Broad-leaved Helleborine*
  Draycott.
Epipactis purpurata Sm.   *Violet Helleborine*
  Campden.
Anacamptis pyramidalis (L.) Rich.   *Pyramidal Orchid*
Orchis mascula (L.) L.   *Early Purple Orchis*
  Dovedale.
Orchis morio L.   *Green-winged Orchis*
Dactylorchis fuchsii (Druce) Vermeul   *Spotted Orchis*
  Aston Magna; Blockley; Dovedale and Tallyho Quarry.
Dactylorchis maculata subsp. **ericetorum** (E. F. Lontin) Vermeul
                                                  Heath Spotted Orchis
  Orchis ericetorum (E. F. Linton) E. S. Marshall
  Broad Campden.
Ophrys apifera Huds.   *Bee Orchid*
Ophys insectifera L.   *Fly Orchid*
  Bourton Wood.
Caeloglossum viride (L.) Hartm.   *Frog Orchid*
  Campden.
Platanthera bifolia (L.) Rich.   *Lesser Butterfly Orchid*
  Campden.

IRIDACEAE

Iris foetidissima L.   *Gladdon; Stinking Iris*
  Campden.
Iris pseudacorus L.   *Flag; Yellow Iris*
  Paxford.
  The "flower-de-luce" of Shakespeare.

AMARYLLIDACEAE

Galanthus nivalis L. *Snowdrop*
  Not yet found wild at Blockley; recorded from Snowshill.
Allium ursinum L. *Wild Garlic; Ramsons*
  W.I. List.

DIOSCOREACEAE

Tamus communis L. *Black Bryony*
  Dovedale.

LILIACEAE

Ruscus aculeatus L. *Butcher's Broom*
  Campden.
Polygonatum multiflorum (L.) All. *Solomon's Seal*
  The W.I. List records "Solomon's Seal" but the species is not given.
  Dovedale (1972), leaves only seen. It appears to be this species.
Convallaria majalis L. *Lily of the Valley*
  The W.I. List says "leaves only".
Endymion non-scriptus (L.) Garcke *Bluebell*
  Scilla non-scripta Hoffmanns. & Link
  Dovedale.
  Shakespeare's "Harebell".
Lilium martagon L. *Turk's-cap Lilly*
  Dovedale; Bourton Woods
  One of our most interesting species. Well-established in the upper part of
  Dovedale and possibly native.
Colchicum autumnale L. *Meadow Saffron*
  Dovedale.
Paris quadrifolia L. *Herb Paris*
  Upper Dovedale.

JUNCACEAE

Juncus acutiflorus Ehrh. ex. Hoffm. *Sharp-flowered Jointed Rush*
Juncus articulatus L. *Common Jointed Rush*
Juncus bufonius L. *Toad Rush*
Juncus conglomeratus L. *Common Rush*
Juncus effusus L. *Loose-flowered Soft Rush*
Luzula campestris (L.) DC. *Field Woodrush*
Luzula pilosa (L.) Willd. *Hairy Woodrush*
  Bourton Wood.

TYPHACEAE

Typha latifolia L. *Reedmace*
  Campden.

SPARGANIACEAE

Sparganium erectum L. *Branched Bur-reed*
  Dovedale.

ARACEAE

Arum maculatum L. *Cuckoo-pint; Lords and Ladies*

LEMNACEAE

Lemna minor L. *Lesser Duckweed*
Lemna trisulca L. *Ivy-leaved Duckweed*

ALISMATACEAE

Alisma plantago-aquatica L. *Greater Water Plantain*

JUNCAGINACEAE

Triglochin palustris L. *Marsh Arrowgrass*
  Campden.

Potamogeton crispus L.   *Curled Pondweed*
  Aston Magna.
Groenlandia densa (L.) Fourr.   *Opposite leaved Pondweed*
  Potamogeton densus L.
  Dovedale.

CYPERACEAE

Carex disticha Huds.   *Soft Brown Sedge*
  Campden.
Carex flacca Schreb.   *Glaucous Sedge*
Carex hirta L.   *Hairy Sedge*
Carex nigra (L.) Reichard   *Common Sedge*
Carex otrubae Podp.   *Common Fox Sedge*
Carex paniculata L.   *Paniculate Sedge*
  Dovedale.
Carex remota L.   *Remote-spiked Sedge*
  Campden.
Carex spicata Huds.   *Common Prickly Sedge*
  Campden.
Carex sylvatica Huds.   *Wood Sedge*
  Dovedale.

GRAMINEAE

Phragmites communis Trin.   *Common Reed*
Glyceria plicata Fr.   *Plicate Sweet Grass*
  Dovedale.
Festuca arundinacea Schreb.   *Tall Fescue*
  Dovedale.
Festuca gigantea (L.) Vill.   *Giant Fescue*
  Dovedale.
Festuca pratensis Huds.   *Meadow Fescue*
  Campden.
Lolium multiflorum var. **italicum** (A. Braun) Beck. *Italian Rye-grass*
Lolium perenne L.   *Perennial Rye-grass*
Catapodium rigidum (L.) C. E. Hubb.
  Scleropoa rigida (L.) Griseb.
  Campden.
Poa annua L.   *Annual Meadow Grass*
Poa compressa L.   *Flat-stemmed Meadow Grass*
  Campden.
Poa nemoralis L.   *Wood Meadow Grass*
  Dovedale.
Poa pratensis L.   *Smooth-stalked Meadow Grass*
Briza media L.   *Quaking Grass*
Dactylis glomerata L.   *Cocksfoot Grass*
Cynosurus cristatus L.   *Crested Dogstail*
Melica uniflora Retz.   *Wood Melic Grass*
  Dovedale.
Bromus commutatus Schrad.   *Meadow Brome*
  Campden.
Bromus erectus Huds.   *Upright Brome*
Bromus sterilis L.   *Barren Brome*
Brachypodium pinnatum (L.) Beauv.   *Chalk False Brome*
  Dovedale.
Brachypodium sylvaticum (Huds.) Beauv.   *Wood False Brome*
Agropyron caninum (L.) Beauv.   *Tufted Couch*
Hordeum murinum L.   *Wall Barley*

Helichtotrichon pratense (L.) Pilg.	*Meadow Oat Grass*
Helictrochon pubescens (Huds.) Pilg.	*Downy Oat Grass*
Broad Campden.	
Avena fatua L.	*Wild Oat*
Dovedale.	
Trisetum flavesches (L.) Beauv.	*Yellow Oat Grass*
Koeleria cristata (L.) Pers.	*Crested Hair Grass*
K. gracilis Pers.	
Campden; Bourton Downs.	
Arrhenatherum elatius(L.) Beauv. ex J.&C. Presl	*False Oat Grass*
Holcus lanatus L.	*Yorkshire Fog*
Holcus mollis L.	*Creeping Soft Grass*
Campden; Hinchwick	
Deschampsia caespitosa (L.) Beauv.	*Tufted Hair Grass*
Deschampsia flexuosa (L.) Trin.	*Wavy Hair Grass*
Dovedale.	
Anthoxanthum odoratum L.	*Sweet Vernal Grass*
Much of the scent of hay is due to it.	
Calamagrostis epigejos (L.) Roth	*Wood Smallreed*
Dovedale.	
Agrestis canina L.	*Velvet Bent Grass*
W.I. List.	
Agrostis stolonifera L.	*Creeping Bent Grass*
Agrostis tenuis Sibthorp	*Common Bent Grass*
Phleum pratense L.	*Timothy*
Alopecurus geniculatus L.	*Marsh Foxtail Grass*

GYMNOSPERMAE
TAXACEAE

Taxus baccata L.   *Yew*
There is a particularly fine Yew Tree in the churchyard near the northern entrance.

PINACEAE

Larix decidua L.   *Larch*
Much planted.
Pinus sylvestris L.   *Scots Pine; Scotch Fir*
Various other Conifers are commonly planted: species of *Abies*, *Cedrus*, *Pseudotsuga*, *Sequoia* etc.

PTERIDOPHYTA
DENNSTAEDTIACEAE

Pteridium aquilinum (L.) Kuhn   *Bracken*
Dovedale.

ASPLENIACEAE

Phyllitis scolopendrium (L.) Newm.   *Hart's-tongue*
Northwick.
Asplenium ruta-muraria L.   *Wall Rue*
Ceterach officinarum DC.   *Scale Fern*
Campden.

ATHYRIACEAE

Athyrium filix-foemina (L.) Roth   *Lady Fern*

ASPIDIACEAE

Polystichum aculeatum (L.) Roth   *Prickly Shield Fern*
Dryopteris dilatata (Hoffm.) A. Gray   *Broad Buckler Fern*
Aston Magna.

Dryopteris filix-mas (L.) Schott   *Male Fern*
Dryopteris lanceolato-cristata (Hoffm.) Alston   *Narrow Buckler Fern*
  D. spinulosa (Mull.) Watt
  Campden.

THELYPTERIDACEAE

Thelypteris robertianum (Hoffm.) Slosson   *Limestone Polypody*
  Gymnocarpium robertianum (Hoffm.) Newm.
  Broad Campden.

POLYPODIACEAE

Polypodium vulgare L.   *Common Polypody*

BLECHNACEAE

Blechnum spicant (L.) Roth   *Hard Fern*
  Bourton Wood.

EQUISETACEAE

Equisetum arvense L.   *Field Horsetail*
Equisetum palustre L.   *Marsh Horsetail*
  Aston Magna.
Equisetum telmateia Ehrh.   *Great Horsetail*
  Dovedale.

OPHIOGLOSSACEAE

Ophioglossum vulgatum L.   *Adder's Tongue Fern*
  Springhill; Ebrington.

CHAROPHYTA

CHARACEAE

Nitella opaca (Agardh ex Bruzelius) Agardh
  Dovedale.

IV BLOCKLEY ENTOMOLOGY
By
DR. E. H. EASON M.A., M.B. (CANTAB.), F.L.S.

Gloucestershire entomologists have devoted much of their attention to the Forest of Dean and most of the work in the Cotswolds has centred around Cheltenham, Stroud and Cirencester so we have little positive knowledge of the insects of the Blockley district; but judging from county and vice-county records of some of the better known groups, and the fact that the Blockley district includes some of the North Cotswold escarpment as well as the edge of the Warwickshire Vale, and is nicely balanced between woodland and farm-land with a stream running through, it seems likely that the insect fauna is well represented and that about a third of the recorded British species will be found to occur in the immediate neighbourhood. For example, of the sixty odd species of British butterflies, nineteen are represented in the accompanying list compiled by Mrs Goadby. A similar list of moths is probably less complete as this group includes so many small inconspicuous species that only very intensive collecting will bring them to light. We do, however, have fairly positive knowledge of a group allied to insects, the myriapods; of forty species of centipede recorded from Britain eighteen have been found near Blockley and the comparable figures for millipedes are forty-five and seventeen.

No rarities have been found in recent years. The only conspicuous insects—little known but not uncommon—which have been brought to me for identification are the Large Velvet-ant (*Mutilla europoea*) and the Greater Horntail (*Sirex gigas*), the largest of the wood-boring wasps.

Modern methods of agriculture—pesticides killing insects and herbicides killing the plants on which some of them depend, commercial forestry which abhors derelict woodland, the destruction of hedgerows and the general "tidying up" of the countryside by removal of old stone-walls and clearing of waste-ground must inevitably have caused the diminution or even extinction of some species. But these trends are no worse in Blockley than elsewhere, and, although some species seem to disappear for years they often reappear years later; the number of individuals seems to have declined but I cannot say, from over twenty years' casual observation in the district, that there has been any marked reduction in the number of species.

V BLOCKLEY BUTTERFLIES AND MOTHS
By
MRS K. M. GOADBY FROM THE COLLECTIONS OF JAMES GOADBY

BUTTERFLIES

PIERIDAE

Small White	*Pieris rapae* Linn.
Large White	*Pieris brassicae* Linn.
Green-veined White	*Pieris napi* Linn.
Orange-tip	*Anthocaris cardamines* Linn.
Brimstone	*Gonepteryx rhamni* Linn.

NYMPHALIDAE

High Brown Fritillary	*Argynnis adippe* Schiff.
Red Admiral	*Vanessa atalanta* Linn.
Painted Lady	*Vanessa cardui* Linn.
Peacock	*Nymphalis io* Linn.
Large Tortoiseshell	*Nymphalis polychloros* Linn.
Small Tortoiseshell	*Aglais urticae* Linn.
Comma	*Polygonia c-album* Linn.

Speckled Wood	*Pararge aegeria* Linn.
Wall Brown	*Pararge megera* Linn.
Meadow Brown	*Maniola jurtina* Linn.
Ringlet	*Aphantopus hyperanthus* Linn.

LYCAENIDAE

Small Copper	*Lycaena phlaeas* Linn.
Brown Argus	*Aricia agestis* Schiff.
Common Blue	*Polyommatus icarus* Rott.
Holly Blue	*Celastrina argiolus* Linn.

HESPERIDAE

Dingy Skipper	*Erynnis tages* Linn.

I am indebted to Mr V. R. Hughes for the following additional records: Clouded Yellow, Marbled White, Small Heath, Purple Hairstreak and Large Skipper.

MOTHS

ZYGAENIDAE

Six-spot Burnet Moth	*Anthrocera filipendula* L.

SPHINGIDAE

Humming-bird Hawk-Moth	*Macroglossa stellatarum* L.
Elephant Hawk-Moth	*Choerocampa elpenor* L.
Small Elephant Hawk-Moth	*Choerocampa porcellus* L.
Striped Hawk-Moth	*Deilephila livornica* Esper.
Privet Hawk-Moth	*Sphinx ligustris* L.
Eyed Hawk-Moth	*Smerinthus ocellatus* L.
Poplar Hawk-Moth	*Smerinthus populi* L.

HEPIALIDAE

Ghost Moth	*Hepialus humuli* L.

COSSIDAE

Goat Moth	*Cossus ligniperda* Fabr.

LIPARIDAE

Pale Tussock Moth	*Dasychira pudibunda* L.
Brown-tail Moth	*Euproctis chrysorrhoea* L.

ARCTIIDAE

Cinnabar Moth	*Hipocrita jacobaeae* L.
Ruby Tiger Moth	*Phragmatobia fuliginosa* L.
Common Tiger Moth	*Arctea caja* L.
Buff Ermine Moth	*Spilosoma lubricipeda* L.
White Ermine Moth	*Spilosoma menthastri* Esper.
Oak Eggar	*Lasiocampa quercus* L.
Drinker Moth	*Odonestis potatoria* L.

NOTODONTIDAE

Buff Tip	*Phelera bucephala* L.
Puss Moth	*Cerura vinula* L.

NOCTUIDAE
Subfam. Acronyctidae

Scarce Merveille-du-Jour	*Diphthera alpium* Osbeck
Coronet Moth	*Acronycta ligustri* L.

Subfam. Orthosiidae

Clay Moth	*Leucania lithargyrea* Esper.
Brown-line Bright-eye	*Leucania conigera* Denis
Southern Wainscot	*Leucania straminea* Treitschke
Uncertain Moth	*Caradrina alsines* Borkh.
Ear-Moth	*Hydroecia nictitans* Borkh.
Herald Moth	*Scoliopteryx libatrix* L.

Subfam. Agrotidae

Broad-bordered Yellow Underwing	*Triphaena fimbria* L.
Lesser Broad-bordered Yellow Underwing	*Triphaena ianthina* Denis
Lunar Yellow Underwing	*Triphaena orbona* Hufnagel
Common Yellow Underwing	*Triphaena pronuba* L.
White-line Dart	*Agrotis tritici* L.

Subfam. Hadenidae

Reddish Light Arches	*Apamea sublustris* Esper.
Grey Chi Moth	*Polia chi* L.
Angle-shades Moth	*Brotolomia meticulosa* L.

Subfam. Xylinidae

Grey Shoulder-Knot	*Xylina ornithopus* Hufnagel

Subfam. Cuculliidae

Mullein Moth	*Cucullia verbasci* L.

Subfam. Plusiidae

Burnished Brass Moth	*Plusia chrysitis* L.
Plain Golden Y Moth	*Plusia iota* L.

Subfam. Catocalidae

Old Lady Moth	*Manica maura* L.
Red Underwing	*Catocala nupta* L.

GEOMETRIDAE

Swallow-tailed Moth	*Urapteryx sambucaria* L.
Pepper and Salt Moth	*Amphidasis betularia* L.
Common Magpie Moth	*Abraxas grossularia* L.

Mr V. R. Hughes has kindly added: Lime Hawk-Moth, Death's-head Hawk-Moth and Convolvulus Hawk-Moth.

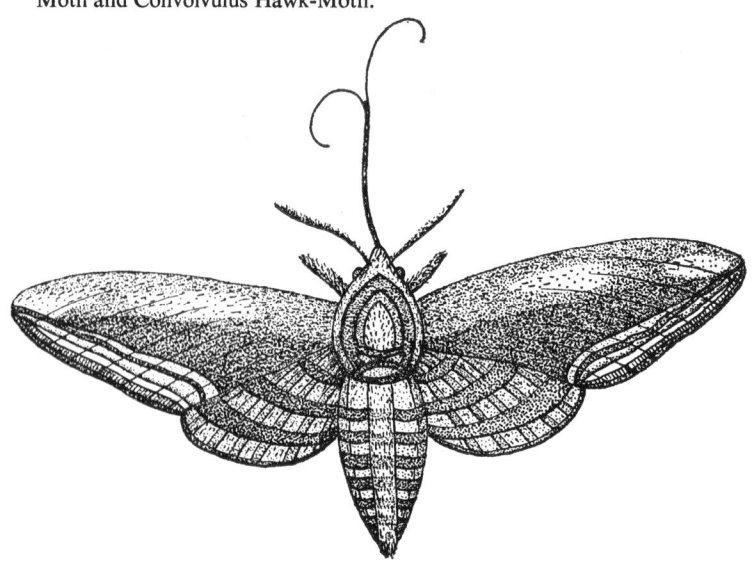

VI BIRDS IDENTIFIED IN BLOCKLEY SINCE OBSERVATIONS STARTED IN 1946

By

MAJOR H. F. COX

Blackbird
Bullfinch
Buzzard (definitely)
Chaffinch
Crow, Carrion
Crow, Hooded
Cuckoo
Dipper
Dove, Collared
Duck, Mallard
Dunnock (Hedgesparrow)
Fieldfare
Flycatcher, Spotted
Geese (unidentified, flying high
    E.N.E. by S.S.W. and vice versa)
Goldcrest
Goldfinch
Greenfinch
Hawfinch
Hedgesparrow (Dunnock)
Heron
Jackdaw
Jay
Kestrel, Lesser
Kingfisher
Lapwing (Peewit)
Linnet
Magpie
Martin, House
Moorhen
Nightingale
Nuthatch
Owl, Barn
Owl, Little
Owl, Tawny
Partridge, Grey
Partridge, Red-legged
Peewit (Lapwing)
Pheasant

Pochard
Redstart
Redwing
Robin
Rook
Seagulls (probably Blackheaded
    Common or Herring)
Skylark
Sparrow, House
Sparrow, Tree
Sparrowhawk
Starling
Swallow
Swan, Mute
Swift
Thrush, Song
Thrush, Missel
Tit, Blue
Tit, Coal
Tit, Great
Tit, Long-tailed
Tit, Marsh
Tree Creeper
Turtle, Dove
Wagtail, Grey
Wagtail, Pied
Warbler, Grasshopper
Warbler, Willow
Wood Pigeon
Woodpecker, Green (Yaffle)
Woodecker, Greater Spotted
Woodpecker, Lesser Spotted
Wren (large and small variety)
Yellowhammer
All seen from the Manor House
Garden except the Grasshopper
Warbler, the Redstart and the
Yellowhammer

Domestic Birds

Budgerigars (flying free from
aviaries) Duck, Aylesbury,
Khaki Campbell, Muscovy, and
Tufted
Goose, Chinese
Goose, Grey
Goose, White
Peacock
Pigeon (racing)
White Doves (Tumblers, Fantails)

I am indebted to Mr V. R. Hughes for the following interesting additions: the
Great Grey Shrike, the Landrail or Crake (along the railway line), Siskin, Lesser
Redpoll, Whinchat (along the railway), Stonechat (once), Canada Goose (on
Northwick Lake), Teal, Wigeon, Little Grebe, Goldeneye, Reed Bunting (Knee
Brook), Snipe (Northwick Park), Woodcock (Dovedale), Garden Warbler, Black-
cap Warbler. Mrs Speakman has recorded the Waxwing and this has been confirm-
ed by Mr Hughes.

VII THE MAMMALS OF BLOCKLEY

By

V. R. Hughes, Chipping Campden School

Despite an increasing population in the region of the North Cotswolds which includes the Parish of Blockley, twenty-nine species of mammals may still be found in its beautiful countryside. This, regardless of large numbers of motorists and other visitors who often penetrate into those secluded areas so necessary for wild life to prosper, is quite remarkable. Probably the number could be increased if more experienced naturalists, were available to carry out a thorough survey of a considerable acreage of land which has never been properly investigated.

Such elusive creatures as bats are easily overlooked, especially as they are most active in the darkened skies of night. Perhaps it is for this reason that the two species of Horseshoe Bats are missing from this list, although the author suspects that both do occur. Likewise the Harvest Mouse has not been authentically recorded during the last ten years but it is likely that some out-of-the-way bit of wilderness holds a colony or two of these attractive little rodents who love to weave their nests among ears of ripening corn.

The semi-domesticated Fallow Deer lies up in local woods and spinneys and audaciously sallies forth after dusk and it will be interesting to note how the recently introduced Roe Deer fares in its new territory. Most people wish it well and indeed, if it prospers and behaves as seemly as the shy and secretive Muntjac or Barking Deer, it will be a most welcome newcomer.

Sad it is, that the Otter appears to be doomed animal in our area but in 1972 and again in 1973, a dog Otter was seen on a number of occasion, surfacing in a deep, conifer-fringed pool within two miles of Blockley. In the same years depressing events took place—otter hunts were held not far from this threatened species' secret hideout. Alas! the fate of this animal, or maybe that of his mate, is not known.

Given reasonable sympathy and consideration, none of our local mammals need become extinct and the wonderful Pattern of Life that has been intricately woven about us since time first began, should continue to be as interesting and varied for posterity as it is for us.

The Fox. Vulpes vulpes.

One can safely say that of all the British mammals foxes are the ones that engender the most controversial views. Poultry keepers and farmers justly dislike them as in a single night they can swiftly destroy a pen of hens or a score of ducks and leave behind a shocking scene of indescribable carnage. Although described as wise and cunning animals, many are killed by hunts and traps. Huntsmen naturally wish to preserve the species, and, indeed may well have done so in the intensively farmed shires of England where he is certainly more hated than loved. A number of local 'earths' recently inspected, provided ample evidence that poultry is not the fox's staple diet. Until myxomatosis drastically reduced their numbers he preferred rabbits but nowadays he had has to change to other fare. Being very untidy housekeepers, the remains of crows, owls, brown rats, magpies, pigeons, grey squirrels and occasionally, especially after prolonged spells of frosty weather, even those of cats are left scattered around their front doors. But the sight of a hungry vixen intently mousing in a bit of rough pasture or longingly eyeing a flock of circling lapwings, is a very amusing spectacle.

Because of powerful scent glands at the base of the 'brush' or tail, foxes are always surrounded by a distinct and pungent smell which is apparent even to human nostrils. It is this scent trail that so easily keeps a good pack of hounds hard on the heels of its quarry. During January the yapping and barking of dog foxes and unearthly wailing screams of vixens engrossed in mating rituals, are frequently heard in our wintry fields and spinneys. The gestation period lasts for approximately two months and the litter of about four blind cubs is born in late March or early April. Pretty little things are fox cubs and fairly easy to watch as they innocently fool around in the quiet twilight of a pleasant summer's day. Often, when songbirds have gone to roost and owls hoot from stands of larch and pine, observant motorists entering or leaving Blockley, glimpse in the light of headlamps, a bushy-tailed, red-brown form drift shadow-like into some gloomy hedge-bottom or leap lightly as a feather over a broken wall. That's how many people see and remember him. May this be always so for undoubted rascal though he is, our countryside would duller be if he were seen no more.

The Badger. Meles meles.

It is surprising how few people have ever seen a live badger in its natural habitat. This is probably because it is a truly nocturnal animal which seldom ventures abroad in daylight. Yet badgers are not uncommon and may still be seen within the Parish boundary if one is prepared to sit in darkness and exercise certain simple precautions. Such enthusiasts should first look for trees where the bark has been vertically scratched and scored. These marks are caused by badgers rearing on their hind legs, whilst cleaning and sharpening their claws in the trunks. They also denote the presence of a 'set' or underground burrow which ramifies deeply into the earth. This consists of a number of branching passages or galleries with two or more secret backdoors, and an imposing front entrance, which is partly hidden by a large mound of earth and old bedding material. Not quite so conspicuous are the faint paths which lead from one set to other neighbouring ones, for badgers are fond of visiting each other. This habit is responsible for the increasing numbers of these timid creatures being knocked down on busy roads and highways. Also examine particularly any low strands of barbed wire in the vicinity, for tufts of tell-tale grey hairs.

A fully-grown badger will sometimes be three feet long, and although little more than a foot high at the shoulders, its chubby, bear-like body weighs between thirty and forty pounds. It is a clean, inoffensive, retiring animal, expert at keeping out of sight, yet fascinating to know. Nothing in the way of food seems to be scorned by a badger, Hedgehogs are caught and cleverly skinned, young rabbits, voles, frogs, wasp grubs, beetles, and even grass snakes are eaten. It is advisable to bury the carcasses and offal of birds and animals deeply in the ground otherwise, if badgers are around an exhumation is likely to take place—they simply cannot resist carrion.

Being rather a slow animal, Master Brock is usually only able to capture weak or wounded prey, but the sharp-pointed canine teeth in the powerful jaws are characteristic of a true carnivore. In the depths of a snowy winter, a badger was seen on an icy moonlit night busily digging for bluebell bulbs at the edge of a wood near Batsford. The lovely black and white striped cheeks fitted in exactly with the silvery moonbeams as it lumbered back to its set. Male badgers are called 'boars' and females are referred to as 'sows'.

It is regrettable that some people object to the presence of this species on their land and place loops of strong wire along the animal's pathways. The mutilated body of a badger with pelvic area almost severed from the abdomen by a thin strand of this encircling material, is a revolting sight and one that the writer will never forget—or forgive.

The Otter. Lutra lutra.

These days otters seldom put in appearance in the area around Blockley and those who do are lucky to continue their wanderings without being unmolested in some way or another. But these long, lithe, close-furred animals are known to have visited Northwick Park Lake, the streams which converge at Bran Mill and the long meandering length of Knee Brook until it joins the infant River Stour. Not so very long ago, whenever Knee Brook became unruly and flooded low-lying fields, one expected to see an otter cavorting among the flotsam and jetsam to the consternation of dabchicks and other waterfowl.

As otters are great travellers and can cover several miles in a night, it is likely that a wanderer does occasionally visit hereabouts without being observed.

208

Luckily one that did sojourn for a few days in 1972 and again in 1973, in a secluded local pool, was spotted and recorded but his actual habitat remains a secret known only to a few.

Unpolluted waters with a healthy fish population offer the greatest attraction to this creature, who is one of the most expert and agile swimmers of the animal world. The webbed feet and slightly flattened tail help to propel it through the water fast enough to catch a fish with ease. During diving, a rising string of silver bubbles marks the underwater course until the small flattened, bewhiskered head and face surfaces, and captured fish or eel is landed. After carefully scenting the air to make sure that there is no danger, a vigorous shake rids the pelt of water. The first bite is taken into the spine behind the gills and the fish is consumed down to the tail which is discarded. Sometimes, for a change from a purely fish diet, meat in the form of voles, moorhens and young mallards is eaten.

Young otters may be born in any month of the year and the cubs, which are blind at birth, remain in the cunningly concealed waterside 'holt', or burrow, for several weeks. A bitch otter, playfully gambolling in mid-stream with her family, is an unforgettable sight, but one which is not quite so pleasant to anglers. Perhaps of all the calls of British mammals, that of the otter is the most unusual, being a queer flute-like whistle, which may be heard at dusk or dawn. To stand beneath a lowering December sky with the bitter East wind moaning in Neigh Brook's willows, and hear once more an otter whistling its erring mate is something I should dearly love to do.

The Rabbit. Oryctolagus cuniculus.

The wild rabbit is not the familar animal it used to be. Indeed, in former heavily rabbit-infested areas, such as the large private estates bordering Blockley, its numbers have been drastically reduced by the horrible disease of myxomatosis. This disease is caused by a virus, Myxomatosis cuniculi, which after an incubation of about a week manifests itself by a feverish condition and a discharge from nose and eyes that transmits the disease by contact to other rabbits. It is interesting to note that a buzzard was seen killing and later feeding on the carcass of an infected rabbit in Northwick Park.

'Conies' or adult rabbits live in underground communities known as 'warrens'. In these the does excavate special blind-ended burrows or 'stops' where they make nests of fur plucked from their own breasts, for their young. These are at first blind and helpless, but at about ten days their eyes are open, and when one month old they are independent of the mother. The males or 'bucks' take no part in the rearing of their families, and sometimes actually destroy them if a stop is accidentally found and entered, for usually the doe plugs the entrance with dried grass to protect the young. When danger threatens, rabbits stamp a warning with their hind feet, and soon all follow each others' bobbing white tails to safety underground. Their food consists of grass, clover and various farm and garden crops. They are very prolific breeders, producing litters at monthly intervals between February and September, so that the damage they do by feeding on the vegetation can be enormous.

The rabbit population around Blockley waxes and wanes as myxomatosis strikes first in one area and then forsakes it for another. But one thing is certain: increasing numbers of these destructive rodents lie above ground and seem to live a hermit-like existence. Perhaps it is they, who, by avoiding constant contact with infected relatives, defeat the annihilating threat of the pestilence and ensure the continuance of their kind.

The Hare. Lepus europaeus.

There should be no difficulty in distinguishing between a rabbit and a hare. Both are certainly similar in appearance and general structure, but the former is a sociable burrowing animal, whilst the latter is a lover of open fields and meadows. Also the hare is much larger—about two feet in length, with black tips to its long peg-like ears, and a black tip to its tail. The fur is mostly sandy-coloured, but tends to be redder on the neck and flanks, whilst the underparts, except on the chest and loins, are pure white. Few animals, besides the hare, have such prominent eyes at the sides of the head, and so a very wide field of vision.

The male or 'Jack' is slightly smaller than the doe, who is often referred to by countrymen as the 'Jill'. During the mating season which is early in the year, the Jacks behave in a ridiculous manner to impress the females. These amusing antics have given rise to the saying, 'Mad as a March Hare.' Leverets, or young hares are pretty creatures, who quickly learn to fend for themselves. They are born during the months of April to October, with their eyes open, in a 'form' which is merely a depression that is cunningly concealed in a tussock of grass. The doe soon isolates the young into separate forms to prevent a prowling fox, stoat, or weasel from destroying all the litter, should a form be found accidentally. In addition, to avoid this catastrophe happening, she takes enormous leaps to the left and right to break her scent trail, whenever visiting or leaving her offspring. The adults are true vegetarians, feeding on clover, sow-thistle, cereals, carrots, roots, young grasses and especially parsley.

Hares still abound in the Blockley area and a lonely rambler trudging the surrounding, bleak mid-winter fields and fallows, is likely to flush at least one, or even two and as I have often done. He will stand enthralled to watch the lissom creatures sprint uphill—they prefer to run uphill—with the speed of a racehorse.

The Stoat. Mustela erminea stabilis.

Many readers at some time have seen a small, short-legged, red-brown animal, about fourteen inches long, suddenly cross their path and rapidly disappear into the bordering herbage. It was probably a stoat. Identification is made easy by the conspicuous finger-length, black-tipped tail or 'pencil'. The stoat is a hunter of rabbits and game, both furred and feathered, such as rats, mice, and small birds. They even take grey squirrels when the opportunity occurs. The hunting is done by scent, and the quarry, after being relentlessly pursued seems to become hypnotised and so is able to offer little resistance to being killed.

The young are usually born in April or May, and by June accompany their parents on hunting excursions. Young stoats are educated in a particularly callous manner, as the following incident shows. While walking quietly down Galloping Lane, a noise in the verge attracted my attention. It was a litter of young stoats playing with a number of short-tailed field voles. Each time a vole escaped from the circle of excited youngsters it was tossed back into the arena by an adult only to be torn to pieces. A stamp of my foot soon put an end to the orgy and a closer inspection revealed that all the tortured voles had been incapacitated by having their limbs bitten off at the elbows. Also very noticeable was the strong, musky odour, typical of this species that pervaded the atmosphere. Local gamekeepers' gibbets always have a few shrivelled stoats among their grisly exhibits and these fierce little animals are still found in the district.

In the winter snows of the northern latitudes the skin of the stoat becomes pure white, except for the black tip on the tail. The fur is then known as ermine. There are pensioners in this area who can remember seeing in the long, frosty winters of many years ago, stoats frequenting the ditches and snow-bound fields in the splendid pelage of the ermine.

The Weasel. Mustela nivalis.

The weasel is our smallest carnivore, having a body the thickness of a man's thumb and from eight to ten inches long. Two inches of this length is tail, which always lacks the black tip of the stoat. The general colour is reddish-brown above and pure white below. So small are the legs and so narrow the head, that at first sight a weasel looks like a snake, especially as it moves with a gliding sinuous action. It hunts small rodents such as field mice and water voles but even rats and rabbits are easily killed and eaten. Tall trees are climbed without difficulty to reach the highest nests, where eggs and young are slaughtered and stolen. However, mice form the chief diet and therefore weasels play an important part in checking the increase in numbers of these very destructive and prolific rodents.

Weasels are accomplished charmers and will perform all kinds of amusing antics in front of flocks of feeding birds. These stupid creatures become enthralled and wake up to the peril when one of their number has been pounced upon and despatched.

The litter is born during the late spring and early summer in a nest of dried grass and leaves, which is cleverly concealed in a variety of places ranging from the hollow clay pipes of land drains, to cavities in stone walls and holes in ivy-covered banks. It has often been said that this tiny hunter who can easily disappear down a mole's run when chased, is in proportion to its size the world's most savage creature. True it is, that if the weasel was as big as the average dog, the British countryside would be a dangerous place to live in. Hardly a day goes by without someone, somewhere in the Parish spotting a weasel stealthily pursuing its blood-thirsty business.

The Hedgehog. Erinaceus europaeus.

It is not necessary to describe the spiny, muscular, pig-like ball of flesh known as the Hedgehog. It is a familiar figure almost everywhere, and at dusk may be seen ambling across gardens or exploring ditches along the lane in search of beetles, worms, slugs and similar creatures, which are readily eaten. It is the largest British member of the mammal group called Insectivora. Despite the short legs and cumbersome body, the hedgehog can move at speed when necessary but prefers to roll itself into a ball and thus presents an array of formidable prickles to an enemy. This habit is unfortunately no protection against night traffic on busy roads, where many fine hedgehogs perish by being runover.

Between the end of June and late August, the young are born. At first they are blind and helpless with a coat of soft, rubber-like spines, but they soon grow and learn to prowl in the summer dusk with their parents. One does not expect the hedgehog to be a swimmer, yet this is so. Young and old have been seen crossing a pool at Hinchwick. By October and November the 'boars' and 'sows'—this is the correct names for the sexes—are fat and round as dumplings in preparation for winter hibernation. This commences according to climatic conditions, and the body temperature of the animal drops, the heart slows down, and the internal reserves of fat are gradually drawn upon to enable the hedgehog to survive until the following spring. Careful examination of any hedgehog will reveal that it has a large population of tiny flea-like creatures moving energetically among its dense forest of spines. This fact very often results in Master Hedgehog being called a lousy animal but many biologists are of the opinion that these so called parasites are really beneficial because they act as combs by scavenging between the prickles and helping to keep the animal clean.

The Red and Grey Squirrels

The Red Squirrel. Sciurus vulgaris leucourus.

A little over twelve years ago the last authenticated record of a red squirrel was obtained at Aston-sub-Edge. Since that date the author has no knowledge of a red squirrel occurring in this area although on several occasions he has been out on wild goose chases to confirm what proved to be erroneous reports. Accordingly, this attractive species does not find a place in the List of Blockley Mammals.

The Grey Squirrel. Sciurus carolinensis.

At the end of the last century a number of alien grey squirrels from North America were liberated in various parts of Britain. Regrettably they succeeded in establishing themselves so well that they have now become an abominable nuisance, owing to their increasing numbers and exceedingly destructive habits. All kinds of forest trees in particular suffer enormous damage. The bark of sycamores and beech seems to be irresistible and woodlands have untold numbers of saplings rendered useless every year by these relentless gnawers. A word of two, about grey squirrels and their behaviour, with the head forester of nearby Batsford Estate, will convince one that this introduction from the U.S.A. is a truly bad character. Not only is the damage it does confined to vegetation, but the eggs and young of song-birds are relished as well.

Grey squirrels are too well known to need describing but their nests or 'dreys', made of twigs, moss, bark and leaves are built into branches, or cavities of hollow trees, early in the year. Litters which are at first blind and helpless, may be found in dreys as early as February and again in early summer. Grey squirrels are frequently seen in wooded Blockley gardens despite the fact that many are destroyed annually. It is consoling to know that this species cannot withstand prolonged hard weather and a bad winter considerably culls their numbers.

Bats. Chiroptera, which is the order of flying mammals.

Of the twelve species of British Bats, only six are known to have been reliably identified in this locality. Being mostly crepuscular flyers and usually living in rather inaccessible places, the order Chiroptera is not so popular with naturalists as other more easily studied branches of natural history. The British members of this family feed mainly on night-flying insects, although they are sometimes observed hovering and picking off spiders and caterpillars from vegetation. Street lamps which attract swarms of moths on summer evenings, provide happy hunting grounds for species such as the tiny Pipistrelle and Long-eared Bats. All bats hibernate, and some, especially in mild winter weather, fly for brief spells during daylight.

Below are given some hints to help in distinguishing the six local species on the wing.

1 The Pipistrelle is the smallest bat, with a wing span of about eight inches. It seems to have a definite hunting territory, which it circles with a quick, erratic flight, and is common throughout the North Cotswolds.
2 Leisler's Bat. This species has a wing-span of ten-and-a-half inches, and an injured one was captured at Paxford. Although it was pampered in captivity it died of its injuries and is now preserved in the Biology Department of Chipping Campden School. The flight is erratic and seldom at a height greater than thirty feet. Not being an easy subject to identify in the field, the tendency to depress the wings below the body on the downward beat is a useful aid.
3 The Long-eared Bat presents no problem of identification. Its ears are very distinctive, as their length is equal to the head and body combined. On mild winter days it will often break its hibernation to drink or hawk for insects over pools and ponds. Before many mature trees were felled on the Northwick Estate, a breeding colony always used a hollow tree there for a summer den.
4 The Whiskered Bat is similar in size and flight to the pipistrelle. One was seen cleverly weaving in and out of the wooden palings at Blockley Station, taking spiders from webs hung between the uprights (this seems to be a typical method of hunting). Their flight is generally quick and unsteady, but may change to skilful hovering over low herbage, or to a slower hunting beat, during which insects are actually picked off leaves and grass in flight. A dead specimen picked up at Campden had prominent whiskers which were a very useful feature in its identification.
5 Daubenton's Bat because of its restriction to the vicinity of water, is often known as the Water Bat. It is an expert flyer and skims the water before dipping and taking drowning caddis flies and other aquatic insects from the surface. It is this species that has been known to take the late angler's fly as he tried for a rise in the gloaming. Pools and streams with well-wooded surroundings form its favourite habitat, and during the summer, dens may be found in hollow willows containing from twenty to forty bats. Not so very long ago, when Captain Spencer Churchill was at Northwick Park, I often sat in the twilight of a summer's evening watching Daubenton's Bats snatching their suppers of drowning insects from the placid surface of the lake.
6 The Noctule Bat has a large wing span being in the region of thirteen-and-half

inches. Its ears are wide apart and broader than long and there is hair on the wing under the forearm. These facts can only be determined by actually handling a specimen. In the field this bat is a high flier and its course is remarkably straight for a bat, indeed at times it has been mistaken for a swift. The writer on occasions has paused in the rides of Bourton Wood to gaze enthralled at a pair of this species actually flying high against the setting sun in the company of a squadron of screaming swifts.

Moles and Shrews

The Mole and Shrew are also members of the order Insectivora. Of these, perhaps the black, velvet-coated mole is the most familiar. Mounds of excavated soil—mole hills—are thrown up in fields and gardens much to the annoyance of farmers and gardeners. Vegetation and crops are not eaten, but their roots are seriously disturbed by the numerous underground tunnels driven through them by this tireless and highly skilled 'miner' of he animal world. It is about four to five inches long and has a pair of immense and powerful forelegs equipped with stout claws. These are the spades, which together with its tough pig-like snout, force a passage through the earth in search of worms and insects. Moles cannot see well, but they are not blind and if the dense, vertically-set fur is carefully parted on the head, two tiny black eyes may be found.

The Mole, Talpa europaea, is common in this area and its habit of feverishly working before and after hard spells of wintry weather is often remarked upon by countryfolk.

The Common Shrew. Sorex araneus castaneus.

The Common Shrew is adept at keeping out of sight, yet this tiny, long-snouted, mouse-like creature is very plentiful hereabouts, and spends its short life (shrews are only annuals) scurrying through tussocks of grass and low herbs in search of insects. The nest is a loose ball of hay and leaves well concealed from view, and the litters of about six young occur several times in a season. Every autumn numbers of shrew corpses are observed and commented upon by naturalists, which bears out the belief that these tiny creatures have a life span of a little over one year, and this ends conveniently before the start of adverse wintry conditions.

The Pygmy Shrew. Sorex minutus.

Britain's smallest mammal—the Pygmy Shrew, has been captured alive and several corpses found, in various parts of the Blockley, Paxford, and Batsford areas. Compared with the common species, these were found to be three-quarters of an inch shorter in total length. Shrews have special glands which secrete offensive odours. It is for this reason that cats sometimes kill them but very seldom consume their victims, although owls capture and eat large numbers.

The Water Shrew. Neomys fodiens bicolor.

Although all shrews are good swimmers, the Water Shrew is the only one that is really aquatic in habits. It has been found in the waters of Neigh Brook, Northwick Park Lake, Hinchwick Pool, and even been seen bathing in the overflow of a septic tank at Stretton-on-Fosse. The head and body length is about three-and-three quarter inches, so it is the largest shrew. The upper fur is slaty-black and waterproof whilst the underside is almost pure white. The long tail has a keel of rows of hairs top and bottom, and the toes are also hair-fringed. These hairs assist in swimming. Freshwater shrimps, caddisfly grubs, and other aquatic creatures form the principal diet.

A water shrew caught and weighed during October was exactly 11.7 gm (a little over half an ounce), whilst a common shrew taken in the same month weighed 8.25 gm. (about one third of an ounce).

Voles, Mice and Rats.

The smaller rodents likely to be found in this district are three species of voles, a similar number of mice species, and the ubiquitous brown rat.

213

The Water Vole. Arvicola amphibius amphibius.

The water vole, very often wrongly called the water rat, is common in most local streams and pools which have a good fringe of aquatic vegetation for it is almost entirely a vegetarian. The vole is stouter and of heavier build than the rat, with a blunt, rounded muzzle and much shorter tail. It can be further recognised by its diving and the fact that it is more often in water than out of it.

The Short-tailed Vole. Microtus agrestis hirtus.

Rough, tussocky pastures, damp meadows and swamps, all provide cover and suitable habitat for this very numerous species. It is about four inches long (an inch-and-a-quarter is tail), with the typical, blunt snout and short ears of the vole family. The brownish-grey fur blends well with the rough herbage that forms its home, and, in a ball of dried grass, litters of about six young are born several times in a season.

The Bank Vole. Clethrionomys glareolus britannicus.

Difficulty may be experienced in identifying the bank vole because it is much less common that the previous species. One captured in Bourton Wood measured three-and-three quarter inches from the snout to the end of its body, plus a tail which was one-and-a half inches long. It was much more agile and alert than its relative, and immediately after capture settled down to a meal of biscuit crumbs and was soon busily constructing itself a nest out of chewed fragments of cloth. The general colour was reddish brown with a much darker upper-tail surface.

The Long-tailed Field Mouse. Apodemus sylvaticus.

A very common mouse which frequents hedges, gardens, fields and woods. Its appearance is similar to the house mouse but differs, in that the fur is more yellow-brown, the eyes are larger and prominent, and the ears are bigger. This very active little rodent climbs bushes and shrubs with ease. It very often uses leaves and moss to make a roof over the old nests of birds, and then uses them for winter store houses, containing nuts, acorns, berries and seeds of all descriptions.

The Yellow-necked Field Mouse. Apodemus flavicollis wintoni.

A typical yellow-necked field mouse was captured in a Longworth Trap set in Bourton Wood. It was larger than the long-tailed variety and seemed to be brighter and smarter in appearance. The upper parts were certainly redder than its close relative and it possessed a definite chest-spot on its snowy-white under-parts. This chest-spot was expanded on either side to form an incomplete collar. What was rather puzzling was the later capture of mice which seemed to be hybrids between the yellow-necked and long-tailed species. Probably, although there was no proof, these two do interbreed.

The House Mouse. Mus musculus.

Most readers will be familiar with the ever-present house mouse and its annoying habits, so that a description here is quite unnecessary. During the summer it often leads an alfresco life, and may be found living quite happily in orchards, hedge-rows, gardens, ricks of hay and similar outdoor situations. It can truly be said that this species is omnivorous. I have even found it busily collecting the pupae of the cabbage white butterfly from ledges and sills of buildings, and watched it sitting on its haunches busily nibbling the same, while tightly held in its forepaws.

The Brown Rat. Rattus norvegicus.

We in this country area, have our fair share of brown rats. They are so common as to be easily known and recognised by most people. It, too, is very adaptable, and can live equally well indoors as well as outdoors—in deserted rabbit warrens, refuse dumps, ricks of hay and straw, and even in woodlands, where it often ruthlessly plunders the eggs of ground-nesting birds. Unfortunately its feeding habits take it into many unhygenic situations, particularly the open refuse disposal sites used by local authorities, which not only provide it with rich breeding grounds, but also enable it to spread all manner of bacterial diseases.

214

Deer.

There are three species of deer in the area but being timid creatures they are seldom seen during the daylight hours although numbers may be present in a small woodland area.

Fallow Deer. Dama dama.

This semi-domesticated species is occasionally met with on the Batsford and Northwick Estates. The ones seen are usually escapes from large country properties where herds are kept for ornamental purposes.

Muntjac or Barking Deer. Muntiacus (?)

The Muntjac or Barking Deer—so called because of their dog-like bark which is uttered when they are alarmed and during the rut, has lived in the vicinity of Blockley for at least fifteen years. They are not native to England, but were brought to Woburn Park, Bedfordshire, by the Eleventh Duke of Bedford. About 1900, they began to spread to surrounding areas, and now, over seventy years later, they have established themselves in several local woods and are extending their distribution. The muntjac is a small animal of a uniform foxy-red colour in summer and olive-brown in winter, with a prominent white patch under the tail. Due to colour and size—about that of a large dog—they have been shot sometimes in mistake for foxes. Fourteen years ago I was phoned by a local keeper and asked to identify a strange creature that he had flushed in his wood and killed as it ran for safety. This proved to be a muntjac, the first so far as is known, to be recorded in this area. I still have the photograph of the dead beast in my possession.

Woods with thick undergrowth are the most likely places for them to be found, and the careful observer may find winding paths tunnelling through the thicket of bracken, bushes and grass. Their tracks are small and fairy-like, especially when seen in a fall of snow, with characteristic uneven cleaves. They feed on grass, shrubs, and fallen fruits such as rowan, hawthorn, crab apple and ripe sloes. They do not strip the bark off trees, as is the case with some other deer species. Early morning or late evening is the best time to go looking for muntjacs.

Roe Deer. Capreolus capreolus.

It is pleasing to report that a nearby public-spirited and enlightened landowner has recently introduced Roe Deer into his estate. On very reliable authority, it is possible to state that some breeding has taken place because a 'kid' as roe deer fawns are called, has been seen on more than one occasion. This charming little animal, provided that it does not make a nuisance of itself by unduly damaging forestry trees and other cultivated plants, will be a most welcome addition to our local fauna.

VIII A BLOCKLEY FAMILY
By
Sir Edward Warner k.c.m.g, o.b.e.

A number of Blockley families became early Quakers and their scattered descendants can trace back to their origins through the Quaker registers, and then, through the Parish Registers, which are almost complete right back to 1538, save for gaps in births in 1544–54 and general deficiencies in 1665–79. One such family is the Warners, few, if any ,of whose descendants are still in Blockley, but who are numerous in the United States and of whom two branches are known to exist in this country, with descendants living near Worcester and Winchester.

2 The Warners were not among the families—such as the Freemans, Walgraves and Mansels—who had leases of land from the Bishop of Worcester under the Great Lease of Blockley Demesne Lands in 1539. They first come to notice as people of substance in the Will of Rychard Warner, who died in 1546, predeceased by his wife Johane in 1545. They had three daughters and a son and the number of "flocke beds", pairs of sheets, pewter and brass pots and candlesticks, bequeathed to the daughters are evidence of well-being. The son, Thomas, was residuary legatee and presumably did better, and it is a fair assumption that the family were cloth-workers. The Bishop of Worcester's lease of Blockley Manor in 1589 to Queen Elizabeth which records "one ffulling mill with all the Lands thereto belonging in the occupation of Thomas Warner" probably refers to the same Thomas.

3 Thomas died in 1595 and left a Will from which, together with the parish register, we know that he married Frances Dennys in 1557 in the Parish Church, that she probably came from Ripple (Ryple) south of Worcester, that her brothers were William and Leonard Dennys (the latter was buried at Ripple in 1613), and that they had eleven children between 1561 (the first registered) and 1588 when Thomas lost his "virtuous wife". 1573 was a tragic year for them. They lost their eldest daughter, Johane, aged 12, who was buried on the same day, and perhaps on the same occasion, as their daughter Elizabeth was baptized. The latter only survived for a week. Some years earlier they had lost a boy twin, and we do not know what losses there may have been in the first few years of marriage when no entries appear in the parish register. Seven children survived to be mentioned in the Will. Robert, who was executor and may have been the eldest, John, who receives first mention for a legacy and may have been the youngest (judging from the pattern of the latter's own Will), Thomas (1567), Richard, Joseph (1574), Johane and Elizabeth (replacing their dead namesakes). When Thomas died, Joseph promptly took out Letters of Administration before the Will was found. He described himself as a yeoman of Whichford, Warwicks, but a search of the Whichford register has failed to reveal a single Warner in the 16th or 17th centuries, so that his career as a yeoman remains a mystery. Apart from John, of whom more below and Thomas, who had a shop and house near the church gate and Richard, who had a house and pigsty there, nothing is known of the fate of the other children. After Frances' death, Thomas remarried a lady of substance, the widow Johane Mansel, who had two sons and a daughter. Her dowry, apparently put up by her sons, seems to have been considerable and they had not finished paying it when Thomas "sick in bodie but of perfect remembrance" made his Will in 1595 and bequeathed to his wife the unpaid portion of her dowry!

4 Blockley Manor Leases were customarily for three lives and there is accordingly no mention of the property passing by assignment, and no reference to the fulling mill, in Thomas' Will (nor in Rychard's who may have had it before him or John's who had it after him). Thomas' actual lease has not so far been traced, but we know from a collation of manorial surveys made in about 1750 (Worcester archives 2236, Doc. 44, 040) that Thomas' mill eventually went to John and, when he died, to his son Robert. We also know from the Lay Subsidy Returns (i.e. tax assessments) that Thomas was assessed for £6. 11s. in 1558, £4 in 1567, £5. 8s. 4d. in 1571 and £6. 6s. in 1572 (PRO/E179/200).

5 Before coming to the main story of John and his issue a digression is needed to

deal with another branch. Thomas had a contemporary, probably a first cousin, Richard Warner married to a Margaret. There were seven children headed by a John born in 1582 who may have died in 1620 without isssue. Richard's second son, William, married Marie Merie in 1612, and the third son, Simon, married Ann Peart the same year (children: Ann, Thomas, Mary, Francis and Doritey). In 1631 Simon was in trouble with the law owing to a quarrel with his in-laws and was bound over to keep the peace—happily the only Warner of Blockley who so figures in the Calendar of Quarter Sessions, 1591 to mid 17th century. Next year Ann died, perhaps overcome by the family quarrel and in 1635 Simon married Frances East, by whom he had four more children (Simon, Margaret, William and Mary). We do not know what became of any of them, except that the first Mary must have died young as did Simon and Margaret.

6 To revert to John, son of Thomas, he was likewise a fuller by trade, married a Margaret, and was Church Warden from 1641–46. John and Margaret had twelve children between 1612 and 1638, of whom the parish register shows two (Anthony and a first Isack) as dying in infancy and of whom a third (a first John) must also have died, though unrecorded. The surviving seven sons all appear in John's Will but not the daughters Jane and Mary who were perhaps married elsewhere and received dowries. All seven sons married and had issue, continuing, in the case of three of them, to the present day.

7 No property is mentioned in John's Will, in which he is described as "of Dracott", since it passed by assignment under lease. But we know from the Manorial Survey of 1647 that he then occupied, in addition to the fulling mill in Blockley, the following in Dracott: "One messuage and one yard land called Knivers and one toft and one yard land called Condyes with appurtenances," totalling 20 acres of arable land, 2 acres of mead and 6 acres of pasture. From the Bishop's Lease of the Manor to Queen Elizabeth in 1589, we know that this property was then leased to Agnes White, widow (who did not however have the "French Mill", wrongly attributed to John Warner in the 1647 Survey and corrected in the 1750 collation of survey material mentioned above). In addition, we know from the Blockley terrier of 1635 (Worcester archives) that John Warner had leased the Church meadow in Blockley, probably together with one of a "range of houses lying near unto the Church between . . . on ye East and William Webbe on ye West now in occupation of Mr George Durant, Vicar, Richard Wacke and John (a mouse has unfortunately eaten the surname) together with certain outhouses and gardens and backsides thereto belonging." And it may be of interest to add that the fulling mill in Blockley and the property in Dracott were under "Lopez Leases". What was a Spanish landlord doing in Blockley at the time of the Armada?

8 In fact Roderigo (anglicised to Roger) Lopez was the Queen's Portuguese Jewish chief personal physician—believed by some to have been the original of Shylock. He appears to have had great influence with the Queen and to have accumulated considerable property, including some or all of the Manor of Blockley, which the Queen obtained on lease from the Bishop of Worcester in 1589 (there is reason to suppose that some of the manorial property had already been obtained on lease from the Bishop the previous year and made over to Lopez "for good and faithful service done and hereafter to be done unto us"). Unfortunately for him Lopez was accused of high treason in 1594, allegedly being involved in a Spanish plot to poison the Queen, sent to the Tower, and executed at Tyburn, despite the Queen's reluctance to sign her doctor's death warrant. The Queen intervened on a petition from the widow to enable her to retain certain property rights which do not seem to have included those in Blockley (Hatfield MSS). But the Worcester Archives have documents prolonging the validity of certain "Lopez Leases" in the county though again not in Blockley.

9 We come now to the fate of John and Margaret's sons and their issue. The eldest, Thomas (1616) married Ursula and had five children. We do not know what he did, but he may well have farmed for his father at Dracott, while the latter plied his trade as fuller in Blockley. Thomas's second son, John (1655) founded the Warner Clockmakers of Dracott, it is said making clocks in a big stone barn

(possibly the one known at the time as "the barn called the Long House")—clocks made in Dracott include that of Chipping Campden Church in 1695, for which there was a charge of £8. John's Will (he died in 1727) shows that the Dracott property of John the Fuller had come into his hands. However it was to fare ill for the clockmaker's grandson, another John (1733) moved the clockmaking business to Chipping Campden in 1751 and, in 1757, mortgaged the Dracott property (then standing in the name of his father John, Ben Pierce of Poughton, Glos., and Thomas Hyorn — probably his cousin) to Mary Loder, widow, for £30 for the life of his elder brother William. No doubt the money was urgently needed for business and family requirements—he had just married. John's eldest son, yet another John (1757–1821) set up as a clockmaker in Pershore and Evesham, and then in London near Marble Arch, but his brother Isaac and the latter's son Thomas Evans (1805-79), followed by his son, Thomas Proctor (1847), continued the clockmaking business in Chipping Campden until about the end of the century. The present descendant, Mr Thomas William Reginald Warner (1893) went into the Civil Service, his father, Thomas Penson, having abandoned clockmaking for the teaching profession, in which he was headmaster at the time of his death.

10 The next son, Richard (1622) married Sarah and had four children, but the absence of further reference to them save for a legacy of two shillings in John's Will suggests that they may have left the neighbourhood. The next, Robert (1625) married Eleanor and had three daughters. He was a clothworker and dyer. His father's fulling mill in Blockley was in due course assigned to him and the lease was formally put in his name in 1684, when he was 59, together with his nephew Robert aged 28, son of William (see below) and William, aged 1, son of William Dyde— almost certainly William's brother-in-law. Robert appears to have been quite prominent, for he was among those who signed a memorandum to the Bishop of Worcester transmitting the 1664 Survey of Manorial Leases.

11 William (1627) was certainly the most sensational member of the Family. According to family tradition on the other side of the Atlantic, he was a captain in Cromwell's army and emigrated to America in 1658 following the death of the Lord Protector and the death of both his parents in 1657, when he was executor of his father's Will, having to go to London for Probate. It may be wondered whether that visit to London did not decide him to emigrate for he may have been unimpressed by his prospects in Blockley and by those of his younger brothers John and Isack whom he would have met in London (see below). That members of the family emigrated was common tradition throughout the family, but it is to the American branch that we are indebted for details including the information that he married Anne Dyde of Blockley, and a copy of his Will of Sept. 8. 1703, proved at Philadelphia Oct. 18, 1706, showing that he had two houses in Dracott purchased from Joseph Woodward. These he left to his son, Robert (1656–1709) who was sent back from America to join Uncle Robert at the family fulling mill (see above) where he became a dyer. Anne and the other children—John, William, Isaac and Mary (who married James Kite) stayed in America. One curious feature of Williams Will was that, in consideration of the two Dracott houses, Robert was required to pay his Uncle Isack (see below) "five pounds sterling money of England or to his Assigns." Judging from Robert's Will and that of his wife Sarah, they prospered. Robert's Dracott property passed on his death to his son Isaac, who had apparently gone to America to join William in Pennsylvania where he had founded an American Blockley, now a suburb of Philadelphia. But Robert also had some houses in Blockley, Worcs., and some other houses in Dracott which he left to his wife, Sarah. When she died in 1712 she passed her Dracott property to Isaac, and also lands in Blockley leased from the Bishop of Worcester. To her daughters Anne (who married William Minchin) and Mary, she gave two houses in Blockley occupied by Edward Warner junior and Joan Eden. It is not clear what became of Isaac but there is a belief that he died in America so that the whole of his property in Dracott and Blockley may have passed to his sisters, Anne and Mary, with the extinction of the male line. William's other sons, John, William and Isaac married in America and founded American lines of Warners, many descendants of which

are alive today, including Mr Hayward Dare Warner (1879), historian of the American branch. For generations the family were Quakers on both sides of the Atlantic which has facilitated genealogical research. Whilst there is no evidence that William became a Quaker before emigrating—it was early days in 1658—he probably became a Quaker in America, for his son and principal heir, Isaac, is known to have been a Friend. William was Deputy Sheriff for Upland and Dependencies and a Justice of the Upland Court. He sat in the first Provincial Council and in 1682–3 was Member of Assembly for Philadelphia.

12 The most prominent Quaker member of the family was the next son, Edward (1629), who was imprisoned in 1660 by Sir Thomas Overbury (vide Quaker Book of Sufferings) for refusing to take the oath of allegiance, along with other Blockley Quakers. When, in 1663, the Friends first Meeting House was acquired at Broad Campden, Edward was made Chief Trustee (see deed in Gloucester County Archives). Edward married another Anne, and they had ten children the first five of which are recorded in the parish register as births, not baptisms, and the latter ones in the Quaker register for Warwickshire South. He seems to have died suddenly at the Mill in 1698 where he presumably worked as a dyer. He died intestate and his elder brother, Robert, took out letters of administration of his estate which came to only "two pounds for his apparell and money in his pocket" and £15 for "good debts". His son Edward married Mercy Hartell and they had eleven children but all trace of them soon vanished from the Blockley scene. No doubt Edwards senior and junior had families beyond their means and this, together with devotion to the Quaker cause, persecution under the Restoration, and the decline of the wool trade effaced them.

13 Whatever happened to Edward, the decline in the wool trade doubtless accounted for the departure of the last two sons. John (1632–78) took the road to London in 1648, the year of Pride's purge and the year before the execution of Charles I. Isaac (1638–1704) followed him in 1654, the year after Oliver Cromwell became Protector. In London John was apprenticed to a cooper. The reason for this choice of trade has not emerged, but it may have been a family connection with a Robert Warner, then on the Court of the Coopers' Company. However, John was not apprenticed to a Warner but to John Girney, duly serving his seven years before being admitted to the freedom of the Company by redemption in 1655. Isaac was apprenticed to John Girney's widow, Ann, whom John married sometime between then and 1661, when Isaac was admitted to his freedom (see Minutes of the Court of the Coopers' Company in Guildhall Library). This must have been a business marriage for Ann was 19 years John's senior and no doubt a woman of some substance. All concerned were by now Quakers and Isaac duly married a fellow Quaker, Ann Packwood of Northampton, in 1668, daughter of Simeon, deceased, a fellow cooper, whose name has dogged the Warners for generations. John died of consumption in 1678 and Ann the following year of "stoppage of the stomach". There were no children of the marriage.

14 Isaac and Ann had six children spaced every two years and all but one survived and married. Isaac seems to have prospered as a cooper in Whitechapel, living and working "At the Sign of the Bathing Tub and Milk Pail". He had a subsidiary business interest at the Court Yard and at St. Saviour's Dock in Bermondsey, where he imported building stone (according to family papers), no doubt taking advantage of the demand due to the rebuilding of the City after the Great Fire, and also timber. His eldest son, Simeon, appears also to have been apprenticed to the Cooper's Company, but developed his father's timber importing activities in Bermondsey. The timber trade took him overseas and he married Anna Geisbets a fellow Quaker in the Dutch trading port of Friedrichstadt in Holstein, originally an émigré Dutch Arminian Remonstrant settlement. Their eldest daughter Anna looked in the same direction and married Jacob Hagen of Hamburg: they have Quaker descendants to this day. Simeon became an active and respected Minister, visiting Quaker communities in Holland and Germany on several occasions, and accompanying Joseph Gurney, in 1718, on a visit to the West of England. The second son Isaac (1670) was presumed lost at sea in about 1701 by the London

Friends. The body of an Isaac Warner was in fact washed up on the American island of Tinicum in 1698, and recorded as that of a carpenter, who had had a survey made of 400 acres in Chester and Newcastle counties and had married one Catherine (Jordan's 'Colonial and Revolutionary Families'). The third son, John (1674–1760), married a fellow Quaker called Mehetabel and had six children. He was a merchant and noted horticulturist of Rotherhithe who has earned entries in the Dictionary of National Biography and Musgrave's Obituaries, and a reference in the large Oxford Dictionary on account of his introduction into this country of the Black Hamburg Hothouse Grape and other horticultural developments. From Simeon and Anna descend several branches still extant. Their sons, Isaac and Jacob, founded merchant establishments in Bermondsey, that of Isaac being Hambro Merchants and that of Jacob going first into the coal trade and then, with another Jacob (1747–1831) and Joseph (1752–1831), into City business with the import of spices, becoming members—and in due course masters—of the Grocers' Company. Descendants of this branch later went into the Law, the Army, the Church and the Foreign Office.

15 The Parish Registers show graphically the drift from Blockley of the Warners: 86 recorded births from 1561–1704, but only 40 burials and only 8 marriages. Whilst the Friends Meeting House at Broad Campden may account in part, the Vicar registers a good many Quaker births and some Quakers backslid and were married in Church—a backsliding for which not a few Quaker Warners were to be in trouble elsewhere.

The American Warners of Blockley: Living Descendants

So far as is known to the writer, all are descended from the three sons of William the Pioneer who settled in America. The fourth, Robert, returned to Blockley, Worcs, and his male line quickly died out. But it is more than possible that other members of the family went out to join cousins in America.

The following short list of living descendants is submitted with apologies to the many others, of whom the writer has unfortunately not yet heard.

1. John, 1649-1717, and Anne Campden
John was the eldest son of William, and his descendants were noted silversmiths and clockmakers. Living descendants include Gordon Warner of Baltimore and Lt. General Leroy Lutes, CBE, of Washington.

2. William, 1653-1714, and Christina Schute
Their descendants were bankers, coastal shipping people and founders of the Warner Company of Philadelphia, still operating on a large scale in sand, gravel and building materials. The head of the firm in 1932 was Charles Warner and Irving Warner Jr. became a director in 1955.

3. Isaac, 1662-1727, and Anne Craven
were the ancestors of:
Hayward Dare Warner (1879), his son Robert Collett and grandson Peter David, of Denver, Colorado. Gardiner Arthur Warner (1917) and his son Gardiner Arthur jnr. (1957) – the Haverford Warners.
John Winthrop (1916), son of Robert Cecil Winthrop (1885) and the late John Warner Winthrop (1916), and Robert C. Winthrop Jnr. son of Robert John Warner Winthrop (1916), and Robert C. Winthrop Jnr. son of Robert Cecil Winthrop (1885) and the late Rebecca Jane Warner, both of Haverford.
Lyttelton Gould jnr (1919) of Conneticut and New Jersey, married to Mary Esther Krech, and their four children.
Mildred C. Bain, married to William J. Bain, of Seattle, their sons: Dr Robert Clark Bain (three children) and another son (with four children); and daughter (with one).

IX THE BLOCKLEY SURVEY—1972

By

CHIPPING CAMPDEN SCHOOL

This survey was carried out in June 1972 by members of Chipping Campden School, at the request of Blockley Antiquarian Society, to provide an appendix to Mr Icely's History of Blockley and to make a comparison with Eyre's Blockley Guide of 1827.

Aims

The aims of the survey were to discover what kinds of employment were followed by the people of Blockley, what proportion were in part time employment and what proportion were employed outside Blockley. Further aims of the survey were to gather information on the methods of transport used by those travelling to work outside Blockley, to gather information from employers on how many of their employees came from outside Blockley, and to gather information on the pattern of local farming.

Method

The information was gathered by means of questionnaires. These questionnaires were delivered to every house in Blockley on a Saturday morning and collected the following day. The area covered was that of Blockley Main Ward: this included Blockley village and a number of outlying farms and cottages; it included no other centre of population, although the ward boundary does include a couple of houses at Draycott. 437 questionnaires were delivered of which about half (see Table 1 a, b, c) were returned completed.

Results

(Numbers and letters in brackets refer to the tables of figures, and the items in those tables).

The questionnaires yielded information on 422 men and women. We are very grateful to them for taking the trouble to fill in the questionnaires. Although we specifically excluded those in full-time education, the survey did, intentionally, bring returns from a number of retired people. This, however, did lead to problems when considering the number in part time employment, or the number travelling outside Blockley to work, as a proportion of the total return. To take account of this, certain occupations such as retired or housewife were excluded from the total returns (1 d, e) to give, without disrespect, totals of those in gainful employment (1 g, h, i). Details of those excluded to give these figures may be seen marked * on tables 6 and 7. As can be seen, this adjustment makes a very considerable difference especially as far as the number of women is concerned.

It was hoped that the information summarised in Tables 2 and 3 would indicate a pattern of movement of, on the one hand, those living inside Blockley and seeking work elsewhere, and on the other hand, those working in Blockley but living elsewhere. From Table 2 it can be seen that *two thirds of those in gainful employment travelled out of Blockley to work.* The small number of returns for table 3 make it difficult to draw any valid conclusions about the proportion of employees working in Blockley but living elsewhere. However, it is perhaps reasonable to say that the two tables together show that the prevailing pattern is one of people leaving Blockley village to work and not of people coming from outside to find work in Blockley.

The figures in Table 4 are largely straightforward and the pattern they present is self-evident. The very small part played by public transport in getting people to work is of interest, but scarcely surprising to people who live in rural areas.

The survey received information from 5 farms, and the aggregate figures of their replies appear in table 5. All five farms engaged in arable cultivation. Four farms had dairy herds in excess of 50 head of cattle, but three-quarters of the cattle were kept on just two of the farms. Similarly, more than 80 % of the sheep were kept on one of the farms, and more than 90% of the pigs on another.

Tables 6 and 7 give the details of occupations of men and women respectively.

For convenience, both lists have been divided into those occupations which appeared more than once in the survey and those which appeared once only. It is not easy to come to any very definite conclusions from these returns. The advantage of using a questionnaire which asks the single question, "What is your occupation?" is that the widest range of replies is received, from the very specific to the rather vague. The disadvantage of not using a more exact means of questioning is that subsequent categorisation of occupations becomes very difficult. Where, for example, does one place electricians? In an industrial occupation or in a service occupation? However, the following broad divisions may be of interest: about 1 in 9 of the men was engaged in an agricultural occupation of some sort, while the rest of the men were divided fairly evenly between industrial and service occupations. As far as the women were concerned, those in service occupations outnumbered those in industrial occupations by about a quarter.

TABLE 1. General Information

a.	Number of questionnaires delivered	437
b.	Number of completed questionnaires returned	213
c.	Percentage of completed deliveries	48.74%
d.	Number of men who gave information	202
e.	Number of women who gave information	222
f.	(d+e) Total	424
g.	Number of men in gainful employment	154
h.	Number of women in gainful employment	92
i.	(g+h) Total	246
j.	Number of men employed part-time	24
k.	Number of women employed part-time	42
l.	(j+k) Total	66

Table 2. Those working outside Blockley

a.	Number of men who worked outside Blockley	101
b.	Number of women who worked outside Blockley	56
c.	(a+b) Total	157
d.	Number of men who worked both in Blockley and outside Blockley	6
e.	Number of women who worked both in Blockley and outside Blockley	6
f.	(d+e) Total	12

TABLE 3 Information from employers

a.	Number of employers who gave information	27
b.	Number of full-time male employees	14
c.	Number of part-time male employees	15
d.	Total of male employees	29

e.	Number of full-time women employees	...	...	...	...				4
f.	Number of part-time women employees	...	...	...	...				40
g.	Total of female employees	...	...	...	...	...	...		44
h.	Number of male employees living outside Blockley			...	...				4
i.	Number of female employees living outside Blockley			...	...				6
j.	Total number of employees (d + g)	...	...	...	...				73
k.	Number of those employees living outside Blockley (h + i)				...				10

TABLE 4

Methods of transport used by those working outside Blockley to get to work.

a.	Public Transport	...	...	...	...	...	...	...	10
b.	Works Transnort	...	...	...	...	...	...	...	70
c.	Private Car or motor-cycle	...	...	...	...	...	...	...	72
d.	Bicycle	...	...	...	...	...	...	...	12
e.	Foot ...	...	...	...	...	...	...	...	9
f.	Total ...	...	...	...	...	...	...	...	174*

*It will be noticed that this total exceeds slightly the total of those requiring transport (2c + 2f = 169). A small number of people listed more than one means of transport.

TABLE 5. Information from farmers

a.	Number of farms which gave information		...	...	...			5
b.	Total arable acreage	...	...	...	...	...		829
c.	Total pasture acreage	...	...	...	...	...		922
d.	Total acreage of woodland and scrub	...	...	...	...		31
e.	Total number of cattle	...	...	...	...	...		803
f.	Total number of sheep	...	...	...	...	...		435
g.	Total number of pigs	...	...	...	...	...		130
h.	Total number of poultry	...	...	...	...	...		30

TABLE 6. Details of occupations (Men)

a.	Retired*	42	p.	Bricklayer ...	...	3
b.	Brickworks labourer	10	q.	Gardener ...	...	3
c.	Farmer	9	r.	Carpenter ...	...	3
d.	Builder/decorator	9	s.	Grocer	...	2
e.	Welder	8	t.	Company Director	...	2
f.	Electrician	7	u.	Personnel manager	...	2
g.	Teacher	6	v.	Architect ...	...	2
h.	Factory worker	6	w.	Plasterer ...	...	2
i.	Farm labourer	6	x.	Sales manager	...	2
j.	Machine operator	5	y.	County Council employee		2
k.	Labourer	5	z.	Engineer ...	...	2
l.	Unemployed or no occupation*	5	aa.	Civil Servant	...	2
m.	Painter	4	bb.	Stock checker	...	2
n.	Driver	4				
o.	Butcher	4				

The following occupations appeared in the survey ONCE each:

Production controller
Agricultural fitter
Jeweller
Design Engineer
Press Operator
Scientific research
Government service
Police officer
Packer
Cook
Electrical fitter
Printer
Drystone Waller
Sales Correspondent
Army
Manager
Technician
Civil Engineer
Antique Dealer
Market Gardener
Mobile Sewerage

Fibre-glass laminator
County Council roadman
Water board employee
Dental Surgeon
Artist
Warehouseman
Plant hire operator
Self employed
Company Representative
Excavator
Bank manager
Technical representative
Production manager
Metal polisher
Husband*
Garage proprietor
Estate bailiff
Plumber
Business man
Forklift truck driver

Total 202

* = Those subtracted from total to give number in gainful employment (1 g).

TABLE 7. Details of occupations (Women)

a.	Housewife*	... ...	96
b.	Retired*	... ...	31
c.	Domestic work	... ...	13
d.	Factory worker	... ...	8
e.	Packer	... ...	6
f.	Clerical worker	... ...	6
g.	Machinist	... ...	4
h.	Teacher	... ...	4
i.	School meals service	...	4
j.	Hotelier	... ...	4
k.	Secretary ...	... ...	4
l.	Shop Assistant	...	4
m.	Cleaner	... ...	3
n.	Postwoman	... ...	3
o.	Hairdresser	... ...	3
p.	Nurse	... ...	3
q.	Inspection viewer ...	...	2
r.	Unemployed or no occupation*	... ...	2
s.	Stained glass artist	...	2

The following occupations appeared in the survey ONCE each:

Cashier
Electro-plater
Laboratory assistant
Mother's help
Physiotherapist
Nursery assistant
Disabled*
Personnel Manager
Laundry Worker
Engineering worker

Casual labour
Hotel worker
Grocer
Supervisory assistant
Orthoptist
Company Director
Canteen assistant
Housekeeper
China repairer
Cook

Total 222

*Those subtracted from the total to give the number of those in gainful employment. (1 h).

Form sent to each household

1) OCCUPATIONS

Please complete one line for each person who is no longer at school or in other full time education.

MEN: What is your occupation?	Full time or part time?	Do you work outside Blockley?
....	....	....
....	....	....
....	....	....
....	....	....
....	....	....

WOMEN: What is your occupation?	Full time or part time?	Do you work outside Blockley?
....	....	....
....	....	....
....	....	....
....	....	....
....	....	....

2) MEN AND WOMEN WORKING OUTSIDE BLOCKLEY ONLY

How many people living in your household and working outside Blockley travel to work by each of the following methods?

a) a) by public transport   ....

b) by works transport   ....

c) by private car or motor cycle   ....

d) by bicycle   ....

e) on foot   ....

(2)
BLOCKLEY SURVEY

3) FOR EMPLOYERS OF LABOUR ONLY

How many full-time people do you employ?
          Men   ....   Women   ....
How many part-time?
          Men   ....   Women   ....
How many come from outside Blockley?
          Men   ....   Women   ....

4) FOR FARMERS ONLY.

Please give estimates of your acreage of:
          Arable   ....
          Pasture   ....
          Woodland and scrub   ....
Please give numbers of cattle   ....
                    sheep   ....
                    pigs   ....
                    poultry   ....

225

X BLOCKLEY AND THE ELECTRIC LIGHT
By
Dr. A. W. Exell

Blockley has a quite well-founded claim to be the first village to have electric light but it is difficult to produce absolute proof. Gorseinon in South Wales claims that its church was lit by electricity in August, 1888 according to an article in *Midlands Electricity* August, 1961. Blockley was certainly earlier than this but Mr Ray Shekell, the editor of the magazine, says in a letter to Mrs N. Marshall dated August 11, 1961 "I should warn you not to boast too soon about Blockley. We have another entry into the lists, from Staffordshire, which claims a church first lit by electricity in 1876." We have never had any further news about this unspecified Staffordshire church.

The first Blockley electricity supply, powered by a water wheel, was started by Lord Edward Spencer-Churchill at Dovedale House. From this the house was lit and by all accounts the church and the shop which is now the Post Office and Bolt's store. The late Captain E. G. Spencer-Churchill of Northwick Park wrote in a letter to *Midlands Electricity* (loc. cit.) "I am afraid I cannot be precise about the date on which my father helped to light the Blockley Church with electric light; but my family left Dovedale, Blockley, in 1887, and I well remember that my father harnessed a waterfall just below the house and took electricity from it to light his own house, and the church, well before then. I think it was about 1884 or 1885, but I cannot be more definite than that."

It may be that we shall be unable to date the first installation more precisely than 1884–85.

A note in the *Evesham Journal* for 13 May 1911 gives the date as 1880 (probably too early) and says that when Lord Edward, who wound the dynamo himself, was fixing it at the bottom of the shaft, the carpenter helping him (probably Charles Baldwin, father-in-law of the late Horatio Webb and a former child silk-worker) dropped an axe, cutting the dynamo and Lord Edward's fingers.

One of the three Humphries brothers later added a dynamo at Webb's mill and the batteries were charged by Mr Marks then living at Dovedale House as secretary to Captain Churchill.

Old residents have said that the old tariff was an inclusive charge of 12s. 6d. per year for each light not exceeding 40 watts.

About the second installation, at Mill Close, we have much better information. The Memorandum of Association of the Blockley Electric-lighting and Manufacturing Company was dated 12 December 1887.

The Articles of Association are curiously reminiscent of the South Seas Bubble not through the slightest implication of fraud but from the language used in the prospectus. The objects of the proposed company were ". . . sale, letting on hire, and maintenance of electrical engineering and other goods and apparatus connected with the production of light, heat, sound and power by electricity, galvanism or magnetism, or otherwise . . ." The only method they apparently did not contemplate was the time-honoured one of stroking the fur of a cat with an ebony rod but this too may have been included in "or otherwise."

For this purpose they proposed to "acquire a lease of a mill, at Blockley, in the County of Worcester, or elsewhere, with water or other power, and to acquire lands, works, property and premises wherever convenient, machinery, patent rights and other property, and to acquire and establish other businesses and property as may seem expedient." This you may think cast their net sufficiently widely, but not so! They gave themselves far greater scope for they proposed to take powers "to construct, maintain, carry out, improve, work, control and manage any tramways, railways, roads, tunnels, waterworks, canals, gasworks, reservoirs, watercourses, wharves, piers, docks, furnaces, stamping works, smelting works, factories, warehouses and other works and conveniences." The Blockley Electric-lighting and Manufacturing Company clearly bid fair, at least in its prospectus, to become Great Britain Ltd.!

The proposed capital was £20,000 divided into 4,000 shares of £5 each.

The signatories to the Memorandum and Articles of Association were:

Edward Spencer-Churchill, Dovedale, Moreton-in-Marsh
Alexander William Hall, St. Thomas', Oxford, M.P.
Henry Barter, Clerk in Holy Orders, Shipton-under-Wychwood, Oxon.
William P. Warburton, Canon of Winchester
Henry Montagu Spencer, Gentleman, Paxford, Moreton-in-Marsh
Charles Barter, Electrical Engineer, Shipton-under-Wychwood
Hugh Nigel Warburton, Electrical Engineer, The Close, Winchester

The signing of the document, dated 12th day of December, 1887, was, one may hope, a convivial occasion, for all the signatures were witnessed by William Henry Havers, Butler, St. Thomas', Oxford.

Presumably the original idea came from Lord Edward Spencer-Churchill and Alexander William Hall, as a Member of Parliament, was to be responsible for "arrangements with any Governments or authorities, supreme, municipal, local or otherwise" as envisaged in the Memorandum. There is an interesting double link between Church and Industry. We have Canon Warburton of Winchester and Nigel Warburton (his son?) an electrical engineer and similarly Henry Barter of Shipton-under-Wychwood, a Clerk in Holy Orders and Charles Barter, electrical engineer of the same village. The maiden name of Lord Churchill's wife was Augusta Warburton, daughter of Major C. D. Warburton. Hugh Nigel Warburton was Lady Augusta's nephew and his friend Charles Barter (the other electrical engineer) became closely connected with Blockley life by marrying Canon Houghton's daughter. Their son, C. Barter, often stayed at the vicarage with his grandfather and has recently given us a copy of a note by his father which is of such general historical interest that we are glad to quote it almost in full.

"The mill we took over [in 1888] had been used for silk throwing when the Coventry ribbon trade was at its zenith, but had been un-used for several years. There were the rotting remains of two over-shot water-wheels 22 ft. in diameter & as the repairing of these would have cost a good sum of money, it was thought better to replace one of them by the latest form of water turbine.

In order to get the best results, the old wooden water flume was replaced by cast iron pipes; the old wooden flume had been made of green elm & though it had been in the ground for very many years, it was perfectly sound and quite difficult to break up when it was underground or water but quite rotten when exposed to the air in the wheel house.

Sufficient power was available from the turbine for lighting the Church, vicarage, school, three or four houses & the street, Be it noted that it was not often that all of these would be wanted at full load at one & the same time; the streets were not lighted when there was moonlight & were switched off at 10 p.m.

During the day, a large battery of accumulators were kept charged; the machinery was run with the battery in parallel till 10, after which time current was supplied by the battery.

We were sufficiently enterprising to make our own dynamo; the mains for the street lamps were bare wires supported overhead on posts planted at the roadsides, their bases being well charred and creosoted before erecting. Previously the village had depended on oil lamps, candles, etc., so the change-over at that date was revolutionary.

Blockley was one of the first villages in England to have electric lighting from the natural water power sources."

This second installation was known as the Astral Works. *Plate* 51

The coming of electric light coincided with the deep depression at Blockley due to the collapse of the silk industry (see p. 139). Whether this was one of the deliberate efforts to relieve unemployment or not it certainly had a psychological effect. In a local poem of the time we are told that the days had gone "when Blockley with the world could cope" but it ends on a note of triumph and consolation:

Our church is lit
It is a wondrous sight
For we can manufacture
The electric light

A large lamp was placed on the top of the church tower which illuminated the surroundings by a "moonlight glow" which could be seen from four counties. The village was not slow to take advantage of the new wonder. J. Joyner, Grocery Wine and Spirit and Provision Establishment published an advertisement (*Plate*51) that on and after October 27th (year unfortunately not mentioned) his shop would be "Illuminated by Electricity! What at present will not be found in Worcester, Gloucester, Hereford, Oxford, Warwick or in many Cities or Towns in England and Wales".

As the electricity was distributed by overhead cables the meters were often in the attics. When the time came to read the meters we are told that the attics were frequently found to be occupied by old ladies who had just been taken seriously ill!

Further evidence about the installation is contained in an interesting extract of a letter from Charles Stowe of Warburton, Cambs. sent to Mrs Marshall in 1966, reading as follows:

"All I remember about the place (Mill Close) was the huge water-wheel underneath the building. This would probably be about 1897. The water-wheel was not usable then—a turbine driven by water from the adjacent mill-pond had been installed at the lowest possible level (to get a good fall of water) & this turbine generated electricity by driving a dynamo on the same low level. I have started that turbine many, many times by the wheel control which was on ground floor level. Later on, an oil engine was installed (at normal ground level) which also generated current—this engine was *in* the old mill—another much more powerful gas engine was set up in a newer shed alongside the mill proper. This engine was a wonderful thing to me—Harry Humphries bought a fine old organ & erected it in this engine shed—we used to play and make an awful din whilst the engine thumped away near by. An anthracite gas-making plant supplied the engine from another shed at the back. This would be in the early years of the century (say from 1901)."

During his period as Manager of the Works, the late Mr Morley Smith installed an additional turbine at Snugborough Mill and we have been told that there was yet another one at Mill Dene.

The mainly aerial distribution of the electricity naturally led to many failures and the village was disfigured by posts and overheard wires. The overhead line poles are said to have been old tram standards from the Black Country but these were probably not the earliest ones.

In 1901 H. J. Paintin had offered to light the streets for £45 and after the adoption of the Street Lighting Act Spencer Flower of Stratford agreed to do it for £60. The undertaking was bought by the Shropshire, Worcestershire and Staffordshire Electric Power Co. in 1931.

The Midlands Electricity Board, now our supplying authority, has recently (1970–71) put most of our cables underground with much improvement to the appearance of the village. The change is admirably shown by two photographs of the High Street printed side by side in the *Evesham Journal* for 30th September 1971.

How history can repeat itself is shown by one small incident. The Square was lit for many years by an old-fashioned electric lamp on the corner of Church Gates which also helped to illuminate the churchyard. This was replaced by a very tall and ugly standard of the tram standard type at the gateway to the churchyard. Now with the latest improvements the Midlands Electricity Board has replaced the lamp on the corner of Church Gates where it used to be many years ago.

With regards to the installation of telephones in Blockley, Mr W. S. James, who was in charge of the project, has kindly informed us [that a rural automatic exchange, 50 lines through Morton, was installed about 1923 in the former Boys' School. This was only the second of its kind in England.

XI REMEMBRANCE OF THINGS PAST
By
Norah Marshall, F.L.A.

I have been privileged to know many fascinating Blockley characters and it seems only right and proper, in a definitive history of the village such as this, that some of their recollections of times past should be recorded. They testify to a world which has gone for ever, as when George Eastbury spoke lovingly of the ox team at Spring Hill, kept for purely sentimental reasons, which justified the faith of all connected with it during the last war, when it ploughed the ancient sheep pastures, too hard and steep for tractors to work safely, and made a grand job of it. Many memories centred around horses: the father of Mrs Wheeler of Snugborough walked to Gloucester and back in a day to attend a horse sale and an eight-horse team, which hauled wheat and corn to Chipping Norton and belonged to his grandfather Harris, figured large in the memories of Henry Sale, who was born in 1864.

Farm wages of 9/- or 10/- a week made even a rent of 1/- so difficult that some men worked Sundays, making it a seven-day week to get their cottage free, as Charles Dee remembered. George Nobes' father brought up twelve children on 10/- weekly and their greatest treat was a bloater between three of them, at a time when they cost 1/- for 30. Ernest and William Purser, whose family had a long farming connection with Aston Magna, lived largely on their home-reared pork, so that breast of lamb was a Sunday treat. Looking back to the 1880's, they recalled skimmed milk at 1d. a quart and a 4lb. loaf at 4d. Paton Keyte began herding cattle at the age of seven for wages which seem to have varied from a penny and an egg a week to tuppence a day. When George Nobes left school, he worked a 12-hour day, first scaring birds from the beans on Colonel's Piece and then protecting the young wheat from feathered marauders in Keeley's Hollow, where he made himself a little sundial with a stick and stones to keep some touch with time and ensure that he did not eat all his bread and cheese too quickly.

The shops also had to open for long hours and Charles Dee remembered an old shepherd who bought a penny-ha'p'orth of tobacco and matches at 6.45 every morning. Early rising was universal and shepherds would be about at 5 a.m. Craftsmen had few labour-saving tools; Keytes, the Paxford wheelwrights, cut timber by hand in their saw-pit until 1926. Joseph Bates worked a 60-hour week tailoring, at a time when coachmen, footmen and game-keepers wore elaborate and superb individually-tailored livery. The day of the car was approaching and George Rouse's reminiscences of early motoring days included stuffing a faulty tyre with straw after thirteen punctures and paying 6d. for a bucket of water for a boiling radiator at the Inn at the top of Fish Hill, at a time and place where water was in greater demand than beer.

Woman's lot was, needless to say, no easier; as a child, Ethel Worthington's mother bought a small bag of coal after school each Friday and carried it up through Dovedale to their remote cottage so that they might enjoy their weekly treat of a roast dinner on Sunday. Mrs Horatio Webb cleaned the Church for eleven years for 1/- a week plus Boxing Day gifts from hassock-holders, which could realise as much as 25/-. A Blockley woman walked to Aston Magna and back to do similar work for the same wage, but it must be remembered that the stipend of the Vicar there was only £45 per year as his daughter, Mrs William Purser, recalled. Mrs Horatio Webb treasured a stool, the underside of which was scored with countless cuts, made by her mother's chisel, as she cut slits for buttonholes. She was an out-worker for the collar factory and was paid 3d. per dozen collars, three buttonholes on each. She rose earlier than her family and on fine mornings sat on a low wall outside her cottage to work.

In spite of prodigiously long hours of work, there was still time for pleasure. The late Mrs Gould of Worcester, formerly Mary Herbert, was born at the Crown Inn in 1865 and had vivid recollections of the Mummers Play performed there at Christmas and of the sale in the Club Room of some of Joanna Southcott's possessions, including a magnificent cradle prepared by her for the expected birth of

229

the Holy Child Shiloh. Ernest Purser recalled a dancing bear coming to Aston Magna and boys climbing a greasy pole over Mill Close Pond as part of the Friendly Society revels on Whit Monday. Dancing was always popular; Henry Sale had happy memories of "treats" at Northwick, where they danced to the tunes of William Lively, the blind fiddler and basket-maker, who had returned from Liverpool Blind School in 1817, able to support himself and to give great pleasure to the village with his music. He led the Church choir from the gallery. The choir also contributed choruses and glees to the Penny Readings remembered by Mrs Gould about a century ago, held in the new Girls' School; entrance cost a penny, except for the gentry, who paid sixpence for reserved seats in the front row. The Service on the Church tower at 4.45 a.m. on Ascension Day, followed by breakfast for the ringers at the Coffee Tavern opposite Balhatchet's butcher's shop, was a great occasion. It seems to have been a holiday, as Mrs Horatio Webb recalled that the boys and girls went for walks afterwards. She also told of a musician and of the cry of the young people; "Master Cother, shall you be there to-night?" and the joy when he agreed to be sitting on the stone stile in Back Ends (or the Fair Ground, as it was once called) to play for a variety of dances, including lancers and quadrilles, on his concertina. The last remnants of what had once been a 16-day Fair ceased to appear, with its delights for the children, only about six years ago. Mrs Downing spoke of a maypole and a skittle alley at the Dovedale End.

George Clifford, foreman stone-mason at Northwick, contributed a poem to an entertainment held in 1889 in aid of the newly-formed Blockley Workmen's Club; the MSS is in the possession of his great-granddaughter, Mrs H. Clifton. The show apparently included an elaborate version of "Mrs Jarley's Waxworks" with Diogenes, Pepper's Ghost, Sleeping Beauty, Paganini, Sairey Gamp and a group on a station platform. Apparently a financial success, as indicated in verse 18:

To Patroness, to Presidents and our supporters all.
Deep gratitude and thanks are due from members one and all
Of the Blockley branch of the Union known as 'Blockley Workmen's Club'
Who now with tightened purse-strings can the coin together rub.

Private residents also provided entertainments; Miss Sylvester, of Dovedale House, organised Human Whist and Chess and (a practical joker) played ghost around the village until one evening, having knocked on the Humphries' door in Northwick Terrace, she fled down the path, abandoning her enveloping white raiment entangled in a thorn bush and leaving proof of identity in the family name on the linen sheet.

Larger-than-life characters linger in many memories: Harry Humphries, born in 1885, who worked for the Blockley Electric Lighting Co. in what is now Mill Close and who emigrated to Canada, recalls a bachelor named Wilks, who lived in a cottage with the minimum of furniture and grew mushrooms under his table. In spite of limited education, he was a "Village Hampden" and, discovering that his neighbour, Timms, received no pension in spite of previous army service, took up his case and obtained for him a small pension back-dated to the time of his discharge. After this, he pinned up a notice on Rouse's stable door commencing, "To whom it may concern" stating that he was prepared to undertake correspondence of a business or private nature; liberally sprinkled with such words as "whatsoever" and "whomsoever", it ended with "confidential & free. God Save the Queen". Incidentally, Blockley's penchant for music was evident in the Astral Electric Light Works, where an organ stored there was frequently used for Music While you Work! Minor poets, led by the redoubtable H. J. Paintin, also flourished and Mrs Peyton Checketts, daughter of Thomas Banbury of Colebrook Mill, treasured a poem dated 1888, thought to be by Joseph Taylor of Draycott, which includes these lines:

Our church is lighted, that's what few can say,
And so will be our streets without delay,
Though tortuously winding are our ways
The Electric Light will pierce them by its rays.

Another old Blockley man who emigrated, Arthur Taylor, recalls Town Crier Harvey Hopes crying a reward of a pound of liver, offered by Balhatchets, whose shop faced his cottage, for news of a missing drover, later found drowned. Mr Taylor's brother, pad-groom to Lady Churchill, had driving lessons from the first garage opened in London (at Notting Hill) and later became mechanic to the Hon. R. S. Rolls. Years later, he took over an Inn at Stow and started a taxi business.

At a time when wages were only barely sufficient for day-to-day living, charity was very necessary and was forthcoming: Lady Northwick regularly gave blankets and clothing. Charles Baldwin, Mrs Horatio Webb's father and a former coachman was visited during his last illness by her, bearing the carriage rug, trimmed with jackal skins, as a gift. "Too heavy for him to bear it on his legs", said his daughter, "but he made me hang it over the rail at the foot of the bed so that he could look at it; he was so pleased that her Ladyship brought it herself instead of sending one of the servants". During a particularly bad time, Mrs Herbert ("Liz") Pain remembered that they took pillow-slips to Batsford, which were filled with food and that Mrs Joyner made untold gallons of soup. Illness was helped by private medical schemes, including one run by Herbert the ironmonger, where patients paid 1d. per week; George Hale recalled that they had a choice of four doctors. Self medication, of course, was much practised and George Nobes mentioned the habit of bandaging blisters with cabbage leaves.

The village's reputation for lawlessness rests mainly on the riots and the bad name of that part of Dovedale End known as "Hell's Corner", its inhabitants notorious for poaching, drinking, gambling and playing "pitch & toss". George Nobes, who delivered milk there for fifteen years when a young man, said that it was dangerous for a prosperous-looking stranger to go there, as he was likely to be set upon and robbed. An old man named Hale, now living in America, who was born in the Red Lion, visited the village several years ago and said that his grandfather, who was the licensee at the time of the grim Blockley riots in 1876, told him that the trouble was started at his Inn by men who came down from the hills, doubtless the tree-fallers (you "fall" a tree in these parts) mentioned by Mrs Gould, who were working on General Lygon's estate. Everyone agrees that the worst trouble was at the Crown Inn and a remarkable account exists, taken down in shorthand many years ago by Miss Mary Dee from the recollections of Mrs Hancock, who was nine years old when it happened. An unpopular and over-zealous policeman named Drury was determined to clean up the village and declared war on the poachers. "Why, if you kicked a stun along the street he wur after you . . . Every time there was a magistrates' meeting at Shipston, he wur theer wi' ten or twelve Blockley men. One day the magistrate told 'im, 'If you bring such paltry cases 'ere agen, I won't 'ear 'em.' Now that day, the day of the riots, he 'ad took about a dozen Blockley men to Shiptson . . . Mrs Pate Keyte in Lower Street was servant at the Crown and 'er see it all . . . at 10 o'clock 'e must needs goo up into the Crown and peep over the settle. Theer they was, a -sittin' and a-drinkin', many on 'em half drunk and when they seed 'is 'ead come over the top of the settle, somebody banged a quart pot 'o beer at it and 'it it . . . he took to 'is 'eels and they arter 'im along the 'igh Street . . . every doer along that street opened and out come somebody else to join in. He made off straight down the churchyard to 'is 'ome, they followin'. My mother were a-darnin' stockings and when 'er 'eard the runnin' off 'er went and of course I 'ad to follow 'er . . . and got upon the mill wall and dangled me legs over the top . . . I could see all as went on. Well, 'e got to 'is 'ouse and got inside . . . they was a 'owling mob and they was determined to get 'im . . . battered the door down and got in. Them as couldn't get in, throwed stuns at the winders. Well, they fetched 'im out and they mauled 'im and then they dipped 'im in the brook . . . a time or two and then Pate Keyte, 'is father and Oliver Eastbury as 'ad 'elped to knock 'im about, 'e carried 'im in and carried 'im upstairs, washed 'im . . . and 'e *wanted* washin' and stayed by 'im all night. You know, they'd 'a killed 'im if somebody 'adn't fetched 'im away from 'em for by that time they '*ad* very nearly killed 'im . . . Five got away, but five were took; four on 'em got 18 months . . . Now when all them men 'ad done thur time at

'Ooster, theer was great doins the days they came 'ome. They closed the mill . . .
and all the women wi' tin cans and kettles and pots and pans and trays went down
to the station to meet 'em and drummed 'em up into the village". Many were fugi-
tives for years and were never caught: the policeman recovered and ultimately
became Chief Constable of Malvern.

To end on a lighter note: George Nobes recalled that "beer was tuppence a pint
or three-ha'pence if you grumbled".

XII CAMPDEN PETTY SESSIONAL DIVISION
List of Magistrates resident in Blockley Parish
By
F. C. Spurgin

William Childe of Northwick (died 1600), twice High Sheriff of Worcester. Both
   his son William and his grandson Thomas were also J.P.'s in their day.
Sir John Rushout (1730–1770)
The Rev. C. J. Selwyn (1760–1790)
The Rev. W. Boughton (1795–1828)
Admiral Sir Edward Collier, K.C.B., J.P., D.L., (1851–1872)
George, Third Lord Northwick (1860–1885)
J. C. Reynolds of Paxford (1900–1905)
Capt. E. G. Spencer-Churchill, M.C., D.L., (1912–1931)
Dennis Holton of Paxford (1924–1945)
W. Heath of Paxford (1942–1951)
Dame Janet Campbell, D.B.E., M.D., (1943–1953)
Mrs F. C. Spurgin, O.B.E., (1943–1970)
Michael Hope (1960–1971)
Adrian Bolt (1972–   )

In 1931 the Campden Petty Sessional Division was transferred from Worcestershire to Gloucestershire.

XIII DOCTORS PRACTISING IN BLOCKLEY FROM 1939
By
F. C. Spurgin

* Dr. Jacob (Blockley) L.R.C.P., L.R.C.M.
* Dr. Nicholson, M.D., M.B.E., M.C., M.A., B.M., ch.B., (noted for his pelvimetry)
   lived and practised in Blockley before moving to Moreton.
* Dr. Jameson, B.A., M.B., B.ch., (Dublin) B.A.O., D(obst.), R.C.O.G. (Moreton)
   Dr. Brownridge, M.B., ch.B., (B'ham), D.(obst.), R.C.O.G., D.A.(Eng.), (Moreton)
   Dr. Lieber, M.B., B.S.(Lond.), D(obst.), R.C.O.G., D.A.(Eng.), (Moreton)
   Dr. Saxton, M.R.C.S., L.R.C.P. (Moreton)
* Dr. Fenton, B.M., B.ch.(Oxon.), D(obst.), R.C.O.G. (Moreton)
   Dr. Jean Haine M.B., ch.B(Edin.) (Blockley)
   Dr. Frank Haine F.R.C.S. (Eng.), M.R.C.S., L.R.C.P. (Glas.), (Blockley)
   Dr. Ian Reekie, M.B., B.S. (Lond.), D.(obst.) R.C.O.G. (Blockley)
   Dr. Birts, M.B., B.S. (Lond.), D(obst.), R.C.O.G. (Bourton-on-the-Hill)
   Dr. Jennifer Olliff, M.B., ch.B. (Bristol) (Campden)
   Dr. Donald Oliff, M.B., ch.B. (Bristol) (Campden)
* Deceased.

Moreton District Hospital is the local hospital for General Practitioners with a
broad variety of Consultants aligned with Oxford and Cheltenham.

BLOCKLEY (AX)

Alcock, Frances G. K., Paxton Hse
Alcock, Richard, Paxton Hse
Allen, Annie L., Tredwells, High St
Allen, Elsie, 5 Buchan Hse
Andrew, Mary L., 9 Orchard Bank High St
Angel, Cecil I., The Glen High St
Angel, Estelle, The Glen High St
Angwin, Dorothy G., Bridge Cottage Mill Lane
Armstrong, Harold, 39 Park Road
Armstrong, Inez C., 39 Park Road
Arrowsmith, Joan M., Oldborough Farm Draycott Moreton-in-Marsh Glos
Arrowsmith, Nigel P., Oldborough Farm Draycott Moreton-in-Marsh Glos
Arthurs, Betty C. A., 1 Sunnybank
Arthurs, Thomas C., 1 Sunnybank
Ashley, Hebe, Bath Orchard School Lane
Ashton, Marion H., 4 Mill Close
Aston, Gladys M., Forge Cot Lower St
Aston, Norah E., Forge Cot Lower St
Aubrey, Barbara A., 6 Park Road
Aubrey, Enid M., Southcot Lower St
Aubrey, John A., 6 Park Road
Aubrey, Joseph W., South Cott Lower Street
Aubrey, Michael J., Ferndale Park Rd
Aubrey, Sheila A., Ferndale Park Rd
Avery, Frances D., High Street
Balhatchet, Andrew F., 7 Springfield
Balhatchet, Dashwood A., Dene Close School Lane
Balhatchet, Dashwood A. Jnr., Dene Close School Lane
Balhatchet, Dorothy P., High Street
Balhatchet, Edward G., 7 Springfield
Balhatchet, Hilda G., 2 St Georges Terrace
Balhatchet, Morris W., High Street
Balhatchet, Nancy W., 7 Springfield
Balhatchet, Nora G., Dene Close School Lane
Balhatchet, Sally E., 7 Springfield
Balhatchet, Shirley, Dene Close School Lane

Ball, Agnes L., Archway Cottage High Street
Ball, James W., Garron Cottage High Street
Ball, Jean M., Garron Cottage High Street
Ballard, Maud B., Cherry Orchard Cottage Greenway Road
Balsom, Florence B., 2 Landgate Cottages
Banning, Jessie M., Malvern Cot High St
Barbour, Allan, Cotstone High St
Barbour, Joan Cotstone High St
17/11/74 Barbour, Sabina M., Cotstone High St
Barlow, Dennis E., 3 Arlington Terrace
Barlow, Janet, 3 Arlington Terrace
Bartlett, Olive E., The Cottage Blockley Court
Bartlett, William A., The Cottage Blockley Court
Bartlett, William O. S., The Cottage Blockley Court
14/5/74 Bates, Jonathan M., 20 Springfield
Bates, Phyllis W., 20 Springfield
Baxter, Henry T., 26 Park Rd
Baxter, Joan E., 26 Park Rd
Beasley, Albert H., Farthing Cottage Greenway Road
Beasley, Elsie M., 13 Springfield
Beasley, Godfrey C., 3 South View Flats Blockley Court
Beasley, Harry, Farthing Cottage Greenway Road
Beasley, Jack, 3 North View Flats Blockley Court
Beasley, Margaret F., 3 South View Flats Blockley Court
Beasley, Wilfred J., 13 Springfield
Beechey, Annie, 4 Buchan Hse
Benfield, Henry A., 32 Winterway
Benfield, Margaret J., 32 Winterway
Bickell, Edith A., Nut Tree Cot Bourton Rd
Bird, Helen J., Jessamine Cot
Bishop, Ian R., 2 Springfield
Bishop, Marjorie F., 2 Springfield
Bishop, Mavis A., 2 Springfield

Bishopp, Alice E., 6 Buchan Hse
Blundell, Arthur J., Rosedale High St
Blundell, Doris I., Rosedale High St
Bolt, Adrian E. A., Post Office Stores
Bell Lane
Bolt, Mary D. C., Post Office Stores
Bell Lane
Boulton, Albert F., 4 Mount Pleasant
Boulton, Georgina E., 4 Mount
Pleasant
Bourdillon, Pernette, 1 Beverley
Dovedale
Bowell, Arthur H., 9 Station Road
Bowell, Cynthia D. E., 9 Station Road
Bowell, Kenneth A., 9 Station Road
Bowen, Eileen P., Daleside Chapel
Lane
Bowen, John H., Daleside Chapel Lane
Brackenbury, Alan S. H., 1 Sheafhouse
Cottages Draycott Road
Brackenbury, Cecily, 1 Sheafhouse
Cottages Draycott Road
Bradwell, Frances M., North End Hse
Park Rd
Brady, Albert L., 34 Park Road
Brady, Hilda R., 34 Park Road
Brazenor, Louis F., Colebrook Cot
Lower St
Brooks, Albert W., 17 Station Road
Brooks, Allan D., Garron Cot High St
Brooks, Beryl E., 17 Station Road
Brooks, Eva, 24 Winterway
Brooks, Horace, 26 Springfield
Brooks, Kelvin G., 26 Springfield
Brooks, Phyllis A., 17 Station Road
Brooks, Reginald, Rock Bank High
Street
Brooks, Robert C. W., 24 Winterway
Brooks, William, Rock Bank High
Street
Brotherton, Annie E., 8 Mount
Pleasant
Brotherton, Barbara J., 10 Mount
Pleasant
Brotherton, Cyril F., 10 Mount
Pleasant
Brotherton, John H., 8 Mount Pleasant
Brown, Alexander, 24 Springfield
Brown, Arthur H., Winterway
Brown, Diane, 51 Park Rd
Brown, Doreen, 20 Winterway
Brown, Dorothy M., 24 Springfield
Brown, Gillian, 24 Springfield
Brown, Michael A., 51 Park Rd
Brownbill, Samuel, The Chequers
Draycott Moreton-in-Marsh
Bryan, Margaret, 12 Park Rd
Bryan, Peter B., 12 Park Rd

Bryson, Carmen C. F., Colebrook Cot
Lower St
Bryson, Gerald J., Colebrook Cot
Lower St
Bryson, Noreen A., 4 Park Rd
25/3/74 Bugler, Bryan K., 54
Springfield
Bugler, Derek R., 12 Winterway
Bugler, Kathleen M., 12 Winterway
Bumford, Georgina M., 13 Station
Road
Bumford, Leslie J., 13 Station Road
Butler, Amy L., 52 Springfield
Butler, Derek E., 52 Springfield
Butler, Jeanette M., 52 Springfield
Butler, Peter A., 9 Winterway
Butler, William H., 1 Winterway
Butterworth, John R., Tredwells High
St
Butterworth, Joyce P., Tredwells
High St
Button, Clifford E., Hillside Cottage
Station Road
Button, Phyllis C., Hillside Cottage
Station Road
Cadle, Edith M., 19 Station Road
Cadle, Emily L., Snugborough Mill
Cadle, Gwendoline M., 34 Springfield
Cadle, James C., 34 Springfield
Cadle, Robert D. P., 19 Station Rd
Cadle, William C., 19 Station Road
Carter, Lise, 5 Mount Pleasant
Carter, Ronald J., 5 Mount Pleasant
Chaning-Pearce, Blanche F., Greenhill
High Street
Chant, Tom J., 27 Park Road
Chapman, Hetty, High St
Chapman, James L., 32 Park Rd
Chapman, Leslie J., 32 Park Rd
Chapman, Marcel E., High Street
Cheers, Linda H., 8 Orchard Bank
Claydon, Grace K., Halfa High Street
Clayton, Mabel, Hawthorn Cot High
St
Cluley, John, Peartrees St Georges
Terrace
Cluley, Susan V., Peartrees St Georges
Terrace
Cole, Ronald H., 2 Sheafhouse Cotts
Draycott Rd
Cole, Sarah A. L., 2 Sheafhouse Cotts
Draycott Rd
Coleman, Stanley F., Wayside Station
Rd
Collins, Francis T., 40 Springfield
Collins, James W., 23 Station Rd
Collumbine, Barabara M., Barmaur
Station Road

Collumbine, Gillian, Barmaur Station Rd
Collumbine, Maurice, Barmaur Station Road
Compton-Smith, Cecilia E. A., Garden Cottage High Street
Compton, Ernest A., 49 Park Road
Compton, Hilda C., 49 Park Road
Cook, Evelyn J., Malvern Mill High Street
Cook, Robert H., Malvern Mill High Street
Cook, Violet C., Hangmans Hall Broad Campden Chipping Campden Glos
Cooke, Aubrey B., 5 Chapel Row
Cooke, Margaret D., 5 Chapel Row
Cooper, Eileen M., 1 Upton Cottages Upton Wold Moreton-in-Marsh
Cooper, Samuel T., 1 Upton Cottages Upton Wold Moreton-in-Marsh
Cooper, William H., 1 Upton Cottages Upton Wold Moreton-in-Marsh
Corden, Christopher J., 2 Riverbank High St
Corrie, Adam, Laggan Cottage Upper High Street
Corrie, Anne E., Laggan Cottage Upper High Street
Cother, Alan C., 1 Coneygreen Greenway Road
Cother, Charles J., 8 Northwick Terrace
Cother, Frederick J., 9 Springfield
Cother, Ian, 9 Springfield
Cother, Jean E., 8 Northwick Terrace
Cother, Marguerite, 9 Springfield
Cother, Patricia M., 1 Coneygreen Greenway Road
Cother, Shirley P., 9 Springfield
Courtney, Susan M., 15 Winterway
Courtney, Walter C., 15 Winterway
Cox, Henry F., Manor House
Cox, Hester J., The Manor House
Coxhill, Doris K., 1 Arlington Terrace High Street
Coxhill, Frank, 1 Arlington Terrace High Street
Coxhill, Sidney E., 12 Springfield
Criddle, Amy 16 Winterway
Criddle, Leslie T., 16 Winterway
Crocker, Bernice A., Millbrook Hse
Crocker, Kenneth R., Millbrook Hse
Cross, Mabel L., Bijou Cottage High Street
Cullumbine, Agnes M., 2 Northwick Cottages Station Road
Cuthbertson, Florence, 2 Orchard Bank

Dale, Geoffrey D., Widdowes Close High St
Dale, Margaret C. K., Widdowes Close High Street
Dale, Michael D., Widdowes Close High St
Dale, Robin J., Widdowes Close High St
Dalrymple, Kathleen M. B., Fish Cottage Dovedale End
Dalrymple, Walter B., Fish Cottage Dovedale End
Danilina, Paraskova, 5 Mill Close
Dare, Barry S., Blockley Mill School Lane
Dare, Wendy A. V., Blockley Mill School Lane
Da Silva, Harold B., Wessington Station Rd
Da Silva, John, Silver Rose Station Rd
Da Silva, Rose, Silver Rose Station Rd
Da Silva, Thelma D., Wessington Station Rd
Davenport, Dawn D., 11 Mount Pleasant
Davenport, Peter, 11 Mount Pleasant
Davey, Anthony G., 8 Greenway Rd
Davey, Frederick H., 8 Greenway Road
Davies, Joyce O., Vale Cot High St
Davies, William E., Vale Cot High St
Davis, Clifford J., 10 Springfield
Davis, Marina E., 10 Springfield
Davis, Winifred R., Greenhill High St
Day, Ena R., Sunrise Cot Greenway Rd
Day, Linda M., Sunrise Cot Greenway Rd
Day, William D., Sunrise Cot Greenway Rd
Dee, Henry M. J., Park Farm
Dee, Joan, Park Farm
Dee, Zillah, Park Farm
Dicks, Albert E., Peace Haven Greenway Road
Dicks, Christabel J., Peace Haven Greenway Road
Dicks, Olwen, Sleepy Hollow
Disley, Barbara G., 5 North View Flats Blockley Court
Disley, Frank C., 5 North View Flats Blockley Court
Dolphin, John H., 6 Springfield
Dolphin, Phyllis, 6 Springfield
Draper, George R., 2 Summerfield Close
Draper, Ila M., 2 Summerfield Close
Drinkwater, Anthony J. F., Gawsworth High St
Drinkwater, Frances M., Gawsworth High St

Duerden, Adrienne M., 3 Mount Pleasant
Duffy, Jessie, 28 Park Rd
Duggan, Maisie E., High Street
Duggan, William A., High Street
Dunn, Nellie V., 45 Park Road
Dutton, May, 2 Mill Close
Dyer, Janet E., 8 Summerfield Close
Dyer, Roger C., 8 Summerfield Close
Dyer, Stewart J., 32 Winterway
Dyer, Susan, 32 Winterway
2/3/74 Earl, Christine, 3 Station Rd
Eastbury, David J., 43 Park Road
Eastbury, Elsie E., Pasture Cottage Pasture Lane
Eastbury, Harry, 54 Park Road
Eastbury, Harry, 1 Mill Row Station Road
Eastbury, James A., Flat 2 Lady Northwick Homes
Eastbury, John, 17 Springfield
Eastbury, Maurice J., 17 Springfield
Eastbury, Morris, Pasture Cottage Pasture Lane
Eastbury, Patricia A., 43 Park Road
Eastbury, Sarah, 4 Brook Lane
Eastbury, Susan G., 17 Springfield
Eastbury, Sylvia J., 17 Springfield
Eastbury, Winifred M., 54 Park Road
Eden, Alice M., 10 Summerfield Close
Eden, William E., 10 Summerfield Close
Edgington, Emily, 9 Winterway
Edgington, Herbert, 30 Winterway
Edgington, James T., 5 Springfield
Edgington, Kathrine B., 5 Springfield
Edgington, Lewis J., 2 Northwick Cottages Station Road
Edmonds, Alice L., 3 Northwick Terrace
Ellis, Albert E., 53 Park Road
Ellis, Anne E., 5 Bungalow Station Road
Ellis, Dorothy M., 53 Park Road
Ellis, Edward G., 20 Park Road
Ellis, Eileen J., 20 Park Road
Ellis, Frank C. J., 53 Park Road
Ellis, Roland, 5 Bungalow Station Road
England, Gordon, The Stone House High Street
England, Junay R., The Stone House High Street
Ephgrave, Alex R., Crown Cot High St
Ephgrave, Peggy M., Crown Cot High St
Exell, Arthur W., Church Gates The Square
Exell, Mildred A., Church Gates The Square
Fairhead, Eleanor, Beggars Roost High Street
Fairhead, Richard, Beggars Roost High Street
Fairhead, Susan M., Beggars Roost High Street
Faulkner, Patricia A., Hayford Station Road
Faulkner, Victor A., Hayford Station Road
Figgures, Gwendoline M., 6 Northwick Terrace
Fisher, Janet, Hangmans Hall Broad Campden Chipping Campden Glos
Fisher, Ralph L., Northwick Hill Farm
Flaherty, Bryan C., Pilgrim Cot High St
Flaherty, Pamela J., Pilgrim Cot High Street
Fletcher, Emma, 55 Park Road
Fletcher, Frederick T., 55 Park Road
Fletcher, Peter B., 4 Blockley Court Cotts
Fletcher, Rose E., 4 South View Flats Blockley Court
Fletcher, Rose E. D., 4 South View Flats Blockley Court
Fletcher, Yvonne D., 4 Blockley Court Cotts
Ford, Florence P., The Steps High St
Forss, Rodney, Ginger Hse High St
Franklin, Dorothy V., 1 Greenway Rd
Franklin, Harry, 1 Greenway Road
Fry, Gerald L., 7 Mount Pleasant
Fry, Norman L., 7 Mount Pleasant
Fry, Pamela A. M., 7 Mount Pleasant
Gaden, Alan J., Rosebank High St
Gaden, Catherine M., Rosebank High Street
Gaden, David I., 2 Mount Pleasant
Gaden, Joan C., 2 Mount Pleasant
Gaden, John A. E., 32 Springfield
Gaden, Joseph L. G., 2 Mount Pleasant
Gaden, June, 32 Springfield
Gaden, Stanley T. J., 41 Park Road
Galt, Brenda E., Dovedale Farm
Galt, David A., Hailstone Farm
Galt, Donald H., 8 Upper Terrace
Galt, Elizabeth M., Hailstone Farm
Galt, Linda J., Pasture Farm
Galt, Martin J., Pasture Farm
Galt, Sandra J., 8 Upper Terrace
Gardner, Albert, 6 Summerfield Close
Gardner, May M., 6 Summerfield Close
Garrood, Frederic R., Guessens School Lane

236

Garrood, Hilda L. M., Guessens
School Lane
Gasside, Frederick H., 4 North View
Flats Blockley Court
Gasside, Hilda M., 4 North View Flats
Blockley Court
Gasside, James E., 4 North View Flats
Blockley Court
Gasside, Neil, 4 North View Flats
Blockley Court
Germaine, John F., The Old Bank
Dovedale
Germaine, Shirley A., The Old Bank
Dovedale
Gibson, Florence E., 3 St George's
Terrace
Gibson, James, 3 St George's Terrace
Gibson, Mary E., 2 South View Flats
Blockley Court
Gibson, Matthew S., 2 South View
Flats Blockley Court
Gill, Edna M., 2 Coneygreen Greenway
Road
Gill, Jacqueline, 2 Coneygreen Cotts
Gill, John, 2 Coneygreen Greenway Rd
Gill, Lyndsey, 2 Coneygreen Cotts
Greenway Rd
Gillett, Brenda, 8 Springfield
Gillett, Carol, 8 Winterway
Gillett, Charles E., 58 Springfield
Gillett, David G., 8 Springfield
Gillett, Donald E., 58 Springfield
Gillett, Elizabeth F. M., 58 Springfield
Gillett, George, 25 Winterway
21/3/74 Gillett, Grant, 25 Winterway
Gillett, Gwendoline F., 25 Winterway
Gillett, Omar J. F., 8 Winterway
Glastonbury, Margaret J., Police Hse
Greenway Rd
Glastonbury, Paul W., Police Hse
Greenway Rd
Goadby, Kathleen M., Boveton Hill
Godson, Baden G., 2 Winterway
Godson, Constance M., 18 Winterway
Godson, Ellen, 2 Winterway
Godson, George S., 18 Winterway
Godson, Heather M., 14 Park Road
Godson, Ronald, 14 Park Road
Goodall, Ivy E., 13 Park Road
Goodall, William, 13 Park Road
27/4/74 Gooderham, Alan J., 10
Winterway
Gooderham, Marie E., 10 Winterway
Graham, Alexander H., The Square
Graham, Mary R., The Square
Gray, Margot, 5 Park Road
Green, Barry J., 13 Summerfield Close
Green, Edith M., 41 Park Road

Green, Janet J., 13 Summerfield Close
Green, Malcolm P., Violet Cot Days
Lane
Green, Mary J., 16 Springfield
Green, Patricia M., Tudor Hse High St
Green, Robin J., 16 Summerfield Close
Green, Sheila H., 16 Summerfield Close
Green, Thomas P., Tudor Hse High St
Green, Veryan R., Violet Cot Days
Lane
Green, Wilfred, 41 Park Road
Greenstock, Gillian M., Lower Brook
House
Greenstock, Robert I., Lower Brook
House
Grew, May R., Cotswold Cottage
Tally-ho Hill
Gunn, Gwendoline M., Park Hse
Park Rd
Haine, Francis H., Box Cottage
Haine, Marjory J., Box Cottage
Hale, Edith N. M., Snugborough Mill
Hale, Moses E., 11 Park Road
Hale, Winifred J., 11 Park Road
Hall, Dorothy J., The Cot Far Upton
Wold Farm Moreton-in-Marsh Glos
Hall, James M., The Cot Far Upton
Wold Farm Moreton-in-Marsh Glos
Halliwell, Brian S., 1 Mill Close
Halliwell, Dorothy, 1 Mill Close
Hancox, Ambrose P., 44 Springfield
Hancox, Gladys, 44 Springfield
Hanman, Shirley G., Snugborough
Mill
Harbord, James C., 3 Chapel Row
Harbord, Jennifer A., 3 Chapel Row
Harris, Albert E., 64 Springfield
Harris, Daisy M., 24 Station Road
Harris, Florence R., 64 Springfield
Hart, Thomas E., 6 Orchard Bank
High St
Hartland, Helen H., Beckwood High
Street
Harvey, Alice M., 1 Summerfield Close
Harvey, Charles E., 1 Summerfield
Close
Harvey, Edith E., 5 Winterway
Harvey, Francine E., 3 Park Road
Harvey, John H., Old Jockey Stables
Moreton-in-Marsh
Harvey, Joyce, Old Jockey Stables
Moreton-in-Marsh
Harvey, Karen C., 2 Old Jockey
Stables Springhill Moreton-in-
Marsh
Harvey, Roger J., 3 Park Road
Harvey, Sidney G., 5 Winterway
Harwood, Lilian A., 3 Upper Terrace

237

Haseler, Jean M., 56 Park Rd
Hawtin, Carol A., 29 Winterway
Hawtin, Emily, 29 Winterway
Hawtin, Marion J., 33 Winterway
Hawtin, Ronald J., 33 Winterway
Haydon, Alice E., Church Gates
The Square
Hedges, Christopher J., 5 South View
Flats Blockley Court
Hedges, Lynda E., 5 South View Flats
Blockley Court
Heming, Ivy V. G., The Chequers
Draycott Moreton-in-Marsh
Heming, William J., The Chequers
Draycott Moreton-in-Marsh
Hemming, Beatrice, Red Lion Cot
High St
Hemming, Maureen W., 24 Station
Rd
Henshaw, Gary G., Flat A & M. Bolt
High St
Henshaw, Helen F., Flat A & M Bolt
High St
Heritage, Anthony, 60 Springfield
Heritage, Linda M., 3 Winterway
Heritage, Pearl, 60 Springfield
Heritage, Peter E., 16 Station Rd
Heritage, Robert, 3 Winterway
Heritage, Tsing F., 16 Station Rd
Herniman, Simon J., 1 Downs Farm
Cot Moreton-in-Marsh
Hicks, Annie, 1 Pitt Cot High St
Hicks, Doris A., 1 Pitt Cot High St
Hicks, Ernest, 1 Pitt Cot High St
Hicks, John R., Porch House
Hicks, Ursula K., Porch House
Hill, Elsie M., 62 Springfield
Hill, Walter J., 62 Springfield
Hitchman, Albert 22 Winterway
Hitchman, Anthony A., 17 Winterway
Hitchman, Arthur J., 6 South View
Flats Blockley Court
Hitchman, Dorothy E., 17 Winterway
Hitchman, Molly, 6 South View Flats
Blockley Court
Hitchman, Valerie M., 6 North View
Flats Blockley Court
Hodgkins, Annie V., 23 Station Rd
Hodgkins, Beryl J., 3 Station Rd
Hodgkins, John F., 3 Station Rd
Holder, Albert W., Upton Wold
Moreton-in-Marsh
Holder, Bernice, 23 Park Rd
Holder, Florence N., Upton Wold
Moreton-in-Marsh
Holder, Raymond S., 23 Park Rd
Holloway, Rowland, 7 Park Road
Holloway, Ruby K., 7 Park Road

Holmes, Doreen E., Peyton Cottage
Lower Street
Holmes, Gerald S., Peyton Cottage
Lower Street
Holtom, Beatrice, 2 Greenway Road
Holtom, Ronald D., 2 Greenway Road
Hooke, May E., 4 Orchard Bank High
Street
Hooper, Albert, 4 Upper Terrace
Hooper, Lillian F., 4 Upper Terrace
Hope, Colin A., 3 Springfield
Hope, Helen P., Colebrook Hse Lower
Street
Hope, Michael, Colebrook House
Lower Street
2/3/74 Hope, Rosemary E., 3
Springfield
Hope, Ruth E., 3 Springfield
Hopes, Algie W., Blaythorn Station Rd
Hopes, Amy, 27 Park Road
Hopes, Sybil, Blaythorn Station Rd
Hopkins, Arthur W., 13 Winterway
Hopkins, Diane V., 10 Station Rd
Hopkins, Doreen M., 13 Winterway
Hopkins, Edward C., 30 Winterway
Hopkins, Hilary J., 30 Winterway
Hopkins, John A. U., 56 Springfield
Hopkins, Kenneth A., 10 Station Rd
Hopkins, Rita E., 13 Winterway
Hopkins, Roy L., 13 Winterway
Hopkins, Veronica J., 56 Springfield
Hoskins, Caroline M., Broad Close
Hoskins, Herbert R., Broad Close
Hoskins, Joan C., Broad Close
Hoskins, Kathleen E., Holland Cottage
High Street
Hoskins, William W., Holland Cottage
High Street
Hotchkiss, Walter E., 3 Bungalow
Station Road
Howe, Agnes H., 6 Greenway Road
Howe, Colin C., 6 Greenway Road
Howe, Hilary R., 2 Upper Terrace
Greenway Road
Howe, Robert D., 2 Upper Terrace
Greenway Road
Humphreys, Janis W., Greenways
Greenway Road
Humphreys, John, Greenways
Greenway Road
Humphries, Eric M., Hangman's Hall
Broad Campden Chipping Campden
Glos
Hyatt, Edward, Rose Cottage Pasture
Lane
Inseal, Florence I., 1 North View Flats
Blockley Court
Jackson, Maureen F., 58 Springfield

238

Jackson, Michael S., 58 Springfield
James-Carrington, David W., Elm
House St Georges Terrace
James-Carrington, Phyllis, Elm House
St Georges Terrace
Jeffrey, Anthony B., North End Hse
Park Road
Jeffrey, Fabiana C. J., North End Hse
Park Road
Johnson, Arthur R., 7 Summerfield
Close
Johnson, Florence E., 7 Summerfield
Close
Johnson, Irene M., 4 Lower Terrace
16/9/74 Johnson, Julie, 4 Lower
Terrace
Johnson, Malcolm T., Barton Cot
Station Road
Johnson, Peter D., 4 Lower Terrace
Johnson, Violet, 7 Summerfield Close
Jordan, Mary E., 12 Summerfield Close
Joyner, Agnes M. L., 3 Mill Close
Kadel, Nigel, 52 Park Road
Kay, Freda B., Japonica Pasture Lane
Keay, Pamela J., 1 Court Cot
Keay, Raymond G., 1 Court Cot
Keeley, Barry R., 28 Springfield
Keeley, Edith B., 14 Summerfield Close
Keeley Ellen M., 28 Springfield
Keen, Beatrice L., 2 Park Road
Keen, Katherine A., 2 Lower Terrace
Keen, Lewis W., 2 Lower Terrace
Keyte, Constance E., 30 Springfield
Keyte, Gertrude M. M., 4 Greenway
Road
Keyte, Harry, 46 Springfield
Keyte, Joan M., 46 Springfield
Keyte, Margaret E., 4 Greenway Road
Keyte, Patricia M., 4 Summerfield
Close
Keyte, Reginald H., 30 Springfield
Keyte, Richard T., 4 Summerfield
Close
Keyte, Sara C., 30 Springfield
Kilmister, Don, 21 Winterway
Kilmister, Georgina, 11 Summerfield
Close
Kilmister, Margery J., 29 Winterway
Kilmister, Sheila, 21 Winterway
Knapper, Elizabeth F. M., 20 Station
Road
Knapper, James, 20 Station Road
Knight, Audrey A., 37 Park Road
Knight, Frank, The Bank High Street
Knight, John H., 37 Park Road
Knight, Kate, The Bank High Street
Knight, Ruth, Acorn Cottage Days
Lane

Knott, James M. S., Woolstaplers
High Street
Kryssa, Elizabeth G. J., Marygreen
Station Road
Kryssa, Eugene, Marygreen Station Rd
Kucek, Karel J., Stable Court Dovedale
Kucek, Mary M., Stable Court
Dovedale
Lake, Seymour E., 48 Park Road
Lane, Steven J., Hangmans Hall Broad
Campden Chipping Campden Glos
Langley, Lorna L., Paxton House
Ledbetter, Dora M., 4 Winterway
Ledbetter, Harry C., 4 Winterway
Leeson, Edward G., Crown Hotel
High Street
Leeson, Elsie G., Crown Hotel High St
Levick, Frank, Byways Brook Lane
Levick, Winifred G., Byways Brook
Lane
Lewis, Esther M., 1 Orchard Bank
High Street
Lewis, Kathleen M., Porch Cottage
Linstead, Marjorie, Bishop's Barn
Lockwood, William C., 5 Mill Close
Luckett, Eva W., Brook Cot Pasture
Lane
Luckett, Francis L., Brook Cot
Pasture Lane
Lusty, Eileen M., Old Silk Mill
Lusty, Robert F., Old Silk Mill
Lydiatt, Sheila J., Dovedale Ridge
Lydiatt, Sidney L., Dovedale Ridge
Lyne, Ruth, High Street
Lyne, William R., High Street
Macdonald, Alastair, The Cot Pasture
Lane
Macdonald, Mary B., The Cot Pasture
Lane
MacGillivray, Daisy L., 22 Station Rd
MacGillivray, Hugh, 22 Station Rd
Malin, Barbara, 21 Station Road
Malin, Elizabeth A., Corner House
Old Jockey Stables Moreton-in-
Marsh
Malin, Evelyn M., 25 Station Road
Malin, George S., Old Jockey Stables
Moreton-in-Marsh
Malin, Gordon, Old Jockey Stables
Moreton-in-Marsh
Malin, Hilda M., Old Jockey Stables
Moreton-in-Marsh
Malin, Janet V., Old Jockey Stables
Moreton-in-Marsh
Malin, John, 21 Station Road
Malin, Leslie J., 25 Station Road
Malin, Malcolm P., Corner House Old
Jockey Stables Moreton-in-Marsh

Mansell, Daisy I., 11 Winterway
Margetts, Kathleen M., 3 Orchard Bank
Marks, Margaret S., Troopers Lodge
Marks, Nellie, Landgate Cottages
Marlow, Reginald H., 1 Lower Street
Marshall, Norah M., Lansdowne High Street
Massey, Albert D., 35 Winterway
Massey, Nora, 35 Winterway
Matcham, Carol A., 2 Park Rd
Maxwell, Mary E., 36 Springfield
Maxwell, Thomas J., 36 Springfield
Mayo, Albert, 15 Station Road
Mayo, Alfred E., 1 Station Road
Mayo, Cynthia R., Newhaven Greenway Road
Mayo, Douglas A., Newhaven Greenway Road
Mayo, Edith A., 1 Station Road
Mayo, Edith E., 2 Station Road
Mayo, Elsie, 4 Station Road
Mayo, Ethel M. M., 4 Rose Row
Mayo, Gladys E., 1 Buchan Hse
Mayo, Gladys I., 15 Station Road
Mayo, John B., 36 Park Road
Mayo, John H., 36 Park Road
Mayo, Joseph G., 2 Station Road
Mayo, Kate, 36 Park Road
Mayo, Maureen J., 11 Station Road
Mayo, Michael J., 11 Station Road
McCallum, Robert, Jockey Stables Springhill Moreton-in-Marsh
McCallum, Valerie M., Jockey Stables Springhill Moreton-in-Marsh Glos
Medlock, Mary E., 20 Winterway
Meredith, Cyril T., Dovedale House
Meredith, Karman, 6 Station Rd
Meredith, Robert G., Dovedale House
Meredith, Timothy N. B. S., 6 Station Road
Miles, Amy V. M., Arreton Cot
Miles, Angela J., 11 Springfield
Miles, Bernard L., 56 Springfield
Miles, Michael J., 11 Springfield
Millard, Harry S., Stapenhill Farm
Millard, Rosalind, Stapenhill Farm
Milton, Duncan C. W., Bankside High Street
Milton, Sylvia M., Bankside, High Street
Minett, Allan H., Downs Farm
Minett, David H., Downs Farm Cottage
Minett, Harold G., Downs Farm
Minett, Hester M., Downs Farm
Minett, Margaret D., Downs Farm Cottage

Moore, Carol A. M., Brown Hse Station Road
Moore, Jean M., Brown House Station Road
Moore, Joy F., The Old Mill
Moore, Marjorie C., Cedarwood Cottage Lower Street
Moore, Strafford M., Brown House Station Road
Morgan, Diana E., 18 Park Road
Morgan, Huw, 18 Park Road
Morley-Smith, Cyril F., 3 Rose Row
Morley-Smith, Douglas J., 3 Rose Row
Morley-Smith, Gladys M., 3 Rose Row
Morris, Albert J., 5 Upper Terrace
Morris, Eva N. L., 23 Winterway
Morris, James F., 24 Station Rd
Morris, Joan, 5 Upper Terrace
Morris, Joseph F., 23 Winterway
Morris, Levi A., 2 North Flats Blockley Court
Morris, William A., 23 Winterway
Moulder, Albert E., 38 Springfield
Moulder, Brenda E., 28 Winterway
Moulder, Leslie, 28 Winterway
Moulder, Sarah A., 38 Springfield
Mumford, Catherine A., 8 Station Rd
Mumford, Iris E., The Square
Mumford, Percy J., 8 Station Road
Nobes, Albert W., Jockey Stables
Nobes, Christopher J., 4 Gate Hse Old Jockey Stables Moreton-in-Marsh Glos
Nobes, Doreen A., Old Jockey Stables Moreton-in-Marsh
Nobes, Elizabeth M., 3 Summerfield Close
Nobes, Jeniffer A., Gate Hse Old Jockey Stables Springhill Moreton-in-Marsh Glos
Nobes, Jessie M., 4 Gate House Old Jockey Stables Moreton-in-Marsh
Nobes, Margaret A., Old Jockey Stables Moreton-in-Marsh
Nobes, Peter J., Old Jockey Stables Moreton-in-Marsh
Nobes, Walter H., 3 Summerfield Close
Nobes, William, 4 Gate House Old Jockey Stables Moreton-in-Marsh
Nobes, William D., 4 Gate Hse Old Jockey Stables Moreton-in-Marsh
Northall, Barbara, The Vicarage
Northall, Malcolm W., The Vicarage
Northall, Michael J., The Vicarage
Oliver, Minnie, 9 Park Road
O'Neill, Hilda M., Philongley Station Road
Ongley, Richard, 20 Springfield

Ongley, Sylvia W., 1 Northwick Terrace
Owen, Grace E. M., 24 Park Road
Owen, Norman T., 24 Park Road
Pain, Alice E., 5 Lower Terrace
Pain, Annie, Wul-Gath-Rin Springfield
Pain, William G., 5 Lower Terrace
Pain, Nellie M., 6 Greenway Rd
Pallister, James C., East End Cottage Snugborough Lane
Pallister, Peggy, East End Cottage Snugborough Lane
Payne, Allan C., 5 Greenway Rd
Payne, Dorothy M., 26 Winterway
Payne, Geraldine L., 1 The Court
Payne, Gwendoline R., 1 Rose Row
Payne, Ivy L., 3 Brook Lane
Payne, James, 1 Rose Row
Payne, Keith M., 2 Northwick Terrace
Payne, Mabel D., Blockley Court Hse
Payne, Norah M., Pear Tree House Lower Street
Payne, Ralph W., 2 Northwick Terrace
Payne, Reginald S., 26 Winterway
Payne, Sidney, Blockley Court House
Payne, Terence C., 1 The Court
Payne, Winifred M., 2 Northwick Terrace
Peach, Beverley E., 5 Jockey Stables Springhill Moreton-in-Marsh Glos
11/8/74 Peach, Jayne E., 5 Jockey Stables Springhill Moreton-in-Marsh Glos
Peach, Thomas H., 5 Jockey Stables Springhill Moreton-in-Marsh
Pearson, Alan, 2 Sunnybank Station Road
Pearson, Atholl A. F., 50 Springfield
Pearson, Christine, 2 Sunnybank Station Road
Pearson, Dorothy A., 50 Springfield
Pearson, Harvey E., The Woodlands Dovedale
Pearson, Jane, 50 Springfield
Pearson, Margaret A., The Woodlands Dovedale
Phillips, Mabel, Cedarwood Cottage Lower Street
Philpott, Carmen T., 5 Mill Row Station Road
Philpott, Dorothy B., Jador Station Rd
Philpott, John, Jador Station Rd
Philpott, Michael J., 5 Mill Row Station Road
Pickering, Susie, 11 Park Road
Pickford, Nellie, 2 Mill Close
Pither, Annie A., Belmont Station Rd
Pither, Beryl, Belmont Station Rd

Pither, Ronald C., Belmont Station Rd
Pither, Sybil, Belmont Station Road
Playle, Elizabeth J., 3 Mill Row Station Road
Playle, Eric W., 3 Mill Row Station Rd
Polkinghorne, Ethel M., 7 Orchard Bank High Street
Powell, Frank A., Southwold The Greenway
Powell, Jean M., Southwold The Greenway
Prew, Barabara I., 4 Chapel Row
Prew, Colin J. J., 4 Chapel Row
Price, Margaret T. G., 7 Northwick Terrace
Priest, Basil J. G., The Limes Station Road
Priest, Carmel C., The Limes Station Road
Proctor, Dennis W., 5 Bungalow Station Road
Pyke, Ruth P., Bell Bank Bell Lane
Pyke, Stephen P., Bell Bank Bell Lane
Rathbone, Eileen R., Arreton Station Road
Rathbone, Reginald B., Arreton Station Road
Read, Susan L., Lower Brook Hse
Reekie, Ian, Wold Hse
Reekie, Sarah E. R., Wold Hse
Rice-Oxley, Mark A., Vine Cot High St
Rice-Oxley, Susan B., Vine Cot High St
Richardson, Ivy P., 14 Winterway
Richardson, Walter, 14 Winterway
Richford, Edward W. C., 1 River Bank High Street
Richford, Maragaret E., 1 River Bank High Street
Righton, John H., Holt Farm
Righton, Ruth M., Holt Farm
Rimell, Dennis E., 5 Greenway Road
Rimell, Joan V., 5 Greenway Road
Robinson, Grace E., Hainault High St
Rochfort, Andrew J., Clogrenane Station Road
Rochfort, Horace A. F., Clogrenane Station Road
Rochfort, Margaret E., Clogrenane Station Road
Rochfort, Phillip M. A., Clogrenane Station Road
Rochfort, Sarah, Clogrenane Station Road
Rollinson, Keith, 2 West View Chapel Lane
Rollinson, Louise A., 2 West View Chapel Lane

Rosenfled, Edith J., Temporary Bungalow Station Road
Rouse, Graham G., 12 Station Rd
Rouse, Jennifer, 12 Station Rd
Rouse, Winifred E., Fair View Cottage High Street
Russell, Albert E., 10 Upper Terrace
Russell, Amy M. A., 10 Upper Terrace
Russell, Victor J., 10 Upper Terrace
Sandford, Frederick D. G., 8 Park Rd
Savage, Walter, 16 Springfield Estate
Shackleton-Bailey Dorothy, The Old Mill
Shackleton-Bailey John, The Old Mill
Shadbolt, Doreen J., 15 Summerfield Close
Shadbolt, Elsie K., 19 Park Road
Shadbolt, Frederick G., 56 Springfield
Shadbolt, Henry J., 19 Park Road
Shadbolt, Mabel, 56 Springfield
Shadbolt, Peter J., 15 Summerfield Close
Shaw Close, Beatrice, The Crows Nest Greenway Road
Shaw Close, Courtenay C., The Crows Nest Greenway Road
Shepherd, Katie L., 19 Winterway
Sheppard, Henrietta, 2 Hillcrest High Street
Sims, Fay, 1 St George's Terrace
Sims, Harold, 1 St George's Terrace
Small, Irene, Sunnyside Station Road
Small, Robert, Sunnyside Station Road
Smedley, Alan A., The Old Royal Oak High St
Smedley, Joyce M., The Old Royal Oak High St
Smeeton, Christine H., Broughton Cottage
Smeeton, Reginald A., Broughton Cottage
Smith, Eric G., Troopers Lodge
Smith, Leonard, 27 Winterway
Smith, William, 27 Winterway
Sollis, Alfred H., The Steps High St
Sollis, Doris K., The Steps High St
Sollis, Graham A., 16 Park Rd
Sollis, Jean D., 16 Park Rd
Sollis, Roger, 1 Brook Lane
Sollis, Rosemarie M., 1 Brook Lane
Speakman, Dorothy C., The Old Quarry Greenway
Speakman, John D., The Old Quarry Greenway
Spice, Sara G., Melrose Station Road
Spiers, Margaret J., Temporary Bungalow Station Rd

Spiers, Winnie R., Temporary Bungalow Station Rd
Spittle, John, Sheaf House Farm
Spittle, Wendy A., Sheaf House Farm
Spray, John R., 40 Park Rd
Spray, Olive M., 40 Park Rd
Spurgin, Frances C., Boveton Hill
Stanley, Alice M., 7 Station Road
5/4/74 Stanley, Andrew J., 31 Winterway
Stanley, Arthur H., 44 Park Road
Stanley, Blanche, 40 Springfield
Stanley, Clara E., Waterside High St
Stanley, Florence K., 44 Park Road
Stanley, Ian J., 31 Winterway
Stanley, Leslie G., 31 Winterway
Stanley, Margaret K., 31 Winterway
Stanley, Norman T., 31 Winterway
Stening, Elizabeth E., 5 Northwick Terrace
Stewart, Leslie V., Great Western Arms Station Rd
Stewart, Rose, Great Western Arms Station Rd
Strachan, Alexander J., 14 Springfield
Strachan, Andrew, 14 Springfield
Strachan, Catherine, 2 Buchan Hse
Strachan, Derek, 14 Springfield
Strachan, Joan H., 14 Springfield
Strain, Eileen H., Arlington House High Street
Strain, Mary, Arlington House High Street
Strange, Basil J., Greystones High St
Strange, David J., Greystones High St
Strange, Margaret J., Greystones High Street
Stroud, Bessie E., 19 Springfield
Stroud, Harvey, 19 Springfield
Stuart-Turner, Margaret R., Central Garage Bell Lane
Stuart-Turner, Richard, Central Garage Bell Lane
Stuart-Turner, Roy S., Central Garage Bell Lane
Taplin, Albert G., 18 Springfield
Taplin, Eileen P., 18 Springfield
Tarplett, Doris A., 33 Park Road
Taylor, Alec R., 25 Park Road
Taylor, Archibald E., School House
Taylor, Elsie E., 6 Lower Terrace
Taylor, Geoffrey M., 4 Springfield
Taylor, George E., 2 Upton Cottages Upton Wold Moreton-in-Marsh
Taylor, Hazel, 4 Springfield
Taylor, Herbert, Southcot Lower St
Taylor, Janet, 17 Park Rd
Taylor, Millicent, School House

Taylor, Philip S., 17 Park Rd
Taylor, Reginald A., 4 Springfield
Taylor, Richard F., 9 Mount Pleasant
Taylor, Rosina B., 2 Upton Cottages
  Upton Wold Moreton-in-Marsh
Taylor, Sheila J., 9 Mount Pleeasant
Taylor-Gill, Simon P., 3 St George's
  Terrace
Terry, Diane Y., 54 Springfield
Terry, Stuart B., 54 Springfield
Thomas, Charles A., Warren Cotts
Thomas, David G., The Warren
  Dovedale
Thomas, Eva E. G., Salcombe Cottage
  High Street
Thomas, Mary E. F., Warren Cotts
Thompson, Glen, 49 Park Rd
Thompson, Sidwell J., 4 Northwick
  Terrace
Thomson, John C., Brookdale Brook
  Lane
Thomson, Margaret N., Brookdale
  Brook Lane
Thursfield, Jane, Gentian Cot Days
  Lane
Thursfield, John, Gentian Cot Days
  Lane
Thurston, George W. H., The Puffers
  St George's Terrace
Thurston, Nair V., The Puffers, St
  George's Terrace
Timms, Allan C., 14 Station Rd
Timms, Colin J., 14 Station Rd
25/9/74 Timms, David J., 14 Station Rd
Timms, Gertrude E., 14 Station Road
Timms, Lavinia M., 15 Springfield
Timms, Lewis G., 14 Station Road
Timms, Rodney L., 15 Springfield
Tomes, Austin G., 7 Winterway
Tomes, Florence E., 7 Winterway
Tomes, Muriel A., 2 Court Cottages
  Blockley Court
Tomes, Percy L., 2 Court Cottages
  Blockley Court
Turner, Alice M., 3 Greenway Road
Turner, Martin L., Red Lion Cottage
  Dovedale End
Turner, Olive, Red Lion Cottage
  Dovedale End
Turner, Robert E., Green Pastures
Turner, Violet M., Green Pastures
Turvey, Elsie, Northwick Mill Farm
Turvey, John E. B., Northwick Mill
  Farm
Turvey, Mabel R., 5 Station Road
Tustin, Florence B., Hill View High St
Tweed, Malcolm P., The Bungalow
  Bell Bank

Tweed, Norma R., The Bungalow Bell
  Bank
Udell, Edith A., 7 Greenway Road
Vale, Alfred E., 1 Mount Pleasant
Vale, Mabel J., 1 Mount Pleasant
Van Moppes Victoria R., Wold Hse
Vick, David J., 1 Springfield
Vick, Sheila A., 1 Springfield
Wadsworth, Edward T., Polls Perch
  High Street
Wadsworth, Grace E., Polls Perch
  High Street
Waine, Allan C., Old Mill Dene
Waine, Ilfra M., Old Mill Dene
Waite, Gwendoline M., 47 Park Road
Walker, Bernard J., 46 Park Rd
Walker, Brenda W., 2 Brook Lane
Walker, Derrick, 9 Summerfield Close
Walker, Evelyn, 46 Park Rd
Walker, Frederick D., 2 Brook Lane
Walker, Mildred S., 9 Summerfield
  Close
Warby, Brian J., Gable House Station
  Road
Warby, Margaret, Gable House Station
  Road
1/3/74 Ward, John K., Dovedale Hse
  Dovedale
Ward, Lilian A., Ginger Hse High St
Warner, Alfred W., Landgate House
Warner, Conrad, Orchard Cottage
  Draycott Road
Warner, Ellen E., 42 Park Road
Warner, Esther R., Orchard Cottage
  Draycott Road
Warner, Hilda, Landgate House
Warner, Joan, Rodneys
Warner, John W., Rodneys
Warner, June E., Pear Tree Cottage
  Lower Street
Warner, Leslie H., 42 Park Road
Warner, Peter B., Pear Tree Cottage
  Lower Street
12/10/74 Watkins, Graham V.,
  Millview High St
Watkins, Kenneth F., Millview High St
Watson, Clement A. G., Half Crown
  Cot High St
Watson, Gabriel A., Half Crown Cot
  High St
Watson, Grace W., Cherry Orchard
  Greenway
Watson, John S. F., Cherry Orchard
  Greenway
Webb, Alfred V., Woodleigh Station
  Road
Webb, Catherine E., Dovedale
Webb, Edith M., Woodleigh Station Rd

243

Webb, Ernest, 42 Springfield
Webb, Ellen L., Flat 1 Lady Northwick
Homes
Webb, Jane, Colebrook Cot Lower St
Webb, Jonathan, Colebrook Cot
Lower St
Webb, Leslie J., Dovedale
Webb, Rosalie, 42 Springfield
Webb, Ruth, Colebrook Cot Lower St
Webster, Florence, 5 Orchard Bank
High St
Wheeler, Ernest J., Draycott
Moreton-in-Marsh
Wheeler, Violet A., 3 Greenway Road
White, Annie, 5 Summerfield Close
White, William C., 5 Summerfield
Close
Whitehouse, John B., Hilters Greenway
Road
Whitehouse, Vera B., Hilters Greenway
Road
Whitford, Elsie M., 2 Red Lion Steps
High Street
Whittington, Eliza A., The Vicarage
Whitworth, Robert B., 9 Summerfield
Close
Whitworth, Susan J., 9 Summerfield
Close
Wilders, Annie E., 38 Park Road
Wilders, Reginald J., 38 Park Road
Williams, Betty D., 35 Park Road
Williams, Charles D., Wilum Cot
Station Road
Williams, Daniel W., 35 Park Road
Williams, Edna M. E., The Studio
High Street
Williams, Hubert J., The Studio High
Street

Williams, Olive M., Wilum Cot
Station Rd
Williams-Wynne, Herbert B. W.,
Dene Cot High St
Williams-Wynne, Phyllis M., Dene
Cot High St
Winter, Arthur H., 18 Station Road
Winter, Gladys M., 18 Station Road
Winter, Iris., 12 Station Road
Winter, Nicola., 18 Station Rd
Wise, Alice H., 1 Station Rd
Withers, Betty., 30 Park Road
Withers, John W., 1 West View
Chapel Road
Withers, Violet A., 1 West View
Chapel Road
Withers, Walter J., 30 Park Road
Wood, George E., Middle Cot
High St
Wood, Linda B., Middle Cot High St
Workman, Dorothy J., 6 Winterway
Workman, Frederick J., 1 North
View Flats, Blockley Court
Workman, Wilfred F., 6 Winterway
Woskett, Arthur J., Little Manor
Woskett, Beatrice R., Little Manor
Wright, Agnes M., Widdowes Close
High Street
Yates, Christopher J., Lower Farm
Yates, Rosa M., Lowre Farm
Young, Keith R., 22 Springfield
Young, Lorna M., 22 Springfield
Yoxall, Doris E., Pinner-s Quarry
Yoxall, Nora A., 1 Red Lion Steps
High Street

Abbotts, Agnes E., Old Manor Cotts
Abbotts, Denis T., Old Manor Cotts
Abbotts, Winefred, Old Manor Cotts
Aizlewood, John A., Paxford Manor
Aizlewood, Margaret D., Paxford Man.
Allen, David, Northwick Park
   Mansion Blockley Moreton-in-
   Marsh Glos
Allen, Robert, Northwick Park
   Mansion Blockley Moreton-in-
   Marsh Glos
Atkinson, Janette, 4 Clay Lane
Atkinson, Terence K. G., 4 Clay Lane
Aves, Robert, Manor Cot
Aves, Violet, Manor Cot
Bailey, John, Northwick Park Mansion
   Blockley Moreton-in-Marsh Glos
Ball, John E., Northwick Park Mansion
   Blockley Moreton-in-Marsh Glos
Ball, Linda E., Northwick Park
   Mansion Blockley Moreton-in-
   Marsh Glos
Beasley, Doris A., 2 Plum Cottages
Beasley, Edith A., The Folly
Beasley Jesse T., The Folly
Birch, Richard, Northwick Park
   Mansion Blockley Moreton-in-
   Marsh Glos
Black, Margaret, Northwick Park
   Mansion Blockley Moreton-in-
   Marsh Glos
Bothamley, Ann, Northwick Park
   Mansion Blockley
Bothamley, Kenneth, Northwick Park
   Mansion Blockley Moreton-in-
   Marsh Glos
Bradshaw, John E., Manor Farm
   Homestead
Bradshaw, Julie A., Manor Farm
   Homestead
Brown, Doreen, Northwick Park
   Mansion Blockley Moreton-in
   Marsh Glos
Brown, Roger, Northwick Park
   Mansion Blockley Moreton-in-
   Marsh Glos
Bryan, Charles A., 16 Brookside
Burnett, Guy, Northwick Park
   Mansion Blockley Moreton-in-
   Marsh Glos
Chan, Rufus, Northwick Park Mansion
   Blockley Moreton-in-Marsh Glos
Clark, Arthur, Northwick Park
   Mansion Blockley Moreton-in-
   Marsh Glos

Cook, Gladys L., The Stores and Post
   Office
Cooper, George H. A., 15 Brookside
Cooper, Hilda E., 15 Brookside
Courtney, Lily L., Wells Farm Cottage
Courtney, William G., Wells Farm
   Cottage
Davenport, Paul, Northwick Park
   Mansion Blockley Moreton-in-
   Marsh Glos
Dunn, Alan, Northwick Park Mansion
   Blockley Moreton-in-Marsh Glos
Fletcher, Charles, 5 Brookside
Fletcher, Joyce, Upper Folley
Fletcher, Ruth, 5 Brookside
Gandy, Alice, Vine Cottage
Gandy, Francis G., Vine Cottage
Gregg, Hector W., The Folly
Griffin, Ann E., 3 Brookside
Griffin, Beryl M. E., 13 Brookside
Griffin, Frank T., 13 Brookside
Griffin, Geoffrey F., 1 Wells Farm
   Cottages
Griffin, Hilda M., Paxford
Griffin, Ivor A., Paxford
Griffin, Sheila D., 1 Wells Farm
   Cottages
Hall, Anne R., Northwick Park
   Mansion Blockley Moreton-in-
   Marsh Glos
Hall, Dorothy E., The Laurels
Hall, Leslie P., The Laurels
Hall, Martin N., The Laurels
   Brookside
Hall, Robin L., The Laurels Brookside
Hall, William H., Northwick Park
   Mansion Blockley Moreton-in-
   Marsh Glos
Hancock, Charles T., The Lane
Hancock, Kathleen A. M., Rosebank
Hancock, Mary A., The Lane
Harlock, Pamela A., 4 Manor Cots
Harlock, Roger E., 4 Manor Cots
Harris, Bryan, Paxford
Harris, Doris H., Paxford
Harris, Frances L., 2 Bank Farm
   Cottages
Harris, Mervyn M., Paxford
Harris, Rita J., Paxford
Harris, Robert A., 2 Bank Farm
   Cottages
Harris, Thomas H., Paxford
Hicks, Christine M., The Firs North-
   wick Park Blockley Moreton-in-
   Marsh Glos

Hicks, Harry M., The Firs Northwick Park Blockley Moreton-in-Marsh
Higgins, Fergus, Northwick Park Mansion Blockley Moreton-in-Marsh Glos
Higginson, James, Elm View
Hill, Angela M., 7 Brookside
Hill, Douglas J., 7 Brookside
Hill, Vera J., 7 Brookside
Howard, Glennis, 2 Wells Cotts
Howard, Richard R., 2 Wells Cotts
Hutchings, Charlotte, Northwick Park Cottage Blockley Moreton-in-Marsh
Jackson, Ian M., Wellacres Station Road Blockley Moreton-in-Marsh
Jackson, Sybil J., Wellacres Station Road Blockley Moreton-in-Marsh
James, Doris E., 3 Brookside
James, Gordon P., 3 Brookside
James, Susan M., 3 Brookside
James, William J., 10 Brookside
James, Winifred N., 10 Brookside
Jugg, Peter, Northwick Park Mansion Blockley Moreton-in-Marsh Glos
Keen, Gordon, 9 Brookside
Keen, John, 9 Brookside
Keen, Joseph, 9 Brookside
Keen, Mary A., 9 Brookside
Keepence, Sarah A., 2 Lower Folley
Kelly, Douglas J., Neighbrook Moreton-in-Marsh Glos
Keyte, Donald C., Field View
Keyte, Doreen M., Field View
1/10/74 Keyte, Lynette S., Fiedlview
Lamdin, David R., Holtom House
Lamdin, Zara P., Holtom House
Larner, Elizabeth A., 4 Brookside
Larner, Ethel M., 4 Brookside
Leage, Allan D., Northwick Park Mansion Blockley Moreton-in Marsh Glos
Leage, Rita M. L., Northwick Park Mansion Blockley Moreton-in-Marsh Glos
Marlam, Wendy A. M., Northwick Park Mansion Blockley Moreton-in-Marsh Glos
McAteer, Doreen E., 11 Brookside
21/2/74 McAteer, Elaine S., 11 Brookside
McAteer, John, 11 Brookside
McAteer, Stephen J., 11 Brookside
Melville, George A., Upper Folly
Melville, Rosalind, Upper Folly
Mennell, Harold, 8 Brookside
Mennell, Louisa M., 8 Brookside
Mennell, Michael G., 8 Brookside

Mitchell, Gerald, formerly of: 1 Clay Lane
Newitt, Derek J., 1 Clay Lane
Newitt, Donald E., 1 Clay Lane
Newitt, Mary E., 1 Clay Lane
Newman, Harry, The Folly
Newman, Jessie, The Folly
Nicklin, Albert H., Upper Folly
Nicklin, Gertrude A., Upper Folly
Odling, Thomas G., Paxford House
O'Sullivan, Beatrice, Paxford Manor Cottages
O'Sullivan, John, Paxford Manor Cottages
Page, Hilary J., Northwick Park Mansion Blockley Moreton-in-Marsh Glos
Palmer, George C. L., Hillside
Palmer, Jessie M., Hillside
Parnell, Margaret A., 14 Brookside
Payne, Christine J., 3 Clay Lane
Payne, Frank J., 2 Clay Lane
Payne, Martin E., 3 Clay Lane
Peacock, Elizabeth J., The Walnuts
Peacock, John R., The Walnuts
Peacock, Robert J., The Walnuts
Percival, Geoffrey, Northwick Park Mansion Blockley Moreton-in-Marsh Glos
Powell, Edward R., Paxford Farm
Powell, Evelyn G., Paxford Farm
Pullen, Jessie E., 12 Brookside
Richardson, Arthur G., Sandown Cottage
Richardson, Winifred C., Sandown Cottage
Robinson, Charles J. O., Lambsdell
Robinson, Freda M., Lambsdell
Rouse, Ernest J., 1 Brookside
Rouse, Jessie, 1 Brookside
Rumbold, Venetia, Northwick Park Mansion Blockley Moreton-in-Marsh Glos
Searle, Heather, Northwick Park Mansion Blockley Moreton-in-Marsh Glos
Smith, Michael, Northwick Park Mansion Blockley Moreton-in-Marsh Glos
Smith, Roselea, Northwick Park Mansion Blockley Moreton-in-Marsh Glos
Stokes, Hilda L., Bank Farm
Stokes, John S., Bank Farm
Stokes, William, Bank Farm
Tandy, Paul J., Northwick Park Mansion Blockley Moreton-in-Marsh Glos

Tarplett, Mary, The Bakery
Tarplett, William E., The Bakery
Taylor, Alice M., The Grey House
Taylor, Anthony C., The Grey House
Taylor, Charles H., The Grey House
Tebbutt, Janet M., Northwick Park
Mansion Blockley Moreton-in-
Marsh Glos
Toon, Andrew, Northwick Park
Mansion Blockley Moreton-in-
Marsh Glos
Traynor, Stephen, Northwick Park
Mansion Blockley Moreton-in-
Marsh Glos
Turner, Alfred M., 6 Brookside

Turner, Angela, 6 Brookside
Turner, Olive I., 6 Brookside
Turner, William, 6 Brookside
Unwin, Allen, Northwick Park
Mansion Blockley Moreton-in-
Marsh Glos
Waring, Thomas E., 2 Brookside
Wilson, Frank, Northwick Park
Mansion Blockley Moreton-in-
Marsh Glos
Wilson, Shirley, Northwick Park
Mansion Blockley Moreton-in-
Marsh Glos
Young, Doris M., Bridgefield
Young, John E., Bridegfield

Baggaley, Anthony C., Bran Mill
Ball, Susan J., Ditchford Farm Hse
Baranowski, Henry, 21 Church View
Aston Magna
Beasley, Alan R. M., 10 Wydelands
Draycott
Beasley, Ann L., 10 Wydelands
Draycott
Beasley, Beatrice A., 11 Wydelands
Draycott
Beasley, David J., 16 Wydelands
Draycott
Beasley, Keith A., 11 Wydelands
Draycott
Beasley, Mary R. K., 16 Wydelands
Draycott
Beasley, Reginald C., 5 Post Office Lane
Draycott
Beasley, Winifred M., 5 Post Office
Lane Draycott
19/12/74 Bennett, Lynn D., Manor Hse
Aston Magna
Bialosiewicz, Edwarda T., 11 Church
View Aston Magna
Brooks, Jackie, 12 Aston Magna
Brooks, John D., 12 Aston Magna
Clarke, Carol R., Two Bays Draycott
Clarke, Edgar A., Two Bays Draycott
Clifford, Barbara, Ditchford-on-Fosse
Clifford, Francis, Ditchford-on-Fosse
Clifford, Frederick W., 3 Wellacres
Cottages Draycott
Clifford, Kathleen A., 3 Wellacres
Cottages Draycott
Clifford, Mary A., 2 Wellacres Lane
Draycott
Clifford, Michael L., 3 Wellacres Cotts
Draycott
Clifford, Rita M., 2 Cot Ditchford-on-
Fosse
24/8/74 Clifford, Rosemary, 2
Ditchford-on-Fosse
Clifford, Walter T., 2 Wellacres Cotts
Draycott
Colbourne, Alison J., 1 Wellacres Cotts
Draycott
Colbourne, Peter, 1 Wellacres Cotts
Draycott
Coldicott, Bramble M., Ditchford-on-
Fosse
Coldicott, John H., Ditchford-on-
Fosse
Coldicott, Henry C., Ditchford-on-
Fosse
Coldicott, Jessamy A., Ditchford-on-
Fosse
Coldicott, Stephen M., Ditchford-on-
Fosse

Cooke, Alice B., 5 Wydelands Draycott
Cooke, David G., 12 Wydelands
Draycott
Cooke, Edna G., Wimbourne Cot
Draycott
Cooke, Maud E. R., 12 Wydelands
Draycott
Cooke, Norman D., Wimbourne Cot
Draycott
Cother, Arthur, 15 Wydelands
Draycott
Cother, Bernard, 4 Church View Aston
Magna
Cother, Edith L., 4 Church View Aston
Magna
Cother, George H., 4 Church View
Aston Magna
Cother, Irene L., 15 Wydelands
Draycott
Digweed, Christopher J., 5 Wydelands
Draycott
Digweed, David, J., 9 Wydelands
Draycott
Digweed, Francis J., 5 Wydelands
Draycott
Digweed, Phyllis M., 5 Wydelands
Draycott
Dudfield, Mary E., Compton Cottage
Draycott
Edgington, Bertram C., Two Bays
Draycott
Edwards, Ivy I., Barn Cot Aston
Magna
Edwards, William H., Barn Cot Aston
Magna
Foster, Albert B., Draycott
Foster, May E., Draycott
Garne, Dorothy M., Fir Tree Cottage
Draycott
Garne, Robert, Fir Tree Cottage
Draycott
Gasside. John H., Draycott Farm
Cotts
Gasside, Kathleen, Draycott
Gladwin, Alan, Rushbrook Draycott
Gladwin, Olwyn F. M. L., Rushbrook
Draycott
Hardiman, Basil W., 9 Aston Magna
Hardiman, Elizabeth M., 9 Aston
Magna
Harris, Gwendoline A., 9 Church View
Harris, John A., 4 Draycott
Harris, Marylyn, 4 Draycott
Harris, Ronald V., 9 Church View
Harrison, Leonard A., Rose Villa
Draycott
Hawtin, Dorothy M., Post Office
Stores Draycott

Hawtin, Percy F., Post Office Stores Draycott
Hemming, Maureen W., 9 Church View Aston Magna
Herbert, Harry, 1 Aston Magna
Herbert, Ivy W., 3 Church View Aston Magna
Herbert, Lynn M., 3 Church View Aston Magna
Herbert, Margaret, 1 Aston Magna
Herbert, Maurice, 3 Church View Aston Magna
Hessel, Arthur E., Newlands Farm Hse Aston Magna
Hessel, Patricia K., Newlands Farm Hse Aston Magna
Hookham, Catherine E., 24 Aston Magna
Hookham, Glenn, 24 Aston Magna
Hookham, Joseph, 24 Aston Magna
Hooper, Pamela W., 2 Middle Ditchford Cottages
Hooper, Rodney P., 2 Middle Ditchford Cottages
Hope, Kate, 8 Aston Magna
Hope, Kenneth, Dorn Hill
Hope, Victor, 8 Aston Magna
Hope, Winifred M., Dorn Hill
Hopkins, Elizabeth K., 8 Church View Aston Magna
Hopkins, Graham G., 8 Church View Aston Magna
Humphreys, Lilian R., 2 Bran Mill
Hurdiss, Harry, Manager's House Glos Brick Co Aston Magna
Hurdiss, Rhian, Manager's House Glos Brick Co Aston Magna
Ireland, Clifford, H., Aston Hale Farm
Ireland, Harold J., Church Farm Aston Magna
Ireland, Iris M., Aston Hale Farm
Ireland, Joyce, 6 Aston Magna
Ireland, Margaret, 23 Aston Magna
Ireland, Robert C., Aston Hale Farm
Ireland, Ronald C., 23 Aston Magna
Ireland, Ronald W., 6 Aston Magna
Ireland, Valerie G., Aston Hale Farm
Jackson, Basil G., 14 Aston Magna
Jackson, Patricia, 14 Aston Magna
James, Charles A., Draycott
James, Ethel F., Draycott
James, Marion P., Draycott
Jasinska, Danuta M., 13 Church View Aston Magna
Jasinski, Richard S., 13 Church View Aston Magna
Jeffrey, Barry H., Harpers Hse Draycott

Jeffrey, Ernest H., The Laurels Draycott
Jeffrey, Peggy A. B., The Laurels Draycott
Jeffrey, Teresa J., Harper's Hse Draycott
Johnsey, Elizabeth P., 4 Post Office Lane Draycott
Johnsey, Ronald W., 4 Post Office Lane Draycott
Johnsey, Rowan J., 4 Post Office Lane Draycott
Judge, Muriel E., Ends Cottage Draycott
Kelly, Henry, 20 Aston Magna
Kelly, Rose V. I., 20 Aston Magna
Kipplewhite, Patricia A., 6 Wydelands Draycott
Knight, Ethel, Draycott Farm Draycott
Knight, Georgina M., 4 Wydelands
Knight, Joseph, 4 Wydelands
Knight, Michael J., 4 Wydelands Draycott
Knight, Stanley C., Draycott Farm Draycott
Knight, Nicholas J., 4 Wydelands Draycott
Lindsell, Christine, The Long Barn Draycott
Lindsell, Ivor C. M., The Long Barn Draycott
Lindsell, Lisa, The Long Barn Draycott
Lindsell, Patricia, The Long Barn Draycott
8/6/74 Lootes, Angela J., 9 Wydelands Draycott
Lootes, Audrey J., 9 Wydelands Draycott
Lootes, Frederick C., 9 Wydelands Draycott
Lowe, Ida, 6 Woolaway Bungalows Aston Magna
Lowe, Francis J., 10 Church View Aston Magna
Lowe, Patricia A., 10 Church View Aston Magna
Marshall, Richard P., 5 Aston Magna
Marshall, Suzette, 5 Aston Magna
Mayo, Barbara J., 13 Wydelands Draycott
Mayo, Janet, 13 Wydelands Draycott
Mayo, Roderick A., 13 Wydelands Draycott
McLelland, Decima J., The Old Vicarage Aston Magna
McLelland, Douglas H. W., The Old Vicarage Aston Magna

McLelland, William A., The Old
Vicarage Aston Magna
Miles, Edna, 7 Wydelands Draycott
Miles, Gordon T., 7 Wydelands
Draycott
Morgan, Frances M., Tudor Hse
Draycott
Morgan, Thomas C., Tudor Hse
Draycott
Mozgowiec, Adam J., 22 Church View
Aston Magna
Mozgowiec, Jozef, 22 Church View
Aston Magna
Mozgowiec, Maria, 22 Church View
Aston Magna
Nowakowski, Jerzy, 18 Church View
Aston Magna
Parnell, Joan P., Norton Cottage
Aston Magna
Parnell, Jonathan L. A., Norton Cot
Aston Magna
Parnell, Kenneth W., Norton Cottage
Aston Magna
Peach, Alan R., 2 Wydelands Draycott
Peach, Christine M., 2 Wydelands
Draycott
Peach, David, 2 Wydelands Draycott
Peach, Florence M., 2 Wydelands
Draycott
Peach, Leonard, 2 Wydelands
Draycott
Peach, Richard J., 2 Wydelands
Draycott
Peck, Letitia E. A., Rose Villa Draycott
Penn, George H., 6 Post Office Lane
Draycott
21/7/75 Penn, Philip G., 6 Post Office
Lane Draycott
Penn, Vera K., 6 Post Office Lane
Draycott
Perry, Charles O., The Long Hse
Draycott
Perry, Colleen M., The Long Hse
Draycott
Pockett, Gillian A., 2 Church View
Aston Magna
Pockett, Peter W., 2 Church View
Aston Magna
Potter, Albert E., Home Farm Draycott
Potter, Frances M., Home Farm
Draycott
Potter, John E., Home Farm Draycott
Potter, Richard M., Home Farm
Draycott
Pulley, Alice M., 25 Aston Magna
Pulley, Benjamin, 26 Aston Magna
Pulley, Dorothy M. M., 26 Aston
Magna

Pulley, Reginald J., 25 Aston Magna
Purser, Alexander T., 4 Aston Magna
Purser, Annie E., 4 Aston Magna
Quartermaine, David J., Bungalow
Ditchford Hill
Quartermaine, Doreen M., Bungalow
Ditchford Hill
Rainbird, Geraldine A., Tin Hau
Draycott
Rainbird, Seamus W., Tin Hau
Draycott
Randall, Iris J., 2 Aston Magna
Randall, William J., 2 Aston Magna
Read, Anne, Two Ends Cot Draycott
Read, Cecil W., Two Ends Cot
Draycott
Read, Denis W., 14 Wydelands
Draycott
Read, Doreen A., 14 Wydelands
Draycott
Read, Frances E., Two Ends Cot
Draycott
Reid-Adam, Randle, 2 New Row
Draycott
Reid-Adam, Rita A., 2 New Row
Draycott
Richards, Derek L., Two Trees
Draycott
Richards, Mary, Two Trees Draycott
Rodgers, Charles L., 7 Woolaway
Bungalows Aston Magna
Rodgers, Margaret C. C., 7 Woolaway
Bungalows Aston Magna
Rodgers, Rowland L. C., 7 Woolaway
Bungalows Aston Magna
Sabin, Anthony, J., 6 Church View
Sabin, Beatrice W., Corner Cottage
Aston Magna
Sabin, June, 6 Church View Aston
Magna
Sabin, Flora M., 8 Church View Aston
Magna
Sabin, George, Corner Cottage Aston
Magna
Sabin, Herbert, Corner Cottage
Aston Magna
Sabin, William C., 8 Church View
Aston Magna
Sass, Stephen B., 8 Wydelands
Draycott
Simon, Geoffrey M., Manor Hse
Aston Magna
Simon, Jeanette M. J., Manor Hse
Aston Magna
14/10/74 Smith, Alison M., 7 Church
View Aston Magna
Smith, Jennifer A., 1 Draycott Farm
Cotts Draycott

Smith, Margaret J., 7 Church View
Aston Magna
Smith, Raymond B., 7 Church View
Aston Magna
Smith, Stephen J., 3 Wydelands
Draycott
Smith, Sylvia, 5 Wollaway Bungalows
Aston Magna
Smith, Trevor A., 3 Wydelands
Draycott
Starsiak, Helena S., 20 Church View
Aston Magna
Swallow, Andrew C., 1 Cot Middle
Ditchford
Swallow, Mavis E., 1 Cot Middle
Ditchford
Swallow, Paul A., Cot Middle
Ditchford
Taylor, Algy L., Old Farm Aston
Magna
Taylor, Cyril J., Old Farm Aston
Magna
Taylor, Gerald A., Old Farm Aston
Magna
Taylor, Henry A., 21 Aston Magna
Taylor, Naomie M., 21 Aston Magna
Taylor, Patricia M., Old Farm Aston
Magna
Taylor, Stephen, 21 Aston Magna
Turtle, James M. de Bec., Northwick
Cot Draycott
Turtle, Lynda A., Northwick Cot
Draycott
Vale, Edith M., Bran Mill
Vale, Ernest T., Bran Mill

Walker, Marjorie E., Norman Chapel
Aston Magna
Walker, Noel O., Norman Chapel
Aston Magna
Wallace, Anita J., Dorn Cot Draycott
Wallace, John M. L., Dorn Cot
Draycott
Wells, Belinda J., Bank Farm
Wells, Janet, Bank Farm
Wells, Jasper, Bank Farm
Wheeler, David T., 11 Aston Magna
Wheeler, Ernest J., 4 Post Office Lane
Draycott
Wheeler, Robert W., 11 Aston Magna
Wild, Sandra D., Ditchford Mill
Wild, Stephen, Ditchford Mill
Withers, Annie M., 5 Church View
Aston Magna
Withers, Clive D., 7 Church View
Aston Magna
Withers, Henry J., 5 Church View
Aston Magna
Withers, Jessie E., 13 Aston Magna
Withers, Margaret, 1 Church View
Aston Magna
Withers, Phoebe M., 7 Church View
Aston Magna
Withers, Rodney, 5 Church View
Aston Magna
Withers, William J., 1 Church View
Aston Magna
Wright, Anthony J., Ditchford Hill Cot
Ditchford-on-Fosse
Wright, Stephanie J., Ditchfor Hill Cot
Ditchford-on-Fosse

Index

No detailed index of the appendices is included

252

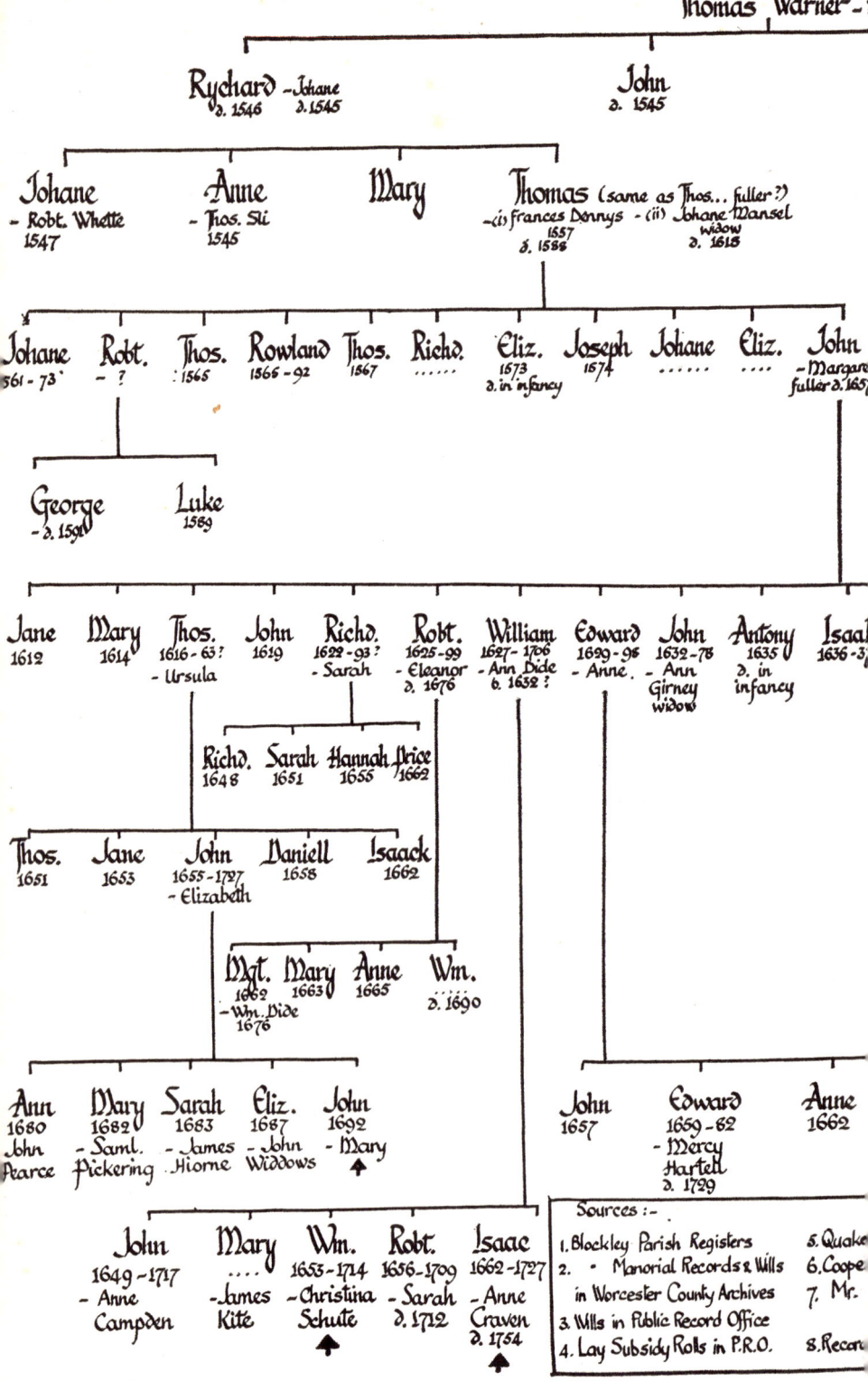